Whitney M. Young, Jr.,
and the Struggle for
Civil Rights

Whitney M. Young, Jr.,

and the Struggle for Civil Rights

Nancy J. Weiss

PRINCETON UNIVERSITY PRESS

Princeton, New Jersey

ISBN 0-691-04757-X

This book has been composed in Linotron Caledonia type

Clothbound editions of Princeton University Press books are printed
on acid-free paper, and binding materials are chosen for
strength and durability. Paperbacks, although satisfactory
for personal collections, are not usually suitable
for library rebinding

Printed in the United States of America by Princeton
University Press, Princeton, New Jersey

Library of Congress Cataloging-in-Publication Data

Weiss, Nancy J. (Nancy Joan), 1944–
Whitney M. Young, Jr., and the struggle for civil
rights / Nancy J. Weiss.
p.   cm.
Bibliography: p.
Includes index.
ISBN 0–691-04757-X (alk. paper)
1. Young, Whitney M. 2. Civil rights workers—United
States—Biography. 3. Afro-Americans—Biography.
4. National Urban League—Biography. I. Title.
E185.97.Y635W45 1989
323'.092—dc20
[B]   89-4045

TO BURT

Contents

Illustrations

Frontispiece: Whitney M. Young, Jr. (Whitney M. Young, Jr., Papers, Rare Book and Manuscript Library, Columbia University)

Following page 128

Whitney M. Young, Sr., and Laura Ray Young (Whitney M. Young, Jr., Papers, Rare Book and Manuscript Library, Columbia University)

Newlyweds (Whitney M. Young, Jr., Papers, Rare Book and Manuscript Library, Columbia University)

Kentucky GIs at leisure in Germany (Whitney M. Young, Jr., Papers, Rare Book and Manuscript Library, Columbia University)

Company C,. 1695th Engineer Combat Battalion, at Versailles (Whitney M. Young, Jr., Papers, Rare Book and Manuscript Library, Columbia University)

Dean of the Atlanta University School of Social Work (Whitney M. Young, Jr., Papers, Rare Book and Manuscript Library, Columbia University)

With fellow civil rights leaders, 1963. *Left to right*: John Lewis, Whitney M. Young, Jr., A. Philip Randolph, Martin Luther King, Jr., James Farmer, and Roy Wilkins. (The Bettman Archive, Inc.)

Leaders of the March on Washington (Moorland-Spingarn Research Center, Howard University)

At the White House following the March on Washington. *Left to right*: Whitney M. Young, Jr., Martin Luther King, Jr., Rabbi Joachim Prinz, A. Philip Randolph, President John F. Kennedy, and Walter Reuther. (The Bettman Archive, Inc.)

With President Lyndon B. Johnson and Roy Wilkins in the Oval Office (Whitney M. Young, Jr., Papers, Rare Book and Manuscript Library, Columbia University)

With President Lyndon B. Johnson at the White House (Whitney M. Young, Jr., Papers, Rare Book and Manuscript Library, Columbia University)

Preface

THIS BOOK tells the life story of Whitney M. Young, Jr., the executive director of the National Urban League from 1961 to 1971, the civil rights leader whom contemporaries described as the "inside man" of the black revolution, the man who served as bridge and interpreter between black America and the businessmen, foundation executives, and public officials who comprised the white power structure.

Whitney Young led no demonstrations and changed no laws. He accomplished much of his best work out of the public eye. His soapbox, the Associated Press said,

was the podium of plush executive suites. When he clenched his fist, it was around the hand of a white executive who had agreed to provide more jobs for Negroes.

If Young marched, he was usually being ushered into the office of a corporation president, and his sit-ins took place around a table with company executives.[1]

Young took on what Jesse Jackson called the toughest job in the black movement: selling civil rights to the nation's most powerful whites. A black man who grew up in a middle-class family in the segregated South, he spent most of his adult life in the white world, transcending barriers of race, wealth, and social standing to build bridges between the black ghetto and the white establishment. He took it on himself to interpret the needs and desires of blacks struggling to make it in American society to those whites who were in a position to help them or to stand in their way. His methods were reason, persuasion, and negotiation; his goal was to gain access for blacks to the basic elements of a decent life—good jobs, education, decent housing, health care, and social services.[2]

With race briefly at center stage in American national politics, Young brought the National Urban League into the civil rights movement and made it a force in the major events and debates of the decade. Among his colleagues in the civil rights leadership, he played an important role as strategist and mediator. He understood keenly the value to the movement of creative tension between moderates and militants, and he took good advantage of that understanding to advance his goals. His style and his convictions led contemporaries to call him a moderate, a label he would have preferred to shake. He insisted that he was just as angry at racial injustice as anyone else; what distinguished him were the means he chose to express that anger and to advance the social and economic welfare of black Americans.

Andrew Young said of Whitney Young that "he was a man who knew the high art of how to get power from the powerful and share it with the powerless." How he managed that, and with what consequences, is the central theme of this book.[3]

Acknowledgments

LIKE MOST scholarly enterprises, this book has profited greatly from the generosity and good judgment of many people. I am indebted, first, to the directors and staffs of the Rare Book and Manuscript Library at Columbia University and the Manuscript Division of the Library of Congress, repositories where I did the majority of the research on which this study is based. I am grateful, as well, to their counterparts at the many other libraries and institutions where I worked: the Atlanta University School of Social Work; the Blazer Library, Kentucky State University; the W. Dale Clark Library, Omaha; the Ford Foundation Archives; the Lyndon B. Johnson Library; the John F. Kennedy Library; the Library and Archives, Martin Luther King, Jr., Center for Nonviolent Social Change; the Louisville Free Public Library; the Minnesota Historical Society; the Moorland-Spingarn Research Center, Howard University; the National Urban League; the *Omaha World-Herald* Library; the Rockefeller Archive Center; the Schomburg Center for Research in Black Culture; the St. Paul Public Library; the Taconic Foundation; the University Library, University of Illinois at Chicago; the Walter Library, University of Minnesota; and the Robert W. Woodruff Library, Atlanta University Center. In addition, archivists at the Military Reference Branch and the Nixon Presidential Materials Project, both at the National Archives, provided copies of material that I requested, and the Federal Bureau of Investigation and the U.S. Army Reserve Personnel Center responded to requests for records under the Freedom of Information/Privacy Act.

A number of individuals graciously allowed me to use material in their private files. I am grateful to Clarence D. Coleman, Daniel S. Davis, Alexander D. Forger, Sam H. Jones, James A. Linen, Eleanor Young Love, Arthur B. McCaw, William R. Simms, Eugene W. Skinner, Percy H. Steele, Jr., and Margaret B. Young for important assistance in this respect. John E. Jacob permitted me to consult records in his office at the National Urban League. John C. Kenefick opened doors for me in Omaha, and Harold W. Andersen gave me access to the *Omaha World-Herald* Library. Lawrence G. Crowley, M.D., and Albert Rothenberg, M.D. consulted on medical issues. Cora Drewry of Hoechst Celanese, M. Louis

Camardo of Ford Motor Company, Richard T. Erickson of J.C. Penney, and R. R. Hailes of Texaco Inc. responded most helpfully to my requests for information about their companies.

The Rare Book and Manuscript Library at Columbia University granted me permission to quote from documents in the Whitney M. Young, Jr., Papers, and to publish photographs from that collection. The National Urban League allowed me to quote from documents in the National Urban League Papers at the Library of Congress, as well as those at the League's headquarters in New York. The Ford Foundation permitted me to quote from documents in the Ford Foundation Archives.

Generous grants from the Princeton University Committee on Research in the Humanities and Social Sciences helped importantly to facilitate my research. An idyllic year at the Center for Advanced Study in the Behavioral Sciences, supported in part by the National Endowment for the Humanities, provided the perfect environment for writing the manuscript. Carol Cairns Baxter taught me to use the computer, encouraged me to keep my eye on achievable objectives, and helped me to strike a healthy balance between work and play. Margaret Amara and Roseanne Torre cheerfully produced all manner of arcane information and elusive sources. Leslie Lindzey translated draft after draft into clean copy with great competence and good humor. Back at Princeton, Anne Holderried generously took on the same task. My editor at Princeton University Press, Gail Ullman, provided unfailing encouragement and help of all kinds. Carolyn Wenger, Jenna Dolan, and Sterling Bland shepherded the manuscript through various stages of copyediting and production, and Cindy Hirschfeld helped me to locate important photographs. Phyllis Marchand prepared the index with characteristic skill and dispatch. I thank all of these good people for their essential assistance and their confidence in this book.

The men and women who consented to be interviewed for this project brought Whitney Young alive for me in ways that would not have been possible had I relied solely on the written record. For all the frailties of human memory, for all the allowances that need to be made for the gap between what was and what people would wish this author and her readers to believe, the portrait that emerges here is much richer and more complex because of the recollections of Whitney Young's family, his friends and colleagues, and those individuals in the public and private sectors with whom he worked. The names of the people who shared their memories with me are recorded in the Note on Sources; I owe them a great debt. I want to make special mention here of the members of Whitney Young's family: his sisters, Arnita Young Boswell and Eleanor Young Love; his daughters, Marcia Young Cantarella and Lauren Young Casteel;

and most of all his wife, Margaret Buckner Young. Each one, in her own way, contributed unstintingly to this effort while keeping the distance necessary to insure its scholarly credibility. Maintaining that balance is a challenge, and I am very grateful to them for handling it so gracefully.

I owe a special debt to John Hope Franklin and August Meier, who planted the seed for this project by inviting me to contribute an essay on Whitney Young to their book, *Black Leaders of the Twentieth Century*. Their faith in me, and their helpful comments, have been of inestimable importance. So has the assistance of the generous friends who read all or part of this manuscript at various stages in its evolution: Carol Cairns Baxter, Alan Brinkley, George Butler, Kenneth B. Clark, Frank Freidel, Louis R. Harlan, Hylan F. Lewis, Arthur Mann, Deborah H. Bacon Nelson, Andrew M. Scott, Anne Firor Scott, Florence D. Shelley, W. J. Trent, Jr., and Roger Wilkins. The strengths of this book reflect their careful, critical reading and their wise counsel. Its weaknesses, of course, remain my own responsibility.

My husband, Burton G. Malkiel, brought to this project the gift of style and the talent for asking the right questions that infuse his own remarkable scholarship. His encouragement, support, and practical assistance made the critical difference in my ability to complete my work amid compelling distractions and obstacles. The dedication only begins to suggest the depth of my appreciation for the contributions he has made to the book and for the joy he has brought to my life.

Princeton, New Jersey
February 1989

Whitney M. Young, Jr.,
and the Struggle for
Civil Rights

Prologue

IN THE FALL OF 1966, two dozen of the most influential business leaders in the United States went to Eastern Europe under the auspices of *Time* magazine. Their trip was one of a series sponsored by the magazine to foster communication and understanding between American businessmen and those individuals who wielded political and economic power in other parts of the world. All but one of the American travelers were the chairmen and chief executive officers of Fortune 500 companies: North American Aviation, Bendix, Goodyear Tire & Rubber, Alcoa, Caterpillar Tractor, Mobil Oil, Borg-Warner, and the Ford Motor Company, among others. The exception came from outside the corporate sector. He was a forty-five-year-old black man, Whitney Moore Young, Jr., a social worker by training, who for the past five years had been executive director of the National Urban League, one of the two oldest organizations for black advancement in the United States.[1]

A man of medium complexion, Young was six feet two inches tall and weighed about two hundred pounds. His size and his manner struck people immediately; big and impressive, he cut an imposing figure, conveying a palpable sense of authority, self-confidence, and personal security. He spoke in the accents of his native Kentucky; no matter how diligently close associates at the league tried to change his pronunciation, regionalisms ("cain't," "hep," "particula'ly," "po'ly) peppered his informal conversation as well as his formal speeches. Everyone who knew him remarked on his style: frank, without pretense; exuberant, eager to take on the challenges and pleasures of life; aggressive, indefatigable, a study in perpetual motion. His staff members said that when they walked into the National Urban League headquarters in midtown Manhattan, they could tell immediately whether he was around just by the electricity in the air.

For a black man to spend twelve days in intimate contact with some of the most important leaders of the American corporate establishment was unprecedented. But with civil rights in the headlines in the United States, there were symbolic as well as practical advantages to including a black American in the group. Young was chosen because of the close ties between the National Urban League and Time Inc. The president of Time,

James A. Linen, headed the league's corporate support committee and would, in 1968, become the league's president. W. J. Trent, Jr., who arranged the invitation to Young, was both a member of the National Urban League's board and the top black executive at Time.

The trip gave Young an opportunity to establish human relationships with men who had never spent time exchanging meaningful ideas with a black person. As the trip progressed, the executives felt at ease with Young and sought him out. Several told him, "if more Negroes were like you there wouldn't be any problem." He responded, "If more white people were like me there wouldn't be any problem."[2]

The trip also gave Young a chance to do what he did best: sell his organization and his cause to the white establishment. These were men who were in a position to improve the economic status of black Americans, and Young took full advantage of the opportunity to influence their actions. He had done his homework—he knew about each company's black employment record and its contributions to the Urban League. He tackled the executives one by one and made his pitch. "I never saw a man work a crowd as hard as Whitney did," recalled the chairman of Time Inc., Andrew Heiskell. He exhorted the men to get involved in racial progress, to do better, to try harder. He used tough talk and charm to make his case. Young had a knack for knowing when to stop, when to change his tack and soften his approach, how to use a joke or a story to turn his listener around. "He had the ability," Heiskell said, "to push you right up against the wall, and you're about to get mad, and at that point he smiles and laughs and you smile and laugh and you're the greatest buddies in the world." The technique was irresistible. "By the end of the trip," Heiskell said, "there wasn't a person who didn't think that Whitney Young was one of the great guys they'd ever met."[3]

The Young approach paid off. He came back from the trip with promises of fifty thousand new jobs for blacks and financial support for the Urban League. (He also had offers of corporate vice-presidencies for himself, which he declined.)[4] Probably the most unexpected benefit of the trip was a friendship with Henry Ford II. The two men sat together on the bus trip into Hungary, talking and arguing the whole way. When they got off in Budapest, Ford was carrying Young's briefcase. The item made its way into the gossip columns of major American newspapers. Young delighted in the irony; as his administrative assistant, Enid Baird, remembered, "Whitney used to love to tell people that Henry Ford was his bag carrier." That Christmas, Ford wrote to say how much he had enjoyed getting to know Young: "You are a great guy and run a wonderful organization." As tangible evidence of his admiration, he enclosed a check to the National Urban League for $100,000 with instructions to Young to spend the money any way he wished. A $100,000 gift from Ford arrived each year until Young's death.[5]

Not only did Young hold his own with the executives on the trip, but he managed in a relatively brief time to forge friendships and affect attitudes among a group of influential whites whose backgrounds, experiences, and relationships to the centers of power in the United States were very different from his own. To do that took exceptional personal qualities: extraordinary charm, an unusual degree of self-confidence, a strong ego, and a gift for understanding and relating to people from walks of life very different from his own. Those qualities came from many sources, including the happenstance of imposing size and unusual physical attractiveness; the nurturing of a loving, supportive family; and the professional training of a social worker. To understand how the elements of personality evolved and blended in this man, one needs to begin in the 1920s, in Lincoln Ridge, Kentucky, where Whitney Young grew up.

I

Growing Up at Lincoln Institute

❧

WHITNEY YOUNG'S first encounter with racial prejudice affected him so deeply that he would recall it in vivid detail for the rest of his life. It happened when he was five years old.

He grew up in the sheltered world measured by the 444-acre campus of Lincoln Institute, a boarding high school for blacks in rural Shelby County, Kentucky, where his father was a member of the faculty. The Institute's address, Lincoln Ridge, was simply a post office. The nearest village, Simpsonville, was a mile and a half away; the closest town of any size, Shelbyville, and the nearest city, Louisville, were respectively eight miles to the east and twenty-two miles to the west. Whitney was accustomed to seeing black and white faculty and staff mixing freely on the Lincoln Institute campus, and to seeing his parents treated with respect. Nothing he had experienced had prepared him for the day his parents took him to the movies in Shelbyville.

While his mother and father were buying tickets, the boy walked into the lobby of the theater, where he attracted the attention of an usher. "What are you doing here?" the usher asked angrily. Realizing what was happening, Whitney's mother and father hurried over, scolded the boy, and took him up to the "crow's nest," the segregated balcony reserved for blacks.

The child was bewildered and close to tears. Why did he and his family have to climb several flights of stairs to the balcony? Why did they have to sit in the dirtiest section of the theater? Why, above all, were his parents angry at him instead of at the white man who had questioned him?

"I later understood that they were angry at me out of their concern for me," Young said. "Their anger had to do with the early training that all black youngsters received. How do you survive? How do you get along? You survive by not talking back. You get along by 'staying in your place.'"

It made no difference that Whitney's father was an educator who held a position of respect in the community. He, too, had his place. Uneducated white men from rural areas, unkempt and wearing overalls, were free to take seats on the main floor of the theater. Whitney's father, educated, well dressed, courteous, could not sit with them. "Even at the age of five," Young said later, "I recognized the hypocritical nature of it, the inconsistency of it."[1]

Racism and discrimination in Kentucky may have been less virulent than in the states of the Deep South, but the more civilized tenor of race relations did not change the fact that blacks and whites lived, for the most part, in separate worlds. Kentucky law contained few provisions requiring segregation (the Day Law of 1904, mandating segregated private schools, was the major exception), but the force of custom and, sometimes, city ordinances made up for a relative lack of racism in the state statute books. In schools, parks, places of amusement, libraries, welfare institutions, hospitals, places of employment, and public conveyances, segregation was standard practice.[2]

For a young black child in Kentucky in the 1920s, as for any child, parents were the first and most significant links to the larger society. Caring black parents played a special role as mediators between their children and a usually hostile white world. Interpreters, strategists, molders of values, sources of security and confidence, they gave their children the wherewithal to make their way through the complex patterns of American race relations. In order to understand Whitney Moore Young, Jr., then, one needs to begin with his parents, Whitney, Sr., and Laura Young.

WHITNEY MOORE YOUNG, SR., was born in 1897 in Midway, Kentucky. His father, Taylor Young, earned a living as a farm laborer, road builder, and sometime horse trader. His mother, Annie Henderson Young, worked as a laundress, a maid, and, later, as a cook at a country club in Lexington. The boy was named for Whitney Moore, the young son of a family for which Annie worked at the time her son was born.[3]

Whitney, Sr., went to elementary school in Frankfort, where he boarded with an aunt, and then attended a normal school in Lexington for two years. In 1912, he enrolled at Lincoln Institute, a boarding high school recently founded by the trustees of Berea College to provide an education for black students who had been excluded from Berea by state law. He worked year-round doing odd jobs in the engineering department to cover his fees and expenses.

The curriculum of the institute was primarily vocational. For girls, the emphasis was on home economics. A model rural home gave students experience in planning a budget, preparing meals, decorating, making clothes, caring for babies, and cleaning house. As well, girls could take a course in pre-nurse's training. The curriculum for boys offered vocational training in agriculture, the building trades, the industrial arts, business administration, and steam and maintenance engineering. In addition, a six-year teacher-training course was available to both sexes.

Whitney, Sr., studied engineering and graduated in 1916. He stayed at Lincoln to teach for a year and then went to Detroit to work as an engineer for the American Car and Foundry Company and the Detroit United Railway. In June 1918, he married Laura Ray, a girl two years his junior whom he had met at Lincoln. Laura came from Lebanon, Kentucky, where her father, Richard Ray, earned his living as a farmer and realtor and served as president of the Marion County Chautauqua. Laura had taken the teacher-training course at Lincoln, and she would teach briefly before her children were born. When Whitney and Laura married, he was three months short of his twenty-first birthday; she had not yet turned nineteen.

Inspired by a U.S. Army recruiting poster—"Don't Read History, Make It"—Whitney, Sr., enlisted in March 1918 and served overseas for the final months of World War I. He was one of more than 12,500 black Kentuckians who served in the armed forces during the war—14 percent of Kentucky's servicemen. Young was attached to the Ninety-second Division, Company 317 Engineers, which saw action in the Vosges Mountains near Alsace and in the Argonne Forest. He was discharged at the end of April 1919.

Following the war, he took a job as an engineer with Ford Motor Company in Detroit. Soon afterward, when Lincoln Institute asked him to come back to join the faculty as a teacher of engineering, he accepted the offer, took a substantial cut in pay, and returned to Kentucky with his wife and their baby daughter, Arnita, who had been born in Detroit on April 19, 1920. Two more children were born on the Lincoln campus: Whitney, Jr., on July 31, 1921, and Eleanor, on October 10, 1922.[4]

In fact, the offer of a teaching job turned out to be a ploy. When Young arrived at Lincoln, the principal, a white man, called him into his office and said that the board, most of whose members were white, had decided that engineering was too advanced a subject for high school students, but that Young could stay on as the engineer for the school. Young asked what that meant and discovered that he was being offered a job as the school janitor.

Young said that he would think about the offer. Determined to turn the situation to his advantage, he remembered the blacks he had seen sweeping and mopping floors in the new apartment houses in Detroit. As cities grew, there would be many more janitorial jobs available. With proper training, black men could find real opportunities for employment.

Several days later, Young returned to the principal's office and agreed to take the job on the condition that he also be allowed to develop a new course in janitorial engineering. He and his students would take responsibility for tending the school's boiler and doing painting and repairs. But first they would learn the trade from experts who would be brought in to lecture to the class. The trustees were delighted with the idea, and Young got the job as a teacher in addition to his duties as chief campus engineer. Soon he had learned enough from the visiting experts to teach the course himself.[5]

Young taught janitorial engineering, coached football, and served as dean of men. In 1935, he became the school's fifth principal (later called president) and the first black man to head the institute since its founding. He took over at a time of crisis for Lincoln. The school had been attempting to do too much. Enrollment in the six-year teacher-training course, run as a junior college program, was precariously low, and there were too few faculty members to sustain college-level instruction. There was no trained librarian, and the library's holdings were meager. In 1934–1935, the school discontinued its junior college work and narrowed its focus to vocational education.

Even so, the institute was in financial trouble. Its outstanding bills came to $10,000. Enrollment had dropped from a maximum of 131 in the 1920s to 81 in 1934–1935. The physical plant was in very poor condition. There was no prospect of state aid, and the board was ready to close the school.

Young persuaded the trustees to postpone the closing for a few weeks so that he and the school's business manager could operate the institute under what they called the "Faith Plan," whereby faculty and staff would give up their regular salaries on the understanding that they would get a percentage of whatever funds were raised.

Young was confident that they could find a way to keep the school in business, because he knew that Lincoln offered blacks a unique opportunity. Getting a high school education in Kentucky was no easy matter; integrated schools were out of the question thanks to the Day Law, and many counties were too poor to provide separate high schools for blacks. With its boarding facilities, Lincoln could meet the educational needs of black children throughout the state. It had only to find a sufficient number of students.

Young and his faculty and staff traveled across the state to recruit students. They needed to overcome significant obstacles; black families were reluctant to send their children away from home, and whites were not inclined to let the energies of potential farmhands be diverted into book learning. In each community he visited, Young found a large, strong black man to accompany him, both to provide protection against intimidation from whites and to establish some credibility with blacks. He approached black families with a simple message: "You need to give your kids an opportunity to go to high school." The effort paid off with 125 new students signed up to come to Lincoln. By the 1937–1938 school year, enrollment was up to 221.

Within two weeks after the beginning of the "Faith Plan," a black man in Lexington, William Henry Hughes, died and left Lincoln a bequest of $10,000, exactly the sum of the school's outstanding debts. To the staff of the institute, this was a miracle. Hughes had also set up a scholarship fund of almost $100,000, with half of the annual income to go to the University of Kentucky for the education of white students, and the other half, to Kentucky State for the education of blacks. This unexpected generosity changed the minds of the Lincoln trustees. If Hughes would do that much for white students, surely they ought to do what they could for the institute.

Young needed to supplement the Hughes gift to keep his school afloat. He sent teachers and students, often accompanied by one of the campus singing groups, to churches and civic organizations to appeal for funds. The nickels and dimes they collected, as well as some larger contributions, gave the institute sufficient financial support to carry on. Later, partly at Young's urging, the state legislature took steps that ensured the institute's long-term survival. In 1941, the General Assembly passed a law requiring local boards of education to provide all students in their districts with the opportunity to acquire a high school education. A local board could fulfill its obligation by providing high school facilities itself, by transporting students to a nearby school system, or by paying students' tuition and board at a private school. The law enabled the institute to contract with local boards of education to educate their high school–aged blacks. Later, after a fire destroyed the boys' dormitory at Lincoln, Young appealed to the legislature to take over the school, oversee its operations, and provide it with an annual appropriation, changes that were realized in 1947.[6]

Young not only saved the school but set an important example for the community in the process. "My father taught me and all of his students how to accept the unpleasant and to cope with it instead of running away from it," Whitney, Jr., later said. Straitened circumstances meant that everyone had to pitch in to help. Even during his presidency, Young doubled as chief engineer; there were many nights when he had to repair the furnace and the water pumps so that there would be heat and hot water in the dormitories.[7]

At the same time that Young struggled to keep his school afloat, he was determined to see that his own children got a good education. They started off with a tutor, the white woman in charge of the Lincoln Ridge post office. In 1926, at the age of five, Whitney, Jr., entered the second grade at the Lincoln Model School in nearby Simpsonville. The Model

School enrolled about thirty black children from Simpsonville, Shelby-ville, and the Lincoln campus. A partition divided the small wooden building into two classrooms, one for the first through fourth grades and the other to accommodate grades five through eight. There was no lunch room, so the children all carried lunch buckets; instead of indoor toilets, there was an outhouse behind the school. With just one teacher to cover the range of grade levels in each room, it was important for the older students to help the younger ones with their lessons. Whitney and Arnita were in the same grade while Eleanor was two years behind.[8]

By example and precept, Whitney and Laura Young taught their chil-dren to handle themselves with a feeling of self-worth in a rigidly segre-gated society. Lincoln itself was a kind of oasis. Although the students were all black, the faculty and staff were integrated, and the campus was largely free of racism. ("The white teachers in the school were kind of self-styled missionaries," Whitney, Jr., later wrote, "and their manner toward us was at the worst, patronizing.") Living on the campus meant that the Young children grew up relatively shielded from the more blatant aspects of Southern race relations. Whitney, Jr., reflected that he "only slowly became aware of the limitations placed upon the opportunities open to Negroes." But there was never any doubt in his mind that segre-gation was man-made, and he said that he never felt inferior to whites.[9]

For all the security of the campus, it was impossible to escape the preju-dice and discrimination typical of the South in the 1920s and 1930s. The incident at the movie theater in Shelbyville had given Whitney a stark introduction to the rules governing relations between the races. At the age of eight he learned another lesson, this one about the roles available to black women and black men.

Whitney, Sr., took the boy to town to buy some clothes, and a white salesman sold them an ill-fitting suit. When Laura saw it, she was furious. It fell to her to go back to the store to insist that someone alter the suit or take it back. At first, Whitney, Jr., felt completely bewildered, for it ap-peared that his mother was the stronger of his parents. Then his bewilder-ment gave way to sorrow and shame for his father as he came to see that black women carried the burden of doing battle with whites. But as he looked back on the experience years later, he understood how much strength it took for his father to restrain himself. If Whitney, Sr., had gone back to the store and expressed anger at the white clerk, he would have marked himself as "uppity" and jeopardized his work at the institute; if he had been insistent, he might well have been lynched. Laura, like other black women, had more latitude to speak her mind without appearing to threaten the delicate hierarchy of relations between the races.[10]

A strong, imposing woman, Laura Young was the matriarch of Lincoln Institute. She presided over the president's house, a comfortable, three-story, white-columned frame building in the heart of the campus. Faculty, staff, and students responded quickly to her obvious warmth and her outgoing nature and affectionately called her "Mother, Dear." In addition to raising her children and doing whatever she could for the community, she was postmistress of Lincoln Ridge, a job to which she had been appointed in 1929.[11]

By her own example, Laura taught her children about the possibilities for open defiance of the conventions that governed the separation of the races. Going into town, whether to Shelbyville or Louisville, meant confronting the ever-visible reminders that in Kentucky, like the rest of the South, black people were treated as second-class citizens. Signs designating rest rooms and drinking fountains for "White" and "Colored" spelled out the segregation that prevailed in public facilities of all kinds. Laura would have none of it. She persisted in using rest rooms and drinking fountains intended for whites. She tried on clothes in stores, despite the customary prohibition against it in establishments that catered mainly to whites. She refused to allow people to call her by her first name, openly flouting the conventions about forms of address between whites and blacks. She carried herself with such dignity that she commanded a certain measure of respect in return.

Despite the more complex relationship of black men to the established conventions of race relations, Whitney, Sr., also stood outside those conventions in significant ways. As president of Lincoln, he presided over an integrated staff. The children were accustomed to seeing him as a leader—not only of blacks, but of whites as well. "We didn't see a father who had a white boss," Eleanor observed; "it didn't strike us to think that we couldn't be boss."[12]

Young occupied a unique position in the community. The institute was an important source of business for the white merchants in Lincoln Ridge. Therefore, they gave its president more consideration than they ordinarily gave black men. "Everyone knew that my father could, with a word, change the buying habits of a great many people," Whitney, Jr., said. "So he was always accorded a certain amount of courtesy. They could never bring themselves to call him 'Mister,' but it was always 'Professor Young' or 'Doctor Young,' or even 'Reverend Young,' even though he wasn't a preacher."[13]

Whitney, Sr., was also a skilled diplomat who knew how to negotiate in the world of Kentucky politics in order to secure funds for his school. He contended successfully with the expectations of whites about what constituted appropriate education for black people. When the white members of the school's board of directors came out to the campus, he pulled the students out of their regular classes. The board members found the girls in the home economics room, learning to cook and sew and do laundry.

The boys were out in the fields, practicing their farming skills. As soon as the visitors left, the students went back to studying mathematics, science, English, and history.

Outwardly, then, as Whitney, Jr., saw it, Whitney, Sr., "honored the rules of the white man's game." But he did so in a way that preserved his dignity and allowed him to accomplish his essential purposes. It was a lesson that his son would later translate into his own terms.[14]

Beyond the examples inherent in the roles he played, Whitney, Sr., gave his children explicit rules by which to guide their lives in a world of prejudice and discrimination. Chief among them was the injunction not to hate whites. Hatred was an expression of fear, of weakness; any fool could hate. It meant emulating the worst habits of white bigots. "I never heard my father utter a word of hatred toward white people," Whitney, Jr., said. Arnita remembered her father's constant admonition: "Never let anyone drag you so low that you hate."[15]

Along with that injunction went other commands: to worship God, to value education, and to be compassionate toward other people. "I believe in the education of the head, the heart, and the hand, with special emphasis on moral and spiritual values," Whitney, Sr., once said in explaining his philosophy. He was a Baptist, and Laura was a Methodist. Following the traditions of Lincoln Institute, they raised their children as nondenominational Christians with a strong belief in God. Whitney, Sr., began family dinners by offering a long prayer, and the children were expected to come to the table prepared to recite verses of the Bible. After asking everyone at the table to tell about something that had happened in his or her day, Whitney, Sr., would review the major developments in the news and expect each child to have something to say about them. The dinner table discussions were part of his philosophy about educating his children. "My father . . . believed," Whitney, Jr., later wrote, "that knowledge was the most powerful weapon a man could possess and that education was a principal path to the gateway of freedom. He believed—and it is the validity of these beliefs which has served my life and work—that the most important step in moving toward any goal was to be prepared for opportunity when it presented itself."[16]

Whitney, Sr., insisted that his children take their studies seriously. At home, in the evenings, Whitney, Jr., and his sisters did their homework at the dining room table while their parents, reading the newspaper in the living room, kept a watchful eye on them. The children heard the same message that their father preached to his students: read books, work hard, and strive for excellence. "If you want to improve yourself, your community, your state, your country, and the world, start with yourself," Whitney, Sr., liked to tell the students at Lincoln. "A trained mind will make the task much easier." He consistently put his ideas into practice. A long campaign to persuade the trustees of the University of Louisville of the need for better educational opportunities for blacks resulted in the opening in 1931 of the Louisville Municipal College for Negroes. Whitney, Sr., quickly took advantage of the new opportunity. Courses at night and during the summers earned him a bachelor's degree in education in 1938. Through summer courses, he received an M.A. from Fisk University in 1944.[17]

In contrast with Whitney, Sr.'s, emphasis on education, Laura's great concern in life was people. She gave her children daily lessons in human relations. There were the orphans she took into the house at Lincoln so that they could get an education; her care of the elderly and the sick; her willingness to feed tramps just off the railroad cars who came to the house to beg for a meal. She taught the children to share what they had as she stretched the family's limited resources to help needy students on the campus and took packages of food and clothing to people in rural communities nearby. Whitney, Jr., described her practice of sending cards or notes, with dimes or quarters tucked in the envelopes, to friends who were sick or who had an anniversary or a birthday. He remembered, too, getting a spanking at the age of four when he failed to speak to someone they had passed on the street. "My mother's love of humanity, her unyielding faith in the power for good in man and her incredible talent for discovering it—in the face of a society malignant with fear and hatred—was a major influence in the development of the views I hold and practice today," he said later. He hoped that he represented the qualities of both parents: the "appreciation for study and for excellence and for academic preparation" instilled in him by his father, and the "feeling for people that was generated in me by my mother."[18]

Through Laura and Whitney, Sr., the Young children also gained firsthand knowledge of the world of highly educated, middle-class blacks. The Youngs' friends tended to be other black professionals, including faculty and administrators from Lincoln and Kentucky State, school principals and teachers from nearby communities, the head of the Louisville Urban League, and a handful of doctors and dentists from Louisville and more distant cities. The families visited back and forth in each other's homes, partly for pleasure and ease of association, partly as a way of shielding themselves and their children from the indignities of overt segregation. When the public parks in Louisville were officially segregated in 1924, for example, black leaders protested vigorously but unsuccessfully. To express their opposition to the new policy, they declined to use the small park that had been set aside for blacks. Harvey Russell, the son of the head of the Louisville Normal School, remembered his family packing a picnic lunch and driving out to Lincoln Institute to spend the day with the Youngs instead of visiting the segregated park in the city.[19]

As a refuge, as well as a comfortable place for recreation, Lincoln Institute became a favorite gathering place for the circle around the Youngs. At the same time, Whitney, Sr.'s, professional activities exposed his children to people outside the orbit of family friends, people who included some of the most important black leaders of the period. As a child, traveling with his father to annual meetings of the Kentucky Negro Education Association, for example, Whitney, Jr., would have had an opportunity to hear W. E. B. Du Bois, Mary McLeod Bethune, Adam Clayton Powell, and others of stature who came to address the meetings. Such experiences provided important role models for the Young children.

When Whitney was a little boy, Julius Thomas, the industrial relations director of the National Urban League, made a trip to Louisville. Whitney, Sr., had taken his son to the city, and they came upon Thomas standing on a corner, with a crowd gathered around him. Whitney looked at the handsome, dapper man and told his father, "I don't know what he is, but whatever he is, that's what I want to be." A family friend, a physician from out of town, inspired the boy's early interest in medicine. The man's elderly mother-in-law lived along the railroad tracks near the institute; Laura Young and the children looked in on her regularly and made sure that she had what she needed. The man came to visit frequently, took an interest in Whitney, and encouraged him to think about becoming a doctor. Whitney spent several summers working as an assistant in the physician's clinic.

Beyond providing specific role models and mentors, the world in which Whitney Young grew up carried a message about the lives the children were expected to lead. "We were told that we were the chosen few families," said Harvey Russell, a lifelong friend. Not only were the parents of these children college graduates, but most of them had advanced degrees. They took an active interest in their children's education, their social development, and the formation of their attitudes. They carefully structured the children's social lives, guiding them toward friends from reputable families in their group. They sheltered them from overt racism so that they never felt that all whites were evil. And they pushed their children to lives of accomplishment. "We were told that we had to succeed, we had to do our best," Russell remembered; and through knowledge of the struggle of parents and grandparents (many of whom had been born in slavery) to better themselves, the children became more fully aware of their own responsibility for making something of their lives.[20]

Whitney, Sr., believed in ambition. It was one of his basic precepts: "Never be the guy who's satisfied to just get by." While accomplishment was important, it was also essential not to accept limits prescribed by color. The Youngs instilled in their children the conviction that they could do anything they wanted to do and were just as good as anyone else. With it came the corollary—rarely put into words but always implicit—to prove to themselves and to others that skin color was irrelevant to their achievements. Both Whitney, Sr., and Laura provided support and examples; Laura added the encouragement of competitiveness among the three children, and unbounded praise. The lesson in success would be handed down through the generations. The main thing she learned from her grandparents, Arnita's daughter, Bonnie, said years later, was "to be number one. . . . I grew up feeling a tremendous kind of responsibility to be a leader of some sort or another. . . . Because they were, and there was a tradition to uphold."[21]

The support and encouragement gave Whitney, Jr., and his sisters a great sense of security. They remembered their childhood as being unusually happy and comfortable, and their home as full of laughter. Their mother had a contagious, hearty laugh and was always quick to smile; their father's usual impassiveness overlay a keen sense of humor; and the children themselves were playful and given to kidding.

Whitney, Sr., showed no temper; while he never raised his voice, he had a way of putting things ("using psychology," Eleanor called it) that caused the children greater shame than they would have felt had he confronted them in hot anger. Laura, too, kept her control. Although she fussed at the children to show her displeasure, her voice was too tiny and ladylike to be intimidating; but she still managed to choose her words in such a way as to make the children feel terrible when they had done something wrong.

The children participated in activities on the campus: movies, basketball games, Sunday school, and vespers. They took music lessons (Whitney studied piano and, to his dismay, violin for a couple of years, until he managed accidentally to break the violin) and often gathered around the piano in the evening to sing. Together the family planted the garden, picked and canned fruits and vegetables, and played croquet, cards, and baseball. Laura helped the children with their homework and taught them to dance and later to drive. Whitney, Sr., often took them for walks in the evening along the Louisville-Nashville railroad tracks, telling family stories along the way.

The children enjoyed the pleasures of a rural setting: there were trees to climb, pets to take care of, and the campus farm to play on, with its fields of lespedeza, barley, wheat, and alfalfa, its apple orchard, vegetable and flower gardens, and its dairy cattle, horses, poultry, and swine. During the summers, all three of them (Whitney, Jr., included) went to the Girl Scout camp on the Lincoln campus. There were family trips to visit friends and relatives in Louisville and Lexington as well as Indianapolis, Chicago, and other distant places; as the children got older, they often spent part of the summer out of town staying with family or friends.

While the family was never wealthy (Whitney, Jr., later estimated that his parents together earned about $100 a month), and the children were taught to be frugal, they were never made to feel any insecurity. Whitney, Jr., recalled his father's admonition: "You're a Young! You stand tall boy! We may be broke . . . but we're not poor." In many ways, their lives were unusually comfortable. Needy students working their way through Lincoln came to the house to cook, clean, wash, and iron in order to earn extra money. While Laura Young insisted that Arnita, Whitney, Jr., and Eleanor take turns helping with the dishes or the laundry, the regular presence of student workers made their chores less onerous.[22]

In 1933, at the age of twelve, Whitney, Jr., enrolled at Lincoln Institute as a freshman in high school. He was a short, curly headed, handsome boy, who was said to resemble his mother's brothers. Just as his outlook and values had been shaped by both of his parents, his personality combined the best features of each of them. The boy was friendly and outgoing. Even as a child, he exuded a sense of security and self-confidence. It came, in part, from growing up in such a warm, close-knit family; in part from the fact that, as the only boy, he tended to be pampered and made the center of attention; and in part from seeing the respect that other people generally gave his parents. "He was always sure of himself," his childhood friend Harvey Russell said. "If you looked back, you could almost have predicted that he was going to be a leader in something." He was rarely a follower; if he decided that he wanted to do something, he usually did it. He drew other people to him; people of all ages seemed to want to be around him, and they were willing to follow him. Whitney was a happy child, slow to anger; like his father, he did not like arguments, and, as Eleanor remembered, "if he couldn't talk his way out of [a situation], he'd just walk away from it." He knew almost intuitively how to handle people; he had a knack, for instance, of persuading his younger sister to do things she did not want to do and making her feel good about it in the process. He was very close to his mother, and he knew how to make her melt. He would tell her "how sweet she was, how beautiful she was," Eleanor said, and Laura would "forget what she was fussing about. So he was a manipulator from way back."[23]

By enrolling at Lincoln, Whitney became an official member of a community of which he had long been a part. When he became a student, at the depth of the depression, enrollment was well below one hundred; by the time he graduated, he was among more than two hundred students, most of them from Kentucky, but some from Michigan, Illinois, Indiana, and Ohio. Nearly two-thirds of the students boarded on campus; the rest were day students from nearby towns. The faculty, which numbered about a dozen men and women, lived in cottages on the campus. During his childhood, the principal of the school had been white, and the faculty had been integrated, the legacy of the Berea connection. By the time he graduated, his father was running the school, and all of the faculty members were black; only the business manager and his clerk/secretary were white. Students and faculty ate in a large dining room in the basement of the boys' dormitory, with faculty tables set apart in one corner. Faculty members and students were extremely close; students usually found one teacher who became a special mentor, almost a substitute parent. Teachers took groups of students on picnics, on trips for sightseeing and recreation, and to visit colleges. It was a serene, supportive atmosphere—in the words of one faculty member, "a very close-knit, family-like situation."

It was also a highly structured, carefully regulated world, full of rules and restrictions. The institute asked entering students to present evidence of good moral character; it required them to attend daily chapel, Sunday school, and Sunday vesper services; it prohibited them from using alcohol or tobacco; and it demanded that they observe all proprieties between the sexes.

For boys who boarded on campus, there was a two-hour study period every night, except Saturday and Sunday. The recreation room was open in the afternoons and again for a half hour before lights-out at ten o'clock. To leave the campus, students needed to obtain permission from the dean of men. For girls, there were additional restrictions. The girls were not to be in the main academic building, Berea Hall, or in the library after 4:30 P.M. unless they were accompanied by a faculty member. They were not allowed to stand in the corridors of Berea Hall and converse with boys. They were required to be in their rooms on school day afternoons when they were not in class, on study nights, like the boys, and for an hour on Sunday afternoons, when they were expected to remain quiet and meditate. Girls under the age of seventeen were not allowed to have male callers or to have male escorts to and from their dormitories; older students were permitted to have callers in the girls' reception room every other Saturday night. There were socials or other activities on alternate Saturdays. Girls and boys could sit together at vesper services if they kept quiet; they could go for walks together after vespers only if they were chaperoned. Under no circumstances were girls permitted to leave the campus without a teacher.

Students who violated campus regulations, as some always did, might be put on probation, reprimanded publicly during chapel, deprived of their social privileges, or expelled, depending on the severity of the offense.

Within the bounds of these rules and restrictions, students created a varied extracurricular life. There were many different campus organizations: the student council, literary society, choral society, honorary societies, press club, Hi-Y, YMCA, and a championship basketball team. Students enjoyed parties, movies, and picnics on campus, as well as carefully supervised outings beyond it. Most students held campus jobs in order to earn money for fees and personal expenses; in addition, following the precepts of the founders, the institute expected all students to work for an hour a day without pay to contribute to the upkeep of the school.

The institute offered the academic subjects typical of a high school curriculum: English, French, mathematics, biology, chemistry, and history. There were also classes in music and religious education. Reflecting the school's continuing emphasis on vocational training, all girls had to study home economics and all boys had to learn some trade, whether carpentry, engineering, or agriculture.[24]

Whitney Young, Jr., stood out as an athlete and student. Smaller than most of his classmates, he nevertheless threw himself into sports, especially tennis and basketball. Proving his physical prowess became his way of establishing his identity on the campus. He fell under the influence of LaMont Lawson, a graduate of Fisk University who taught mathematics, coached basketball, and served at different times as principal and dean of men. Lawson was not only a good teacher and coach but a role model for the boy. "My father . . . and LaMont were about the only men I knew who were strong, effective, competent, and masculine," Young said, "and it was they who inspired me to make something of my life."

As the years passed, Young forgot the algebra and geometry that Lawson taught him. But Lawson's personal presence and human qualities— the way he dressed and behaved, his assurance and composure—remained vivid in Young's memory. Lawson taught his students "great lessons—how to be competent, competitive, good sports, and men." He "gave me dignity," Young said; he "made me feel that I was somebody."[25]

Young graduated from Lincoln in 1937, only fifteen years old and valedictorian of his class. Arnita had been chosen as the salutatorian. That was cause for embarrassment for their father, who worried that someone might think that the faculty had shown favoritism because they were his children. Whitney, Sr., tried to have the selections changed, but the faculty refused.

Being named valedictorian was a dubious honor in light of his father's position, Whitney, Jr., thought. He looked forward to college, where he would have the chance to show what he could do without the question raised by his father's rank.[26]

II

Kentucky State

WHITNEY ENROLLED in September 1937 at Kentucky State Industrial College in Frankfort, one of two four-year colleges open to blacks in Kentucky. Arnita began as a freshman at the same time, and Eleanor followed two years later.

For the Young children, Kentucky State was in many ways a continuation of Lincoln Institute. Lincoln had been not only a school, but a home and a family. At Kentucky State, Whitney and his sisters found much the same atmosphere. The college was considerably bigger, of course; enrollment totaled 590 when Whitney and Arnita entered as freshmen. Nearly 90 percent of the students came from Kentucky, and the remainder were drawn from fifteen other states. But despite the difference in size, the college seemed entirely familiar. There were many Lincoln graduates among the students, as well as good friends of the senior Youngs among the faculty and administration. That gave Whitney and his sisters places to go for a home-cooked meal and people to turn to for help in an emergency. The result, in Eleanor's words, was that they felt "very safe, very comfortable."[1]

Like Lincoln, Kentucky State had a dedicated faculty that took a strong personal interest in students. They were highly qualified for the time. Thanks to the efforts of President Rufus Ballard Atwood, a specialist in agricultural education, over 60 percent of the faculty members whom Whitney would have encountered held advanced degrees, a sharp contrast to the situation Atwood found when he arrived at Kentucky State in 1929, when more than a quarter of the faculty held no college degree and none had an earned doctorate. Like the teachers Whitney knew at Lincoln, the faculty members at Kentucky State lived nearby, frequently ate their meals in a separate area of the college dining room, and were readily available outside the classroom. Like their counterparts at Lincoln, they took a paternalistic attitude toward their students, carefully supervising them and working to shape their behavior and values.[2]

Where Kentucky State differed most significantly from Lincoln Institute was in its curriculum. The college devoted itself to three principal aims: to train public school teachers, administrators, and supervisors; to train workers in agriculture and home economics; and to prepare students for graduate and professional education. The curriculum reflected its purposes. The Division of Education offered courses in elementary and secondary education, music education, and art education; the Division of Applied Sciences gave training in agriculture, home economics, and mechanic arts; and the Division of Arts and Sciences taught English, French, history, government, sociology, economics, natural science, and mathematics.

Whitney's interest in medicine led him to follow the prescribed course of study leading to a bachelor of science degree with a major in natural science. That meant eighteen set courses in the Department of Natural Science and Mathematics comprising four semesters of mathematics, four of physics, three of chemistry, two of biology, and one each of bacteriology, botany, comparative anatomy, genetics, and zoology. Whitney took nine additional semester courses in the Division of Arts and Sciences (two each in English composition, English literature, and modern European history, and introductory courses in the humanities and the social sciences), one in the Division of Applied Sciences, and six in the Division of Education. Students were allowed a limited number of electives and were encouraged to use them to obtain a minor in some field of interest. Whitney chose to minor in education.[3]

There was nothing distinguished about Whitney's academic performance. In his freshman year, he got five Cs and four Bs in academic subjects, as well as a D in French. The first semester of sophomore year was worse: Cs in four courses and a D in general chemistry. The situation began to improve in the second semester, when he pulled his grades up to four Bs and a C. And in his junior and senior years, he managed a solid B average, including an occasional A. His friends attributed the improvement not to greater studiousness but to the influence of the young woman he was dating, who tutored him and edited his term papers.[4]

Where Whitney stood out was in the force of his personality and in the gifts he demonstrated for making friends and for exerting leadership. He found his niche in a campus environment like the one he had experienced at Lincoln Institute and characteristic of other black colleges throughout the South.

Student life at Kentucky State revolved around dormitories, the dining hall, the library, fraternities and sororities, and sports. There were two dormitories for women, Kentucky Hall and Memorial Hall (a third one opened in 1939–1940); men lived in Atwood Hall, a three-story brick building constructed in 1935 through Public Works Administration funds.

Each weekday morning, the campus bell rang at 6:00; breakfast followed
in the dining room in Kentucky Hall at 6:45. Classes began at 8:00, continued until lunchtime, and resumed again from 1:00 until 4:00. Students
and faculty sat down to dinner at 5:30. There were evening study hours
from 7:00 until 9:00, with lights-out at 10:00. Moral and religious training
assumed an important place in the program of the college; students were
required to attend the college assembly every Tuesday morning, chapel
every Thursday, Sunday services on the first three Sundays of the month,
and vespers on the fourth and fifth Sundays. Attendance was optional at
Sunday school and Wednesday night prayer services. Student behavior
was carefully regulated, especially for women: possession and consump-
tion of alcoholic beverages by men or women was strictly prohibited;
women students were not allowed to smoke on campus; the deans of men
and women walked the halls of the dormitories at night to make certain
that students were in their rooms studying; women had to sign out of their
dormitories to go to the library at night, and they were prohibited from
making overnight or weekend visits to the city.[5]

The tight restrictions on social life during the week gave way to a varied
program of extracurricular activities, sporting events, and parties on the
weekends. Clubs and organizations—the YMCA and YWCA, the debating
society, the Kentucky Players, the college chorus, college band, and other
musical groups—held meetings, put on performances, and sponsored socials. Football and basketball were the biggest sports. There was a lively
rivalry between Kentucky State and Tennessee State, Wilberforce, and
other black institutions, and home games drew large, enthusiastic crowds.
Campus dances, put on by the Athletic Council, usually followed football
games. As the campus newspaper, the *Kentucky Thorobred*, put it, take
"one football game, one football social; mix together well and you will
have something that will always remain dear to you, the good old Kentucky State spirit."[6]

Movies in the Health Building drew many students on Saturday nights,
but the main focus of weekend social life lay in the fraternities and sororities. The campus had a heavy Greek letter orientation; rush, pledge parties, smokers, and socials (all technically without alcohol) dominated the
calendar. The college insisted that participation in fraternities and sororities not interfere with students' academic lives. Whenever the academic
standing of a fraternity or sorority fell below the minimum acceptable
collective gradepoint average for a semester, the group was put on probation; if its standing failed to improve after a semester, it lost its right to
pledge or initiate new members or to hold social functions. Each semester's academic averages were usually published in the *Thorobred*; the
chapters competed with each other for the highest standing.[7]

It was a protected, carefully structured world, where a paternalistic
faculty and administration established rules, kept a watchful eye on be-

havior, and tried actively to shape the moral as well as the intellectual development of their students. "I don't think you can imagine a college setting where the faculty members watched the students so carefully," Benjamin Shobe '41 recalled with a chuckle. "There were watchdogs all over," said Harvey Russell '39. "With my father being the dean, I couldn't do anything. And with Mr. Young being right down the road about twenty-five miles, neither could Whitney." Students generally accepted the paternalism and close supervision as facts of college life. For those who had gone to Lincoln or similar institutions, they were certainly familiar, and it was clearly understood that real misbehavior would carry serious consequences. The restrictions were to be expected—evaded from time to time if possible, of course, but on the whole, tolerated.

Campus protest was practically unknown, and when it occurred, it, too, was blunted by the all-encompassing paternalism of the institution. Russell remembered a strike to protest the quality of the food. The protesters went to make demands of President Atwood, who closed the dining hall. Atwood refused to see them that day and again the next. "By the end of the second day," Russell said, "we were so hungry we decided we wanted to negotiate," but Atwood still would not see them. "By the third day, we were in begging President Atwood, 'Please open up the dining room, we didn't mean it.' "[8]

Living in such a sheltered environment also meant living at a distance from the racial and social concerns of the world outside the campus. On the whole, the students were not especially attuned to current events. The college made some effort to bring such issues to their attention; the annual observance of Negro History Week, for instance, involved inviting a prominent black speaker to the campus to address issues of topical importance. The president and faculty talked about racial issues to some extent, but their message was usually conveyed in the language of Booker T. Washington, not that of W. E. B. Du Bois. There was no talk of protest, or, for that matter, any special encouragement to organize to change the law. Instead, the stress was on personal preparation as the key to self-improvement and to racial uplift: "Equip yourself to go out and make something of yourself" was what the students heard. But there was optimism about a better future in that Washingtonian message. The faculty "used to say over and over, 'You've got to move into the mainstream,' " Young remembered. " 'In the mainstream, you have to compete with all kinds of people. So, therefore, we can't teach you simply what is so-called useful and necessary only in the black world. You must also learn mathematics and physics, even though opportunities for their use are not presently open.' "[9]

On campus, students were insulated from firsthand contact with racism and discrimination. Shobe remembered seeing cross burnings on the hills in the distance, but students were generally free from harassment by local whites. The faculty members were anxious to protect them, and they also wanted to prevent trouble. Accordingly, they kept the students from getting too involved in matters beyond the campus. But the city limits of Frankfort were just three hundred feet down the hill, and when students went into town to shop or eat or go to the movies, they came face to face with the realities of Southern race relations. "They sent us to the back door or pushed us out the front door," Young said. "If we rode a bus, we had to ride in the back. Or if we wanted to take a taxi, we had to find one operated by black people." Going to the movies—probably the most popular reason to go to town—always meant sitting upstairs in the crow's nest.[10]

The proximity to the state capital created special complications, since the college depended on the state legislature for funding. "There was always this problem of how we behaved, what model students we had to be," Russell explained, "because the legislature and the governor were looking over our shoulders." Some students believed that Atwood was overly accommodating, if not sometimes obsequious, to the governor. When Governor A. B. "Happy" Chandler staged a pageant on the lawn of the governor's mansion to celebrate the sesquicentennial of Frankfort, the Kentucky State choral society was invited to participate. Its members were to wear bandannas, act as though they were picking cotton, and sing the old slave spiritual, "Nobody Knows the Trouble I've Seen." Incensed at being so demeaned, some of the students refused to participate. "This really put President Atwood in a bind," Russell recalled; "he didn't know what to do. He almost threatened to put us out of school." Most of the group finally bowed to the president's pressure and agreed to sing the spiritual, but without the bandannas and the simulated cotton picking. When Chandler had a dinner party at the governor's mansion, he often called Atwood and said, "I want your boys and girls to come down and sing for us." After the college's double octet presented a selection of classical numbers, the governor invariably said, "Now how 'bout singing some of those nice spirituals." Once the singing was over, he would send the students to the kitchen for fried chicken prepared by his black cook. "We always blamed Rufus Atwood for putting us in this position," Russell said, "but at that time, he almost had to do it. He tried to do it gracefully, but this was the requirement."[11]

Whitney Young knew the indignities of going into Frankfort and facing the constant reminders of his second-class status. He also knew that there were drawbacks to living in the protected, segregated environment on the campus. The competition and the challenges were simply not as acute as they were going to be in the larger society. His father kept reminding him of star baseball players whose batting averages plummeted when they made the leap from the minor leagues to the majors. But there were also advantages to going to school in an all-black environment. The students had the chance to form close associations with other highly motivated, talented black students who were at Kentucky State because their families could not afford to send them to more expensive colleges. The experience cemented lifelong bonds; the "Kentucky mafia" was a tight group of friends who visited back and forth and relied on and supported each other throughout their adult lives. Going to an all-black school also gave the students opportunities to test their leadership abilities in a wide range of extracurricular activities.[12]

Whitney seized those opportunities with gusto. Like most students, he needed to earn some money to help defray his expenses. While tuition was free to in-state students, there was an incidental fee of $15.00 per semester, and room, board, and laundry cost between $18.50 and $20.50 a month, depending on the size and location of the room. Whitney waited on tables, washed cars, and earned money as student manager of the football team. He loved athletics, especially basketball and tennis. Barely sixteen when he entered college, he was neither big enough nor strong and quick enough to win a starting spot on the varsity basketball team (he would grow to his full height after college, during his army service in World War II). Still, he participated enthusiastically in practices and eventually saw some floor action in intercollegiate competition. He captained the tennis team, managed the football team, and spent much of his time with players and coaches.

Young joined Alpha Phi Alpha fraternity in the fall of his junior year; as a senior, he was vice president of the campus chapter. During his senior year, he was elected class president, a testament to his personal popularity. He was highly regarded as a campus leader. Arthur Walters, two years behind him, thought of him as being especially serious about his responsibilities and his goals. He seemed, Walters said, "to already envision himself making an impact on something broader than Whitney." Reviewing the graduating class, the *Kentucky Thorobred*, poking fun and yet conveying admiration, wrote about him this way: " 'Hitler,' no, not Adolph, but Whitney Young, the President and youngest boy of the graduating class. It burns him up to be called Hitler, but he should take it easy, because he is only called that in recognition of his ability to get things done."

Whitney was fun to be with; "he was a very happy fellow," his friend Ben Shobe said, "as full of laughs as anybody on the campus." In addition to athletes, his particular friends were also campus leaders: Harvey Russell was president of the student council and of the senior class in 1938–1939; Shobe, who roomed with Young during Whitney's freshman and sophomore years, was president of the student council in 1940–1941, a makeup editor of the *Thorobred*, and one of two senior males elected to the Tau Sigma Honor Scholarship Society—distinctions, in the judgment of the *Thorobred*, which made him "the most outstanding student in the Senior Class."[13]

Whitney was also extremely popular among the women students. Since Arnita had started at Kentucky State in the same class (she later had to drop out because of illness, and she earned her degree two years later than Whitney, in 1943), he had easy access to the freshman women, and he made a big hit. "Anywhere Whitney was, was fun," said one of Arnita's sorority sisters. "He was radiant and just carried happiness with him." "Everybody spoiled him to death," Arnita's freshman year roommate, Ersa Poston, said. "He was the kind of person you just had to love. He was like a big brother to everybody."[14]

As a junior, Whitney took an interest in one particular sophomore woman, an interest that was far from brotherly. Margaret Buckner had come to Kentucky State from Aurora, Illinois. She was the fifth of six daughters (one of whom had died before her birth) of Frank and Eva Buckner, Kentuckians who were living in the small town of Campbellsville at the time of Margaret's birth in 1921. Frank Buckner taught in a one-room schoolhouse and ran the local grocery store. When Margaret was four, the Buckners moved to Aurora, a working-class, factory town of just over thirty-six thousand people located forty miles southwest of Chicago. Frank, whose normal school training in Kentucky did not prepare him for teacher certification in Illinois, took a job as a fireman in a power plant. Eva stayed home to raise her five daughters. During the depression, she worked for a time as a domestic servant to supplement the family income.

Margaret finished high school in 1938, in the same class as her next older sister, Virginia. Her father believed in sending his daughters to college, but with the depression, paying two tuitions was beyond the family's reach. Virginia, an accomplished pianist, enrolled at a music school in Chicago. Margaret set aside her dream of studying journalism at Northwestern or the University of Illinois and followed the urgings of her oldest sister, Eugenia, to return to Kentucky for college. Ten years older than Margaret, Eugenia had attended Louisville Municipal College and had stayed on in Kentucky to teach in an elementary school. Kentucky State had the virtue of being inexpensive; perhaps equally important, in Eugenia's view, it was an all-black institution. "She felt that with the kind of background that I had had that coming to a black college might be an enriching experience for me," Margaret said. Aurora was predominantly white—only 2 percent of the town's population was black. While there was a black church, there were no black teachers in the school system, and there were only a handful of black students in Margaret's graduating class at East Aurora High School. "I didn't have too much color awareness," Margaret said. "I didn't feel [it] in terms of my achievements in school; I didn't feel it in terms of activities; I didn't feel it in terms of where we lived."

Going south to Kentucky State raised her racial awareness in dramatic ways. Her father took her to Chicago and put her on the train to Louisville, where she changed to go to Frankfort. "All of a sudden I was aware that there was a sea of black faces in one car of the train," she explained later. "I had never seen things like that before." For the first time, she was struck forcibly by segregation. It dawned on her that blacks had congregated in the car because they had to; "there was no place else that [they] could sit." Her parents had not told her what to expect. Perhaps they thought she knew. Margaret wished that she had been given some warning to prepare her for the shock.

It took a while to get used to the new environment. At first, when the other Kentucky State students went to home football games on Saturdays to cheer their team, Margaret stayed in her room to listen to Big Ten games on the radio. "It was just different, it was just so vastly different," she said. "I didn't know how to relate." Gradually, she came to appreciate her new experiences: being exposed to black artists who came to the campus, watching a black football team play, having black teachers, making a wide range of black friends. But there were still some difficult adjustments. Margaret continued to chafe at racial conventions that were unfamiliar to her, and there were situations in which she could not contain her anger. Like most students, she needed to earn money to pay her college expenses, and she held a National Youth Administration job in the college business office. As a Northerner, she was accustomed to blacks being addressed as "Mr." or "Mrs."; when people called and asked, "Is Spurlock* there?" she told them, "There's no Spurlock here," and hung up. Her boss tried to restrain her: " 'Miss Buckner, please,' " he told her, " 'if they call from the state capitol, would you please let somebody else answer the phone?' " But such incidents were the exception; on the whole, she adjusted to her new environment and made the most of it.

Margaret seemed to excel in everything she attempted. She made the honor roll in her freshman year, the top student among only six in the entire college to be selected. She majored in English, earning her B.A. magna cum laude, with departmental honors. The *Thorobred* listed her among the ten outstanding seniors in the class of 1942; she was president of Tau Sigma Honor Society, president of the Kentucky Players, corresponding secretary of the student council, secretary of the Pan-Hellenic Council, associate editor of the *Thorobred*, and a member of at least five other clubs and committees.[15]

Talented, pretty, popular, Margaret attracted considerable attention from the men on campus. One Sunday after the college church service, at which Margaret sang in the choir, Whitney went to her dormitory and left a note in her mailbox: "Please forgive me for staring at you in church this

---

* Langley Augustine Spurlock was superintendent of buildings and grounds.

morning. But I couldn't take my eyes off you. I would very much like to meet you." But Margaret was dating someone else, and there was no response.

Still determined to get to know her, Whitney tried another tack. Margaret's roommate, Ersa Poston, seemed a likely person to introduce them, and Whitney pursued her constantly. He finally succeeded in meeting Margaret on Homecoming Weekend, when Ersa and Margaret were on their way to the railroad station in Frankfort with a friend who had been visiting them. Whitney spotted them in a taxi, opened the door, and jumped in. Later, Margaret found out that Whitney's roommate had bet him that he could not get a date with her. By the time she made the discovery, she said years afterward, "it was too late."

Despite Whitney's boldness, the relationship grew slowly. Since she was seeing another man, Margaret had some reluctance about a new suitor. Whitney, too, had been dating someone else. While he and Margaret saw each other from time to time, they did not begin dating seriously until months after they met.

By Whitney's senior year, however, they were seeing a great deal of one another. "Junior" and "Pookie" became a campus item. "Mr. W. Y. and Miss M. B. seem to be a clear case of 'can't do with and can't do without,' " the *Thorobred* reported on its campus gossip page. "For the time being everything is rosy." The "Kampus Komics" columnist wrote,

> Can you imagine
> Bull without Ionia.
> Sporty without Frances
> Junior without Pookie.

The flowering of the private, personal relationship spilled over into their academic lives. Margaret was clearly the stronger student; "we'd kid her and say that when she and Whitney started [going] together," Poston said, "her grades went down and his went up." By the end of his senior year, thanks in significant measure to Margaret's influence, Whitney stood thirty-first among eighty-seven students in the class of 1941, just below the top third of the class.[16]

On Tuesday morning, June 10, 1941, still seven weeks short of his twenty-first birthday, Whitney Young graduated from Kentucky State College. On Sunday afternoon, along with his classmates, he had listened as Benjamin E. Mays, president of Morehouse College, delivered the baccalaureate address at the traditional services in the school auditorium in Hume Hall. On commencement morning, the procession marched onto the basketball court in the Health Building to the strains of the "Festival March" from Wagner's *Tannhäuser*. After greetings from the governor of Kentucky and selections by the college chorus, the most prominent black

woman of the day, Mary McLeod Bethune, founder-president of Be-
thune-Cookman College, president of the National Council of Negro
Women, adviser on Negro affairs in the National Youth Administration,
and unofficial convener of the Black Cabinet during the New Deal, delivered the commencement address. President Atwood conferred the degrees and awarded scholarships and prizes, the chorus sang the "Hallelu-
jah Chorus" from Handel's *Messiah*, and the class of 1941 marched out to
Mendelssohn's "March of the Priests," now alumni of Kentucky State College. Some of them may have pondered the parting words of the editor of
the *Thorobred*. Kentucky State had equipped them to be leaders, he
wrote in a farewell editorial. "You, singularly and collectively, will now
take your places in the world as the backbone of the Negro race."[17]

III

World War II

YOUNG HOPED to go to medical school. "I was not driven by any burning desire to become a great healer," he said later. He saw medicine as a pragmatic choice given the alternatives available to young blacks in the South. He admired the freedom of black doctors to speak and act as they wished without fear of whites. And he liked the fine houses and fancy cars that they owned. He could not imagine another profession that would provide as much independence or as comfortable a life.[1]

In order to earn some money to finance his medical studies, Young took a summer job at a hotel in Louisville, working as a busboy during the day and a dishwasher at night. But he caught pneumonia, which meant that he had to postpone further schooling. Once he recovered, he got a job teaching mathematics and coaching basketball at Rosenwald High School in Madisonville, Kentucky. Madisonville was over one hundred miles from Frankfort, where Margaret was in her senior year of college, but the two managed to see each other reasonably frequently. He went up to Kentucky State on weekends and came with his team for basketball tournaments; she cut vacations short in order to spend a few days with his family before returning to school. Neither one had yet made a commitment to an exclusive relationship, but each remained very much interested in the other. "I was struck," Margaret said later. "I really was struck."[2]

Pearl Harbor changed Young's plans for the immediate future. Once the school year had ended, he enlisted in the army. He did so with some hesitation because it was a Jim Crow army, with segregated battalions commanded by white officers, and with black troops relegated to the dirtiest, most menial jobs. He was reluctant to join, but he did not want to be a conscientious objector. In July 1942, he went to work for the War Department as a mechanic learner in the Signal Service at Large at the Lexington, Kentucky, Signal Depot. In October, he was reassigned as a junior repairman trainee, and in January 1943 he became an assistant radio mechanic technician. In May 1943 he was ordered to active duty and was assigned to the Army Air Force Basic Training Center at Kearns Field, Utah. "My motivation wasn't as patriotic as it sounds," he said later. He still wanted to become a doctor, and he thought that the Army Specialized Training Program (ASTP) would be a means of going to medical school. But places at Meharry and Howard—the medical schools for blacks in the South—were filled, so the army sent him to the Massachusetts Institute of Technology to study electrical engineering as preparation for assignment to a combat engineering unit.[3]

Blacks rarely qualified for admission to ASTP. The program required a score of 115 or better on the Army General Classification Test, a level achieved by only 2.5 percent of the blacks in the army. At ASTP's peak, in December 1943, just three quarters of 1 percent of the enrollees were black, or 789 men.[4]

Young arrived at MIT in October 1943, along with three other blacks, the first to take part in ASTP there. "At first they didn't know what to do with us," he recalled, "so they put us off in a room while they had a meeting." The four blacks figured out that the officers in charge of the program must be discussing how to house them, and they decided that they would resist being segregated. As expected, the officers came back and said, "Of course, you fellows want to stay together." The new recruits replied that they did not unless the army or MIT had a rule requiring segregation. The officers had to admit that there was no such rule, and they agreed to house the men where there were vacancies. Accordingly, Young was assigned to a room with two white roommates.

He walked in with his duffle bag, said hello, and announced that he was to be their new roommate. One of the whites, a Mississippian, walked out and went to complain. He told the officer in charge that he could not room with a black.

"Why not?" said the officer.

"Because," said the soldier, "where I come from . . . blacks and whites just don't live together."

"Well," said the officer, "you're not home now. You're in the Army, and *we* give the orders. So get back upstairs!"

The Mississippian did not speak to Young for three weeks. Then they spoke occasionally. When he found out that Young had taught mathematics, he asked him to help him with a few problems. Before long, they became good friends. Six months later, the Mississippian asked Young to be the best man at his wedding. He even told Young that he would not mind if he married his sister. "I told him that was the ultimate gesture," Young said, "but that if his sister looked anything like him, I wasn't remotely interested."[5]

In January 1944, Young did marry. Margaret was still at Kentucky State, teaching freshman composition and working as the school cashier.

Young had written from Kearns Field to ask her to marry him. He had also
written to her father to ask for his daughter's hand. At Christmas time, he
got a five-day pass and traveled by train from Boston to Chicago and then
on to Aurora. Margaret was waiting for him on the station platform.

They had planned to get their marriage license on Friday, December
31, after Whitney's arrival, but the train was late. The county clerk's office
would not open again until Monday morning. With Whitney on a five-day
pass, they could not afford to wait.

On the morning of New Year's Day, Margaret's father phoned the
county clerk at home and asked him to do a special favor for a soldier. The
clerk agreed to come downtown and issue the marriage license. Margaret
later remembered, "Whitney said he'd never seen such a relieved expression on anybody's face as he did on my father's."

The wedding took place the next day in the parlor of the Buckners'
house. Margaret wore a yellow suit, Whitney had on his army uniform.
After the ceremony Laura Young hugged Whitney. "Junior," she said,
"I'm like every other mother. I always thought that no girl would be good
enough for my son. But there *is* one, and you've found her."

Whitney and Margaret spent the night at a hotel in Chicago. Then they
went to Kentucky for a day, and he went back to ASTP, this time at Rhode
Island State College in Kingston, while she returned to Kentucky State.[6]

When personnel shortages led the army to dramatically reduce enrollment in ASTP by the spring of 1944, Young was assigned to a black company, the 1695th Engineer Combat Battalion. Like most units of black
troops, the 1695th went into World War II under the command of a white
officer. It was nominally a combat engineering unit, but most of its work
involved building roads. Young reported for duty at Camp Pickett, near
Petersburg, Virginia.

"I'll never forget the day I walked into the company commander's office," he said. At first his commanding officer looked pleased; Young was
over six feet tall, 190 pounds, ideally suited for the sort of work that the
unit would be doing. "He could see me heave-hoin', totin' dat barge 'n'
liftin' dat bale." But then the officer looked at Young's records, and his
face fell. This black man was a college graduate who had been to MIT.

"I wasn't in the field two weeks when they said they'd make me the first
sergeant," Young said. "They were doing the same thing to me that they
did for my father. They saw me as a threat to their authority. Well, I took
it because I didn't want to be out there in the hot sun, pushing those rocks
around." While the unit was stationed in the United States, the officers
ruled by fear. "They had the authority and the means to enforce their
will," Young said, "so they were able to dominate the men, but they never
won their respect." That was true partly because the black troops naturally felt antagonistic toward the white Southern officers who reminded

them of racists they had known at home. It was true, too, because they knew that the officers were their superiors because of color rather than merit or achievement.

Margaret remembered traveling to Virginia to visit Whitney. She took a train from Kentucky to Washington, and then changed to go to Petersburg. She never forgot the trip. Her coach was so crowded that she sat on her suitcase all the way to Petersburg; the next coach was empty, but it had been reserved for whites.

Young's battalion sailed for England on the *Sea Tiger* on October 22, 1944. It took twelve days to make the journey. The *Sea Tiger* traveled in a large convoy, changing direction many times to avoid German submarines. The 1695th trained in Ivybridge, outside London. In early February 1945, it shipped out to France. Subsequently, it was reported in Belgium, Holland, and Germany. Most of the time, following army practice with respect to segregated black units, it remained behind the lines, but saw some limited combat in the last major campaigns of the European theater: in the Ardennes, the Rhineland, and in central Europe. The battalion's activities in Germany in the early spring of 1945 were probably typical of its wartime experience. In a four-week period in late March and April, the unit moved from Erkelenz to Bedburg, Rotgen, Aachen, and finally to the east of the Rhine River. The 1695th devoted its major energies to road construction and maintenance. At Rotgen it blocked approach roads in order to require all civilian and military traffic leaving Germany to travel on prescribed guarded routes. Near Aachen, it constructed obstacles, roadblocks, and craters to destroy the usefulness of secondary exits from Germany. At Erkelenz and Bedburg, it operated water points where potable water was made available to combat troops—in some instances, by means of laborious and continuous pumping from deep wells. In addition, the 1695th was responsible for reconnaissance of the Rhine River for obstacles to navigation.

While First Sergeant Young occasionally took over company field responsibilities, his major duties with the 1695th involved headquarters administration. He supervised the preparation of personnel records and carried out the assignment of duties and orders to the men of his company.

Probably more important, Young played a critical role as a liaison between the officers and the men. Going overseas brought a drastic change in race relations in the 1695th. The black soldiers vastly outnumbered the white officers, and the officers could no longer rely on fear to keep the men in their place. The men were not only free from the conventional bounds of Southern race relations, but they were armed, and they were angry at the inequities in the way they were treated. The camp bristled with racial tension. "The white officers would say, 'Fall in,' " Young recalled, "and the men would say, '—— you.' " The men became much

more difficult to control; the officers, in turn, became more heavy-handed
in their attempts to keep order. Things reached the point at which the
officers "were terrified of the men, afraid to speak to them, even afraid to
come out of their tents at night."

Since their careers depended on their ability to keep their men under
control, the officers had a vested interest in seeking Young's help. Young
negotiated between the two sides. He tried to persuade the officers to
treat the men with respect. Of the black soldiers, Young said, "I would say
to the brothers in the company, 'I agree you're getting a bad deal, but
what's it going to take to get you to fall out tomorrow morning and do the
job?' They'd tell me and then I'd go to the officers. 'The men ain't goin'
nowhere,' I'd tell them, 'unless you do so-and-so. You can put them in the
guardhouse but you're going to look bad. It's going to look like you don't
have the skills of leadership.' So we'd extract the conditions."

Young made some headway; he got the men to do their jobs in return
for greater civility from the officers, fairer assignments, more frequent
passes, and a share of the officers' liquor allowance. Slowly, the fear and
tension in the camp began to dissipate. Still, Young got some flak from
some of the men. "You're just brown-nosin' or Uncle Tomin'," they would
say. "O.K.," he would reply, "you take over," but none of them ever
volunteered to negotiate in his place.

In recognition of his service, Young was awarded the American Theater
Ribbon, the European-African-Middle Eastern Theater Ribbon with
three Bronze Service Stars, the Good Conduct Medal, and the World War
II Victory Medal.[7]

Young's experiences as a negotiator gave him a new direction. Instead
of medicine, he would make race relations his life's work. "I began to feel
the first flicker of hope that if justice could be won for the American Negro
in a foreign land, then it could, and must be won in his own country," he
said. It struck him that he might be able to be of some use in that struggle.
"I was convinced," he said,

that this was a problem which called for education on both sides: education for the
Negro in skills to make up for centuries of slavery and discrimination; and education for white people in exposure in human relations and to teach them appreciation and respect for the Negro as an individual.

I had seen how people could modify their attitudes when it became necessary
for them to do so, and I had seen how simple contact with Negroes had wrought
deep changes in individuals who had never before questioned the myths about
race they were brought up to believe.[8]

On December 16, 1945, after almost a year in the European theater,
Young's company boarded the army troop ship *Eleazar Wheelock* for the
long trip back to the United States. "We were going home," he later

wrote, "we were alive—we had come through an indescribable hell victorious." It was hard to contain feelings of elation:

The tyrant was crushed, and once again we could begin to build a new world—a world free of terror, suppression, prejudice. . . . Nothing was impossible. We would be greeted as returning heroes, by a country proud of our achievement, grateful for our sacrifice. The color of a man's skin no longer mattered. He was an American, he had proved his worth and would take his rightful place in our society. The war was not in vain.

But the long days and nights aboard the ship allowed the doubts bred in the reality of American race relations to temper that elation. Young wrote,

I . . . suddenly realized that, even though we were all soldiers in a common cause, we were black soldiers in a segregated Army. Would anything really be different?
    Would we be accepted, or would my fellow Americans continue to go about "business as usual" with an old indifference we knew only too well?[9]

Young decided to keep a log in the form of nightly letters to Margaret, which he would mail to her as soon as the ship docked in New York. "This afternoon a dream of 18 months became a reality," he wrote the first night. "As I walked up the gangplank I couldn't help but breathe a sigh of relief and for a moment I closed my eyes and sincerely whispered a prayer of thankfulness for at last I was returning home to you." He reflected on the significance of the experiences he was leaving behind. "As I stood on the deck and watch[ed] the lights from France & Belgium blinking through the mist," he wrote,

the full impact of how fortunate I was came home to me. For in those countries . . . men's blood had freely flown, men's honor & pride had either been sustained or left crumbling in the dust, and yet for what. To appease mad politicians in their thirst for power, maybe, to prove or disprove racial or national superiority, maybe, but I still would rather think of it as the most vivid portrayal of a man's convictions as to what is right & what is wrong.

The days passed slowly, and Young remarked with concern on the habits and preoccupations of the men. They talked about what they had left behind in Europe, but to Young's dismay, their conversation focused almost exclusively on women. "I have yet to hear anyone speak of the beauties in nature, the never to be forgotten works of art, the heirlooms of great painters, the cleanliness of Holland, the energetic Germans," he wrote, "and yet to me that is all I have left behind." Young observed the men in the ship's recreation room. The piano sat untouched, the books and magazines in the library went unread, while the men—sweaty, smelly, cursing if they spoke at all—occupied themselves by playing poker and blackjack and shooting dice. Worst of all was the condition of the men's quarters. "I guess it is here," Young wrote, "that my disgust really reaches its zenith. No amount of inducements, threats, or punishment can make these men clean up," he went on. "They are content to lie day after day in their bunks, their clothing dirty, their bodies, the floor all around them. It really is embarrassing when the Major asks me why."

Here Young showed most strikingly how little, beyond color, linked him to his fellow troops. He could represent them and negotiate for them, but at a fundamental level, they produced disgust in him rather than a feeling of solidarity. Extraordinary differences in education, values, and personal habits stood between them. Whitney realized, a bit self-consciously, that Margaret might wonder at his "critical attitude concerning our people." He confessed to having a heightened awareness of "our actual situation, morally, culturally, economically, financially, etc." But he hastened to point out that not everything he observed on the ship left him discouraged. There were some positive signs: some of the men were putting out a daily shipboard paper; others had formed a quartet and a jive band; still others organized daily lectures about procedures for separating from the service and taking advantage of their rights as veterans. The men had taken charge of the church service aboard the ship; it was well attended and intelligently handled. "These things I am proud to note & record," Young wrote. They seemed to him to "represent the faint hope for a successful future for our race."

As Christmas drew near, the ship got caught up in a violent storm that markedly slowed its progress. Young wrote:

Couldn't help but draw an analogy between this and life. Man & the ship. The storm & life's problems. The better prepared we are, the more qualified, the stronger our love, faith & determination the better able we become to withstand the storms of life. With an abundance of the above no storm becomes too rough to even change our course, to say nothing of sinking us. This is my prayer.

The long, slow passage gave Young ample time to reflect on what he hoped to find when he returned home. His hopes mirrored closely the aspirations of other Americans of his generation, white as well as black.

Basically I want happiness. To get that I feel I must have security. I find myself in my day dreams wanting to skip preparation & everything to picture us with a nice home, car, small pretty lawn with a cute little girl & boy playing. Yet I know within me that it will take some time to acquire all that. As an American Negro I don't expect to find any great liberal changes but at the same time I don't intend to use that as an excuse to hold me back.

It was hard to be patient. "Today was really nice and the boat speeded merrily on, so naturally I am in a good mood," he wrote on December 27, "because I know that with every turn of the propeller I am being brought closer to you." He jumped at any opportunity he could find to make the trip appear shorter. He had read half a dozen books and was rereading Dale Carnegie's *How to Win Friends & Influence People*, which he thought might come in handy later.[10]

Carnegie's international best-seller prescribed an approach to human relations that would prove to be remarkably well suited to Young's personal style and his professional needs and goals. Carnegie started from the premise that popularity, happiness, and a sense of worth depended in large measure on skill in dealing with other people. In chatty, exhortatory essays, he laid out a set of simple principles. To open effective dialogue with other people, he instructed, start by emphasizing the things on which you agree. To get people to do something, make them want to do it. To change them, appeal to their nobler motives; to influence them, appeal to their self-interest and show them how to achieve it. To get others to like you, make them feel important and show genuine interest in them. Over the years, Carnegie's principles became an integral part of the way Young operated.[11]

The New Year found Young making some resolutions. In the main, they related to his relationship with Margaret. "Maybe I should just call it, just a confirmation of a constant prayer & my perpetual dream," he confided. "I want to make you the happiest person ever."

Two days later, as the ship approached New York, he made his last entry in the log. "Tomorrow I'll walk down the gangplank, I'll turn once and look back across the mighty Atlantic toward Europe and . . . utter a prayer of thankfulness for my safe return and one of gratitude for all my experience, then turning I shall think only of the future with you, my beloved wife."[12]

IV

St. Paul and Omaha: Early Years in the Urban League

NOW WHITNEY could rejoin Margaret and begin to lay plans for his professional career. She was at the University of Minnesota, finishing the course work for a master's degree in educational psychology. Honorably discharged from the army on January 12, he stopped in Lincoln Ridge to see his parents, and then in Atlanta, where Arnita and Eleanor were both in graduate school, before making his way to Minnesota.

Margaret had found a room with kitchen privileges in the home of an older black couple on Snelling Avenue South in Minneapolis. The house was on a block of small, shingled, two-story homes, most of them built as single-family residences. There was a large mill nearby, and dust from the processing of grain frequently blew through the windows. The neighborhood was mainly black, quite close to the railroad tracks, with easy access by bus to the university. Margaret and Whitney continued to rent the room until after the birth of their first daughter, Marcia, in October 1946; when they outgrew the space, they found an apartment in a duplex a few blocks away.[1]

Like Margaret, Whitney was interested in pursuing graduate studies. He got a temporary job tending equipment and facilities at the Minneapolis Athletic Club and began to explore his options. Friends urged him to get a master's degree in social work and go into community service. He went to talk to the associate director of the University of Minnesota School of Social Work, John C. Kidneigh, about the prospects for professional training for a career in the field of race relations.

The two men discussed Young's background, his experiences during the war, and his professional interests. Kidneigh told Young about the roles that social workers could play in race relations and suggested that the Urban League would be an especially appropriate vehicle. Young had meager academic credentials for admission to the school; his only courses in the social sciences had been an introductory survey and a semester of educational psychology, and his record at Kentucky State had not been distinguished. But he showed Kidneigh a letter from the captain of the troopship that had brought him back from the war, praising the role Young had played in calming the black troops on the unusually long trip home. The letter apparently persuaded Kidneigh to give Young a try. Young's application to the School of Social Work was quickly approved, and he began his studies in the spring quarter of 1946. The GI Bill of Rights paid his tuition, plus $90 a month for living expenses. To earn additional income, he continued to work at the Athletic Club.[2]

Over the next two years, Young followed the program prescribed for candidates for a master's in social work. He took courses in principles of social casework, principles of group work, community organization, social pathology, public welfare, dynamics of human behavior, juvenile courts and problems, legal aspects of social work, and the history of social work, among others.

Given Young's interest in race relations, Kidneigh suggested that his first field placement ought to be in a public welfare agency dealing with large numbers of underprivileged blacks, and arrangements were made for him to work for the Hennepin County Welfare Board. Dorothy A. Whitmore, who supervised the field work unit, remembered him as a very interesting student, far better than average. "The thing that made him a real joy," she said, "was that he had an intuitive capacity for relationships." Young made human connections quickly and easily, in a way characteristic of the best social work students. It was a skill that could not be taught.

Whitmore recalled Young's apprehensiveness at the beginning of his fieldwork. She distributed the cases at random, and Young said immediately, "I don't want all Negro files." Whitmore said that she did not know whether he had any Negro cases at all. In fact, he did not, and when Whitmore met with him before he went on his first visit, he expressed concern about whether the client—a white woman—would allow him in her house. Whitmore reassured him and gave him a card that identified him as a Welfare Board employee. When Young went out to make the visit he drove around the block twice before he could gather the courage to talk with the woman. Once he made the call, he had no difficulty. "It showed me two sides," Whitmore said; "his real pride in his ability to get along with people, and his fear that he might be rejected, even though he was in a helping situation."

Young's experiences sustained his interest in race relations. He often talked to Whitmore about different ways of combating prejudice and discrimination. Would a law prohibiting discrimination really help? Or did one have to work at changing people's hearts and minds? Whitmore remembered Young as "very determined that there had to be a law, that you couldn't just wait for people to be educated and change their minds."[3]

The next year, for his second field placement, Young went to work for the Minneapolis Urban League under the supervision of its executive secretary, James Tapley Wardlaw. The Minneapolis League was among the earliest affiliates of the National Urban League, one of the two most important organizations for black advancement in the United States. Founded just before the massive northward migrations of black people during World War I, the National Urban League quickly established itself as the principal agency dealing with the problems of blacks in American cities. While its counterpart, the National Association for the Advancement of Colored People, concerned itself with the political and legal rights of black Americans, the Urban League strove to open employment opportunities and to provide social services to ease the process of urbanization. Working through a network of affiliates, mainly in the North, the league sought jobs for blacks through personal contacts with private employers. It conducted scientific investigations of conditions among urban blacks as a basis for practical reform. It trained the first corps of professional black social workers and placed them in community service positions. It sought decent housing and adequate recreational facilities for blacks, and it counseled newcomers to the cities on behavior, dress, sanitation, health, and homemaking.

By going to work for the Minneapolis Urban League, Young was associating himself with the premier national social service agency concerned with the problems of blacks. For a young black social worker in training, there could have been no better preparation.

Young took on a range of duties: accompanying the industrial secretary to personnel offices, employment bureaus, and union headquarters; interviewing applicants seeking assistance with employment problems; reporting to the Urban League's board on welfare bills before the state legislature; making field visits to individual clients and to other agencies seeking assistance from the league. Wardlaw thought well of him. Young was sincere and hardworking, and he had the capacity for objectivity in his relationships with clients that a good social worker needed. He had made a good impression on board members and representatives of other agencies. All told, he had clearly grown and learned from the assignment.[4]

Persuaded by his experiences in Minneapolis that the Urban League was the organization he wanted to work for, Young chose the history of the St. Paul Urban League as the subject of his master's thesis. Drawing on interviews with league officials, reports and correspondence from the agency's files, newspapers, records of churches and the local community chest, and other sources, he prepared a ninety-page account of the history of the league and its current activities. Balanced, careful, and generally well written, the study was mainly descriptive rather than analytic; it showed clearly Young's faith in the Urban League as a positive force for black progress. The league, he said, provided a good "example of how a group of interested citizens may cooperate toward alleviating social injustices, thereby making their community a better place for all its citizens." He hoped that his study might help the league gain a long-term perspective on its program, so that it would plan for the future on "a sounder basis of recorded fact." He also acknowledged a personal stake in the project, which dealt with the kinds of concerns that he hoped to make his life's work.[5]

The racial world that Whitney Young described in his report differed in significant ways from the world he had known in Kentucky. In 1940, the 214,000 blacks who lived in Kentucky accounted for 7.5 percent of the state's population; of those, 54.6 percent lived in urban areas. In Minnesota, at the same time, the black population numbered just over 9,900, or 0.3 percent of the population; of those, 88 percent lived in Minneapolis and St. Paul, where blacks accounted for 0.9 and 1.4 percent of the population, respectively. By the time Young was writing, the black population in St. Paul had grown to an estimated 6,000, close to half of the black residents in the state. As late as 1950, the total black population in Minnesota barely exceeded 14,000.[6]

Small numbers, set against the particular history of the region, made for different patterns of race relations than Young would have been accustomed to in Kentucky. In Minnesota, blacks could vote without interference, ride public conveyances without hindrance, walk the streets without fear of attack, and send their children to the public schools. While the state civil rights statute prohibited discrimination in public accommodations, blacks in the Twin Cities still suffered frequent indignities. Years later, local residents recalled such episodes as the day that a group of black professionals was asked to leave a leading local restaurant, or the time that Marian Anderson came to town and had to stay in the Phyllis Wheatley House because she was not allowed to stay in a hotel. They remembered, too, how difficult it was to obtain loans to buy houses, and what an uproar there had been when a black family moved into a white neighborhood. In the Twin Cities, as in so many parts of the country, restrictive covenants and "gentlemen's agreements" fostered residential segregation, and many blacks lived in overcrowded, dilapidated buildings. Probably the most pressing problem facing most blacks was job discrimination; perhaps 10 percent of Minnesota employers hired blacks, and a much smaller percentage hired them free of any restrictions as to type of job and level of skill. While there had been real progress in employment opportunities during and after the war, there were still significant limits on the jobs for which blacks could compete. No breweries or soft drink companies hired blacks above the janitorial level. No producer of flour, cereal, or feed employed them as anything but porters, janitors, and grain shovelers. Packing houses, where blacks had an easier time finding work, relegated them to the dirtiest jobs, like cleaning out hog intestines. Perhaps 12 to 13 percent of the manufacturing firms in St. Paul had ever hired a black worker in any capacity, and knowledgeable people agreed that only a fraction of those gave blacks employment commensurate with their abilities. In Minneapolis, only 6 percent of industrial plants were known to employ any blacks. On the railroads—a principal source of employment for blacks—blacks could find jobs as porters, waiters, red caps, and laborers, but not as engineers, firemen, brakemen, or conductors. There were almost no opportunities for office work in banks or insurance companies.[7]

Convinced by his fieldwork assignment and his research project that the Urban League would give him a real chance to play some role in improving conditions for blacks in the Twin Cities, Young eagerly accepted an appointment as industrial relations secretary of the St. Paul Urban League. He moved his family to St. Paul and took up his duties on September 1, 1947, after completing his degree. His new boss, S. Vincent Owens, was a big, strapping man who exuded energy and force. Dynamic, gregarious, well liked and highly respected, he was a good match for the newly trained social worker. Owens was tough, experienced, and a good teacher. He had an eye for talent; he was very good at developing young professionals, and he cultivated staff members who were likely to make something of themselves. As he wrote to Young's predecessor, Charles F. Rogers, the first man to hold the post of industrial relations secretary at the St. Paul league, "I'm interested in young men who are on their way up."[8]

As the second professional staff member in a two-man office (the league's staff also included a secretary, and there were usually two social work students on fieldwork assignments), Young had a good deal of latitude and responsibility. His particular role was to try to improve employment opportunities for blacks. The industrial relations secretary visited employers, urged them to hire black workers and to upgrade those already employed, and put them in touch with blacks looking for jobs. In cases of discrimination or racial tension, he worked with management and workers to try to resolve the problem.

The largest challenge lay in convincing employers to hire blacks, but Young also had to find applicants to fill jobs that were available. Too often, Young found himself blocked in his placement efforts by not having qualified people to place. In an attempt to change that, he worked with counselors in schools, social agencies, and employment offices to modify the widespread practice of counseling blacks to take training only in those areas where blacks already held jobs. In addition, he provided vocational guidance and counseling to job applicants who came to the Urban League for help.[9]

In finding jobs for blacks, Young had to use ingenuity as well as persuasiveness. He developed his own strategies and borrowed ideas from other industrial relations secretaries. The case of Schuneman's department store illustrates his technique. Young spent several days walking through the store, making a careful count of the number of black shoppers. Data in hand, he went to see the president of the store and told him what he had learned: Schuneman's had many black shoppers, but no black clerks. Persuaded by Young's logic, the president agreed to change the store's hiring policy.

Young's victories were small ones, but they were important departures from past practice. He accomplished the placement of two black saleswomen at Schuneman's, two telephone operators at Northwestern Bell, a beauty operator at Gayman Beauty Salon, a machine tender at Straus Knitting Mills, and a tailor at Robert Hall Clothes, among others. He helped blacks find employment for the first time as taxicab drivers, bus and streetcar drivers, and conductors. As he added to the list of firsts, he helped slowly to increase the number of firms that had black employees— 100 in 1948, 116 in 1949, 128 in 1950. In the words of S. Vincent Owens, it was slowly "becoming possible to match Negroes to jobs best suited for them."[10]

In 1945, when an interracial commission appointed by the governor of Minnesota had undertaken a study of employment conditions among blacks, Young's predecessor as industrial relations secretary, Charles F. Rogers, had collected a good part of the data. The resulting publication, *The Negro Worker in Minnesota*, had provided a comprehensive account of patterns of black employment as well as of attitudes and practices on the part of employers, employees, labor unions, and customers that had some effect on opportunities for black employment. In addition, it had offered constructive suggestions about what might be done to effect some positive changes. In 1949, with the supply of copies of the report virtually depleted, there was a demand for a new edition. There had been sufficient changes over the four years to warrant the collection of new data, and Young, along with the industrial relations secretary of the Minneapolis league, collected the information and prepared the necessary material for the revision, which appeared under the title *The Negro Worker's Progress in Minnesota*.[11]

Young also maintained close ties to social work education. In his capacity as industrial relations secretary, he supervised fieldwork students assigned to the St. Paul league from both the University of Minnesota and the Atlanta schools of social work. That meant consulting with faculty members from those schools about what the students ought to be expected to accomplish, helping the students learn how to do their various assignments and to prepare a detailed written record of their activities, and holding regular weekly conferences with them to discuss their work. [12]

At the same time, Young involved himself in the life of the community in a variety of ways. He was a board member of the Associated Negro Credit Union, the local branch of the National Association for the Advancement of Colored People, and the Crispus Attucks Home, and he was one of the first black members of the Jaycees. He participated in clubs and fraternal organizations that gave him opportunities for social and recreational contacts as well as forums for the discussion of civic issues among black professionals and businessmen. He joined the YMCA Men's Club and Alpha Phi Alpha fraternity and took an active part in the No Name Club, a group of about a dozen black professional men in the Twin Cities who met each month to discuss local and national issues, share concerns about problems they were facing in their jobs, and solicit their friends' opinions on the best ways of handling those problems. [13]

For Margaret, the main focus was at home, as wife and mother. Already pregnant when she completed her graduate work, she chose not to look for full-time employment in order to devote herself to raising her child. She put her counseling skills to work through a part-time job as director of teenage and young adult activities at the Hallie Q. Brown Community House. [14]

Weekend social activities revolved around friends. Many of them were people of the same age—blacks who lived in the same neighborhood or who participated in the same civic activities, some of them veterans with young families, like the Youngs. Others were older professional people who had been in the Twin Cities for years and had taken the Youngs under their wing. They also had white friends, chiefly people Whitney met in graduate school. None of the younger people had much money (Young's starting salary as industrial relations secretary of the Urban League, for example, was $2,700, which was increased to $3,500 within two years), and most of what they did together—playing cards, listening to records, watching football games or westerns on television, sharing potluck chili or spaghetti suppers—took place at the house of one couple or another. Sometimes there were parties or dances. Few of the couples had cars, but it was possible to carry picnic meals to local parks, or walk to shows at neighborhood theaters, or take the bus to concerts or sports events. Much of the social activity took place under the aegis of the Young Marrieds Club, a group of a half dozen or more black couples who got together every weekend for recreation and conversation. It was all low-key, relaxed, and informal; the Youngs spent comfortable, convivial times with other young couples who were raising families and building professional careers.[15]

Once again, Young's gift for making friends stood him in good stead. He was extremely gregarious, almost magnetic in his ability to establish immediate, lasting connections with other human beings—the sort of person who made new friends believe that they had known him all their lives.

One of those friends, Laura Gaskins, remarked especially on Young's sense of humor. He had a great ability to laugh at himself as well as a gift for telling stories on himself. She remembered when Whitney and her husband, Ashby, were supposed to go fishing. Ash Gaskins was an avid, experienced fisherman, but Young was not. Gaskins told him where to go to get a fishing pole. Before too long, Young, laughing uproariously, arrived at the Gaskinses' house and told the story of his adventure. He had made his way from the store to the nearest streetcar stop without incident, but when the streetcar came, he suddenly realized that he could not get the long pole inside. He noticed a white woman with her hand hanging out the window, pushed the pole into her hand, and jumped on the streetcar. Since she was white, it would have been unseemly for him to lean over her to grab the pole, so she continued to hold it. By this time the other people on the streetcar were laughing, but Young was wondering how he was going to get the pole off the streetcar and what he was going to do if the woman got off first. When he reached his stop, he quickly made his way to the door, ran out, and grabbed the pole, to the great amusement of the people on the streetcar.[16]

Young delighted in other human beings. Coleridge Hendon remembered how he loved to meet people. Often the two men would go out at night to visit bars, community centers, and other places where groups of blacks congregated in order to get some sense of what was on their minds. But there was another side to the fascination with other people, and it sometimes caused problems for Young. The warmth and friendliness could be misinterpreted, and some men were jealous of the attention he paid to their wives. He would often say, " 'I like women,' " Bernese Hendon remembered, "and he did." He had an extraordinary magnetism and seductiveness about him; when he walked into a room, Laura Gaskins recalled, acting out the response, women had a way of swooning. Coleridge Hendon liked to tease him about the way women looked at him; Young would take him aside and say, " 'Man, you're starting trouble—don't talk like that in front of Margaret.' "[17]

Young's effectiveness in his work at the Urban League and in his involvements in the community caught the attention of National Urban League officials in New York. He struck up an especially close relationship with the national executive director, Lester B. Granger. Young idolized the older man; Granger, in turn, thought well of his protégé, and in the spring of 1949, he began to explore the possibility of promoting Young to a position of greater responsibility in the Urban League movement. Seeking S. Vincent Owens's evaluation of Young's work, Granger joked, "I know he is only a *fair* tennis player, but I feel he might have some other exceptionally good qualifications which would merit consideration."

Owens responded with fulsome praise for Young's abilities and accomplishments. He had been interested in Young ever since he entered the School of Social Work, he wrote, and had "seen him develop into an excellent representative of the Urban League." He remarked on Young's outstanding personality and his well-balanced relationships with people, white as well as black. In his work as industrial relations secretary, Young had shown himself to be very conscientious and loyal; he had demonstrated creative ability and insight into Urban League methods and philosophy and had had ample opportunity to observe and participate in the administration of the St. Paul league. He had made good progress in opening employment opportunities and in promoting the league's vocational guidance program. In sum, Young was an exceptional young man with a lot to offer; given his ability, knowledge, and interest, he was clearly ready to assume larger responsibilities.[18]

In the fall of 1949, as the executive director of the Omaha Urban League, M. Leo Bohanon, prepared to move on to the directorship of the Urban League of St. Louis, those who ran the Omaha league asked Lester Granger for help in identifying possible successors. They were looking for a person of broad outlook and initiative, someone who would appreciate the opportunities the job offered. They preferred a young man with potential for future growth even though they were unlikely to be able to hold such a person for more than a short time.

The national office forwarded the names of six candidates, including Whitney Young. He was the youngest, but as the associate executive director, R. Maurice Moss, wrote, "his work in the Minneapolis area has stamped him as one of the most promising men in the industrial ranks." He had had an excellent grounding in the league's methods; among his special strengths were an outgoing personality, a quick grasp of situations, and an ability to plan and to carry out programs.

On the basis of the information Moss had assembled, the Omaha board invited Young to come for an interview. They liked him immediately. There was at least one other strong contender, James A. Pawley, the industrial relations secretary of the Washington, D.C., Urban League. But Young stood out. "Whitney was a charmer," said James Paxson, a member of the search committee; "he had a lot of personality. You would take to him immediately." Another member of the committee, Eugene Skinner, described him as poised, self-confident, articulate, dynamic—"the kind of guy that I think would impress whites." And the fact that he was a Midwesterner and familiar with the problems of the region weighed in his favor. On December 30, the board voted to appoint Young as executive secretary, effective February 1, 1950, at a salary of $4,000.[19]

Young was enormously pleased. He had felt ready to take on new responsibilities and yet uncertain about the possibilities for promotion within the league; the enthusiastic endorsement of his qualifications by both the national office and the Omaha board made him feel that he had a good future in the Urban League movement. Expressions of admiration for his accomplishments and regret at his leaving St. Paul poured in following the announcement of his new post. As the *St. Paul Sun* commented, Young had labored long, hard, and effectively in the interests of employment opportunities for blacks; with his departure for Omaha, the Twin Cities would lose "one of its greatest young Negro leaders of the past decade."[20]

The move to Omaha was the Youngs' first as a family. They would be leaving behind good friends and familiar patterns of social activity and community involvement. As a city, Omaha held no special appeal, as Margaret was quick to recall, but the chance for Whitney to run his own agency made the move irresistible.

The Youngs found a temporary house to rent on Wirt Street, in a black neighborhood, and then looked for a house to buy. They found a place they liked a few blocks away on Spencer Street, just on the edge of a white neighborhood. The street remained integrated while they lived there, but it was on the verge of becoming predominantly black. Whitney and Margaret found friends in the neighborhood, among the Urban League's board and volunteers, at St. John's A.M.E. Church, and through Whitney's civic activities (he served on the boards of the NAACP and the Boy Scouts, among others) and his part-time teaching in the Adult Education School at Creighton University and the Graduate School of Social Work at the University of Nebraska. With Marcia in nursery school at the Joslyn Museum, and then in public school for kindergarten and first grade, Margaret spent time with volunteer activities and homemaking. To help supplement Whitney's salary, she began typing theses for graduate students at the University of Omaha and at Creighton. When the *Omaha Star* featured the Youngs as its distinguished family of the week, it described Margaret as an ardent housewife whose greatest pastimes were reading and sewing.[21]

For Whitney, the challenge lay in using the Urban League to make some headway for blacks in employment, housing, and social services in a small, profoundly conservative city in a white, largely rural Midwestern state. Stretched along the west bank of the Missouri River, Omaha had the largest black population of any city west of Illinois, east of California, and north of Kansas City, Missouri. There were just over 16,300 blacks in the city in 1950, 6.5 percent of the total population. Blacks in Omaha had no difficulty exercising their right to vote, and a state civil rights statute prohibited discrimination in public schools and places of public accommodation. Still, there was a significant gulf between practice and theory; with the exception of one hotel and two restaurants in downtown Omaha, blacks had no certainty of admission to places of public accommodation in the city. When the executive director of the Urban League met for lunch with white businessmen, they ate at the YMCA, one of the few places in town where blacks were sure to be comfortable. There were two all-black elementary schools in Omaha, and four out of five black students failed to graduate from high school, compared to a citywide average of one out of two. Residential segregation was the norm, not the exception; 80 percent of blacks in the city lived on the Near North Side, an area thirty blocks long by twelve blocks wide. One out of every two blacks lived in a building that did not meet minimum housing standards.

Improving employment opportunities for blacks was the largest challenge in Omaha. Despite the efforts of the Urban League and others, it had proved impossible to enact a fair employment practices law for the state. While a proposed city ordinance had the backing of labor, some civic groups, the Council of Churches, the NAACP, and the Urban League staff, no member of the city council was willing to introduce it.

With fifteen meat packing plants, Omaha was the second largest livestock marketing and meat packing center in the world. It had one of the world's largest grain markets, and it was a leading agricultural center. The headquarters of the Union Pacific Railroad and the home of the Western division of the Northwest and Burlington lines, it was the fourth largest railroad center in the United States. The home offices of thirty insurance companies were located in the city as well. All told, almost two-thirds of the blacks who worked in Omaha were employed as laborers or service workers. The packinghouses were the best source of employment. The railroads and the insurance industry hired blacks in service jobs but not in skilled or clerical positions.[22]

Young began immediately to make his presence felt. People remarked again and again on the "real go-getter" who had come to town to take over the Urban League. His first priority was to improve employment opportunities. He defined his task in two ways: first, "to sell management on the value of the Negro employee, especially the skilled and educated"; second, "to work with the Negro people, to make them understand that with increasing freedom of opportunity they have increasing responsibilities." Young argued that eliminating racial discrimination in employment was good business; better job opportunities for blacks meant not only better living conditions for them, but an expanded consumer market for white businessmen. "Businessmen should take the initiative in ending job discrimination against Negroes," he said when he took over at the Urban League at the beginning of February. "They have as great a stake in democracy as anybody." At the league's annual meeting two weeks later, he declared, "We are going to give employers here a chance to set a precedent—to show that the Sermon on the Mount is more than just pretty words."[23]

Patiently, persistently, Young began to chip away at the barriers to black employment. Together with his industrial relations secretary, he made the Urban League's presence more visible; the two men made three times as many visits to employers in Young's first year as league officials had made the year before. Omaha was so conservative that whites on the Urban League board had often thought twice about the advisability of taking the black executive director along when they went to call on major employers. With Young, it was different; in the judgment of attorney Milton Abrahams, he had such an effective personality that white employers might recognize "that it was possible to sit opposite a black without bringing a blemish upon themselves." Young was exceptionally good at making his point. He had the facts, and he presented a convincing argument. He talked about the assets that blacks could offer to businesses in Omaha, and he argued that the economic consequences to the city as a whole of not hiring blacks were more harmful than the consequences of hiring them and taking advantage of their skills.

The pace of job placements picked up accordingly. The Urban League had placed only thirteen blacks in clerical positions in 1949, but it found jobs for forty-five in 1950; placements in skilled jobs grew from fourteen in 1949 to thirty-two in 1950; in semiskilled jobs, the number went from thirty-three to fifty-six; in professional positions, the figure rose from three to seven; and in semiprofessional jobs, from zero to six. The numbers were very small, but the growth was unmistakable. The league registered important firsts in job placements: long-distance operators at Northwestern Bell Telephone Company, elevator operators and sales people in downtown department stores, a clerk and an assistant librarian in the Omaha Public Library, a claims official at the Nebraska State Employment Service, clerical workers at public utility companies, secretaries in businesses and banks, driver-salesmen for dairy companies, and taxicab drivers. The league regarded the blacks who filled these showcase positions as exemplars for what black employment could achieve, and so it chose the people it placed with considerable care, making certain to instruct them about the proper way to dress, about punctuality and absenteeism, and about the way to act among white coworkers. And it imbued them with the sense (as Young said of the first blacks to be hired by two large taxicab companies) "that they were crusaders because of the great possibilities for jobs for more Negroes."

All told, during Young's tenure there were ninety-three such firsts—important not so much for their immediate impact in changing patterns of black employment, but for their symbolic value and for what they promised for the future. At a time when employers resisted hiring blacks on the ground that they were incapable of dependable behavior and sustained, disciplined effort, these pilot placements gave the Urban League a chance to show off black employees who were actually succeeding in their jobs. Significant as they were in those terms, the breakthroughs stood as modest accomplishments in view of the distance still to be covered in achieving real equality of employment opportunity. "I remember," Young told a newspaper reporter years later, "how pleased we were at really what represented such small gains at the time."[24]

The schools, too, began to show small but significant changes. There were still no black teachers in the city's high schools, but there had been some progress at the elementary school level. In 1950, when Young arrived in Omaha, there were twelve full-time black teachers in two all-black public elementary schools. Three years later, there were twenty-five, distributed among six schools, teaching whites as well as blacks. Two private parochial schools had hired black teachers. At the same time, race relations in the public schools showed some improvement; after considerable effort on the part of the Urban League, minstrel shows and racial incidents—commonplace in 1950—almost completely disappeared.[25]

Young also made some progress in changing patterns of access to housing and places of public accommodation. In 1951, in response to persistent pressure orchestrated by the Urban League, the Omaha Housing Authority voted to end racial segregation in its low-rent federal public housing. Young, the *Omaha Star* said, had spearheaded the fight. Through painstaking work with the city's Hotel and Restaurant Association, establishments that had not previously served blacks began slowly to accept their patronage. By the end of 1952, Young reported that all hotels and eating places in the downtown area, as well as motels and tourist camps on the outskirts of the city, served blacks without discrimination.[26]

Some of Young's efforts were organized and institutional, as in the case of the campaign for desegregated public housing. Some were more private and personal, the product of one-on-one persuasion. Some involved cooperative attempts to smooth race relations in potentially tense situations. On one occasion, in the fall of 1950, when a black veteran bought a house in a fringe area just beyond the ghetto, the reaction was ugly. White neighbors sent threatening letters to the buyer and made angry telephone calls to the white man who had sold him the house, as well as to the real estate agent and the financing corporation. They threw bricks and stones through the windows and made plain that the black family risked bodily harm if it tried to move in. Young brought the matter to the attention of Rev. John Markoe, a Jesuit social activist on the faculty of Creighton University who served as guide and adviser to the De Porres Club, an interracial group dedicated to working for equal rights for blacks that had been organized in the 1940s by Creighton students. On the morning the moving van was due to arrive, Markoe and Denny Holland, the young white president of the De Porres Club, sat waiting on the front porch of the vacant house. White neighbors asked what they were doing there. Markoe responded, "We're waiting for the new owners. We're helping them move in." When the van arrived, a group of young blacks and whites, members of the De Porres Club, helped carry in the furniture. Later, the club sent some of its older members to call on the white neighbors to try to smooth the way for their acceptance of the black family.[27]

As the housing incident makes clear, Whitney Young was by no means the only—or even the chief—actor working for racial justice in Omaha in the early 1950s. The De Porres Club, with its boycotts, picket lines, and other forms of direct action, took stands that were far more radical than anything the Urban League could espouse. But Young formed a close working relationship with the club that enhanced his own effectiveness—and, in the process, showed his appreciation of the value of different but complementary approaches in accomplishing social change. When, for example, Young succeeded in negotiating the hiring of black cab drivers, there was some uncertainty about how the community would respond. To offset any negative reactions, he deployed members of the De Porres Club to ride the cabs and tell the drivers that they approved of the new hiring practices. In seeking to persuade businesses to integrate their work forces, Young might tell them that he had information that the De Porres Club was thinking of picketing them. When the club staged a month-and-a-half-long boycott of the local Coca-Cola Bottling Company to protest its discriminatory hiring practices, Young stepped in to settle the dispute, with the result that Coca-Cola agreed to hire blacks. The league and the club divided the work of racial advancement, each handling what it could do best.

Young was an adviser to the members of the De Porres Club who were out on the front lines. He went to their meetings and spent many hours talking with them in his office. He came to places where they were picketing, and he honked and waved to them to show his encouragement. He taught them the importance of building a consensus at the same time that they pushed hard for change. As the president of the club, Denny Holland, put it, Young "helped guide us to the concept that setting fire to some building wasn't going to help a lot."[28]

Throughout his time in Omaha, Young made exceptionally effective human connections, with blacks as well as whites. What "impressed me so was how he could relate to the business world and also relate to the man on the street," his secretary, Bettye Corbin, said. Two or three times a month, he walked the length of Twenty-fourth Street, in the heart of the black community. He stopped in at bars, met people on street corners, and greeted taxi drivers waiting for their fares. He always paused to exchange a few words and find out what was going on. His good friend Art McCaw, the chief examiner in the county tax appraiser's office and a member of the board of the Urban League, who often accompanied him, remarked on the force of his personality and his obvious regard for other people. He was "loved by everybody," McCaw said. "Everybody who met him and talked to him a little bit thought they were his best friends." Young's successor, George Robinson, evaluated his human impact in similar terms. "People gravitated to him," Robinson said. "He had a knack for dealing with people in any walk of life."[29]

In dealing with prominent whites in Omaha, Young profited handsomely from what McCaw described as an "overwhelming ability to make people see his point of view." He preached a straightforward message: "Democracy is everybody's business." He wrote in his first annual report that "in view of world conditions today, the need for good racial relations is more urgent than ever. To meet the challenges hurled at it, America must be democratic in fact as well as in theory. Good relations is not a Negro problem; it is a community problem. It can be solved only by cooperative efforts of all races working together." It was a theme he returned to again and again. "It is mandatory that we in America back up our democratic professions with performance!" he echoed in his final report. "It is necessary that our progress in human relations catch up with our technological advances!"[30]

As he would throughout his professional career, Young managed to get people to listen to him because of the way he approached them. In the conservative environment of Omaha in the early 1950s, he needed all the grace and charm and humor he could muster. Milton Abrahams remembered the dinners at his house to which Young and white businessmen were invited. He did not tell the whites in advance that Young would be there, and they did not know what to make of his presence. Was he a waiter, or was he a fellow guest? The whites showed their disdain for Whitney and Margaret and kept very much on their guard. Sometimes it was difficult to get them to sit opposite Young or even at the same table. Abrahams counted on Young's personality and good nature to help bridge the gap.

Slowly, Young helped modernize the old-fashioned images that whites in Omaha held of blacks. Most of the time he did it by the impact of his logic and reasoning, by the security and self-confidence with which he handled himself, by the force of his charm and personality. Some of the time he did it by unexpected behavior; he might, for example, make a point of kissing all the white women when he came into a room—behavior so audacious for the times that observers believed he did it in order to stir people up.[31]

Young also influenced the whites on the board of the Urban League. For many of them, joining the board was a way of acting out their conviction that blacks ought to have a fair chance at good jobs, decent housing, and better living conditions. For others, less certain in their commitments to racial liberalism, service on the board turned into an opportunity to have their horizons expanded, as Young and some of the black board members worked quietly and patiently to educate them and bring them along.

Some of the white employers on the board clearly demonstrated their sincerity. Otto Swanson instituted a policy of hiring and training black salesmen at the Nebraska Clothing Company. Lloyd Skinner broke the color barrier at his macaroni manufacturing company when he joined the Urban League board; as he said at a league meeting, "I can't be going around asking other people to employ blacks unless I do it myself."[32]

The white realtors on the board stood at the other end of the spectrum. They gave only lip service to the principle that blacks ought to be able to live wherever they wanted. As late as 1963, Robert L. Myers, a black undertaker who chose to move outside the ghetto, found that it did him little good to be serving on the Urban League board with leading white realtors. No realtor was willing to show him a house outside the ghetto; none was willing to sell to him. Ultimately, he built a house through a subterfuge in which a white friend handled all of the negotiations with the builder and the workmen and deeded the house to Myers once it was finished. Two years later, Rev. Charles E. Tyler went to N. Phillips Dodge and Alfred C. Kennedy, both prominent realtors who had each been a chairman of the league's board, for help in buying a house. Tyler, also a member of the board, was well known to them, but they were unwilling to help him move beyond the ghetto.

Myers thought that the realtors on the Urban League board engaged in a lot of "two-sided talk," claiming that *they* were trying to achieve some progress for blacks, but that other realtors, stubborn and less enlightened, stood in the way. "Sometimes," he said, "I even wonder if they weren't just keeping tabs on us, seeing what we were up to." Another black board member, Eugene Skinner, at that time principal of Long Elementary School, was sure that service on the board provided the realtors a means of keeping an eye on the people who were most interested in advancing opportunities for blacks in Omaha—and, if necessary, slowing them down. In 1966 when Young, who had long since left Omaha, came back to the city, he remarked that he was appalled that people could tell him the names of the blacks who lived outside the ghetto. "If you can still name them, you're in trouble."[33]

As the example of the realtors suggests, there were clear limits on what even well-intentioned whites were willing to do for blacks in Omaha in this period. No matter how much charm or logic Young used, he could not change those limits dramatically. But he made at least a modest difference in the way some whites understood the race problem. Phil Dodge's comments illustrate the point. "Whitney Young is the man most responsible for prying open my eyes to the disease of segregation and discrimination in our own community," Dodge declared at a dinner honoring Young after he had been chosen to head the National Urban League. Before coming to know Young, Dodge said, he had simply never realized that Omaha had a racial problem. "He did more to wake me up on racial issues," Dodge reflected years later, "than anyone I know." Moved by Young's message, Dodge joined the Urban League board. "Because of his strength and determination and warm friendship," Dodge said, "I was proud to join him and others to nudge Omaha into the realization that the problem existed, first, and secondly, [that] people of goodwill could actually do something about it. Now—with 20-20 hindsight, I wish I'd done more."[34]

The years in Omaha gave Whitney Young the chance to test his skills, develop his gifts as a communicator between the races, and establish some of the patterns he would return to again and again throughout his professional life. "Here he had the opportunity to stretch his wings and learned to fly," Margaret said years later, in a speech about his time in Omaha. "It was here that he learned to soar . . . to find his own identity." Shortly, that identity would lead him away from Omaha and the Urban League to a new set of challenges in the Deep South.[35]

V

Atlanta: Social Work
and Civil Rights

❧

IN THE LATE SUMMER OF 1953, Rufus E. Clement, president of Atlanta University, came to Omaha to talk to Young about becoming dean of the Atlanta University School of Social Work. As soon as Clement left, Young sought out his friend Art McCaw and told him about Clement's offer. The job was certainly attractive, but it paid less money than Young was making in Omaha. Young wondered what McCaw thought he ought to do. McCaw did not hesitate. "Take it," he said. The job would have its own challenges, and it would put Young in a good position for the future. When it came time for Lester Granger to retire, McCaw thought, there was a good chance that the National Urban League would go outside to find his successor.[1]

Founded in 1920 to train black social workers, the Atlanta School of Social Work had opened with fourteen students and a faculty drawn from among professors at Morehouse College and the staffs of local social service agencies. The sociologist E. Franklin Frazier was director from 1922 until 1927, when he was succeeded by Forrester B. Washington, executive secretary of the Armstrong Association of Philadelphia, an affiliate of the National Urban League. Washington brought professionalism to the fledgling institution, broadening the curriculum, raising the requirements for admission, and lengthening the duration of the program of study. A year after he assumed the directorship, the school was accredited by the American Association of Schools of Social Work, the first school for blacks to be so recognized. The school became affiliated with Atlanta University in 1938, but maintained its own board of trustees and continued to operate as an independent organization. In 1947, it relinquished its charter and became an integral part of the university. The school flourished under Washington's leadership. The enrollment—just 10 students when he took over—grew to 90 in 1938–1939 and 266 in 1946–1947. The affiliation with the university brought decreased enrollments because of the university's more rigid entrance requirements, but the quality of the students improved. Washington transformed the curriculum, introducing new courses designed to meet the specific needs of blacks and initiating a six-month block fieldwork assignment to give students practical experience in social service agencies. By the time Washington retired in 1954, Atlanta was still the only professional school of social work in the state of Georgia.[2]

The prospect of the deanship intrigued Young. He was eager for a new challenge. His experiences as a student and teacher of social work had given him ideas about the most effective ways to train social workers; the deanship at Atlanta would provide an opportunity to put those ideas into practice. Besides, the Atlanta School of Social Work was something of a legend in the black community. It had trained the first black social workers. It had sent students to major northern cities for fieldwork assignments before agencies there had begun to hire black social workers. It had placed black social workers in jobs all over the country. Young felt strongly that so important an institution "shouldn't be permitted to flounder."

Another part of the attraction was the prospect of working for an old family friend. Rufus Clement had been dean of the Louisville Municipal College for Negroes from 1931 until his election to the Atlanta University presidency in 1937, and the senior Youngs and the Clements had belonged to the same professional and social circle. To Whitney, the Clements were Uncle Rufus and Aunt Pearl.

The prospect of moving to Georgia frightened Margaret. She had never been south of Kentucky; even there, her world had been largely confined to a college campus. Race relations in St. Paul and Omaha had been relatively tranquil and tension-free; in Atlanta there would be daily encounters with Southern racism. "I really just didn't want to go that far south," she said. "I hated the thought of going." She told Whitney that she hoped he did not get the job, because if he did, he would have to take it.[3]

Whitney took a different view. Moving south would bring him to the threshold of the emerging civil rights movement. During his years in St. Paul and Omaha, he had seen civil rights become a significant issue in American national politics, for the first time in the twentieth century. Pushed hard by civil rights groups, the president of the United States, Harry S Truman, had appointed a committee in 1946 to investigate the status of black rights. Following the release of its report, *To Secure These Rights*, in 1947, the president had urged the enactment of a fair employment practices law, the outlawing of poll taxes and lynching, and the elimination of segregation in interstate transportation. Later, these recommendations had been incorporated into the 1948 Democratic party platform. Although no civil rights legislation had been passed during the Truman administration, the president had issued executive orders before the 1948 election ending legal segregation in the federal civil service and in the armed forces, and the Truman Justice Department had filed an amicus curiae brief in support of the NAACP's position in *Shelley v. Kraemer*, the 1948 Supreme Court case that found privately arranged restrictive covenants in housing to be unenforceable.

Along with the unaccustomed attention to civil rights issues from the executive branch went promising developments in the Supreme Court. For decades the NAACP had been waging two parallel legal battles against racial discrimination: on the one hand was the effort to secure voting rights for blacks, which had resulted in an important victory in 1944 in *Smith v. Allwright*, outlawing the white primary system used by the state of Texas to deny blacks the right to vote; on the other was the attempt to open educational opportunities to blacks, in which a series of cases enlarging the access of blacks to graduate and professional institutions set the stage for an attack on the constitutionality of segregation in the public schools.

As Young contemplated Clement's offer of the deanship at Atlanta, he knew that the Supreme Court would soon be handing down its ruling in *Brown v. Board of Education*, the flagship of the school segregation cases. A favorable ruling would be of monumental consequence—the equivalent of "a second Emancipation Proclamation," Young thought; it "would create an opportunity in the South for either great victory or great tragedy, and leadership would be desperately needed." "I was born in the South," he said. "Many Negroes had stayed South to help me get educated. I felt that I owed it to them, and to others, to be there during the change."[4]

When Lester Granger learned of Young's discussions with Clement, he tried to interest him in the possibility of the executive directorship of the Washington, D.C., Urban League. It was not the first time Granger had raised the possibility of a move to a larger league. In January 1953, Young had interviewed for the executive directorship in Philadelphia, but he had concluded that it seemed premature to think seriously about leaving Omaha and that the Urban League of Philadelphia appeared intent on choosing a more experienced man.[5] Nevertheless, Young remained an attractive candidate for promotion to a more demanding post. He had made real strides toward improving opportunities for blacks in Omaha, and he had clearly invigorated the Omaha Urban League. By every measurement it had grown significantly under his leadership: a membership of 75 in 1950 had increased to over 1,000 in 1953; attendance at the annual meeting grew from 125 to nearly 800; the budget nearly doubled. And the board, initially composed of ministers, social workers, school teachers, and others, gained significantly in access and influence with the addition of leading businessmen, university officials, and labor leaders.[6]

Young was interested in Granger's proposition. The Urban League was his first love, and the Washington job might offer the kind of challenging situation he was looking for. He told Granger that he was not sure what the outcome would be at Atlanta, and that he would like to have more information about the Washington league.[7]

Once the offer came from Atlanta, however, it proved to be irresistible. The school still had a strong reputation, but as Washington's twenty-seven-year deanship drew to a close, it had begun to decline. To Young, that was part of the attraction. "I was challenged," he said later, "by this opportunity to not just salvage but once again make this one of the leading schools of social work—run by black people, in a black university, for black students." Clement had set attractive terms for the appointment. Young would be named dean (the first leader of the school to carry that title) and professor of social work. His basic salary—$5,800 for nine months work—would be augmented by $400 for administrative duties and $800 for summer teaching, just matching the $7,000 he had earned in Omaha. There were plans to build some new houses for the Atlanta University faculty, one of which would be available to the Youngs by late summer. In the meantime, they could take up residence in a furnished suite in one of the dormitories.[8]

On November 10, Young submitted his resignation to the board of the Omaha Urban League. "I leave Omaha," he told them, "with mixed feelings of pride in our progress but with a realization that much remains to be done before Omaha can become the true symbol of democracy which all of its citizens desire."[9]

An outpouring of praise from the people with whom Whitney had worked in Omaha, along with the prospect of new challenges, left him exhilarated as he contemplated going to Atlanta. For Margaret, waiting for the birth of their second child, the move was much less appealing. The baby was a second daughter, Lauren, who came in early December, three weeks late. "Everybody was saying that the reason was because I knew that as soon as I delivered, we would have to move to Georgia. I was fighting it every way I could." The family spent the Christmas holidays with the senior Youngs at Lincoln Ridge and then moved to Atlanta shortly after the New Year.[10]

Coming to the School of Social Work as Clement's protégé might have caused Whitney some difficulties. At thirty-two, Young was probably the youngest member of the school's faculty. His relationship with Clement was well known; as one professor put it, "He was a fair-haired boy, hand-picked. It just happened that he was a good one."[11]

Young succeeded in strengthening the school in significant ways. He quickly immersed himself in the business of the institution, getting acquainted with faculty members and students, assessing the biggest needs in terms of finances and staffing, and laying plans for changes in the cur-riculum. He doubled the budget, enlarged the full-time faculty, and sub-stantially increased faculty salaries. He changed the composition of the faculty by recruiting more men and more whites, and he integrated the student body. He reorganized the school administratively and delegated more responsibility to members of the faculty. Young sought to promote their professional development by urging them to attend social work con-ferences and by fostering shared professional activities with other schools in the region. Through annual class and field institutes in Atlanta, focusing on major issues in social work education, he improved communication between classroom teachers and the agency staff members supervising students in block field assignments. Young himself participated actively in regional and national social work activities, and he sought board member-ships for himself and his faculty members in social service agencies and professional associations. The result, one of his colleagues said, was "a more serious professional approach . . . and greater unity in purpose among the faculty," and greater visibility for the school.[12]

Along with these changes came significant curricular innovation. With Young's encouragement, the faculty undertook a thorough study of the curriculum, which led to major changes to bring it in line with the new curriculum policy statement of the Council on Social Work Education. Supplementing the traditional training in family casework, child welfare, group work, and community organization, federal grants made possible new programs in psychiatric social work, medical social work, and voca-tional rehabilitation, all of which had the enthusiastic approval of the council.[13]

Young also attracted talented students. One of them was John Mack, a senior majoring in applied sociology at A & T College in Greensboro, North Carolina, who heard Young speak about the School of Social Work and decided that he wanted to study there. Young found a scholarship for him, and Mack enrolled at Atlanta. Later, he became an Urban League executive. He called Young his hero—"the most instrumental person whom I can think of in really impacting my life."

Lyndon Wade, a student at Morehouse, found himself attracted to graduate study in social work because of the example Young set. Not only had Young invigorated the Atlanta School of Social Work, but he had made the field of social work come alive. Young demonstrated through his activities in the community ways of connecting textbook learning and real-world needs. "He was kind of like a beacon light," Wade said, "saying, 'Here's a way for you to make a contribution.' "[14]

Wade was talking about Young's immersion in civil rights. That was part of the reason Young had come to Atlanta, and he took advantage of the opportunities the city offered to work actively for social change. He estimated that within a year of his arrival, he was spending 50 percent of his time on civil rights issues.

The *Brown* decision made the climate ripe for such efforts. The legal destruction of separate but equal in public education opened the way for an attack on separate but equal in other segments of public life. State and federal courts began to hand down decisions extending the effect of *Brown* beyond the realm of school segregation. Equally important, the triumph of *Brown* gave black Americans the hope that racial justice might be within reach. For the first time in their experience, an arm of the federal government had come down emphatically on their side. The result was to stimulate the growth of nonviolent protest in behalf of black rights.

Atlanta—the leading industrial city of the New South—provided a laboratory for the struggle. It was a city of thriving black institutions: banks, insurance companies, businesses, newspapers, churches, and educational institutions, whose leaders constituted a powerful black economic and social elite. Here, especially among the younger businessmen and professionals, was the stuff of potential leadership in the battle for black rights.

As a board member of the Atlanta NAACP, a founder of the Atlanta Committee for Cooperative Action, a leader of the Atlanta Citizens Committee on Economic Opportunity and Employment, and the cochairman of the Greater Atlanta Council on Human Relations, Young found ways to make his voice heard. Those involvements brought him into the thick of campaigns to end discrimination in the Atlanta public schools, to hasten the admission of black students to Georgia State and the University of Georgia, to open employment opportunities to blacks, to eliminate segregated rest rooms in public facilities, and to desegregate the city's transit lines and public library system. Three examples illustrate his efforts: his part in desegregating the Atlanta public library; his role in the activities of the Atlanta Committee on Cooperative Action; and his help as an adviser to the emerging student movement in Atlanta.

Despite the fact that no state law or city ordinance mandated it, the Atlanta public library system, following what it described as the "Southern way of life," adhered to a policy of racial segregation in its facilities. Library services were made available to blacks at three "Negro branches"; the other branches, as well as the central library, were reserved for whites.

In 1958, the Atlanta Council on Human Relations, a newly formed interracial organization, began efforts to convince the library's board of trustees to desegregate the library system. Young, cochairman of the group, took a leading role in developing the strategy for waging the battle. In a report to the council, he outlined the situation. The segregated facilities were insulting and embarrassing to blacks. In addition to the indignity of separation on the basis of color, however, the policy put blacks at a real disadvantage. The Negro branches were often inconvenient to get to, and their resources were no match for the holdings of the central Carnegie Library. Blacks were prohibited from using the main card catalog, and they had no means of easy access to material not to be found in the Negro branches. "One need not be a librarian to realize the loss of efficiency and the waste of money which develops in trying to operate complete library facilities on a segregated basis, relating only to color," Young reported. "Any white person no matter how illiterate, dirty, or undesirable may use the main library, while the most learned, cultural and immaculate Negro citizen is denied."

The council tried to talk the library trustees into changing their policy. Its members collected information about the desegregation of other library systems in the South, marshaled data about the differences in library resources available to whites and blacks, kept statistics on patterns of library use, framed arguments about fairness and efficiency, presented petitions to the board, and held private meetings with the director, but to no apparent avail. At the same time, a group of students in the social science club at Spelman College, anxious to translate their theoretical discussions about processes of social change into action, and in need of a wider range of books than they could find in the Atlanta University library, devised a strategy for confronting the segregated library system. Students and faculty members from the Atlanta University system began visiting the Carnegie Library to ask for books that were unavailable in the branch libraries. They expected to be rebuffed, but they were determined to put pressure on the library. The steady stream of Spelman and Morehouse students repeatedly encountered the same response. The librarian asked if the person requesting the book had tried the Negro branch, and then offered assurances that the book would be sent to the Negro branch for use there. Those who insisted that they needed books immediately were permitted to use them in a special room downstairs or in an office behind the main desk in the Carnegie Library, locations where there would be no danger of contact with white patrons.

In the face of continued unwillingness on the part of the director of the library system to move toward desegregation, the next step was to prepare a suit in federal court. There were favorable precedents: recent lawsuits had resulted in the desegregation of the city's transit system and municipal golf courses and had cleared the way for the admission of blacks to the University of Georgia. Young and Howard Zinn, a professor at Spelman and the faculty adviser to the social science club, took responsibility for finding plaintiffs and securing financial and legal assistance. They found two plaintiffs who met the technical requirements necessary to sue and who were unafraid to risk the consequences—intimidation, harassment, and economic reprisal, among others. At the same time, student visits to the Carnegie Library were intensified.

On Tuesday, May 19, a member of the library board called Young to say that he was disturbed to hear about a lawsuit; could not something still be done to head off the action? Young said that it was too late; there had been plenty of opportunity before to negotiate a settlement without resort to the courts. He told the board member that the parties involved in the suit were meeting that very afternoon to discuss their plans. The man said that he would try to call an emergency meeting of the board at lunch. That afternoon, with Zinn in his office, Young got a call from the library trustee. The board had just met and had agreed to change the policy. The trustee told Young to hold off for a few days, just long enough for the director of the library system to inform his staff about the decision to desegregate. Young and Zinn agreed to give them Wednesday and Thursday and to begin testing the new policy on Friday.

On Friday afternoon, May 22, Irene Dobbs Jackson, a professor of French at Spelman College, walked into the Carnegie Library, went to the front desk, and obtained a membership card. At the same time, Carl Sanders, a violinist and music professor, checked out some chamber music records on the second floor. Within days, two Spelman students and a Morehouse student successfully tested the new policy at one of the white branch libraries. Over the following weeks, desegregation proceeded without significant difficulty or disruption. [15]

The desire to speed up progress on civil rights issues and to breathe some new life into the structure of black leadership in Atlanta led Young, along with other young black professionals and businessmen, to form a new organization, the Atlanta Committee for Cooperative Action. The idea was born in the wake of a meeting of the 27 Club, the vehicle of the older black establishment in the city. On this particular occasion, the club had invited a few younger blacks to attend. The speaker was Mayor William B. Hartsfield.

During the question period after Hartsfield's remarks, Young asked him about the problem of segregated rest rooms in the Atlanta airport. The Council on Human Relations and other groups had been pushing to desegregate all of the facilities at the airport. Hartsfield claimed that the city had made some headway; the signs in the new airport for "Colored" and "White" rest rooms were considerably smaller than in the old facility. Young continued to push: Why, he asked, was it necessary to have the signs at all? [16]

After the meeting, Young met a businessman he knew, Q. V. Williamson, on the street and talked with him about the Hartsfield speech. Not only was Hartsfield reluctant to take the sort of action they wanted, but the older black leaders had been protective of the mayor. Young and Williamson were also concerned about the controversy concerning the Nat King Cole television show. The show was important to blacks because it had a black star and presented black artists in a dignified way. But some whites wanted NBC to take it off the air, and Williamson suggested to Young that they ought to start a write-in campaign to keep the show going. They jotted down the names of a few men they knew who would be in a position to write the letters. They called the men together, told them about the television show and the Hartsfield speech, and decided to organize.[17]

The group was made up of black professionals and businessmen, young men who had the independence to speak out on racial issues without the risk of pressure or reprisals. At the suggestion of M. Carl Holman, a professor at Clark College, they called themselves the Atlanta Committee for Cooperative Action.

The committee had three objectives: to shake up, if not supplant, the old guard leadership that purported to speak for black Atlantans; to call attention to racial problems in the city; and to provide research and technical assistance to support the emerging struggle for civil rights. Young said that ACCA was established to challenge the old guard, upper-middle-class blacks "who were doing well and had pretty much been brainwashed into thinking that Atlanta was an oasis in the desert." The younger leaders saw a city whose potential was seriously marred by persistent racism and discrimination, and they set out to gather facts and raise their voices to move the white establishment to make some changes. Their purpose was not to mobilize demonstrations; they envisioned themselves, as Jesse Hill, president of the Atlanta Life Insurance Company, put it, as a think tank, or, in Holman's words, as "a kind of technical assistance/professional arm" of the black movement. Their premise, Hill said, was that "in order to bring about change, in order to build, in order to achieve something, you had to get the facts."

The group met in the evenings, usually once a month at the house of one or another of the members. The members identified problems and set out together to find ways to address them. Following up on the issues that gave rise to ACCA's founding, they mobilized a letter-writing campaign to urge NBC to continue the Nat King Cole show, and they lobbied for the removal of signs designating segregated rest rooms at the airport. When the Los Angeles Dodgers organization came to Atlanta, ACCA tried to get it to hire black players and park personnel for its Atlanta Crackers team and to allow integrated seating at the ballpark. True to their intention to provide technical assistance to other groups, they cooperated in a project initiated by a local women's club with the aim of improved restaurant and rest room facilities for blacks at Rich's Department Store.

Finally the group hit on a major project. Atlanta liked to boast of being a progressive city; the members of ACCA decided to prepare a report that would inject some realism into the boosterism and lay to rest the myth of Atlanta as "the city too busy to hate." Different members of ACCA took responsibility for individual sections of the report. They collected data and sketched out rough drafts, and Holman put the report together. The Atlanta Life Insurance Company paid the lion's share of the cost of production, and the Southern Regional Council did the printing.[18]

After a year and a half of research and preparation, *A Second Look: The Negro Citizen in Atlanta* was ready for distribution in February 1960. It spelled out in stark detail the inequalities that black Atlantans experienced in education, health services, housing, employment, justice, law enforcement, and policy making. The booklet showed conclusively that Atlanta's rhetorical commitment to opportunity and fair treatment diverged substantially from reality.

Atlanta was "a dynamic and generally forward-looking city—potentially a great city," the booklet began. But for all their pride in their city, Atlantans needed to be on guard against complacency and self-delusion. Committed to helping the city realize its fullest potential, the members of ACCA were asking their fellow citizens "to take a second look at Atlanta . . . to take a long, hard, honest look" at problems that most directly affected the city's black citizens, but also threatened "the civic health of the entire Atlanta community." Atlanta would become a truly great city, they said, only as it recognized its problems and took steps to make "the fullest and wisest use of all its human resources."[19]

The committee had accomplished its work quietly; the young men knew that they would be saying some harsh things about racial conditions in the city, and they did not want the older black establishment to know too much about the effort for fear that they might scuttle it. Once the work was done, it was a different story. Young suggested showing the booklet to some of the older leaders. It was too late for them to block the project; why not let them see what ACCA had accomplished?

They arranged a meeting and passed out copies of the booklet. The older men could not deny the truth of what they saw in it. One of them asked how many copies had been printed. There were not nearly enough, he thought, and he encouraged some of his friends to write checks to enable ACCA to print more. To the surprise of the young men, the older leaders, with whom they had expected to do battle, had turned into allies.

Now *A Second Look* was circulated widely: ACCA mailed copies to a long list of elected and appointed public officials, labor unions, businesses, voters' groups, neighborhood associations, fraternal groups, service organizations, ministerial groups, and others, with a covering letter explaining its purposes and inviting comment. Both the *Atlanta Daily World* and the *Atlanta Constitution* gave the booklet's contents detailed coverage, and the city's ministerial organizations instructed their members to use it as the basis for their sermons.[20]

A Second Look won public approbation from the older black leaders ACCA had been trying to supplant. The president of Clark College called it a "statesmanlike document" that provided "a magnificent array of pertinent and relevant facts," and said that "every responsible citizen should be shamed by the ugly picture of inequality, injustice, and unfairness . . . and should be moved to join those who would make every sincere effort to correct these evils." The *Atlanta Daily World* described the booklet as "sober and factual. . . . There is no irresponsible rabble-rousing; it is not key-noted to defeat or despair. While due credit is given for the progress Atlanta has made in certain areas, the major emphasis is on the corrective tasks that lie before all of us."

Equally important, *A Second Look* caught the attention of the students who were about to launch a campaign of sit-ins and demonstrations in Atlanta. The *New York Times* portrayed it as a plan for political action, and the *Atlanta Constitution* thought that it forecast campaigns by blacks to combat segregation in public accommodations. The Atlanta University students read it the same way. It "became a kind of impetus to us," Julian Bond, one of the leaders of the Atlanta student movement, said; it "sort of made people think, gee, maybe there is something here, maybe there is some reason for black people to be upset." *A Second Look* "gave us a basis larger than simple discontent with lunch counter segregation" around which to construct a protest movement; "it gave us an intellectual rationale greater than the desire to eat a hamburger."[21]

The Atlanta student movement drew its immediate inspiration from the student sit-ins that began in Greensboro, North Carolina, on February 1, 1960, when four black freshmen at A & T College sat down at a Woolworth's lunch counter and ordered coffee. When they were refused service, they sat quietly and politely until the store closed. Within a year, more than fifty thousand people would participate in sit-ins in over one hundred cities to protest racial discrimination in public facilities.

News of the student sit-in in Greensboro prompted students in the Atlanta University complex to organize their own demonstrations. Aimed especially at segregated lunch counters and businesses that practiced discrimination in hiring, the student sit-ins, marches, and boycotts kept the city of Atlanta embroiled in racial controversy for the better part of a year.

The Atlanta students announced their intentions in a statement of grievances, "An Appeal for Human Rights," which appeared as a full-page ad in the Atlanta newspapers on Sunday, March 9, 1960. In composing their account of what was wrong in the city, they drew directly on the facts and figures presented in *A Second Look*. That was precisely the sort of influence ACCA had hoped to have.[22]

Rufus Clement, who was then chairman of the Atlanta University Council of Presidents, did what he could to slow the movement. Anxious that the university keep a low profile and avoid controversial issues, he managed, largely by encouraging the students to prepare the statement of grievances, to delay the demonstration until the middle of March. Clement also forbade the students to hold meetings on the Atlanta University campus with white students from nearby institutions whom they had enlisted in their cause. Many faculty members and administrators in the university system counseled the students against engaging in demonstrations. Blacks in the community shared their reservations. "There were many of our elders," John Mack, a student at the Atlanta School of Social Work and one of the organizers of the protests, said, "who thought we were crazy, we were wild, we were fanatical, we ought to cut it out, we were going to bring hell and damnation upon all black people and were going to set the movement back thousands of years."[23]

A small number of Atlanta University faculty members, however, along with a handful of other black adults in the community, willingly embraced the student movement and functioned as informal advisers. From the university came Carl Holman, Howard Zinn, and Whitney Young. Clarence D. Coleman of the Urban League often took part in the discussions. Martin Luther King, too, offered advice when he was in Atlanta. Mack called them major supporters of the protest movement. The group met late at night, usually at the house of one of the faculty members, to discuss strategy and tactics. They talked about the schedule for demonstrations, the best targets, how to mobilize broad support, how to bridge the gap between the university and the larger community. The students trusted the older men not to sabotage them, and communication was direct and candid.[24]

Young was "one of these increasingly rare black academics" who believed that social science ought to have "some immediate relevance," Bond said. He believed in marshaling information and resources to attack problems; he was not afraid of organizing to bring about social change. Accordingly, especially in the view of the student organizers from the School of Social Work, he emerged as a real confidante.

"Whitney was probably the person," Mack said, "who worked—I won't say harder—but at least was perhaps the glue that caused it all to stick and come together." Young was always there when the students needed help. He offered sound advice and moral support, as well as practical assistance in terms of access to money, equipment, facilities, or other resources.[25]

Whenever the students turned to Young, he stood firmly beside them. The night before the first major demonstration on March 15, Mack and another social work student, Johnny Parham, believing that some university officials ought to be aware of their plans, went first to notify the president of Morehouse, Benjamin Mays, and then to see Young. Students at the School of Social Work were concerned about missing classes to join the demonstration. Young said he could not officially excuse them, but that he was fully in support of the protest.

Mack remembered planning a major demonstration at which three groups of protesters would be deployed simultaneously to federal, state, and private facilities to dramatize the demand for change. "There were all kinds of people who thought it was a terrible idea," Mack said; the mayor, the chief of police, and their friends tried to persuade Young, King, and their friends to talk the students out of it. But Young held firm.

Older, conservative blacks, too, tried to lean on Young and his colleagues to stop the protest movement. To C. A. Scott, the publisher of the *Atlanta Daily World*, the fault was not so much with the students but with their adult supporters: "Over there on that campus, it's Whitney Young and Carl Holman puttin' these students up to doin' all this stuff." Scott saw the protests as "jeopardizing his paper by making his good white advertisers mad," Mack thought. When, after a large protest meeting at the Wheat Street Baptist Church, the students raised money for an ad in the *Daily World*, Scott refused to run it. Young tried to prevail on Scott not just to run the ad but to be supportive of what the students were trying to accomplish. Mack remembered the response: "Mr. Scott told Whitney that he was dead in that city as far as he was concerned—he would never get another line of coverage as long as he was there because of his involvement with us."[26]

To a Northern audience, Young sought to explain his understanding of the movement. The bus and lunch counter demonstrations were "dramatic symbols to protest the institution of segregation" and to refute "the lie that the Southern Negro is satisfied with his conditions." Behind them stood "the deeper realities, or the results of segregation; the newborns who die, the talented who are forced to accept menial jobs, the public tax supported educational and cultural facilities closed to citizens because of an accident of birth and the mother who is forced to live in a two-room rat infested apartment with her five children paying $80. per month rent." The disturbances were "symptomatic, not of regression, but of forward movement, bitterly contested," he said. The South's troubles were the "results of an old order's last desperate rally against new forces." The student protesters were behaving "in a dignified, calm and dispassionate manner," quite a sharp contrast to "the leather-jacket, ducktail hoodlums who assault them. . . . The backdoor sandwich so good to eat is now too humiliating to buy," Young continued. "The back seats of buses so comfortable to tired feet are too heavy a burden for a soul seeking dignity." The struggle was not "merely an attempt to escape personal injustice and humiliation"; the demonstrators believed that they were "fighting the cause of America and the preservation of democracy in trying to make this country the moral leader of the world."[27]

The intensity of Young's commitment to the movement surprised some of the people who knew him. "It was Whitney Young's fortune to be underestimated throughout most of his life by people who should have known better," Carl Holman wrote years later. "Even among those of us who were his friends and colleagues in Atlanta back in the late 1950s, Whitney seemed so affable, so much in love with the sheer living of his not uncomfortable life . . . that very few correctly gauged the depth of his concern." Well dressed, suave, he never quite looked the part of the civil rights activist. Perhaps his marvelous exuberance worked against a full understanding of his seriousness of purpose; perhaps it was the fact that he so obviously loved a good party and the company of attractive women. Whatever the reason, those who shared Holman's view did not fully grasp the complexity of the man. As Young's School of Social Work colleague Ginger Hill summed up, "He'd be one of the boys on the corner at the same time as he sat breaking bread with those who led. . . . Kind of rare. I don't know that I've ever known a black person exactly like Whitney. I say that because the sense of comfortableness he had in mobility, not a lot of blacks had, because they hadn't had the exposure or the inner strength to be comfortable with who they were and take themselves wherever they chose to go."[28]

For all Young's personal satisfaction in his leadership of the School of Social Work and in his involvement in the civil rights movement, the years in Atlanta carried real costs for his family. There was comfort and security in the small compound of two-story, red-brick faculty houses on Beckwith Street, two-fifths of a mile from the university and just opposite the winding driveway leading to Holly Hill, the residence of the Atlanta University president. And there was conviviality and good friendship in the circle of well-educated, middle-class black professionals, businessmen, and educators who socialized regularly in each other's houses. For Margaret, however, there was also deep discontent. She found gratification in her family and friends and satisfying professional challenges in her job teaching education and psychology at Spelman College. But the burden of battling the indignities of everyday life in a segregated society became too much to bear.

"I hated it down there", she said years later. "I was angry all of the time. . . . I was just crippled being there." There were so many reminders of second-class status; one could agree to follow the conventions dictated by whites or try to avoid them, but either choice carried pain. Margaret found ways to maintain self-respect. She would not ride the buses. "I tried it once," she said, "taking Marcia to town on the bus, and when I got on the bus and saw this sign, 'Blacks seat from the back,' I got off. I just was not ready for that. . . . I think it hit me too suddenly and too fast." She would not agree to the indignity of segregated rest room facilities; she always told the children to go to the bathroom before they went downtown. She refused to use the public park designated for black people. When the zoo and Stone Mountain—ordinarily segregated—opened their doors on "Black Day," she declined to go. "As far as I was concerned," she said, "if there was only one day, then there was no day." "Perhaps if I had been by myself," she mused, "I would have walked into some of the doors that were shut, but I wasn't going to take my child through."[29]

Another way of maintaining self-respect was to extend respect to other blacks. In later years, Whitney frequently told the story of what happened when they first hired a housekeeper. The woman told Margaret that her name was Carrie. Margaret said, "Then what is your last name?" "Johnson," the woman replied. "Thank you, Mrs. Johnson," Margaret said. When the Young children came home from school on the housekeeper's first day, Margaret introduced them. "Lauren and Marcia, this is Mrs. Johnson." The woman said, "Oh, Mrs. Young, you don't have to do that. I like to be called Carrie. It makes me feel more comfortable, like one of the family, and I can relate better to the children. And after all, white people call me Carrie. So you don't really have to do that." Margaret said, "Mrs. Johnson, we are not doing this for you, as much as we respect you; we're doing it for our children. We don't permit them to call a forty-year-old woman by her first name. We don't let them call any of our friends by their first names, and if we don't let them do it for anybody else why should we let them do it for you? We're trying to teach them that there is no difference between people because of the color of their skin or the kind of work they do."

About an hour later, the phone rang. A small boy asked, "Is Carrie there?" Margaret said, "There is no Carrie here," and hung up. Then she told Mrs. Johnson that she thought the call had come from her son and suggested that she call him back. When the housekeeper phoned to ask her son if he had made the call, the boy said, "Yes, but the lady said there was no Carrie there." His mother answered, "And there isn't. In this house I am somebody."[30]

In the private world of the family, one could find ways to push at the normal boundaries of racial relationships. But in public settings racial conventions were stronger. Accommodations to racism, no matter how defiant, no matter how successful in preserving dignity and self-respect, always carried human costs. One of the most painful was the need to explain segregation to the children. The girls were always asking questions: "*Why* don't we eat downtown anymore? *Why* don't we go on any picnics anymore?" Marcia, seven years old when the family moved to Atlanta, understood. She had a clear sense of the differences between Omaha and Atlanta; some of her favorite pleasures, like eating at the lunch counter in a downtown department store, were no longer possible. And she experienced firsthand some of the limits imposed by segregation. When she read her way through the books on the shelves at the local Negro branch library, it was impossible to go to the central library to get more books.

With Lauren, it was more difficult. A baby when the family came to Atlanta, she was too young to grasp the restrictions imposed on blacks or to appreciate the significance of the struggle to change them. In 1960, in the midst of the boycott of Rich's Department Store, Lauren, then six, announced that she wanted to go to Rich's to buy a record. Margaret said, " 'You can't go to Rich's. We aren't going to Rich's now.' 'Why aren't we?' And Marcia said, 'Lauren, we aren't going to Rich's because they won't let us eat there, and so we don't buy there.' And Lauren said, 'Well, I don't want to eat, I just want to buy a record.' "

Along with the frustrations of living in a segregated society, there were fears about physical safety. Whitney was in the public eye, taking controversial stands on racial issues that angered some whites. They responded with hate letters and threatening telephone calls. One particular incident stood out in Margaret's memory. In the midst of heated debate over the desegregation of the public schools, one of the Atlanta newspapers published an editorial saying that the NAACP was trying to move things along too quickly. Whitney wrote a letter to the editor asking, "Is over a hundred years too fast?" One night, when he had gone out of town, the phone rang, and Margaret heard a voice saying, " 'Is Whitney there?' And I said, 'No, Whitney Young is not here.' And he said, 'When do you expect him?' I said, 'Well, I don't know.' I said, 'He's out of town and he should be in soon. Who is this?' And he said, 'Well, you just tell him I notice he wrote his obituary in the evening paper.' " Then came Young's appearance before the Georgia Commission on Education in March 1960, when he spoke in behalf of the NAACP to urge compliance with the *Brown* decision. "Those were times," Margaret said, "when you were afraid a little bit for your safety."

Margaret made no secret of her feelings about living in the South. On social occasions, when people asked her, "How do you like Atlanta?" she responded, "I don't like it." (Whitney would ask when they got home, "Margaret, can't you just say, you like it better?") She suggested to him at one point that perhaps she should leave to go north; he could follow when he had had enough.[31]

As early as 1958, Whitney began telling friends that the family's time in Atlanta might soon be drawing to a close. He felt strongly about his responsibilities to his job and to the broader community, but he also had a responsibility to his family, especially the children, and he needed to consider their needs and interests. Besides, he had begun to receive some appealing job offers. It was clearly time to begin thinking about his future.[32]

There was good reason to believe that the future held greater opportunities and challenges. In the spring of 1959, the National Conference on Social Welfare honored Young with its Florina Lasker Award for outstanding achievement in professional leadership and public service. A member of his faculty had nominated him some months earlier, praising Young as a teacher, scholar, administrator, professional citizen, and community activist. He noted especially Young's contributions to the civil rights struggle. The nominator (himself apparently white) remarked on Young's characteristic role as the only black person in a group. "Thousands of individuals have had their attitudes changed through this relationship in which these persons were enabled to see Mr. Young not as a gifted Negro, but rather as an outstanding professional and human being." The award committee named Young its recipient for 1959; he was being honored, the committee chairman said, especially for his " 'vigorous, wise and unafraid leadership' in the field of desegregation and civil rights." At thirty-eight, he was the youngest person ever to receive the Florina Lasker Award.[33]

As the Lasker Award implied, Young's future lay beyond Atlanta. He began to make applications for fellowships that might take him away from the city. He could not have known that the speech he would give at the National Urban League's annual conference in Washington in September would set in motion a train of events that would determine his course for the rest of his life.

VI

A Year Off
and a New Job

ONCE YOUNG made up his mind to explore ways of getting out of Atlanta, a number of opportunities began to come his way. Initially, the most appealing prospect involved a combination of a Southern Regional Education Board research fellowship and some part-time teaching at the School of Social Welfare at the University of California at Los Angeles in 1958–1959. The fellowship did not come through, and the dean of the School of Social Welfare encouraged Young to think instead about a visiting lectureship at UCLA for a semester or a year. Young declined, at least for the time being. There had been a number of administrative changes at Atlanta University in the last couple of years, and Rufus Clement was reluctant to have him go. Young's faculty, too, resisted the idea of a leave, in view of the curricular developments then underway at the school. Young told the dean that he was still keenly interested in teaching at UCLA and asked for a rain check.[1]

Whether Young really saw a teaching post elsewhere as consistent with his ambitions remains an open question. He had another attractive invitation—this from the University of Chicago School of Social Work for a full professorship in community organization, with a concurrent appointment as head of the department—which he also declined. There were opportunities outside social work education as well; the executive directorship of the Urban League affiliate in Philadelphia was vacant again, and Young knew he was under consideration for the job. In June 1958, he wrote Lester Granger to ask advice about his future: "My interest, convictions and dedication continue to remain very close to the Urban League program, and I would therefore, consider very seriously any challenging opportunities."[2]

Young kept his league connections in good order. Granger used him as an adviser and sounding board and included him on the program at the

Urban League's annual conferences. Young's most important appearance came when he addressed the annual conference in Washington, D.C., in early September 1959.

Young took as his theme "the role of the Urban League in the current American scene." That role was fundamentally the same as it had always been: to improve the social and economic conditions of blacks through interracial teamwork. But the context in which the league operated had changed. Now there was a national movement for racial advancement that focused on changing the law. No matter how successful it might be, however, there would still be barriers to the elimination of discrimination and second-class citizenship. The first barrier came from people who continued to try, through every subtle device, to thwart equal opportunity for blacks. The second resulted from the long history of suppression, exploitation, segregation, and discrimination, all of which handicapped blacks and left them unable to compete on an equal basis with whites.

The Urban League was the agency best equipped to confront those obstacles. It was a social work agency, Young said, not a civil rights organization; as such, its program properly focused on research and communication. The Urban League needed to have the facts about the situation of blacks in any given community, and it needed to communicate those facts to the people and institutions with the power to do something about them. In addition to acquainting policy-making bodies with the needs of its constituents, the league needed to encourage those constituents to avail themselves of existing services. "It is one thing to eliminate barriers," Young said, "it is another to get effective utilization of the new resources."

What was at stake was not just "adjusting minority citizens to urban cities" and not only "improving the social and economic conditions of Negro citizens"; the real stakes were "America and a truly American way of life."[3]

Young's speech came at a critical moment in the history of the National Urban League. As he doubtless knew, by the late 1950s, the organization was generally acknowledged to be in the doldrums. Granger, already past sixty, had served as executive director for almost two decades. In earlier years he had been a capable leader. But in the judgment of many Urban Leaguers, he had become excessively cautious, unwilling to identify the league with the emerging civil rights movement, reluctant to speak out on major public issues, resistant to pressures from local executives and board members who called for greater activism. The organization could barely raise a modest budget of $300,000 a year. Some weeks it could not even meet its payroll.[4]

Those circumstances made many Urban Leaguers ready to listen to a reassessment of the agency's purposes and prospects, an opportunity that must not have been lost on Young as he prepared his speech. Among them was a particularly influential newcomer to the National Urban League's board of trustees.

Late in the afternoon following his speech, Young found a handwritten note in his mailbox at the Sheraton-Park Hotel. "Admiration and congratulations on a magnificent presentation—imaginative, vigorous, and right to the point," it said. "Worth coming to Washington to hear!" The writer was the new board member, Lindsley F. Kimball, vice president of the General Education Board, later executive vice president of the Rockefeller Foundation, and a longtime philanthropic counselor to the Rockefeller family. Looking after the Urban League had been a Rockefeller family tradition. In its earliest years, John D., Jr., had been the largest single contributor; in the 1940s his son Winthrop, a trustee, had shaped its major fund-raising efforts. A personal gift from Winthrop had enabled the league, in 1956, to acquire its first permanent headquarters building on East Forty-eighth Street in New York. Not long thereafter, Winthrop had moved to Arkansas, where he would later develop a political career. In his absence, and with the league in real difficulty, the Rockefellers suggested that Kimball go on the board and see what he could do to invigorate the organization. He thought that the first priority was to make a change in its leadership.[5]

Young's speech gave Kimball an idea. "I was immediately struck," he said, "by his earnestness, his energy, his constructive imagination and really courageous vigor in dealing with difficult subjects before a mixed audience." Kimball thought Young had the makings of a national leader. The two men spent a couple of hours together, talking, among other things, about Young's future. Was Young satisfied at Atlanta, Kimball wondered? What were his hopes for his career? "He said he was bumping his head against the ceiling at Atlanta. I told him that he belonged in the active arena rather than the halls of academe."[6]

Kimball returned to New York. W. J. Trent, Jr., the executive director of the United Negro College Fund, remembered Kimball's excitement at his discovery. "That's the man we've got to have for the Urban League!" he said. Some weeks later, at Young's request, he and Kimball continued their conversation over lunch at the Rainbow Grill in New York. Kimball suggested that Young take a year's sabbatical and go to a major university on a General Education Board fellowship. It would provide a good chance for him to read and reflect and get to know some people. Afterward, he would be in a good position to make a move professionally.

Young was startled and delighted at the suggestion. He had come for advice, not money; here Kimball was proposing an ideal solution that would further Young's own interests and make it possible for him to take care of his family. The reluctance to leave Atlanta that Young had mentioned in response to the offer from UCLA was no longer there. Perhaps circumstances at the School of Social Work had changed sufficiently to make the timing propitious; perhaps, too, Young finally sensed an opportunity consistent with his aspirations. Whatever the reasons, he embraced Kimball's proposition with "complete elation and enthusiastic expectation."[7]

The two men met a number of times during the fall. Kimball helped Young define his objectives for the year's sabbatical and asked him to think carefully about the best place to spend it. Young had thought that he might want to go back to the University of Minnesota and had corresponded with the dean of the School of Social Work about the possibility of doing advanced work in administration and community organization. Kimball encouraged him to consider a new environment that might give him a greater challenge and a richer experience—perhaps the University of Chicago, the University of California, or Harvard.[8]

In response to Kimball's invitation, Young explained at some length his philosophy of race relations and the rationale for the studies he would undertake during the period of the fellowship. His primary interest, he wrote, was in the field of race relations:

With every fiber in me I desire to see these become obsolete words, to see segregation and discrimination become tragic episodes in the history of this potentially great country of ours. I sincerely believe that I am motivated in this obsession not simply because I am a Negro and suffer many indignities, but because of my more basic concern about human dignity versus human exploitation, about human potential versus human waste, about hope as against despair, and about love as against fear and hate. Finally, I would like to feel motivated by my desire to help America live up to its ideals, not for the purpose of acquiring smugness or ridding us of our guilt but rather so we could serve as an alive, dramatic and honest example of the possibilities for human beings throughout the world.

He proposed to look beyond the elimination of legal barriers—the principal focus so far of the civil rights movement—to examine some of the other problems that would have to be addressed before blacks could achieve first-class citizenship. Could integration be furthered by rewarding compliant institutions? What could be done to strengthen the black family? How could one promote greater aspiration and stimulate pride among black youths? Were there ways to make better use of the health and welfare agencies that had regular contact with those blacks suffering the greatest deprivations? These were only a few of the questions he wanted to pursue.[9]

In early December, Young made formal application to the General Education Board for a grant to support the year's sabbatical. In less than three weeks, he had official approval for a twelve-month fellowship, to begin in September 1960, for study in the social sciences at a university to be chosen in consultation with the officers of the board. He would be paid a stipend of $1,000 a month, and an additional sum of $3,000 would be available to cover costs of tuition and authorized travel expenses connected with the fellowship. It was the largest award of its kind that the General Education Board had ever made, Kimball told Young; "that's a testimonial to our customer!" The GEB was "very happy to boost a good man on his way!"[10]

The question of where to spend the year remained unsettled. Young consulted with friends and visited institutions that he thought might be appropriate. His friend Hylan Lewis, then at the Health and Welfare Council in Washington, argued persuasively for the advantages of choosing Harvard. Young tried out Lewis's logic in a letter to Kimball: The Boston-Cambridge area was unequaled as a center of higher learning; it offered extraordinary human and institutional resources, as well as ample opportunity for cross-fertilization among the disciplines. Given Young's interest in the application of scholarly knowledge to social policy, it would be hard to improve on the programs and people available at Harvard, the Massachusetts Institute of Technology, and Boston University. A trip to Boston confirmed Young's inclinations. He would enroll at Harvard as a special auditor, with a home base in the Department of Social Relations and the freedom to sit in on courses throughout the university as well as at Boston University and MIT. Officials at Harvard approved the arrangements, and Rufus Clement authorized the year's sabbatical from Atlanta University.[11]

During the spring, Young continued to confer with Kimball about his plans. At Kimball's suggestion, he went to New York to meet Dean Rusk, the president of the Rockefeller Foundation, whom Kimball had told of Young's ambitions. Young struck up a correspondence with Rusk, discussing his forthcoming year at Harvard, exchanging ideas on problems of mutual interest, and inviting Rusk's comments on a paper he had written about the role of foundation support in enhancing race relations. He told Rusk that he was a real optimist with great faith that Americans would find ways to resolve the crucial problems of human relations. Young also tried to get Rusk to hire him. He stopped in to see him on his way to Cambridge, and in the course of the conversation, Young made plain that he would like to work for the Rockefeller Foundation as part of an "action program" in social welfare. Rusk told him that the foundation was not engaged in such activities, to which Young responded, " 'Then you ought to be.' "[12]

In early August, the Youngs left Atlanta, reasonably certain that their departure would be permanent. Rufus Clement understood that his dean would not be returning to Atlanta, and at least some faculty members did as well. "We knew he had to go," Ginger Hill said. "He'd done his grow-

ing here and left a legacy, and it was time for him. We regretted it, terribly. We were saddened, but we knew for him, it was time."[13]

As the family traveled north, Whitney and Margaret each had their own
private reasons for anticipation: for Whitney, there was the excitement of
the year ahead; for Margaret, there was the relief of leaving Atlanta. They
spent a good part of the summer in Kentucky with the senior Youngs. In
early September, they arrived in Cambridge. They moved into a Harvard
University apartment at 18 Robinson Street, a building reserved for graduate students and faculty. Sam Westerfield, an old friend from Atlanta
University who was teaching in Cambridge, lived just downstairs. Howard Zinn, another friend from Atlanta, was also at Harvard for the year on
a fellowship. Finding some familiar faces made the new surroundings
seem less strange.

The Youngs enrolled both girls in private school to try to compensate
for some of the limitations in the education they had received in the
South. Marcia, a ninth-grader, went to the Cambridge School of Weston;
Lauren, a first-grader, was enrolled at Buckingham. Margaret volunteered at the International Student Center and immersed herself in visits
to museums and historic sites, hungry for the things that she had not had
a chance to do in Atlanta.[14]

For Whitney, the fellowship year brought precisely the advantages he
had imagined. He made the Department of Social Relations (as sociology
was then called) his home base. Initially, Thomas F. Pettigrew, an assistant professor of social psychology, served as his adviser; in February,
when one of the senior men in the field, Gordon W. Allport, returned
from leave, he took on the responsibility. In the first semester at Harvard,
Young audited Pettigrew's Psychology of Social Processes, economist
John Kenneth Galbraith's Social Theory of Modern Enterprise, and psychologist Timothy Leary's Processes of Social Influences. He also sat in on
courses at nearby institutions. He went to sociologist Adelaide Cromwell
Gulliver's Peoples and Cultures in Africa at Boston University, political
scientist Harold Lasswell's Personality, Society and Politics at MIT, and
social work dean Charles I. Schottland's Social Work and Social Policy at
Brandeis. The second semester brought courses in social relations taught
by Allport, David Riesman, and Talcott Parsons, among others. At Harvard Summer School in 1961, Young enrolled in three more courses in
social relations. Outside the classroom, there were long conversations
with people he thought he could learn from; Howard Thurman, the dean
of Marsh Chapel at Boston University, was a notable example. Young took
the fullest advantage of the human and intellectual resources available to
him. He had an insatiable appetite for knowledge, a great curiosity about
other people's points of view. "He always wanted to know," Margaret
reflected; "he always turned to people who he felt had answers."[15]

Young stayed in reasonably close touch with the Atlanta University School of Social Work. The acting dean, Frankie V. Adams, wrote him frequently about issues of curriculum, personnel, and funding, and he responded in detail to questions and requests for advice. But his thoughts were on the future, and that future did not include returning to the deanship in Atlanta.

Hindsight allows a simple interpretation of the connection between Whitney Young's year at Harvard and his appointment as executive director of the National Urban League. Lindsley Kimball had handpicked Young to succeed Lester Granger, and the sabbatical was part of a plan to groom him for his new responsibilities. As Young told an interviewer in 1970, by the time he went to Cambridge "it was pretty well known" that he would be moving a year later into the executive directorship at the league. The National Urban League board, he said, had decided that "this one year of relaxation and research and reading and refreshment would be a way of preparing me for coming into this job."[16]

A number of Young's friends (for whom he was presumably the major source of information on the subject) told a similar story. John Mack and Johnny Parham, Young's protégés in Atlanta, said that when he left for Cambridge, they knew he was on his way to the top post at the league. Howard Zinn called Young's year at Harvard "part of the grooming process." Carl Holman, Young's colleague at Atlanta University, described it as a way of "prepping him for taking over the League." Louis Martin, an influential black Democrat then serving on the board of the National Urban League, said that "the Rockefeller crowd" had identified Young as "a likely guy" and had sent him to Harvard to add "a little eastern veneer" to his "southern common sense." Another board member, John H. Johnson, the black publishing company executive, said that Kimball arranged the year at Harvard "to smooth off the rough edges, so to speak"; it was clear that Young was his candidate for executive director, but he delayed the selection in order to neutralize those members of the board who were opposed to Young on the grounds that he was too young and not yet enough of a national figure.[17]

In fact, the process of choosing Granger's successor was a complicated one that involved a number of important members of the National Urban League's board. There is no doubt that Kimball knew clearly what he had in mind for Young's future, but Kimball was not a member of the search committee for the new executive director; and for all Kimball's undisputed power as a member of the board, the search committee that eventually endorsed Young's appointment came close to settling on another choice. Accordingly, the story of Young's appointment as the new National Urban League executive needs to be told not as the unfolding of a predetermined plan, but as a progression of events that held within them the possibility of different outcomes.

In November 1959, Young had attended the National Urban League's Equal Opportunity Day banquet at the Waldorf-Astoria Hotel in New York. The next afternoon, he talked at length with Granger. "Your frankness and expression of confidence were appreciated at our conference," he wrote Granger in a letter of thanks. "As I indicated to you, I will of necessity have to proceed with tentative plans for a Sabbatical next year, but will be available for more definite consideration of the position when such time arises. I am confident," he continued, "that the details involving your continuing role can be worked out, primarily because of our relationship." Young alluded to the job again three weeks later in a letter to Kimball. Ever the gifted manipulator of people, he wondered ingenuously just what it was that Kimball had in mind for his future. "As I reflected back on our conversations," he wrote, "it occurred to me that other than very general encouragement you were never at all specific about what you would like for me to do. I appreciated very much this freedom to make my own decisions, but I am also aware that you would not be making an investment of this type unless you had something in mind in terms of a substantial contribution which I might make." Young reminded Kimball that he had had "several job possibilities, including the Urban League post." Some of them might still be available after the year at Harvard; it seemed to make sense to shape his program of study to some degree in anticipation of the job he would be likely to take. "What I am really asking you," he wrote Kimball, "is, 'What would you see as the type of position in which I could make the greater contribution, consistent, of course, with my interest?' "[18]

It seems plain that Granger had talked to Young about the executive directorship of the National Urban League, if not at the November meeting, then on some subsequent occasion. In March 1960, as the league prepared to search for Granger's successor, he wrote the chairman of the search committee to make some suggestions about the process. "Whitney Young, the Dean of the Atlanta School of Social Work, is actually interested in the post." He then added, "I consider him to be one of the better prospects."[19]

Convincing Granger to retire was no simple matter. There was no doubt that it was time for him to go; after two decades as executive director of the Urban League, he was too old and too tired to meet the challenge of heading the league in the era of the civil rights movement. Kimball came up with a formula that would satisfy Granger and allow him to save face: the General Education Board would give him a two-year travel grant, and he would step down from the Urban League post. Granger's retirement was set for 1961, thus clearing the way for a search for a new executive director.[20]

In September 1959, Theodore Kheel, president of the National Urban League, asked his board for authority to name a committee to handle the search. He got immediate agreement, but the committee had not yet been appointed when Kheel reported to the board in late January, and the board authorized the executive committee to act as the responsible group.

The search committee consisted of four members of the executive committee, all officers of the board. The magazine publisher Henry Steeger, Sr., senior vice president of the league, who would succeed Kheel as president in 1960, was chairman. The other members of the group were Mollie Moon, a vice president and the longtime head of the Urban League Guild; Regina Andrews, the head librarian of the Washington Heights branch of the New York Public Library and the secretary of the board; and Burns W. Roper, president of Elmo Roper & Associates, public opinion analysts, then serving as the league's treasurer.[21]

Granger began immediately to make suggestions about how to run the search. In early March, he wrote Steeger, "I hope that I have not been presumptuous in setting a schedule for The Committee To Do The Impossible Job Of Finding A Qualified Successor To The Retiring Executive Director." That same day, Granger also wrote Young to bring him up to date on the appointment of the search committee and to encourage him to submit materials to support his candidacy. The committee would begin its deliberations in early April, he advised, so Young ought to have his materials in Steeger's hands before the end of March.[22]

Young wrote Steeger on March 28, enclosing copies of *A Second Look*, his speech to the National Urban League's annual conference the previous September, and a current autobiographical sketch. He described briefly his administrative responsibilities as dean of the Atlanta University School of Social Work, underscored his continuing responsibilities in the field of race relations, and noted his participation as a panelist or speaker at the annual meetings of the National Urban League and a number of affiliates. He told Steeger about his most rewarding recent professional experiences, chief among them the Lasker award and the grant for the year at Harvard. Steeger responded two weeks later that he had studied the materials Young had sent him with the greatest possible interest.[23]

The search committee met on May 18 for a preliminary screening of the names compiled from recommendations and applications. There were seven men on the list: Alexander J. Allen, the forty-four-year-old director of special projects for the National Urban League, who had just been confirmed as associate director; Warren M. Banner, fifty, associate director of the National Urban League since 1957 and, for two decades before that, director of research; Edwin C. Berry, forty-nine, executive director of the

Chicago Urban League since 1955; M. Leo Bohanon, fifty-three, executive secretary of the Urban League of St. Louis since 1950; Nelson C.
Jackson, fifty-three, associate director of the National Urban League since
1957; Reginald A. Johnson, fifty-two, director of housing for the National
League since 1952; and Whitney Young. At thirty-eight, Young was by far
the youngest of the candidates. With three years at the St. Paul Urban
League and three in Omaha, he also had the most limited Urban League
experience. Each of the other men had spent many years as a local executive and/or a member of the national staff. Johnson had taken his first job
with the Urban League in 1930; Banner had served in various posts in the
national office for twenty-four years; Allen and Berry each had eighteen
years of experience, while Bohanon and Jackson each had fourteen.

The committee spent more than two hours in an intensive discussion of
each individual on the basis of materials made available by the candidates
themselves and supplemented by Granger. They agreed as a next step to
interview each of the prospects.[24]

The interviews were set for June 15 and 16 in Granger's office at the
national headquarters in New York. There was an eighth candidate on the
list: Alonzo G. Moron, commissioner of education for the Virgin Islands,
who had retired from the presidency of Hampton Institute after a decade
in June 1959. The candidates who were members of the national staff—
Allen, Banner, Jackson, and Johnson—were scheduled for the fifteenth;
those from out of town—Berry, Bohanon, Moron, and Young—were to
come on the sixteenth. The routine called for a get-acquainted session
with cocktails and conversation between members of the committee and
the group of candidates; after that, the prospects would be interviewed
one by one. The candidates who were waiting were expected to make
themselves at home and chat with members of the National Urban League
staff.

Berry recalled vividly what happened on the afternoon of June 16. The
four candidates showed up at the same hour, as they had been directed.
Roper set up a small portable bar and offered them drinks. The individual
appointments were staggered, so that all four candidates sat around drinking and talking, waiting their turn. The committee, too, shared in the
refreshments; Allen remembered that "Whitney used to tell about the
committee being under the influence." All told, in the view of the candidates, the committee's performance seemed exceedingly unprofessional.
They objected especially to the assembly-line nature of the interview
process. To squeeze a group session and four brief interviews into a period
of three hours hardly seemed to do justice to the importance of the search
or the strength of the candidates.[25]

The process moved slowly—probably more slowly than Granger and
the search committee had originally anticipated. In early September,

Granger reported to the full board that the search committee had held lengthy interviews during the summer without reaching any definitive conclusions. He expected that the search committee would make proposals to the executive committee in October, and that the executive committee might be ready to report to the board in November. At the end of October, Steeger reported to the executive committee and named the applicant whom the search committee considered the top prospect. After prolonged discussion, it became apparent that two members of the executive committee were unwilling to accept the search committee's recommendation without further study. The executive committee agreed to allow two weeks for anyone who wished "to pursue discreet inquiries." If, within that period, no member of the committee registered objections, the name of the favored candidate would go forward to the full board as the unanimous recommendation of the committee. In the event of objection, a special meeting of the executive committee would be called in advance of the December 2 board meeting.

Two weeks later, Granger reported to the executive committee that no one had taken advantage of the opportunity allowed for expression of dissenting views. Still, Steeger thought it would make for stronger agreement if the members of the executive committee had a chance to talk personally with the leading candidates, and Granger suggested, in his behalf, that the four men still under consideration be invited to meet with the executive committee prior to the meeting of the full board.

On December 1, the executive committee interviewed each of the four prospects. But Steeger's intention—to be in a position to present a strong consensus to the full board the next day—proved optimistic. The executive committee was not yet ready to agree on a recommendation; instead Steeger told the board he needed more time for further investigation.[26]

What all the postponements and further investigations reflected was the slow process during which the search committee changed its mind about the man it would recommend as the next executive director. After the initial interviews, Steeger had suggested that the members of the committee take a straw vote to see where they stood; each one jotted down a first choice on a piece of paper, and then they compared notes. Three members of the committee preferred Alonzo Moron; the fourth, Burns Roper, chose Whitney Young. The others asked Roper to explain his views. Roper said that Young combined enthusiasm, aggressiveness, judgment, and moderation, a balance he found especially appealing. He also liked his ideas—they were original, and they made good sense. Still, Roper was not opposed to Moron. He said that he had no intention of resisting the will of the majority of the committee; there was a three-to-one majority for Moron, so why not recommend him as the new executive director? The other members of the committee were unwilling to act so quickly. They felt strongly that the recommendation ought to be unanimous, and Steeger suggested that another round of interviews might clarify the committee's views on the candidates.

As Roper recalled, Moron and Young reacted very differently to the invitation to come back for more discussion. Moron was a dozen years older than Young, much better known, with an established reputation; he "was sort of offended that we had narrowed it down to him and this young upstart," and he made plain his impatience at being summoned for yet another round of questioning. By contrast, Young, eager for the challenge, "came on like gangbusters."

Moron's attitude did his candidacy no good. He had appealed to members of the executive committee precisely because he was an older, more seasoned, more experienced person. But now, in contrast with Young, he appeared less daring, more set in his ways. Forceful, bold, full of energy, Young gave his interviewers the sense that he would make things happen. Malcolm Andresen was taken with Young's personal magnetism and his persuasive message. "He really convinced me and some of the other influential members of the board that he was the man to lead the National Urban League." Young made by far the better presentation in the final round, so much better that he changed the minds of the committee members who had previously favored Moron.

And what was Lindsley Kimball's role in the search for the new executive director? By his own account, he had full control of the process. He sent Young to Harvard in order to groom him for the position. He arranged for Granger's retirement. Then, at the end of Young's sabbatical year, Kimball had the job waiting for him. And when the selection process nearly went awry, Kimball claimed that he exercised the necessary muscle to get it back on track.

Other members of the board do not recall Kimball in such a central role, however. John H. Johnson said that Kimball "never tried to throw his weight around" in the selection process. Burns Roper said that he had heard that Young was "the Rockefellers' choice," but he could not identify any special role that Kimball played in his selection. Mollie Moon, acknowledging that Young was "Kimball's boy," discounted the notion that Kimball had tried to sell him to the search committee. Malcolm Andresen said, "It was much more touch and go than Lindsley Kimball saying, 'This is the man.' It did not happen that way."[27]

Kimball was by no means the only board member outside the search committee who felt a vested interest in the outcome. George Butler, an economist at the Department of Labor, had come to know Young during his years in Atlanta, and he saw him as the right man for the executive directorship. He knew that other members of the board would be disposed toward Moron on the grounds of his experience as an administrator and fund-raiser. Working behind the scenes, Butler set about the business of promoting Young's candidacy.

Together with his friend, Hylan Lewis, Butler consulted closely with Young, offering support and guidance and suggesting specific strategies and tactics as the search progressed. Butler recommended things for Young to read in preparation for his final interview and advised him about the themes that were likely to appeal to each member of the search committee. "If we can handle this right," he told Young, "we can play these people like a piano."

Young followed Butler's instructions perfectly, and the strategy worked. "By the time Whitney was winding up his presentation," Butler said, "it was very clear that he was the candidate."

But there was still one obstacle to overcome. As Butler told the story, Mollie Moon, a strong supporter of Moron, believed firmly that Young did not have "enough age and balance—he didn't look the part. Furthermore, he had a reputation for being quite fast with the ladies, which he was—his reputation was well earned, I might say." Moon told the board that she had seen Young hugging June Vance in the lobby of the Commodore Hotel in New York. Blond, blue-eyed, and wealthy, Vance had been a member of Young's board in Omaha. Butler deflated Moon's story. He had been on the same elevator with Young; Margaret had also been with them. When the elevator reached the lobby, Vance had just entered the hotel; she spotted Whitney, and they embraced. Then Margaret threw her arms around Vance, and Butler did the same. Butler's account kept Moon from wrecking the bandwagon that was developing for Young.

Butler knew, too, that the same sort of tactic could easily be used to discredit Moron. Moron's wife had a reputation as a heavy drinker, and it was widely assumed that Moron shared her drinking problem. Butler never raised the issue directly; rather, he said that he could not cast a vote for Moron if what he heard was true. He urged the board to give him time to ascertain the truth or falsity of the rumors. If they were false, the board could still appoint Moron; if the stories were true, the board would not want to have acted precipitately.

"I thought I could stall the efforts," Butler said. "Mollie and them were lazy. I knew they weren't going to do any work."

He persuaded his colleagues to delay the decision in order to buy time to reinterview the leading candidates. "What I was trying to do," he later explained, "was to cut off Al Moron as a sure thing and hopefully knock him out of the box, because I was convinced if Whitney could get a chance to come and make a presentation, particularly one that was tailored, he would win in a walk."[28]

On December 9, Henry Steeger wrote Young to say that he had enjoyed his presentation at the executive committee interview the previous week, and that he hoped to have an opportunity to talk further at Young's convenience. Perhaps Young would be coming to New York within the next few weeks? Young wrote back suggesting possible dates. There is no record of when the conversation actually took place, but on January 26, at a special meeting, the board of trustees of the National Urban League unanimously approved the recommendation of the executive committee that Whitney Young be named to succeed Lester Granger as executive director. Young was invited to join the meeting, and he eagerly accepted the appointment.[29]

Young told the board that he was extremely flattered to have been chosen to succeed Granger and to be entrusted with the "professional leadership of this important organization at this crucial moment in history." He felt a deep sense of humility, but he also felt deeply challenged by the opportunities for the National Urban League "to play a major role in making equality of opportunity a reality for all Americans."

"While I have been a victim of your committee['s] diligence," Young said, "I could not help but be impressed by its sincerity, dedication, thoroughness and sacrifice." But they ought not to imagine that their work was done. "Your work, our work is just beginning if we are to make the U[rban] L[eague] meet its great challenges and live up to it[s] rich promise and opportunity for greatness."

Young then told a story that he would use often in the years to come. "A famous painter was once asked to name his greatest painting," he said. "He thought for a while and then answered, 'My greatest painting[?] The next one.' And so it is with the U[rban] L[eague]. While we respect the past and recognize that without a great past there could not be a great present, . . . our eyes must be fixed on the future." If they were ever asked to name the Urban League's greatest year, their answer, like the painter's, would be, " 'Our greatest year [will be] the next one.' "

He was grateful for the "great opportunity for service," Young concluded; "I can only pray that those whom we would serve may someday have great reason to be also grateful for your decision here today."[30]

The next day, Steeger sent Young a formal confirmation of the offer. The appointment would be effective October 1, but Young would join the staff in a consultative capacity on August 1 in order to become familiar with his new responsibilities. His salary would be $18,000 a year.

Steeger announced the appointment at a press conference in New York on January 29. He called Young "a dynamic and vigorous leader" with a "record distinguished well beyond his years." He was convinced, he said, that Young would "move the Urban League forward to exciting new achievements. An organization with a fifty year history of 'firsts' has chosen a man who has blazed for himself one first after another."[31]

Among Urban Leaguers, social workers, civil rights leaders, and others, Young's selection won immediate and enthusiastic praise. Two of the many messages of congratulations proved especially prophetic. Between them, they made plain the challenges ahead and specified the particular role that Young would play. "Certainly if any one can drag the Urban League screamingly into the 20th century you can!" a friend wrote after learning of the appointment. "You've certainly got your work cut out for you and that's for sure! Trying to make rich white folks pay for a program to make them do something they aren't too keen about doing in the first place—oh brother!" Welcoming Young to his new post, the executive secretary of the NAACP, Roy Wilkins, made a similar point from a different perspective. "I don't have to tell a skilled social engineer like yourself that the most demanding times of the race relations front are those ahead of all of us," Wilkins wrote. "Nothing is as simple as black and white any more."[32]

VII

Leader of the National
Urban League

WHITNEY YOUNG swept into the National Urban League like a fresh breeze. The pace quickened noticeably. "We don't work this fast," a long-time staff member protested. "From now on, we will," Young told him. "We've got to, or we'll be left behind."[1]

Young had begun planning for his new responsibilities well before he came to New York. He had first started to formulate his ideas during the search. To enlarge his own perspective, as well as to establish immediate connections with a broad range of Urban Leaguers, he wrote the executive directors of the local affiliates from Cambridge in the spring of 1961 to ask for their thinking about new directions the league ought to be following in the years to come. Not only did this give Young some valuable information, but it told the executives that the new man in charge meant to take them seriously, and it made them feel part of a team effort. They were pleased and flattered to be consulted, and they responded eagerly with suggestions about programming, public relations, fund-raising, staff recruitment and development, and ways of strengthening the relationship between the national office and the affiliates. They were clearly interested in a stronger national movement with more visibility, a more dynamic program, and more effective direction from New York.[2]

Young also sought advice beyond the Urban League circle, consulting black academics, many of whom were working in Washington in various federal agencies, to help him formulate the appropriate role for the Urban League in the decade ahead.[3]

From their temporary residence in Cambridge, the Youngs began to look for a place to live in New York. Soon after the announcement of his appointment, Whitney had begun to get inquiries about his plans. The executive director of the National Committee for a Sane Nuclear Policy, who lived in Scarsdale, wrote to ask whether Young would consider living there in order to provide some momentum toward open occupancy. The director of housing at the Westchester Urban League lined up a number of houses to look at in several Westchester communities. Whitney and Margaret decided that they preferred New Rochelle. Considerably more heterogeneous than other nearby suburbs, the city had a range of class, occupation, and income, a mix of ethnic and religious traditions, and a good-sized minority population—10,479 out of a total of 76,812. New Rochelle was also the site of an important school segregation case.[4]

The case involved de facto segregation at the Lincoln Elementary School, whose student body was approximately 94 percent black. The racial imbalance at Lincoln reflected the increasing concentration of blacks in the school's center-city neighborhood, but it also resulted in some measure from the school board's past practice of gerrymandering the Lincoln district to keep blacks in while sending whites to other schools. Not only was Lincoln an antiquated facility, but its teaching staff and curriculum were plainly inferior to those in predominantly white elementary schools.

In October 1960, a complaint filed in federal court on behalf of black children attending Lincoln asked that the court enjoin the operation of the neighborhood school plan in the Lincoln district, require the New Rochelle school board to transfer the plaintiffs to integrated schools, and block the construction of a new school on the Lincoln site (a plan for which voters had just approved a bond issue) as long as the neighborhood school policy was in effect.

In January 1961, after a long, well-publicized trial, Judge Irving R. Kaufman ordered the school board to develop a plan for the desegregation of the Lincoln School. The board's proposal fell considerably short of accomplishing real desegregation, and Judge Kaufman asked the Department of Justice to join the case as a friend of the court to help formulate a workable plan. In May, following the recommendations of the Justice Department, Kaufman handed down a final order requiring the school board to allow Lincoln students to transfer to other elementary schools on a space-available basis. The board's efforts to appeal the decision failed, and the transfer plan went into effect with the 1961–1962 school year. Two years later, the board closed the Lincoln School and reassigned its remaining pupils.[5]

As the first case in which a northern community was found to have violated the constitutional prohibitions against public school segregation laid down in *Brown v. Board of Education*, the Lincoln School case made New Rochelle the focus of national attention. The successful attack on de facto segregation also made the community particularly attractive to the Youngs. With the implementation of the transfer plan, New Rochelle would become an important laboratory for court-ordered desegregation.

For a professional in the field of race relations, that was an exciting prospect.

The Youngs settled on a house on Mohegan Place, just off the Hutchinson River Parkway in a white neighborhood at the north end of the city. It was a split-level, with seven rooms, in a fairly new development. Whitney liked the house and the neighborhood, but he also wanted to make a point about the possibilities for interracial living.[6]

There had been an incident the year before when a black family had tried to buy the house next door to the one the Youngs wanted. Neighbors had protested, and one night, before the family had moved in, stones had been thrown through the windows. The local neighborhood association had bought the house and sold it, at a loss, to a white family.

This time there were no protests. As Whitney later told the story, the real estate agent made a point of telling the neighbors that the Youngs had been invited to live in many exclusive neighborhoods; Mohegan Place was lucky to have won the competition. "Scarsdale wants him; Great Neck wants him; but we've got him." The tactic muted the tensions that might otherwise have surfaced.[7]

Still there were adjustments to make. In the first days after the Youngs moved in, a number of neighbors came to call. Whitney liked to tell the story of one of his first visitors, who asked if he would like to join the White Birch Association. The invitation puzzled him. He knew about the segregationist White Citizens Council and the far-Right John Birch Society, neither of which he would choose to be associated with. What was this White Birch Association? The man saw that Young was uneasy and explained immediately that he was asking him to join a neighborhood association that took its name from the white birch trees common to the area. The incident showed "that you can get overly sensitive on these things," Young said later; "it pays if you want to keep your balance to keep a sense of humor."[8]

Other neighbors came with more usual gestures of welcome. One woman brought a large box of candy. Another offered to help Margaret unpack. A third invited Lauren to come over to play with her daughter, which gave Lauren a means of meeting some of the white children in the neighborhood who would soon be her classmates in the second grade at the newly integrated Davis Elementary School.

Marcia entered the tenth grade at New Rochelle High School. The high school had been integrated for a long time, but students tended to segregate themselves in social situations. To Marcia's surprise, on the first day of school a black girl asked her to sit at an all-black table in the cafeteria. "I sat with them," Marcia told her father that night, "because I didn't want to sit all alone." But it did not feel right to her—she knew that her father had been fighting against segregated facilities in Atlanta. "We've got to

continue the fight up here," he told her, "even if it is lonely at the beginning." For the remainder of the first week Marcia ate lunch alone. The
next week, a white girl joined her. By the end of the month, the pattern
of segregated tables had been broken.[9]

As the family got settled in New Rochelle, Young began to get his bear-
ings at the National Urban League. He had not been in the office two
weeks when he reported to Frankie Adams in Atlanta: "I am standing up
under my period of orientation, indoctrination and brainwashing amaz-
ingly well, with every indication of understanding and support."[10]

Even before Young officially replaced Granger, he had an opportunity
to begin to communicate a new vision for the organization. In a speech to
the closing session of the league's annual conference in September, he
pledged the league to a war "against prejudice and discrimination, against
apathy and indifference, against rationalization, greed, selfishness and ig-
norance." He promised changes, "some dramatic, some necessarily routine." The league needed "greater visibility—greater public understanding and more dramatic interpretation of its program." The speech was well
received, Young told his father, who had commented appreciatively on a
copy that his son had sent him. "And it seems to have set the tone for my
start in the new job, for thus far everything has gone remarkably well."[11]

Before any of Young's longer-range objectives could be addressed, he
needed to pay attention to the internal workings of his organization. His
first tasks were to restructure the national staff, tighten up the relationship between the national and the affiliates, and, with Lindsley Kimball,
to look for money to keep the league afloat. Then he would be able to turn
his attention to expanding the scope of the agency's program.

Raising money was the most urgent challenge. By any measure, the
organization was in desperate financial straits. Meeting the payroll had
become a sometime thing; labor mediator Theodore W. Kheel, who
served as president from 1956 to 1960, remembered "payroll-less days
and weeks" as typical of the league during his tenure. In the last weeks of
Lester Granger's administration, the agency managed to meet its obliga-
tions only through a series of herculean (some would have said irregular)
measures. It hypothecated some securities, spent some foundation grants
a year in advance, borrowed $17,000 from one of its trustees, and (much
to Winthrop Rockefeller's displeasure) took out a mortgage on its national
headquarters. A special grant of $5,000 from the General Education
Board paid transportation and living costs for members of the national staff
at the agency's annual conference in Dayton, Ohio, in September. All
told, income for 1961—$340,000—fell far short of receipts for the previ-
ous year, and failed by tens of thousands of dollars to cover budgeted
expenditures. "I knew the League was in bad shape (financially)," Young
told Kimball, "but I had no idea it was *this* bad."[12]

In an emergency effort known as "Operation Rescue," Kimball under-took to put the league on a sound financial footing. He estimated that the league needed to raise $500,000 for 1962 in order to maintain its 1961 level of operations. Of that money, he expected $200,000 from founda-tions, $100,000 from corporations, $100,000 from Community Chests and Urban League affiliates, $50,000 from individual contributions, and $50,000 from special events. Kimball began with the sources he knew best, the major foundations.[13]

While Young took part in the conversations, Kimball clearly led the way. Young was new at his job, and he had not yet had a chance to estab-lish the kind of personal connections that he would later use to good ef-fect. Kimball had the contacts, and he also had a proprietary attitude about the Urban League, which he described to the president of the Ford Foundation, Henry T. Heald, as one of his "forlorn causes." Kimball had confidence in Young—the new executive director was very able, he told his colleagues in the foundation world—but Kimball also had an old-fash-ioned, hierarchical sense of the best way to do business in that world, a sense that sometimes put Young in a subordinate role. In arranging a meeting with Heald, for example, Kimball wrote, "Do you want Whitney Young along with me when we meet or can we perhaps be a little more frank with a little more privacy?"[14]

The rescue operation worked. The Carnegie Corporation, the Rocke-feller Brothers Fund, the Field Foundation, and the Taconic Foundation all responded to Kimball's appeal. Only the Ford Foundation declined to contribute money for general support. In the space of a year, the National Urban League's total income from foundations nearly quadrupled.[15]

Foundations might provide seed money or funding for special projects, but the principal source of unrestricted money on a continuing basis would have to be corporations. Here the fund-raising potential was largely unrealized. In 1960, the National Urban League had received $85,600 in corporate gifts; the following year, income from corporations dropped off to $70,000. The league set out to increase corporate support under a "fair share" formula for giving based on annual gross sales. For firms with gross sales of less than $100 million, the recommended minimum contribution was $500; those with gross sales of a billion dollars or more would be asked to give at least $5,000.[16]

To make the fair share formula effective, the league needed to modern-ize its approach. Board members could identify the likeliest donors, but there had to be a better way of capturing their attention. To launch the drive for increased corporate contributions, Kimball asked David Rocke-feller, chairman of Chase Manhattan Bank, and Albert L. Nickerson, chairman of Socony Mobil Corporation, to invite a small group of indus-trial leaders to a luncheon in December 1961 where the Urban League

TABLE 1. INCOME COMPARISON, BY SOURCE, NATIONAL URBAN LEAGUE
(In Thousands of Dollars)

Year	Foundations	Commerce Industry	Government	Individual Contribs.	Affiliate Dues
1961	62	70	0	70	48
1962	239	153	0	106	69
1963	513	527	0	87	75
1964	665	657	0	104	81
1965	701	848	0	152	83
1966	707	888	294	164	112
1967	905	1,056	536	243	134
1968	1,573	1,197	650	376	135
1969	2,898	1,521	3,595	425	204
1970	5,054	1,973	6,913	379	252
1971	3,931	1,796	8,051	450	315
1972	2,228	1,781	13,010	296	314

Source: Fund Department, National Urban League, New York City.

could make its case. Kimball made the presentation. Afterward, Young
said to him, "I see exactly how to do it. You won't have to do it again."[17]

To provide a continuing structure for the league's fund-raising efforts in
the corporate community, the board set up a corporate support committee consisting of the chief executive officers of a dozen major corporations.
David Rockefeller signed on; so did Robert W. Sarnoff of RCA, Thomas J.
Watson, Jr., of IBM, and Edgar F. Kaiser of Kaiser Industries. Nickerson
agreed to serve as chairman.

The corporate support committee did not really function as a committee; membership meant a commitment to lend prestige and help make
contacts for the league in the corporate world. Each member agreed to
host a luncheon to introduce Young to leading corporate executives. Malcolm Andresen, senior vice president of the league and tax counsel of
Socony Mobil, wrote the letters of invitation, and Nickerson signed them.
Young was the featured speaker. He approached his audiences from a
position of strength. Whereas Lester Granger, a different personality who
operated in a different era, had often appeared timid or overly deferential
in his dealings with influential whites, Young projected self-confidence.
That was especially striking, Sophia Jacobs, a member of the National
Urban League board, remarked, because it seemed difficult at that time
to find many blacks "who were secure in the presence of white people and
who were utterly unafraid and who felt equal."

Young impressed corporate leaders with his obvious sense of security,
his candor, and the cogency of his message. "He didn't tell them what
they necessarily wanted to hear," Andresen recalled. "He was very frank.

United Funds & Chests	Labor Unions	Clubs & Orgns.	Special Events	Total	Year
28	16	11	35	340	1961
38	18	18	29	670	1962
52	16	26	114	1,410	1963
47	27	39	31	1,651	1964
53	27	43	23	1,930	1965
71	31	46	12	2,325	1966
72	—	—	—	2,946	1967
75	25	25	—	4,056	1968
71	24	85	—	8,823	1969
110	30	83	55	14,849	1970
86	28	40	28	14,725	1971
155	18	57	521	18,380	1972

He told them there were real problems and that they better do something voluntarily or they soon were going to be faced with a lot of unpleasant problems."[18]

Young quickly demonstrated his gift for combining charm, logic, and an extremely tough message. "He used his courage," Kimball recalled; "he made them mad. And then he would relieve it with a little touch of humor." He had a way of making his audience "feel that they would get a return for their dollar." The purpose of the luncheons was to inform and educate; the solicitations followed later. The approach paid off. Bethlehem Steel, which had contributed $2,500 in 1961, gave $4,000 in 1962; General Electric and General Motors both raised their gifts from $2,500 to $5,000; Kaiser Industries' donation jumped from $100 to $5,100, Western Electric's gift rose from $2,500 to $7,000, and IBM's donation went from $1,650 to $7,500. U. S. Steel, which had not contributed at all in 1961, gave $5,000 for 1962. All told, corporate gifts totaled $153,000 in 1962 and $527,000 the year after. Contributions so exceeded expectations that the fair share formula was abandoned. By the end of 1963, the league had raised over $1.4 million from all sources—more than twice the sum that had come in the year before.

In 1964 the corporate support drive continued, with renewed attention to foundations and a direct mail appeal to individual contributors. As shown in table 1, the efforts continued to pay off; total income exceeded the 1963 level by nearly a quarter of a million dollars. The league's annual budget grew accordingly—$700,000 in 1962, $725,000 in 1963, $1,026,000 in 1964.[19]

The infusion of new money freed Young to focus on problems of organizational structure and program definition. Restructuring the national office proved to be the simplest of the jobs before him. Within weeks of taking office, Young vested significant authority in two associate executive directors: Alexander J. ("Joe") Allen would handle administrative matters, and Nelson C. Jackson would take responsibility for program and field operations. Most of the department heads would be accountable to one or the other. Weekly cabinet meetings among the senior staff—the executive director, the associate executive directors, and the directors of the fund department, public relations, and research—gave opportunities to exchange information and discuss ideas for new programs. Cutting down on the number of people who reported directly to the executive director meant that Young would be freer to focus his attention outside, promoting the league's activities, increasing its visibility, raising money, and making the necessary contacts to advance its programs. Later, the continuing need for Young to do his major work outside, together with the expansion of Urban League programs, led to further staff reorganization. In the summer of 1965, in the interests of better internal communication, more effective supervision, and more rapid decision making, Young appointed a deputy director, Mahlon T. Puryear, who had been associate director for job development and employment.[20]

The tightening up of the relationship between the national office and the affiliates began with the adoption of new Terms of Affiliation at the Urban League's annual conference in September 1961. The point was to chip away at some of the autonomy enjoyed by the affiliates and to create more of a national movement. The new terms gave the national office "more responsibility for the standards of performance in local Leagues" and obligated local leagues "to assume more responsibility for development of the total League program." Unstated was the human role Young would play in making the relationship with the affiliates work. Likeable, approachable, exuding charm and personality, he won the admiration and loyalty of most of the executives with whom he worked. Less authoritarian than Granger, more open to listening to people in the field, ready to offer guidance and share experiences, he encouraged them and reached out to them in a way that gave them a greater sense of importance and enthusiasm for their jobs—and, in the process, made them feel more a part of a national movement.[21]

Hand in hand with the forging of a more effective national movement went an increased emphasis on quality. "We must 'get on the ball,' " Young exhorted in informal remarks to local executives at the 1961 conference. "The day is past when we can play it by ear." The Urban League needed to be more careful and professional about its operations. It also needed an injection of optimism and self-confidence. "We have been suffering too long from 'self-hatred,' " he said. "We have for too long talked or permitted people to talk too long about the fact that we're 'no good.' " Certainly there was room for improvement, "but we've got to project a public impression of believing in ourselves."[22]

In mid-December, Young reported optimistically to Frankie Adams that the structural reorganization within the national office, as well as the "rather radical changes in emphasis and role" for that office within the larger Urban League movement, had "met with enthusiasm and understanding." The job was keeping him "working 20 hours a day," he said, "but I find it challenging and I am quite happy."[23]

What he did not mention was that the structural changes within the movement were not yet complete. In March 1962, as a next step toward achieving greater coherence, the program staff at the national headquarters sent the affiliates a detailed outline of a model Urban League program to give them a standard for assessing their activities and measuring their achievements. Later that year, responding to the widely shared view that unevenness of quality among staff was one of the principal problems across the Urban League movement, Young brought the executive director of the Akron league, Raymond R. Brown, to New York on a temporary basis to work on staff recruitment and in-service training activities.[24]

Young had other ideas for structural changes to make the Urban League more effective as a national movement. By the spring of 1963, discussions were well under way about a regional reorganization involving the establishment of three new regional offices in addition to the already existing ones in the South and the West. With funding promised by the Rockefeller Brothers Fund and the Field Foundation, the new plan was announced in April 1964, to take effect May 1. The regional offices were designed to bring local affiliates closer to the national office, give them better service, and allow for more direct supervision of their activities. Before, it had been difficult to make much headway in servicing local leagues; a visit once a year from a member of the national staff gave no one the personal investment to take direct responsibility for follow-through. With the reorganization, there would be ample opportunity for more frequent, on-the-spot service. Each regional director would be responsible for recruitment and in-service training of professional and clerical staff for the affiliates in his region, as well as leadership training of the volunteers who were so essential in the functioning of the local leagues. He would assist affiliates in program development, budgeting, and fund-raising. In addition, he would be responsible for initiating efforts to establish new leagues in his region.[25]

Putting the National Urban League on a sounder financial footing, restructuring the national office, and tightening up the relationship between the National Urban League and the affiliates positioned the league to undertake significantly expanded activities. With new expectations about the possibilities of progress in race relations, as well as a new federal involvement in economic and social welfare, there was scope for more inventive programming on a larger scale than the Urban League had previously attempted. The challenge for Young and his senior staff was to take an established social service agency with a very conservative tone, rethink its major emphases, and make its programs more effective and more dynamic.

Slowly, year by year, the league's programs took on a different cast. It undertook new projects to improve employment opportunities: the National Skills Bank, for example, matched unemployed or underemployed blacks who had marketable skills with positions that utilized their talents; On-the-Job Training (under contract from the Department of Labor) placed unskilled workers in training slots in private industry; the Broadcast Skills Bank sought jobs for blacks in television and radio; and the Secretarial Training Project prepared women for secretarial employment. The number of people whose economic fortunes the Urban League affected changed significantly. When Young took over the league, progress in employment was still measured in terms of pilot placements. The Department of Industrial Relations boasted of small victories: the placement of a black elevator operator at Rockefeller Center and a black secretary at RCA, the hiring by Gulf Oil of its first black sales representative for the New York metropolitan area, the appointment of the first black sales representative at Trans World Airlines or the first black teacher in a Westchester school. In a single year, the National Skills Bank reported 39,700 registrations, 28,500 referrals, and over 9,600 placements. On-the-Job Training alone trained 50,000 workers in seven years. By the late 1960s, the league reported 40,000 to 50,000 placements annually in new or upgraded jobs.[26]

The league made new efforts to improve the quality of black education and to motivate young blacks to stay in school; it provided individual tutoring for ghetto youngsters, street academies to prepare high school dropouts for college, summer fellowships in industry for black college teachers and administrators, short-term teaching assignments for black executives at black colleges, and transfer plans to bring gifted Southern blacks to finish their high school education at first-rate schools in the North. The agency's traditional housing, health, and welfare services took on new dimensions. It assisted black veterans, campaigned for open housing, offered consumer education and protection, tried to find adoptive families for hard-to-place children, and gave group parent counseling to strengthen black family life.[27]

Finally, the league undertook programs to give blacks a stronger voice in public affairs, for example, in voter education and registration, labor education and advancement, leadership development, and, with the "New Thrust" of the late 1960s, community organizing.[28]

What role did Young play in this proliferation of new programs? Some of the ideas were his, some of them originated with members of his staff. The ideas "came out of dialogue," Joe Allen said. Young was constantly moving, talking to—and thus drawing ideas from—Urban Leaguers around the country, as well as business leaders, labor leaders, and many others.

We would have . . . staff discussions . . . fairly regularly and would react to his ideas and add some of our own. And out of that might come proposals which would be developed for funding. . . . His ideas were an important part of it, but they weren't developed in a vacuum.

Young used to say, "I'm really not the intellectual force [around here]." He listened carefully to "the idea people" on his staff, and when someone "sold him on a notion, he'd go all out to get it done." He had a gift for grasping the essence of issues, shaping and reinterpreting what he heard and articulating it in a clear, convincing fashion. By example and by sheer force of personality, he inspired his staff to push ahead; "he gave you the ability to go out there and fight against all the odds," Betti Whaley, a member and later the director of the program staff said. "You wanted to do it."[29]

Whitney Young's executive directorship was a time of remarkable expansion for the National Urban League. Not only did its programs multiply. In the decade of Young's leadership, the league grew from 63 affiliates to 98; its professional staff grew from 300 to over 1,200; its budget increased tenfold.* Those accomplishments alone would have justified the judgment of a longtime member of the national staff that Young had "stepped the Urban League up from Lester Granger to modern times." Even more important than his impact on the internal workings of the league, he stretched and strengthened the organization through the roles he played outside. The early 1960s were a propitious time to head a racial advancement organization; the civil rights movement and the growing federal involvement in social welfare gave the Urban League a chance to make its greatest contribution. The stage was "uniquely set," Young felt, for the league "to play a major role in making true integration a reality in all aspects of American life."[30]

Toward that end, early in his tenure Young broke from the mold he had inherited and charted new directions by making the Urban League an

* These figures refer to the national office and the affiliates. The income of the National Urban League alone grew from $340,000 in 1961 to $14,749,000 in 1970.

influential voice in the formation of public policy and by identifying it with activism in behalf of civil rights. Those directions, more than any of the changes in the internal workings of the league, set Young apart from his predecessor and shaped public perceptions of his leadership and his organization.

VIII

The Civil Rights
Movement

WHITNEY YOUNG made the National Urban League a civil rights organization. That had not been its function. Since its founding in 1910, the league had been a social service agency dedicated to advancing the economic and social conditions of blacks in the cities. The organization had left the business of political and civil rights to its counterpart, the National Association for the Advancement of Colored People. While the NAACP traditionally dealt in legal action and protest, the Urban League's tools were primarily those of negotiation, persuasion, education, and investigation.

For decades the NAACP had assumed the most prominent public posture in the struggle for black rights. That had been true in the unsuccessful political battles of the 1930s and 1940s to abolish the poll tax in federal elections and to make lynching a federal crime. It had been true in the battle against discrimination in federal employment, which had resulted in the creation of a wartime Fair Employment Practices Commission. And it had been true especially in the legal battles against racial discrimination in public education and in voting rights waged successfully in federal courts.

The National Urban League had no role in these critical legal victories. Nor did it play a part in the direct action protests of the 1950s: the bus boycotts in Montgomery, Baton Rouge, and Tallahassee; the broader protests in Birmingham, Nashville, Petersburg, Shreveport, and other Southern cities against discrimination in hiring and against segregation in schools, public transportation, and places of public accommodation.

As the focus of the civil rights movement shifted from the courts to the streets, new, more militant organizations emerged to lead the protests. At the national level, three were particularly notable. The first of them, the Southern Christian Leadership Conference (SCLC), an organization of

black ministers born out of the Montgomery bus boycott, initially employed a strategy of nonviolent persuasion to dramatize the evils of discrimination; later, most notably in Birmingham in 1963 and Selma in
1964, it shifted to a strategy of aggressive nonviolent coercion, designed
to provoke retaliatory violence, capture the attention of the media, rally
national support for the movement, and thus bring pressure for federal
intervention, including the passage of civil rights legislation.

The second organization, the Congress of Racial Equality (CORE), paci-
fist in its origins, working in the North as well as the South, started out in
the 1940s as a small, interracial band of disciplined activists determined to
apply Gandhian techniques of nonviolent direct action to the problem of
American race relations. The CORE trademark was staging dramatic demonstrations to make plain the injustice of discrimination and provoke
changes in the attitudes and behavior of whites. The best-known of them,
the Freedom Rides of 1961, catapulted the organization to national prominence as a major force in the direct action protest movement. By the
middle of the 1960s, CORE began to lose its faith in the vision of integration
that had powered its earlier efforts; reformist rather than revolutionary, it
promoted the development of black capitalism and of black control over
institutions and services in the ghetto.

The third organization, the Student Nonviolent Coordinating Committee (SNCC), initially composed of Southern black college students, captured national attention through the sit-in movement of the early 1960s.
The most radical of the direct action groups, SNCC focused on the mobiliza-
tion and empowerment of local blacks to force change in the status quo.
Committed in its early years to direct action protest and voter registration
to break the hold of Southern racism, it would come in the latter half of the
1960s to reject nonviolence, interracialism, even capitalism, and to call for
a radical restructuring of society based on racial separatism and the creation of alternative institutions controlled by the poor and the powerless.

As the spectrum of civil rights organizations and approaches broadened,
the NAACP came to be regarded by young demonstrators as too cautious
and old-fashioned in its approach and too firmly middle class in its constituency. The Urban League, which had always been seen as more conservative than the NAACP, now appeared increasingly staid and out of touch
with the struggle.

Young understood clearly the need to change both the public perception of the Urban League and its practical relationship to the movement.
He came to that position in a deliberate fashion. In the 1950s, he had
made plain his conviction that the league ought to distance itself from the
new protest movement. At the National Urban League's annual conference in Omaha in 1958, for example, he had argued that the league ought
to function primarily as a "consultant in the arena of race relations." He

contended that "the Urban League should not be known as a protest, civil rights or civil liberties group."[1]

In the early months of his executive directorship, Young had to come to terms not only with his own views, but with the weight of tradition and the conservatism of the league's trustees. The first official expression under his leadership of the league's position on the civil rights movement, a policy statement on nonviolent direct action approved by the executive committee in January 1962, showed the difficulty of staking out a position that reconciled tradition and conservatism with the realities of the movement. With sit-ins, freedom rides, and protest demonstrations occurring throughout the country, what was the organization to do? The elaborate prose of the policy statement conveyed an unmistakable message: the Urban League meant to keep its distance from the protests.

Racial problems in America are manifested in many ways and at many levels, and therefore a multiplicity of techniques and approaches are required to successfully cope with them. No single organization can profess to have a monopoly in this field or to have all the answers as to methodology.

The Urban League movement is committed to the use of such methods as research, conference, public education and community organization. However, it has no quarrel with other efforts under responsible leadership using legally acceptable methods and seeking the same ultimate goal of a free, democratic and healthy society as does the Urban League.[2]

Slowly, under the intense pressure of day-to-day developments in the movement, Young moved his organization toward a more activist stance. In part he did so through symbolic identification with the movement, as in the case of his address to the annual convention of the Southern Christian Leadership Conference in September 1962, in which he described the league as "a necessary and important ally" in the civil rights struggle. In part he sought to modify the Urban League's sense of its own role. In a memorandum to executives of local Urban Leagues in June 1963, Young spelled out his vision of what the agency ought to be doing. He could scarcely avoid coming to terms with the issue. In April and May, in Birmingham, Martin Luther King and the Southern Christian Leadership Conference had led thousands of blacks in peaceful protests against discrimination in employment and public facilities. When the Birmingham police turned on the demonstrators with clubs, fire hoses, and dogs, their savagery provoked sympathy demonstrations around the country. The league could not remain quietly on the sidelines. Young said that affiliates ought not to initiate or participate actively in picketing and boycotting, but that they needed to be visible and to communicate effectively with the protesters. It was essential for the league to be sufficiently involved to maintain the respect of the black community and to take a leadership role in resolving some of the crises. In years past, the white power structure

might have taken a dim view of the Urban League's active identification
with demonstrators. Now that same power structure would want the
league to be in touch with those groups, indeed, would feel that without
that contact, the league would be "of little value to them on those matters
that concern them most." Urban Leagues had important roles to play in
fact-finding and negotiating between the demonstrators and the power
structure. Young was convinced that the protest movement offered the
league a great opportunity; "some real imagination, creativity and honest-
to-goodness sweat" on its part could pay off handsomely in increased
budgets and staffs.[3]

Persistent pressures on affiliates to participate in demonstrations led
Young to further develop and clarify his position. He did so in an atmosphere of heightened national tension over civil rights. Only days after he
had issued his June memorandum, the assassination of Medgar Evers, the
state chairman of the Mississippi NAACP, had once again sparked sympathy
demonstrations throughout the country. Later in June, in a major, nationally televised address, President John F. Kennedy had deplored the moral
injustice of racial discrimination and had then sent an omnibus civil rights
bill to Congress. In July, in a confidential memorandum to local executives, Young once again addressed the Urban League's role in the protest
movement. He made a distinction between picket lines and more general
demonstrations. Picketing, he said, was "not an Urban League technique
and would violate established agency policy"; peaceful public demonstrations, however, when conducted under responsible leadership, constituted an expression of broad community concern in which the league
could and should be represented.[4]

With the March on Washington in August 1963, the National Urban
League's new involvement in civil rights became a matter of public record. In the early spring, A. Philip Randolph approached the National
Urban League and the NAACP about cooperating in a massive march on
Washington to dramatize the demands of black Americans for civil rights
and economic justice. Randolph and his chief lieutenant, Bayard Rustin,
had begun planning for such a march in December. Randolph, the veteran
labor leader, was the architect of the threatened march on Washington in
the summer of 1941 that had prompted Franklin D. Roosevelt to issue
an executive order prohibiting discrimination on the basis of race in employment in defense industries and establishing a temporary Fair Employment Practices Committee to enforce the order. In its original con-
ception, the 1963 march also had economic goals: the enactment of
fair-employment legislation and the adoption of an increased minimum
wage. By the time Randolph approached the National Urban League and
the NAACP, discussions among his associates and others in the movement
had led to a broader focus. Now the march would attempt to pressure the

Kennedy administration into more aggressive support of civil rights; it would be billed as a March on Washington for Jobs and Freedom.[5]

Both Roy Wilkins and Whitney Young reacted cautiously to Randolph's approach. In a series of letters and telephone calls, Young set out to clarify the terms for the National Urban League's participation. He told Randolph that the league would want to be fully involved from the outset in all aspects of planning and policy making, and that it would insist on a joint decision about the coordinator of the march. He explained that the league's tax-exempt status imposed certain limitations. If the march were to entail out-and-out lobbying or if it were to be focused on specific legislation, the league could not join. If, on the other hand, the march should be designed to convey "a general expression of our concern about the problems of unemployment and infringement of . . . civil rights," the league would be inclined to participate.[6]

In early April, Young informed the league's executive committee of Randolph's invitation to cooperate in the march and laid out the conditions under which he thought the league could participate. The executive committee was extremely skittish; as Young later recalled, the idea left them "pretty shaken up." (One of the trustees put it more bluntly. "At the beginning," he said of the board, "they were nervous as hell.") They had many reservations. Protest was not the Urban League's way. A responsible social service organization had no place in a mass demonstration. As a tax-exempt agency, it was barred from lobbying Congress. Besides, the league had made progress in opening communications with administration officials in Washington; participation in the march might jeopardize those ties. The executive committee decided to retract the league's tentative commitment to participate.[7]

Young understood their reluctance, but from his point of view, the Urban League could not afford *not* to be involved. In subsequent weeks, he undertook a delicate, twofold task: shaping the march so that the Urban League would be able to participate, and selling the enterprise to his board. Young kept in close personal touch with Randolph to make sure that he understood the basic direction in which Young was heading. The league took part in weekly planning meetings, some of which were held at its own headquarters. In discussions with the other civil rights leaders, Young made clear the conditions for Urban League participation. The march would have to focus on dramatizing the general problems facing blacks; it would have to be interracial; and there could be no violence or civil disobedience. There would also have to be agreement beforehand among the participating organizations about the goals of the march, and the leaders would need to discuss their speeches with each other in advance of the demonstration to ensure some basic consistency with the agreed-on objectives.[8]

At the same time, Young worked to build a consensus within his own organization in favor of participation. Some members of the staff shared the executive committee's wariness. The march would be a significant departure for the Urban League; it was not easy to make the leap, especially for older people immersed in the league's social service traditions. As late as July 18, the league's senior staff was still discussing the ramifications of participation. What would it mean for the league's future direction? What were the implications for local affiliates, with their dependence on community chests? What if the league participated and things got out of hand?

Patiently, Young dealt with their reservations. He explained that a decision to join in the march would be entirely consistent with the league's recent memorandum drawing a distinction between pickets and boycotts and general demonstrations. As for the fear that SNCC and others might get out of line, he said that the best way to keep them responsible was to become involved and try to guide the march in a constructive direction. Mainly, he argued that the league had to show where it stood with respect to the civil rights movement. "We have to make a decision," Young told the staff. "We must keep the respect of the Negro people and provide some leadership. The revolution is here. Should we divorce ourselves and let it go as it [is], or intervene and try to bring our experience to bear in these matters? Unless we are in communication with the people, we are not in a position to advise those who give us money on matters of the Negro." Cernoria Johnson, director of the league's Washington bureau, chimed in. It was time to declare publicly that the National Urban League was wholeheartedly in favor of the march. It was worth the risk that things might get out of hand. For the league to have credibility with blacks when "the settling down period" came, it *had* to participate.[9]

Ultimately Young won a consensus that the league would join the march. He persuaded his board "that they were really going to be left behind if they didn't take an active role." Board and staff alike came to see, in associate executive director Alexander J. ("Joe") Allen's words, that "there were too many negatives about not being in it and quite a few positives about being in it, considering the circumstances and the clarity of the issues." It was "a beautiful example of how successful Whitney was," the league's public relations director, Guichard Parris, observed. Young got the board and staff to understand "that even though we'd never done a thing like this before, it was very important for this organization to be part of it. And we had no other choice. If we were not part of it, then we were out, completely out."[10]

By late July, Young was speaking publicly about the league's commitment as a sponsoring organization. In an interview with the other civil rights leaders on National Educational Television on July 22, Young declared that the league would "certainly cooperate with this march." The march would be orderly and all-inclusive—meeting the test of the Urban League's "distinction between picketing and what we would call a 'broadly representative group of people' who are not focused at any particular institution, but are simply witnessing their convictions in support of the President's program." The league's annual conference in Los Angeles at the end of the month offered a good opportunity to assuage any lingering doubts among local executives and their boards. Making the case for participation, Young said:

It is becoming clear now, that if the impatience and the heightened aspirations of the masses of Negro citizens are to be protected and to be channelled along constructive lines, [t]hen the Urban League must of necessity be involved in this feat of social engineering. To divorce ourselves from this would be an expression of irresponsibility; to isolate our organization from this activity would be to deny corporations, foundations and community funds a unique opportunity for representation and participation in a new era of social planning. The Urban League will be value-less to responsible institutions in our society if it does not maintain communication with and the respect of other responsible Negro organizations and the respect of the masses of Negro citizens.[11]

The National Urban League's participation in the March on Washington was critically important both for the success of the march and for the public image of the organization. In the words of John Lewis of the Student Nonviolent Coordinating Committee, Young "literally threw the weight and the influence" of the league behind the march, and its credibility as well as its resources helped significantly to ensure the march's success. Ralph David Abernathy of the Southern Christian Leadership Conference put a finer point on it in describing Young's contribution: "Anybody who could touch the purse strings of the power structure . . . [was] most important to our movement." Bayard Rustin said, speaking of both the Urban League and the NAACP, "Without their money, I could not have put on the march."

Young also played a critical role as a strategist. Lewis remembered him as very active in the decision-making process. Dorothy Height of the National Council of Negro Women declared that he took a major hand in developing the plans. Not the least of his contributions was to engineer the selection of Rustin as director of the march.[12]

As the leader of the proposed march on Washington in 1941, A. Philip Randolph was the logical person to call his colleagues together in 1963. But the seventy-four-year-old Randolph expected to vest responsibility for the day-to-day planning and direction of the march in Rustin's hands. Roy Wilkins objected. Rustin was an experienced organizer, but he was also a radical—a socialist, a onetime member of the Young Communist League, a conscientious objector in World War II. The civil rights movement had enough problems of its own, Wilkins argued; why saddle the march with unnecessary liabilities?

Young engineered the compromise. Before the group met, as Rustin told the story, "Whitney got ahold of Dr. King and explained the situation to him. Whitney said, 'Well, you know, Martin, Bayard's worked with you all this time. Were there any real problems?' " King responded that there were not. " 'Well, then,' " Young rejoined, " 'whatever Randolph proposes, I hope you'll vote for.' "

Young talked to each of the other leaders in turn. To Randolph, Rustin recalled, laughing aloud at the memory, Young proposed a way to settle the dispute: " '*You* be the leader of the march, but you insist that Bayard be your deputy.' "

When the group convened, the script went according to plan. Randolph insisted on Rustin's leading the march, and Wilkins objected. "So Whitney looked at Randolph as if to say, 'The time has come,' and Randolph said, 'Well, Roy, if you feel that way, *I* will be the director, but I want full powers of directorship, which means I have the right to select my deputy.' Roy looked over at Mr. Randolph and said, 'O.K., I've warned you, but if you want him, you take him, and it's *your* responsibility.' " Young said to Rustin, patting him on the back and laughing as they left the room, " 'I'm telling you, black boy, you'd better behave yourself.' "

In the course of planning the march, Rustin turned regularly to Young for advice. With ten different cosponsors (leaders of the six civil rights groups as well as religious and labor leaders) to satisfy, the planning process itself needed to be worked out very carefully. Everything had to be determined collectively—the order of speeches, the amount of time allotted to each speaker, the cost of equipment and cleanup, and numerous other details. Rustin asked Young if he had any ideas about how to structure the process so that the ten chairmen would be consulted at every level of decision making. The two men sat down in Young's office and drew up a plan.

On overall strategy, too, Rustin turned to Young for help. Young had a good sense of tactics, and after Randolph, he was the leader least likely to be held back by confrontations or jealousies between organizations. In addition, he had the best relationships with the leadership of the country.[13]

When the president began to express reservations about the march, Young weighed in to mollify his concerns. Kennedy had submitted his omnibus civil rights bill to Congress on June 19, and he was anxious that demonstrations not interfere with its progress. As he put it at the conclusion of his civil rights message, "Unruly tactics or pressures will not help and may hinder the effective consideration of these measures. . . . I urge all community leaders, Negro and white, to do their utmost to lessen tensions and to exercise self-restraint. The Congress should have an opportunity to freely work its will." Three days later, the president invited the civil rights leaders to the White House to talk about the prospects for the bill. Young noted that people were interpreting Kennedy's comments about demonstrations to mean that he opposed the march. " 'We want success in Congress,' the President replied, 'not just a big show at the Capitol. Some of these people are looking for an excuse to be against us. I don't want to give any of them a chance to say, "Yes, I'm for the bill, but I'm damned if I'll vote for it at the point of a gun!" ' "

The leaders explained their position. Blacks were already in the streets; even if the civil rights leadership tried to call off the demonstrations, it was not at all clear that they could succeed. It was much better to lead the demonstrations in a disciplined, responsible way.[14]

Young discounted the possibility that the march would get out of control. "I tried to point out to the Administration," he said later, "that if black people were violent people inherently, then we would have been violent long before now—or else we have the longest time fuse known to man." Blacks had had plenty of provocation, but they had ordinarily been victims, not perpetrators, of violence. Young tried, too, to quiet Kennedy's fears of possible disruption by the White Citizens Councils and the Ku Klux Klan. Surely nothing of the kind would happen—Kennedy would see to it that the FBI and the police prevented any such interference. As Rustin recalled, Young "sort of blocked the President in." Young told Kennedy that Rustin was prepared to come to Washington to sit down with representatives of government agencies for regular planning meetings. If there was close cooperation between the administration and the organizers of the march, there would be no violence.[15]

Young's intervention smoothed the way for the march. Rustin went to Washington every ten days, met with people in the various federal agencies, and worked out every detail: the number and location of toilets, the number of ambulances that might be needed, a list of suggestions as to what people should bring for lunch to avoid getting sick in the August heat. To take action on the president's concerns about disruption, he met regularly with the Washington police, the Park Police, the FBI, and the CIA to follow up rumors about potential troublemakers.

Whether on large matters or small details, Young's imprint could be found throughout the planning for the march. He helped Rustin devise a plan for policing the march that assigned white police officers to deal with Maryland and Virginia, the likely sources of Ku Klux Klan disruption, and detailed carefully trained black policemen from major East Coast cities to handle the march itself and its perimeters. Young encouraged Rustin to set up an office to provide information and take care of emergencies on the day of the march, and to set aside enough money to cover unexpected needs of marchers for food and for transportation back home. At Young's suggestion, his Washington, D.C., executive director, Sterling Tucker, was put in charge.

As the day of the march approached, Rustin continued to depend on Young's counsel. How would the order of speakers be determined? Young told Rustin not to try to organize it; instead, the speakers themselves should meet to work it out. Who would go to the White House to meet with President Kennedy after the march was over? Many people thought they were entitled to be present, and the makeup of the group became a source of some tension. Rustin drew up several possible lists and went over them with Young. Young considered them briefly and then laughed and told Rustin that they were attempting to do the impossible. There was no way to make sensible choices; the only people who could go to the White House were the ten key leaders.[16]

When John Lewis, the young chairman of SNCC, submitted an advance text of his speech, other sponsors of the march became alarmed. Lewis was planning to say that SNCC could not support Kennedy's civil rights bill; his speech was sprinkled with what they considered to be incendiary words, like "masses" and "revolution," and he had even gone so far as to assert that SNCC intended to "march through Dixie like Sherman"—a clear departure, it seemed to anxious critics, from the consensus not to advocate violence. As late as the day of the march, efforts were still being made to convince Lewis to modify the speech to satisfy others' objections. Young was concerned about some of the words and phrases, but he never came down hard on Lewis the way Wilkins and some others did. Instead, he listened, and he took a firm but conciliatory tack. "John, we've come this far together, let's stay together" was the way Lewis remembered his approach.[17]

Young and the other leaders began the morning of the march with a round of appointments on Capitol Hill. First they visited the Senate majority leader, Mike Mansfield of Montana. Next they paid a call on the minority leader, Everett McKinley Dirksen of Illinois. They met with the leadership in the House of Representatives: the speaker, John McCormack of Massachusetts, and the majority and minority leaders, Carl Albert of Oklahoma and Charles Halleck of Indiana. They then left the Capitol for Constitution Avenue and Seventeenth Street, where they took their places at the head of the line of march. Shortly before noon, they began the long, slow procession toward the Lincoln Memorial.[18]

There is no record of what Young thought as he sat on the platform in front of the memorial that afternoon. Before him, arrayed along the reflecting pool, were more people than the organizers had dreamed would come. Enduring the heat and humidity of an August afternoon, nearly a quarter of a million people, blacks and whites, had assembled to bear peaceful witness to the urgency of racial justice. To Young's right on the platform sat Marian Anderson, the distinguished contralto who, on Easter Sunday, 1939, had sung from the steps of the memorial in a nationally broadcast concert after being denied the use of Constitution Hall because of her race. On his left sat Martin Luther King, whose "I Have a Dream" speech would electrify the crowd before the day ended.

Young took care in his own speech to make plain that by participating in the march, the Urban League had deliberately cast its lot with the civil rights movement. The league's presence, he declared at the outset, "says, and I hope loud and clear, that while intelligence, maturity, and strategy dictate that as Civil Rights agencies we use different methods, we are all united as never before on the goal of securing first class citizenship for all Americans—NOW." Then he laid out an agenda for what it would take to accomplish real equality of opportunity. The country's leaders needed to pass legislation and institute remedial programs to correct the damage of past discrimination. That would enable blacks to march from the ghettos to "decent, wholesome unrestricted residential areas"; from relief to re-training centers; from "underemployment as unskilled workers to higher occupations commensurate with [their] skills"; from inner-city schools that bred dropouts and smothered motivation to "well-equipped, inte-grated facilities." While blacks needed to march in front of city halls and five-and-ten-cent stores to get elementary rights, they also needed to march their children to libraries and march themselves to P.T.A. meet-ings, adult education centers, and voter registration booths.[19]

"Thank God I went to Washington!" an Urban Leaguer wrote Young the next day. "As we were going back to the bus," she added, "a middle aged woman noticed my U.L. sign & came up to me. She said 'I listened to your Mr. Young. He didn't make people stand up and cheer but his words stayed. Now we're standing up and cheering and what we need are words like his that make you think.' " Hobart Taylor, Jr., executive vice chairman of the President's Committee on Equal Employment Opportu-nity, made a similar point. "Yours was the speech with content in it," he wrote Young. "After the oratory evaporates, we've still got to do what you advised."[20]

The March on Washington was a watershed for the National Urban League. From that point forward, Young later reflected, it was no longer possible for people to "think of civil rights agencies without considering the Urban League."[21]

As the civil rights movement heated up, Young kept the Urban League involved. While the league never officially embraced demonstrations or protests, it moved some distance toward modifying its standoffish posture. In February 1964, the board approved the addition of a new paragraph to the 1962 statement on nonviolent direct action. Still concerned to make it "unmistakably clear that the Urban League neither initiates nor partici-pates" in direct action confrontations, it declared the agency's readiness to lend moral support to nonviolent direct action as long as it was undertaken by responsible groups in situations "where inequities are clearly obvious and attempts at persuasion and negotiation have failed to produce any results." Then, as on other occasions, Young took pains to interpret the protests to his board and his colleagues. "For the Negro citizen," he said at the Urban League's annual conference in 1963, "these are acts of bear-ing witness to his faith in democracy through peaceful non-violent demon-stration, and by channelling in constructive ways justified resentments and pent-up frustrated emotions that have been born out of age-old abuses and contemptuous indignities."[22]

Young never got himself arrested as a civil rights demonstrator ("I do not see," he once said, "why I should have to go to jail to prove my leader-ship"), but at critical junctures in the history of the protests, the Urban League was there. When Martin Luther King led the dramatic civil rights march from Selma to Montgomery in March 1965, Young was among the black leaders who spoke from the steps of the Alabama state capitol:

Now I would like to ask one question to the white citizens of Alabama. How long can you continue to afford the luxury of a political system and public officials who by their rigidity and vulgar racism have today been responsible for bringing in federally controlled troops. Who today and even more so tomorrow will cost this state millions of dollars of federal funds for prog[rams] of education, health, wel-fare, agriculture, etc. Who have discouraged dozens of industries from coming into this state. How long, how long will you continue to be the victims of this self-defeating folly? I say you cannot afford this luxury.[23]

Howard Zinn, then a professor at Boston University, had come to Ala-bama for the march, but he had decided to skip the speeches at the state capitol. When he got to the Montgomery airport, he met Young, who was just on his way into town. The old friends stopped to have a cup of coffee together in the airport cafeteria. Zinn was dirty and disheveled after the two-day march; Young, as he recalled, was his usual elegant self. Their waitress, who served them without comment, wore a large button—"The South Says Never." The two men talked about the march. Young told Zinn that "he felt a little funny" coming in at the end to give a speech and be photographed. But those were the constraints that came with his job. When Young got home, he accounted to his board for what he had done. He told them that he had participated in the march "because he felt it was important to give support to the non-violent effort," and he "countered the charge that Communists have gained a foot-hold in civil rights mat-ters."[24]

When James Meredith was shot on the second day of his march from Memphis, Tennessee, to Jackson, Mississippi, in June 1966, leaders of the major civil rights organizations hurried to Memphis to confer on how best to respond to the shooting. The group included familiar figures—King, Wilkins, and Young—as well as two newcomers: Floyd McKissick of CORE and Stokely Carmichael of SNCC. All five wanted to continue the march, but they differed sharply over strategy and goals. Wilkins and Young, strongly committed to integration, interracial efforts, and nonviolence, favored a march that would focus national attention on achieving passage of the 1966 civil rights bill. Carmichael and McKissick, insistent on black separatism and self-determination, took a radically different view: the Johnson administration's civil rights policies were far too weak; instead of supporting the president's latest legislative proposal, the marchers ought to demand that it be revised and strengthened. Beyond that, any statement of purpose ought to look to more important goals, such as the urgency of developing black political power. They argued for deemphasizing the role of whites in the march and for welcoming the participation of black proponents of armed self-defense, such as the Louisiana-based Deacons for Defense.

Carmichael wanted to maneuver Wilkins and Young into refusing to support the march. He resisted their request that the march push for passage of the civil rights bill, and he made plain his contempt for their outdated views. "I started acting crazy," he later recalled. "I just started cursing real bad. Some very terrible things were said about them to their faces in some awful language." For all of Carmichael's rhetorical focus on Wilkins and Young, his real concern was with King. If the moderates participated in the march, it would allow King to "take a middle position among the organizations and appear to be the real arbitrator." Without Wilkins and Young, SNCC would succeed in pulling King to the left and shaping the march in its own militant image.

Remaining silent for the most part, King played into Carmichael and McKissick's hands. He was anxious to preserve at least the appearance of unity in the movement, and he thought that his participation in the march could keep the militants in check. As Carmichael had hoped, Young and Wilkins were driven away.

King turned out to be mistaken about his ability to exert a moderating influence on the march. For more than two weeks, as the marchers pushed on toward Jackson, SNCC and CORE came increasingly to set the tone. At a late-evening rally in Greenwood, Carmichael shouted the words that heralded a major split in the civil rights movement. "We want black power," he cried. "We want black power. We want black power," the crowd echoed. Here was dramatic confirmation of " 'the black nationalist' overtones," as well as the "lack of respect for the principles of non-violence," that Young claimed were keeping the Urban League away.

King made no secret of his reservations about the fiery separatist rhetoric that dominated the march, but he was unable to quiet it. Despite his strong urging, Carmichael and McKissick refused to abandon the black power slogan. As the marchers—now fifteen thousand strong—reached the Mississippi capital, the roar erupted spontaneously: "Black Power! Black Power! Black Power!"[25]

Despite his previous unwillingness to endorse the march, Young decided to join the other civil rights leaders in Jackson for the final rally. He had argued to the league's executive committee that he ought to go (he would not use regular Urban League funds to pay his expenses); the committee gave its "cautious approval." He had come to Jackson, he told the press when he arrived, to show his personal concern for what had happened in Mississippi. Beyond that, he hoped to turn the occasion to the Urban League's advantage. Praising the marchers for their courage, he reminded them that the Urban League was not a marching organization in the traditional sense. Still, when the need arose, they could count on the league to be there:

We are marching with you to conquer fear.

We are marching with you to bring democracy to people who have never known it.

We are marching with you to register Negro voters and help them gain justice through the ballot box.

We are marching with you to show the nation and the world that the poison of hate and fear which for too long has pervaded this state must be eradicated.

And we are marching with you to demonstrate to the Congress that federal action is needed to prevent more shootings, to prevent the martyrdom of more people, both black and white.

Young announced the establishment of a new affiliate of the National Urban League in Jackson, which would work to achieve the aims of the march. The basic problems facing blacks would remain after the marchers left, he said, and the Urban League would deal with them by providing job training and health, welfare, housing, and educational services.

Young made plain his disagreement with the separatist thrust of the march. "I have no intention of retreating into a reverse kind of segregation and abandoning my efforts to get true equality. This is what the segregationists have always wanted, but that is not what they are going to get. . . . This land belongs to all of us, black and white," he continued, "and we won't retreat from one bit of it. Together—Negro and white—we will join hands and work against poverty, discrimination, and hate. Only if men of both races join to make a better nation will we succeed. And only if men of both races work together for it, will success be worth having."

Young's presence in Jackson clearly mattered. "It was a very important show of unity," Andrew Young of SCLC reflected; "by Whitney being there it made it understandable and acceptable to a whole middle-class black and business constituency."[26]

As the Urban League executive committee's caution over the Meredith march makes clear, Young had to walk a tightrope on such occasions. A press release issued before the march pointed up the delicacy of his position. He emphasized that the league's participation would not mean abandoning the principles that set it apart from other civil rights agencies. Each organization had

its own unique role to fulfill within the movement. . . . While others march in the streets and the highways to galvanize support for broad measures, the Urban League marches its people to job training centers, neighborhood development centers and the like. Each organization does what it can do best.

These different activities undertaken by the various civil rights agencies complement each other. Jointly we are working toward the same goals—to close the shocking economic and cultural gap which exists between Negroes and other citizens.

Later, Young sent a confidential report on the march and a copy of his remarks at Jackson to executives of major corporations. Once again, he was walking a delicate line. The communication served two purposes. On one level, Young, fulfilling his role as interpreter, was helping corporate executives understand the latest developments in the movement, developments that could easily appear threatening. On another level—less explicit, but perhaps even more important for the Urban League—he was trying to shore up the league's credibility by accounting for the organization's presence in a setting that people accustomed to its more traditional roles might have found startling.[27]

Young knew, in Urban League executive Joe Allen's words, that "being able to identify with the growing protest" was essential to the league's effectiveness. He also knew, as Andrew Young wrote at the time of Whitney's death, that any move in the direction of protest required "an agonizing appraisal of every action," because the league's affiliates "would feel in their budgets the reverberation of any miscalculation."[28]

Taking some part in major demonstrations was the most public way for Young to claim a role for the Urban League in civil rights activism. At the same time, participating regularly in organized meetings of the leaders gave him some private leverage among his colleagues. Early in 1963, Young began meeting regularly with some of the other civil rights leaders—Roy Wilkins of the NAACP, James Farmer of CORE, Dorothy Height of the National Council of Negro Women, and Jack Greenberg of the NAACP Legal Defense and Educational Fund—under the auspices of the philanthropist Stephen Currier.

Currier and his wife, Audrey Bruce Currier, a granddaughter of Andrew W. Mellon, committed themselves from the earliest years of their marriage to using their enormous personal wealth to benefit social causes and institutions that had generally not attracted other benefactors. The Taconic Foundation, which they established in 1958, concentrated initially in three areas: civil rights and race relations, child welfare, and mental health. Before long, however, civil rights became its main focus. Among its other ventures, the foundation financed a large part of the voter registration drives in the South in the early 1960s.

Currier believed that Taconic's work would be more effective if it understood as fully as possible where money could make the greatest difference to the civil rights movement. Early in 1963, he called in the leaders of the major civil rights organizations to ask their advice about what the foundation's concerns should be.[29]

The leaders proposed that the foundation fund some research as a way of establishing needs and priorities. Taconic did not ordinarily support research, but it took the suggestion and put up some money for what came to be known as the Assessment Project. Currier turned to Young to chair the effort. He was a natural choice. The Taconic Foundation had been supporting the National Urban League since the last years of Lester Granger's executive directorship. The vice-president of the foundation, Lloyd K. Garrison, a prominent New York lawyer, was both an intimate friend and important adviser to Currier and a longtime trustee and former president of the league. Currier and Young, who were both the same age, had first met in mid-January 1961, shortly before Young's appointment was announced. And the National Urban League was the civil rights organization that specialized in documenting and analyzing the social and economic conditions of the black population.[30]

In conjunction with Taconic officials, as well as the other consultants, Young organized the plan of work. Each of the consultants agreed to take responsibility for developing a working paper on one or more of the critical issues the group had identified as needing attention—education, employment, housing, labor relations, voting rights, youth programs, and child welfare. The papers would then be circulated among the consultants and their research associates, and ultimately discussed at a larger conference under Taconic's aegis.[31]

As it happened, the papers themselves were not of major consequence. But the meetings quickly began to serve a broader purpose. "What was compelling," in the words of the foundation's executive director, Jane Lee J. Eddy, was that "everybody got to know each other."

What Eddy meant was that the civil rights leaders came to know one another better as a result of the meetings of the Assessment Project. But the project also gave her and the others associated with the foundation a chance for closer contact with each of the black leaders than they had had before. "We didn't know very many blacks," she commented, "and if we did know them, . . . I don't think we really had much sense of them as people." In that context, Young made a great impact. "You didn't know very many blacks who were as direct, as confident, as determined, and as . . . compelling as Whitney Young was, and he just won everybody's heart, so to speak. People had confidence in him . . . and they liked him. . . . And that was part of his personality. But it wasn't all personality, because he was incisive, never let anybody off the hook, and people weren't used to that in those days."[32]

The assassination of Medgar Evers in Jackson, Mississippi, on June 12, 1963, provided the catalyst that would transform what had begun in meetings of the Assessment Project into a formal organization. When Taconic officials heard the news, they feared that it could mean "a terrible blowup in the South," Eddy remembered, and they wondered what they could do to help. They called Young and asked what he thought. He responded immediately: "Let's get everybody together." Currier called an emergency meeting for that afternoon. It was short notice, and not everyone whom Currier invited was able to attend. Young was there; so were Roy Wilkins, Jack Greenberg, and James Farmer. Young and Wilkins expressed concern "that things might just take a wrong turn [and] be explosive." They underscored the urgency of opening communication with the white establishment.[33]

Currier sent out telegrams inviting corporate and foundation leaders to breakfast at the Carlyle Hotel on June 19. Ninety-six of them showed up. Currier asked each civil rights leader to make a statement about his or her organization and its efforts. While the basic purpose was to help the white establishment understand what was going on in the South, the point was also to raise money. The meeting resulted in pledges of more than $500,000.[34]

With substantial amounts of money coming in, there needed to be a structure to handle disbursements and play a coordinating function. The fact that many of the leaders had already been meeting together periodically under the auspices of the Taconic Foundation laid the basis for a cooperative effort. "It seemed almost providential that we were together," Dorothy Height reflected; without the history of shared conversations, she speculated, "I doubt that it would have been possible to pull that group together." Building on the foundation laid by Currier's meetings, the leaders decided to form a new organization, the Council for United Civil Rights Leadership (CUCRL).[35]

The membership of CUCRL included the operating heads of the seven major civil rights organizations—Martin Luther King of SCLC, James Farmer of CORE, Roy Wilkins of the NAACP, Whitney Young of the National Urban League, Jack Greenberg of the Legal Defense Fund, Dorothy Height of the National Council of Negro Women, and James Forman of SNCC—as well as Stephen Currier and Lloyd Garrison. A. Philip Randolph, an important civil rights leader but not the head of a civil rights organization, was invited to join a year later. Currier and Young agreed to serve as cochairmen. Each organization would "maintain its autonomy and its particular sphere of responsibility," but all would "work in unity towards their shared goal."[36]

The day after Currier's breakfast at the Carlyle, Young reported to the National Urban League executive committee on the plans for the new organization. It made some of the trustees nervous, especially because of the chance that it would undermine the Urban League's own fund-raising efforts. Young took pains to reassure them. He acknowledged that the league was taking a calculated risk by joining CUCRL, but he said that recent events were so frightening that unusual action seemed warranted. He told them that without the league's participation, the cooperative effort would never have come to fruition, which he felt would have been disastrous. Lindsley Kimball, who had attended the breakfast meeting, agreed that the league needed to be represented and said that the times called for the league to assume a larger, not a lesser, role. The executive committee of the league agreed that the funds CUCRL received would be used to meet special, emergency needs, and that the purposes for which the money was being raised would be clearly defined by the participating organizations; it instructed Young "to help fashion those purposes into a constructive program."[37]

The new council served two principal functions: it raised money for its seven constituent organizations, while minimizing the increasingly hostile competition among them for contributors' dollars; and it provided a forum for the leaders to share ideas and coordinate strategy. But there was also a more pointed purpose: to exert a stabilizing influence on the movement. The wealthy white supporters of civil rights had a strong interest in moderating the increasingly aggressive, demanding tone of the movement in the South. Similarly, the leaders of the more conservative civil rights organizations had a strong interest in a regular forum in which they might impress their views on their more outspoken, activist colleagues. As Young put it, the idea behind CUCRL was "to keep direction of the movement in responsible hands, so it doesn't get 'taken over by some of those fellows waiting in the wings.' "[38]

The "Unity" effort, as its members called it, drew a good deal of favorable comment. "The nation's Negro leaders have acted boldly to head off the extremists of their own race," the *New York Herald Tribune* declared. The council offered hope that the "ugly outbreaks of violence" that had increasingly marred civil rights demonstrations could be contained. The council represented "an effort by the more responsible leadership to maintain control," the paper said, and it also promised to "act as a check on the dangerous drift into rivalry among the Negro organizations themselves."[39]

The promise of strengthening responsible leadership proved to be an effective fund-raising device. With $800,000 pledged by mid-July, CUCRL announced a goal of raising $1.5 million by the end of the summer. Contributions to support the agencies that were not tax-exempt came directly to CUCRL; contributions to the three participating tax-exempt organizations would be paid to an allied nonprofit corporation, the Committee for Welfare, Education and Legal Defense (WELD). As the money came in, each organization got its share according to a formula agreed on by the council. The first allocation, announced in mid-July, contained $125,000 in non-tax-exempt gifts for the NAACP, $100,000 for CORE, $50,000 for SCLC, and $15,000 (to be upgraded later) for SNCC. The first distribution of tax-exempt gifts meant $125,000 for the National Urban League, $100,000 for the NAACP's Legal Defense and Educational Fund, and $50,000 for the Educational Foundation of the National Council of Negro Women.[40]

The council continued to disburse funds to the member organizations, but after the fund-raising drive of 1963, the sums were never very large. Contributions came from Currier himself and from a handful of other large donors. Following the March on Washington, Martin Luther King assigned exclusive worldwide recording rights of his "I Have a Dream" speech to CUCRL, which produced an album of highlights of the march. Record sales were not as lucrative as the leaders had hoped, but they brought in a small continuing income. Sales of equality buttons, another fund-raising device, brought in a modest amount of additional money. When King won the Nobel Peace Prize in 1964, he allocated a share of the prize money to CUCRL for division among the other six participating organizations.[41]

For a time, CUCRL held regular meetings, either at the Carlyle Hotel or at the offices of the Taconic Foundation, the National Urban League, or the Legal Defense Fund. The agendas for the meetings were not in themselves compelling; what was important was that the leaders got together. Fund-raising was a perennial concern, but agendas included discussion of other topics—the 1964 Civil Rights Act, other Great Society legislation of special interest to blacks, the Mississippi Summer Project, the Mississippi Challenge. From time to time, the council spoke as a body to try to influence public policy.

More significant were the opportunities the meetings afforded for sharing information, thinking collectively about the movement, and diminishing tensions among the civil rights organizations. The leaders talked about
what their organizations had been doing, outlined their plans for the future, and suggested ways that other organizations might offer help and
cooperation. By coming together on a regular basis, each leader became
more intimately acquainted with the purposes and activities of the other
organizations than would otherwise have been the case. The meetings
gave each of them a chance for reflection and thoughtful analysis, an opportunity to step back from day-to-day preoccupations and look at the
broader civil rights picture.

Just as periodic discussions gave the leaders a chance to think system-
atically about the direction of the movement, the sessions provided some
hope for reducing rivalries and tensions among the organizations. Discussion of interorganizational conflicts, tensions, and differences was a regular agenda item when the council met. Eliminating competition among
the organizations would not have been realistic, but the meetings provided a way to talk out disagreements and keep tempers and jealousies
under better control. John Lewis credited CUCRL with heading off major
misunderstandings among the organizations; it "kept us together," he
said, and gave the movement "that sense of unity and focus that it needed
during that time."[42]

The council went through a number of structural transformations in its
short history. According to plan, one of the cochairmanships rotated
among the leaders of the civil rights organizations. The other cochairman,
Currier, resigned from the council in August 1964. He had played a crucial role in bringing the leaders together and providing financial support,
but he recognized, over time, that as a white and an outsider to the movement, he had less and less of a role to play.[43]

Wiley A. Branton, the executive director of CUCRL, resigned in May
1965 to take a post in the Johnson administration in Washington. Instead
of replacing him, the leaders decided that each of the member organizations would take administrative responsibility for CUCRL for one year.
Gradually, the pressure of other responsibilities and the absence of a central organizing force made scheduled meetings less frequent and attendance haphazard, despite repeated reaffirmations of the value of regular
contact among the leaders. There was no more money to distribute, and
growing tensions within the movement—over black power, over the desirability of joining the cause of civil rights and the issue of the United
States' role in Vietnam—made unity harder and harder to realize. In January 1967, at the instigation of Jack Greenberg, steps were taken to liqui-
date the organization.[44]

Over the years, when the civil rights leaders gathered, Whitney Young emerged as the peacemaker of the group. When the mood was heaviest, when tempers flared, he was the one to interject a note of humor to break up the tension. When divisions arose, he was the one to find some middle ground where the leaders could reunite. He was the negotiator, the mediator, always ready "to work out a difference of opinion," John Lewis said. "He was reasonable, sensible. . . . I think he had a calming effect on all of us."

In functioning as a mediator, Young benefited from his position as head of the Urban League. Throughout the direct action phase of the movement, SNCC, CORE, SCLC, and the NAACP competed vigorously for publicity and position. Tensions festered among the leaders: Who had gotten the most attention in the media? Who had done the most effective job of getting out demonstrators? Who deserved credit for the victories? What was at stake was considerably more than vanity or prestige. Getting the credit for mobilizing demonstrators or negotiating change translated into tangible resources—more adherents, increased financial support, easier access to the white power structure—resources that were essential to a leader's ability to lead and to an organization's ability to survive and flourish. Young was not immune to the competition of egos, but since the league was not involved in direct action, he was somewhat removed from the jealousies and rivalries among the organizations. Lewis described Young as "a swing person" who gave direction to the combined efforts of the civil rights leaders. Rustin called him an essential part of "the concrete that kept the bricks from falling apart."

More important, Young's personal qualities fitted him for the peacemaker's role. Thanks in part to his training as a social worker, he knew how to listen, to understand where someone else was coming from, to avoid being judgmental, to build bridges. He was "the kind of fellow," Guichard Parris observed, "who would say, 'Look, let's get together, fellows . . . we don't agree, but let's get together as rational men and find out how we can achieve our end.' "

He did it with a warmth, a graciousness, and a sense of humor that were positively infectious. "He had a fantastic ability to tell jokes about colored people to colored people," Rustin said. As the leaders gathered for a meeting, the sounds of laughter signaled Young's arrival. At one CUCRL meeting, for instance, he joked with Farmer, who was well aware of Young's reputation as a ladies' man, about Farmer's efforts in his speeches to explode racial myths. "That's fine," he told him, "just keep on doing it, but there's one myth I don't want you to mess with" (referring to the commonly held view of black men's special sexual prowess). "Don't touch that one!" The chemistry that made Young a skillful peacemaker also cemented strong personal relationships. "He was one of my favorites among the civil rights leaders," Farmer said. "I got along so well with him and I felt comfortable with him and I think he felt comfortable with me." They shared jokes and anecdotes about things that had happened in the movement. They had the kind of easy camaraderie that led them to trade knowing smiles in meetings, each one certain that he knew how the other was reacting to what had been said.[45]

Young's talent as a mediator made him more successful than many of his colleagues in understanding and relating to the militants. Jesse Jackson said that he had a "unique ability . . . keep his ears open. He could hear even those he disagreed with." Young had a way of inviting the young people who challenged his views to come up to his hotel room or stop by the office to continue the conversation. He believed in communicating— at the very least, it was important to find out what the other fellow had on his mind. They might not convince each other, might not agree, but it was essential to sit down and talk. Urban League staff members remarked on the succession of young militants from the ghetto, dressed in overalls and sandals, trooping in and out of Young's office. Some of them, like the members of Youth Organizations United, an umbrella for youth gangs from around the country, came to take advantage of Young's connections to the major foundations. Young spoke up for them, supported them, and helped them get money. These were not the sort of people who had traditionally come to call on the executive director of the National Urban League, and Young got a kick out of the anomaly. His administrative assistant, Enid Baird, remembered him laughing and saying that Lester Granger would just die if he could see it.[46]

Young's experience with the emerging student movement in Atlanta helped him to identify with the young people in the movement. John Lewis frequently turned to him for advice. "I could talk to him," Lewis said. "He was helpful. He would weigh both sides." In Rustin's judgment, Young got along with the young radicals much better than most of the other civil rights leaders, including King.[47]

As CORE embarked on its odyssey from interracialism to black separatism, Young kept up his connections. The election of Floyd McKissick to succeed James Farmer as national director in January 1966 signaled the organization's tilt toward an increasingly nationalist stance, and CORE's new program of black separatism led many of its staunch supporters to drift away. With them went the financial support from white liberals that had been essential to the organization. When an antisemitic statement by a black official of the Mt. Vernon, New York, chapter in February alienated prominent Jewish supporters, McKissick turned to Young to help him repair some of the strains. That summer, McKissick moved CORE's national headquarters to Harlem, thus symbolizing the agency's new black image and dramatizing its commitment to improving conditions of ghetto life. No black leader had better connections in New York than Young, and McKissick again turned to him for advice on where to go and whom to see to accomplish his purposes. In several instances, Young established connections for CORE that resulted in significant funding. McKissick thought of Young as someone he could turn to when he was in trouble, someone he could count on to get things done—the person "you could call . . . when you couldn't call anyone else."[48]

Young's ability to get along with the radicals in the civil rights movement related directly to his appreciation of their role in effecting change. He likened the movement to a war—in this case, a war against racism, bigotry, and poverty. "In a war you need a division of labor," he pointed out.

You need a variety of strategies and approaches and weapons. You don't just talk about an air force. You need an infantry, intelligence, a tank corps, and antiaircraft.

There have been moments in the civil-rights struggle when you needed the air force to soften them up—to bomb the shores to permit the infantry to land. One doesn't stand back and say the air force is more militant than the infantry. We recognize the interdependence.[49]

The Urban League, he sometimes said, varying the metaphor, functioned as the State Department of the civil rights movement; the NAACP was the War Department, and CORE and SNCC were the Marines. Each organization and leader had different approaches, abilities, resources, and contacts to bring to bear on the struggle; the complexity of the goals of the movement demanded that everyone's resources be used to achieve real progress. Young frequently spoke to that point. "It isn't Urban League, *or* CORE, *or* NAACP," he said in one speech. "It is Urban League *and*. . . . You need all of these approaches, and one thing without the other is absolutely no good." On another occasion he said that "most advocates of civil rights wish that Whitney Young, Roy Wilkins and Jim Farmer were using identical methods to achieve a common goal. . . . Reality forces us to concede that civil rights is no single-faceted problem, nor is there any monolithic solution." He liked to explain that the day had passed when blacks could entrust their "complete destiny to a single Messianic leader or rely on any monolithic approach. . . . We must think today not in terms of individual leaders or of *the* approach," he said, "but of levels of leadership involving many people, with a variety of approaches and tactics. The issue must now become not *which* approach, but how we intelligently deploy our forces and establish roles and division of labor."[50]

It was SNCC, CORE, and SCLC that supplied the charismatic leadership of the movement, rallied and inspired adherents, and organized them for direct-action protests. The NAACP and the National Urban League supplied bureaucratic stability and professional and technical expertise; their leaders functioned as the ambassadors, negotiators, and bargainers who translated the pressure of direct-action protest into concessions from the white power structure.

While the NAACP did its most important work in the courts and in the halls of Congress, and SNCC, CORE, and SCLC demonstrated in the streets, the National Urban League made its greatest impact in corporate boardrooms and policymakers' offices. "You can holler, protest, march, picket, demonstrate," Young liked to say; "but somebody must be able to sit in on the strategy conferences and plot a course. There must be the strategists, the researchers and the professionals to carry out a program. That's our role."[51]

Just as Young understood clearly the distinct roles of the organizations in the movement, he also had a keen sense of how to play on that diversity in order to accomplish his purposes. As a social worker trained to analyze social processes and to understand and relate to difference, he was especially well equipped to grasp the value to the civil rights movement of tensions between moderates and militants. Dorothy Height spoke about his ability to recognize the interdependence of different approaches, the value of different roles: "He used to have a way of saying, 'Well, you see, the more they [the militants] pound on the table, then the readier other people are to sit at the table and talk to me.' "[52]

Far from crippling the movement, the creative tensions between moderates and militants facilitated the accomplishment of its goals. Without the pressure from direct actionists in the streets, leaders of the white establishment would have been much less ready to negotiate with moderate civil rights leaders. Later, without the rhetoric of black separatism and the resort to violence, the urgency of addressing fundamental issues of civil rights and economic opportunity for blacks would have been much less compelling. Young understood that, and he deliberately used the threat of the militants as a tactic in his dealings with the white establishment. "Whenever anybody got upset about some statement I was making," he once explained, "I would say, 'See who is standing in the wings.' " He made the point again and again: do business with moderate, responsible leaders, or you will have to deal with the radicals in the streets.[53]

Young's relationship with Malcolm X is a case in point. Malcolm stood at the furthest fringe of the black movement of the 1960s. He had no use for nonviolence as a strategy—"this mealy-mouth, beg-in, wait-in, plead-in kind of action," he called it—and he dismissed integration as unattainable without a great deal of bloodshed and, more important, as undesirable (after all, what could blacks gain by seeking to assimilate with their natural enemies, white devils?). Malcolm called himself "the angriest black man in America," and his rhetoric of rage and revolution sustained the description. He disdained mainstream civil rights leaders as "black bodies with white heads!" "Today's Uncle Tom doesn't wear a handkerchief on his head," he asserted; "this twentieth-century Uncle Thomas is a *professional* Negro . . . by that I mean his profession is being a Negro for the white man." In turn, the civil rights leaders generally regarded Malcolm as a danger to the cause of improving relations between the races; they resented his attacks on them and envied his coverage in the white media. "I don't see why they hate me," Malcolm told his friend, the actor Ossie Davis. "I raise hell in the back yard and they run out front and The Man puts money in their hands."[54]

Among the leaders, Young came as close as anyone to having some sympathy with Malcolm's role. Malcolm's lawyer, Percy Sutton, brought them together on a number of occasions; once they got to know each other, they developed some mutual respect, and the public sniping between them stopped. Malcolm's biographer, Peter Goldman, said that Malcolm "rather liked" Young as a private person, although he thought that he "didn't spend enough time around Negroes." Goldman described one occasion when the two men got together:

Malcolm thought Young "more down to earth" than most of the other movement celebrities—blacker, that is, than his board-room manner in public suggested. "I can't say the things you can," Young told him. Malcolm by then had got a bit tired of hearing this from respectable black leaders, but he smiled anyway and kidded about how his hell-raising was frightening the more timid Negroes in droves into the Urban League and the NAACP. "You ought to pay me $5 a head for recruiting," Malcolm said; they both laughed.

Malcolm communicated his view of their relationship this way: to Sutton, he said, "My presence makes the corporate structure much more comfortable with Whitney Young," or, to Kenneth Clark, "I have to play the role I play in order for them to listen to people like Martin and Whitney."

Young understood the interplay between them in precisely the same way, and he used it to his advantage. John H. Johnson, president of Johnson Publishing Company, remembered with considerable amusement Young's description of his approach. Young told Johnson that he was usually able to get a hearing from most of the corporate executives he wanted to see. When he had trouble, he sometimes called Malcolm and asked *him* to call the executive in question. Suddenly access was no longer a problem. "Whitney, what do you think Malcolm wants with me?" the man might ask when he returned Young's call. Young would reply that it would be a good idea if the executive were doing something constructive for blacks in the community so that he would have an answer to whatever Malcolm had to say.[55]

James Farmer, too, remembered vividly Young's effective use of the threat of "the iron fist of the militants" to get corporate leaders to do his bidding. He would tell them what he wanted them to do about hiring, training, and advancing blacks in their companies; "they would hem and hedge, and he'd say, 'Now wait a minute, you've got to do what *I* tell you to do. If you don't, Jim Farmer and CORE will get you.' " The threat usually produced the results Young wanted.[56]

Many of the militants understood plainly that while they were out on the front lines doing the hell-raising, Young was in the background reaping the benefits. Some of them resented him for that; others, like Floyd McKissick, took a more pragmatic stance: Young ought to give CORE and SNCC a percentage of what he got. McKissick recalled Young acknowledging, with a laugh, that he probably did owe them a cut.[57]

By bringing the National Urban League into the civil rights movement, Whitney Young redefined the role of his own organization and made an important contribution to the shape and direction of the larger movement. Young accomplished the transformation of the league from a social service agency to a civil rights organization without abandoning any of its historic commitments to the promotion of the economic and social welfare of black Americans. In so doing, he kept the league from becoming peripheral to the black struggle, and he positioned it to take advantage of a political and social climate conducive to progress on black employment and social welfare. It capitalized on that climate in two different areas: its dealings with the corporate establishment, and its relationships to the federal government.

IX

The Corporate Establishment

"I think there is a dangerous man loose," wrote *Pittsburgh Courier* columnist P. L. Prattis in June 1962. "This man is all the more 'dangerous' because he doesn't look 'dangerous.' He looks urbane and suave. He has a ready-made smile and a glad handshake, but he packs a verbal wallop worse than Sonny Liston's hand. He can really hurt you if you are married to the past."

Prattis had heard Whitney Young speak in Pittsburgh, and he was struck especially by the way Young had handled the whites in his audience.

It has been necessary for some time to have someone who could talk straight to white folks and colored folks, someone who was smart and subtle and incisive. Well, folks, the man has come along. I looked at the white folks as he talked in Pittsburgh the other night. He is so disarming that at first they just sort of smiled and grinned.

Then, as they saw where he was headed, they grew grim and thoughtful. . . . They learned that his outward manner was but a mask for a new and more direct way of looking at the problems of the Negro in the United States. In the language of the street, he laid it gently, but definitely, on the line.[1]

Laying it on the line to the white establishment became Whitney Young's stock-in-trade. Consummate politician, salesman, interpreter, and ebullient personality, he bridged the gulf between the ghetto and the power structure. The inside man of the black revolution, he brought the white establishment to the support of civil rights. The National Urban League gave him a platform. The civil rights movement gave him the establishment's ear. What he made of them became the hallmark of his role as a black leader.

Young first got to know corporate leaders through his efforts to raise funds for the National Urban League. Changes in public policy broadened his contacts. Executive Order 10925, issued in March 1961, required companies holding government contracts to maintain a nondiscriminatory employment policy and to take affirmative action to hire members of minority groups. In its wake, companies began adopting Plans for Progress to bring themselves into compliance. Then the Civil Rights Act of 1964 made equal employment the law of the land. That gave businessmen new reasons to pay attention to Young's message. Few companies had a great deal of experience in hiring blacks in significant numbers; even fewer had experience in hiring them for any but the most menial positions. The Urban League could provide practical assistance in identifying potential black employees, training them, and smoothing the tensions that many people believed were bound to accompany integration in the workplace.

Those circumstances created opportunities for Young to carry his message to corporate America. American Telephone and Telegraph asked him to meet with its senior executives; so did the Corn Products Company and Scott Paper. Management at RCA, anxious to develop a successful program in equal employment opportunity, instituted a series of seminars for its executives with Young as the featured speaker. Bell Telephone Laboratories, committed to a good-faith effort under the Plans for Progress program, asked Young to participate in a seminar on civil rights for senior management personnel. General Electric made him a regular lecturer at its management training courses. Time Inc. invited him to join the group of corporate chiefs it assembled for the tour of Eastern Europe.

At the same time, industrial magazines began to spread Young's ideas more widely. The December 1964 issue of *Factory* magazine printed an interview with him on the subject of integration in industry. Excerpts from his book, *To Be Equal*, were published in the AT&T house organ in February 1965. The winter 1966 issue of *General Electric Forum* carried an article by Young on manpower utilization.

Speeches to industrial associations and chambers of commerce were another way of communicating with business leaders. Especially in the latter part of the 1960s, such groups as the National Industrial Conference Board, the National Association of Manufacturers, the National Association of Home Builders, the Rubber Manufacturers Association, the New York Board of Trade, and the American Chamber of Commerce counted Young among their major speakers.

The receptivity of corporate leaders to Young and his message grew in direct relationship to developments in the racial situation in the United States. To all intents and purposes, the civil rights movement had triumphed by the mid-1960s. January 1964 brought the ratification of the Twenty-fourth Amendment to the Constitution, outlawing the poll tax, which had been a principal means of disfranchising blacks in federal elections. That summer, the Civil Rights Act of 1964, first proposed by John F. Kennedy the year before, finally won approval in the Congress.

Among its other provisions, the sweeping law outlawed racial barriers in employment and guaranteed blacks equal access to places of public accommodation. The next year, the Voting Rights Act suspended literary tests, long used to disfranchise blacks, as a qualification for voting; authorized the appointment of federal examiners to register voters; suspended poll taxes in state and local elections; and made interference with voting or registration a federal crime. Taken together, these provisions constituted an unprecedented assertion of federal power in behalf of racial equality.

But then came an extraordinary outpouring of racial violence. A decade of civil rights activity had brought substantial changes in the legal status of black Americans but very few changes in the deep-rooted social and economic ills of the black ghetto. Blacks in the ghetto were twice as likely as whites to be unemployed, three times as likely to be in unskilled and service jobs, more than twice as likely to be in poverty, and three times as likely to live in overcrowded, dilapidated housing. All around them they saw the affluence of white America, and they were fiercely resentful of the enormous disparity in their fortunes and of their inability to command the power to change them. They focused their frustrations especially on the whites they believed to be responsible for their exploitation: the police, slumlords, and ghetto merchants.

These frustrations finally exploded into a cycle of looting, destruction, and death. The long, hot summer of ghetto rioting became a characteristic feature of the 1960s. At first each summer was defined by one or two major riots: Harlem and Bedford-Stuyvesant in 1964, Watts in 1965. By the summer of 1966, the best-known riots, in Chicago and in the Hough section of Cleveland, were only two among 43 racial disorders of varying seriousness. The summer of 1967 was even more frightening: there were 150 racial outbreaks, the bloodiest in Newark and Detroit; all told, by the time that summer had ended, at least ninety people had died in American cities, more than four thousand had been injured, and nearly seventeen thousand had been arrested.

The racial crisis of the late 1960s frightened and angered white Americans, but it also sparked a desire to find ways to improve the conditions that had caused the violence. Above all, the white establishment wanted to restore calm to the nation's troubled cities. Here Whitney Young and the Urban League—safe, respectable, experienced—looked especially attractive. Young understood and could interpret the frightening developments in the cities; he and his organization were experts in the very problems that industrial leaders now needed urgently to address. Young knew that the times gave him an advantage, and he played it for all it was worth. He put the choice directly to corporate executives: back the efforts of responsible racial advancement organizations like the Urban League, or

fuel the excesses of "the extremists and the irresponsibles." With options
of that sort, it was little wonder that Young got increasing attention.[2]

Now the corporate sector's claims on Young's time increased dramatically. By 1968, he was giving almost three times the number of speeches
to corporate groups and industrial associations as he had in 1965. While
the message varied somewhat according to the audience, he built his appeals around some fundamental themes.

Again and again Young hammered home the obligation of members of
the business community to be responsible corporate citizens. Businessmen had reaped the benefits and rewards of the free enterprise system;
now they needed to step forward to help remedy its defects. They liked
taking credit for the good things that had happened in American society,
but they also had to accept responsibility for its shortcomings and fail-
ures.[3]

Not only were businessmen implicated in the racism and discrimination
that pervaded American society, but they were directly accountable for
the discriminatory practices in their own particular industries. It took
great skill and ingenuity to accomplish racial exclusion. Young used irony
to make his point: "I admire the great ingenuity of American business in
keeping Negroes out of all levels of operation except the most menial. I
admire it because I am a believer in excellence and in creativity, and for
the major part of the American economy to do so well in excluding Negroes over the years reflects an excellence in planning and a creativity far
beyond the bounds which we might reasonably expect."[4]

Now it was time for business to change its attitudes and practices. Here
Young managed deftly to shift ground ever so slightly, to ease up on the
theme of villainy, to focus his audiences' attention on ways of becoming
part of the solution. The principal task of his listeners was to promote
genuine integration in their own industries.

Young urged business leaders to begin by finding out how many blacks
they really employed. "One of our handicaps is our high visibility," he
cautioned. One or two black faces did not add up to integration.

He warned against falling into the common traps that so often militated
against jobs for blacks: "Well, we hired some, but they didn't show up
after the first day," or "They were late on Monday, so they must have a
congenital motivation problem." Black people were motivated like anyone else, he said, motivated "by the knowledge that through persever-
ance, extra study, and hard work they, too, can move upstairs." There was
no problem of blacks not showing up or being late for work in professional
baseball or basketball, because there blacks had role models, stars who
made six-figure salaries. Businesses needed a Willie Mays or a Bill Russell: "You've got to have somebody in a comparable position in your company, that role model, that Exhibit A, somebody at the top."

Whitney M. Young, Sr., and Laura Ray Young

Newlyweds

Kentucky GIs at leisure in Germany

Company C, 1695th Engineer Combat Battalion, at Versailles

Dean of the Atlanta University School of Social Work

With fellow civil rights leaders, 1963. *Left to right:* John Lewis, Whitney M. Young, Jr.,
A. Philip Randolph, Martin Luther King, Jr., James Farmer, and Roy Wilkins.

Leaders of the March on Washington

At the White House following the March on Washington. *Left to right:* Whitney M. Young, Jr.,
Martin Luther King, Jr., Rabbi Joachim Prinz, A. Philip Randolph,
President John F. Kennedy, and Walter Reuther.

With President Lyndon B. Johnson and Roy Wilkins in the Oval Office

With President Lyndon B. Johnson at the White House

Meeting at the White House, 1964. *Left to right:* Roy Wilkins, James Farmer, Martin Luther King, Jr., Whitney M. Young, Jr., and President Lyndon B. Johnson.

Visiting American troops in Vietnam, 1966

With Henry Ford

Meeting with President Richard M. Nixon in the Cabinet Room, 1970

Whitney and Margaret

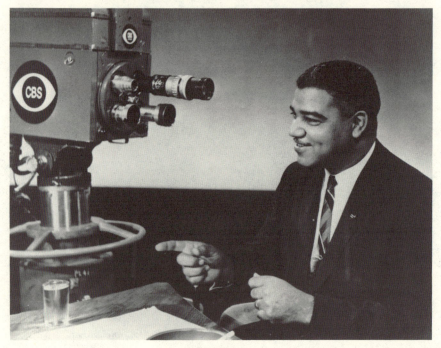

On camera

Important as it was to have some role models, it was essential to create opportunities for black employment throughout industry. Companies needed to hire not just "the Phi Beta Kappas and the Lena Hornes," but "dumb Negroes as you do dumb white people, and mediocre Negroes as you do mediocre white people. We need these jobs at all levels."

Corporate leaders needed to communicate their sense of urgency about the racial crisis right down the line. It was one thing for the chairman of the board to issue a directive about black employment; people throughout the organization needed to know that top management was serious and intended to obtain compliance.[5]

Young used irony and humor to make his arguments come alive. The story of his own efforts to integrate the Urban League was especially effective in underscoring his appeal. When he became executive director, he liked to tell his audiences, 1 percent of the Urban League's employees were white. The agency made a deliberate effort to change that. It began by advertising its commitment to hire people regardless of race, creed, or color. It actively recruited whites in those places where willing and able whites were most likely to be found. It committed itself to a policy of preferential treatment; if two applicants—one black and one white—were equally qualified, the job would go to the white.

The league also reviewed its criteria for employment and came to realize that it would need to modify its expectations if more whites were to qualify. It wanted people who had experienced rejection, who understood the language of the ghetto and the psychology of poor people.

Not many whites met these standards. That seemed to Young to be unfair; the accident of birth ought not to be held against them. Doubtless they had some other qualifications that the Urban League wanted. The agency reviewed its screening and testing process, taking into account the strengths that whites could bring. It decided to hire whites who showed great promise on a provisional basis, give them six months of remedial work, and see what they could accomplish.

The strategy worked. Now 30 percent of the Urban League's employees were white, and they were "well-balanced, well-motivated top people"— as good, if not better, than the blacks who worked for the organization.

"If I can figure this out with my limited capacity and in my very short period of being boss," Young said, "what could the white people figure out, the white American businessmen who have been boss for so long and who are so creative and so imaginative if they will really set out to do it? We wanted to do it. That's the difference. If you want to do it, you could. If you don't want to do it, you will fail."[6]

Young's challenge to businessmen extended beyond integrating their work forces. He urged them to put their plants and retail outlets in the ghetto. He prodded them to press for social legislation to deal with the problems of the ghetto—legislation to attack poverty, to improve the quality of public education, to provide massive appropriations for new construction of housing, to end racial discrimination in housing, and to encourage private investment in the inner city.[7]

There was no flattery of businessmen in Young's speeches, no downplaying of the magnitude of the racial crisis, no pulling of punches in identifying businessmen's responsibilities. It was precisely his forthrightness that captured his listeners' attention. As the president of the National Association of Mutual Savings Banks expressed it at the conclusion of Young's address to the group's annual conference, "At our typical gatherings, we are invariably told what nice people we are, what a great job we're doing. We go away well fed and pretty well satisfied with ourselves. I think your eloquent indictment has done more and will do more for our industry than any number of empty speeches which praise what, I am afraid, will have to be called somewhat empty accomplishments."[8]

Young's candor struck a responsive chord in businessmen acutely concerned about the racial turmoil in their cities. No realistic corporate leader could have doubted the need to try to do something about the crisis. Young was offering practical prescriptions. He succeeded in interpreting frightening developments in ways that made them intelligible and accessible to the white establishment, and he gave his arguments an unexpected twist. "Most of the discussion about riots has concentrated on the negative aspects," he told the Institute of Life Insurance in December 1967. "I think it is time we took a long, hard look at the positives in this situation." What was positive about the explosion of racial violence? The riots made white Americans aware of the problems faced by blacks and brought them face-to-face with the realization that those problems threatened the future of the nation. The resulting racial confrontation, however ugly and painful, was also a positive sign; "for the first time people are saying what is really on their minds. Negroes are freely expressing their resentment and mistrust of white society. . . . And whites feel liberated from having to keep their good manners when talking about racial questions." Bringing hate out in the open was a step in the right direction. "Now an honest dialogue can begin. Stripped of hypocrisy, we can now lay the groundwork for a reconciliation and a rebuilding of our common society."[9]

If riots had positive significance, so did black power. It was a cry for recognition, Young told the Economic Club of Detroit in September 1968, a way of saying, " 'I'm a man. I'm somebody. I have roots. I have pride and I have dignity.' " That was no different from what other ethnic groups had done. "They just didn't make the mistake of shouting it and chanting it. They didn't say Jewish Power, or Italian Power, or Mormon Power . . . or Irish Power. The Irish just kept their mouth shut and took over the Police Department of New York City and Chicago. But it was the same basic concept."[10]

The laughter and applause that interrupted Young's speech after his reference to "Mormon Power" pointed up one of the techniques that served him well. Polite and restrained as Young may have been, there was bound to be some unease when a black man lectured prominent white men on living up to their responsibilities; leavening an otherwise sober message with flashes of humor broke the tension. More than that, humor served to drive home a point that might have been lost through a more direct presentation. Young's anecdotes contained real criticisms of white attitudes and behavior; by making people laugh—at others, and, by implication, at themselves—he took the sting out of the criticisms without vitiating the essential message.

White liberals were a favorite target of Young's humor. He often told the story of whites who claimed to have been alienated from the black cause by riots and demands for black power. He described one such encounter this way:

Shortly after the riots in Detroit, I met a businessman who took very little time to bring our conversation around to riots. "You know, Mr. Young," he said, "I used to be sympathetic to the Negro's cause, but all of this rioting and violence made me change my mind. I've lost my sympathy for the civil rights movement."

"That's too bad," I said, and I meant it for we can't afford to lose meaningful support. But I went on to ask him, "When you did sympathize with us, what did you do? How many Negroes did you hire? How many did you train for jobs? What did you do to help Negroes move into your neighborhood? What did you, as a community leader, do to improve schools and housing in the ghetto?"

"Well," he stammered, "nothing."

"Then we really haven't lost much," I said. "Nothing from nothing leaves nothing."[11]

Another favorite story involved a conversation Young had with a man sitting next to him on a plane. The man said that he and his wife were "great liberals," Young told his audience; "in fact they were wonderful friends of my people. I always get worried when I hear people start off this way." They wanted to express their liberalism by inviting blacks to their house; the problem was that the man's wife felt uncomfortable around blacks, and he did not know what to do about it. Young said he understood completely. "Most people feel odd and uncomfortable, even inferior around Ralph Bunche. I mean here is a man with his Phi Beta Kappa Key and his Nobel Prize and his Ph.D., you know a world figure. . . . Yes, I can understand why she would be uncomfortable around Ralph Bunche." Young told his fellow passenger that he could identify some below-average blacks who might make his wife feel more comfortable. The man got the point.[12]

Young was equally good at telling stories on himself. A vice-president of American Airlines remembered riding with him on the way to a speaking engagement. The driver was having trouble locating the entrance to the hotel. Young said that he could not help in finding the front door, but that he knew the back door of every hotel in the South. Young liked to tell audiences about the time he boarded an African airline and found, to his surprise, that the pilot was black. "I felt some anxiety," he said. "I had spent my life saying these people should be given the chance, but then I wasn't so sure. That shows you how much I had been brainwashed. It was an awful time to have my theories proved wrong."[13]

Getting his audience laughing was a wonderfully effective device, and Young used it to perfection. He had a store of jokes—for instance, a story about Alabama governor George Wallace knocking on the doors of heaven. St. Peter said, "Who dat dere?" Wallace answered, "Oh, hell, never mind." Those who knew his technique watched him play his audience with a sure sense of timing. "I've sat in meetings where he was speaking," Margaret Young said, "and I wanted to just get up and shout, 'Watch out for the upper cut.' " One joke would follow another, "and I'd say, 'Boy, he's getting ready to give it to you on the chin.' "[14]

No matter how cogent Young's analysis, or how practical his suggestions, or how skillful his delivery, his appeal would have fallen flat had he not understood and played to the basic self-interest of the American business community. Good race relations were good business. "I know of no group," he insisted, ". . . that has a greater stake in the preservation of a stable, orderly, democratic society than the American business community." It was in their "own best interest to become deeply involved in the question of civil rights." They had a clear-cut choice: either they could give blacks a stake in society by employing them, "by helping [them] to become productive consumers and producers of goods and services," or they could leave blacks outside the system "as producers of violence and consumers of taxes." A simple analysis of costs and benefits argued for a positive response to racial problems: "You are the one that suffers if this community becomes blacker and poorer. If people become tax eaters rather than tax producers, if people produce crime and welfare costs instead of producing goods and services, you pay the costs." The consequences of inaction also included escalating tensions and conflict—turmoil no businessman could have welcomed.[15]

Young never made his case with a chip on his shoulder. As the chairman of Pepsico, Donald M. Kendall, observed, "He never said, 'You owe this to us because of our past.' " Rather, he said that "it was to the benefit of the company to do it—he put it on a positive basis." It was "good business" to be associated "with the good things in our society," the president of Time Inc., James A. Linen, added; "Whitney preached that morning, noon, and night."

Part of Young's genius lay in fastening on a pragmatic argument that made sense to the corporate leaders who heard him. Part came from the manner in which he made his pitch. He had the ability, in banker Morris D. Crawford, Jr.'s, words, to "tell it like it was" without offending anyone, to tell it "with a kind of grace and sense of humor, and yet with force, that was kind of unique." One of Young's local executives called it "a very skillful way of touching the conscience of people who had resources without making them feel guilty," a way of making them "stretch beyond their normal point of elasticity" and "feel good about . . . what they were able to do in response." His presentation benefited from his careful preparation and from his ability to convey a passionate commitment to his cause. And it succeeded, finally, because of his sense of humor and his instinct for timing and pace. It all added up to what Kendall described as a unique ability to walk into a boardroom, challenge a group of corporate leaders, "give them hell and have them like him."[16]

The racial turmoil of the late 1960s led businessmen to seek out Whitney Young. His gift for combining irony, humor, and hard facts held their attention. His pragmatic appeal to self-interest struck a responsive chord. And the knowledge that the Urban League could deliver in important ways led them to support the organization and its leader.

No one denies that Young enjoyed unusual access to the corporate establishment, that he achieved a level of communication with corporate leaders unprecedented in his time. What is more difficult to document convincingly is the degree to which that made a real difference in the economic situation of blacks or the state of American race relations in the 1960s. Social scientists who knew Young claim that the access and the communication were important in themselves. The black political scientist Charles V. Hamilton credited Young with opening doors to the halls of influence, with keeping channels open that would otherwise have remained closed. In so doing, he made possible dialogue and discussions that "might have been broken off if it hadn't been for his role." But what those discussions actually accomplished seemed to Hamilton to be more difficult to say. The black social psychologist Kenneth B. Clark agreed that it was better to have communication than not, but "the consequences of the communication, the differences that were made," seemed to him harder to evaluate.[17]

What difference *did* it make? While it may never be possible to answer the question with real precision, there are a number of ways of measuring the effects of Young's access and efforts. Three deserve attention here: corporate support for the Urban League; corporate policies with respect to race; and the attitudes and behavior of the corporate executives who knew Whitney Young.

Measuring corporate support for the National Urban League is the easiest way of demonstrating that Young's ability to speak to the corporate establishment paid off in tangible ways. In seeking funds for the Urban League, Young approached donors whom the agency had never previously asked for money, and he set his sights high. To the chairman of the board of National Cash Register, for example, with whom he had traveled to Eastern Europe, he wrote, "This letter comes to fulfill a promise: To stop discriminating against your company by denying it an opportunity to contribute to the work of the National Urban League." Young said he was sure that NCR's failure to support the Urban League came not from lack of interest in civil rights, but because it had never been asked.[18]

In telephone calls and personal visits, Young argued and shamed donors into increasing their gifts. Looking over the list of contributions, he would exclaim to Enid Baird, "So and so only gives us $1,000? That's crazy—get him on the phone!" In a typical incident, he went to call on the head of a major corporation, who offered the company's usual gift of $5,000. Young said he would not take it. "I can't take it because it is not befitting the size and dignity and stature of your company to give us just $5,000. In fact, I won't take less than $50,000." The man agreed to make the gift.[19]

The National Urban League's fund-raising campaign in 1968 and 1969 provides an apt illustration of the way Young did business. To head the campaign, the agency called on one of its board members, the chairman of J. C. Penney, William M. ("Mil") Batten. Sometimes Batten and Young traveled alone; more often they were joined by the president of the league, James A. Linen. They relied on the familiar technique of enlisting corporate leaders to rally their peers for a luncheon or dinner where Young could present the Urban League's case.

Linen or Batten ordinarily made the opening remarks. They were important, because they conveyed to the business leaders around the dining room the commitment to the National Urban League of a highly respected peer. But those speeches functioned as preludes to the main event. "Whitney was our very best salesman," Batten reflected. "The things he talked about, the way he talked about them, and the perception that people gained of him and his views and his integrity and his commitment was really our selling message." Later, the executive who had hosted the luncheon or dinner would write to those who had attended to ask for their support.[20]

Sometimes the increased contributions remained small in terms of dollars; Crown Zellerbach, for example, whose chairman hosted a cultivation dinner in San Francisco in May 1969, raised its annual gift from $1,500 to $2,500. Sometimes the increase was more substantial. Reader's Digest, normally a contributor in the $1,000–$1,999 category, raised its gift dramatically after its chairman, DeWitt Wallace, met Young at a cultivation luncheon in 1969. Now the company sent $50,000, and Wallace himself gave a personal gift of $25,000. Texaco doubled its $10,000 contribution in

1970 after one of its executives heard Young's presentation at a cocktail party in New York for the league's big contributors.[21]

Young had managed to increase corporate support for the National Urban League from the earliest years of his executive directorship. Corporate gifts, just $70,000 in the year he took over, had reached the half-million-dollar level by 1963, and totaled a million dollars by 1967. When the fund-raising campaign began in 1968, annual corporate contributions stood at $1,197,000; in 1970, when it ended, the figure had increased to $1,973,000.[22]

The league was breaking new ground with this kind of fund-raising. The United Negro College Fund aside, racial causes had never rated high with corporate donors. With the onset of the civil rights movement, the Urban League had little competition. Corporate executives were usually not enamored of the more militant civil rights organizations, and the NAACP was not in the habit of soliciting corporate contributions. The association drew its funding mainly from membership dues, contributions from labor unions, and, after the establishment in 1965 of a tax-exempt special contribution fund, foundation grants and direct mail solicitations. The close alliance with the labor movement kept the NAACP from attempting to develop strong relationships with corporations. The upshot was that corporate gifts to the NAACP totaled less than $10,000 a year through the late 1960s. At the decade's end, inspired by Young's successes, the NAACP began to make some tentative overtures toward corporate support; the agency's first organized corporate solicitation effort followed, and by the late 1970s, the NAACP was bringing in roughly $400,000 a year from corporate gifts. It launched its first full-scale corporate campaign in 1979—a decade after the Urban League's effort.[23]

Documenting how many jobs for blacks Young won over the years from the corporate establishment is a more difficult proposition. Still, impressionistic evidence suggests his impact on the employment practices and social policies of major corporations in the United States. The point is not just that Young had the ability to prod corporate leaders into seeing the desirability of some action, but that he encouraged them to act at the very time when public policy and social pressures pushed them in the same direction, and that he had the means to help them make some progress. Young could produce. The Urban League could supply blacks to fill particular jobs; it could review a company's employment practices and suggest ways of hiring more blacks and improving their chances for advancement. These were precisely the sorts of problems corporations were beginning to address in the 1960s, and they were eager to tap Young's expertise.

Mil Batten's firm, J. C. Penney, for example, gave its manager of personnel relations a leave in 1967 to join the National Urban League staff.

His experience at the league led ultimately to the company's formal adoption of an affirmative action plan. Penney's employment of blacks began to grow, albeit slowly. Blacks made up 3.5 percent of its total work force at the outset of fiscal 1965, 3.6 percent in 1967, 4.0 percent in 1970, and 5.4 percent in 1975. At Texaco, where Young had induced a top executive to double the corporate contribution to the National Urban League, employment of blacks increased from 6.8 percent in 1967 to 10.9 percent in 1975. At the Ford Motor Company, employment of minorities stood at 16.6 percent in 1966, the year Henry Ford got to know Young on the trip to Eastern Europe. The numbers inched upward—19.6 percent in 1968, the year Ford founded the National Alliance of Businessmen, 20.1 percent in 1973. General Motors established a program to identify and train minorities to take on dealerships. It invested in minority-owned banks, and it tried to buy from minority manufacturers and suppliers. The company's chairman, James M. Roche, said that the understanding of minority issues that he had gained from his longtime association with Francis Kornegay, executive director of the Detroit Urban League, and his subsequent contacts with Young had a significant influence on his company's efforts.[24]

The experience of the Celanese Corporation was similar. The company's vice chairman, James R. Kennedy, joined the Urban League's Corporate Support Committee in 1966 and, later, its national board. His work with the league paid important dividends: Celanese's annual contribution to the National Urban League ($5,000 in 1964 and $7,000 in 1965) grew to $10,000 in 1966; within a short time, it had reached $20,000. At the same time, Kennedy used his connections in the corporate sector to help Young raise money.

Like many corporations in the late 1960s, Celanese was seeking ways to enhance employment opportunities for blacks. Among other efforts, it sponsored a secretarial training course at Hampton Institute; it joined with the National Alliance of Businessmen to create jobs for the hard-core unemployed; and it provided summer educational and employment opportunities for underprivileged youths. In 1969 the company began its first affirmative action plan; in 1971, it set up a corporate equality committee to review its hiring and personnel practices. The next year, the board established a public responsibility committee to review Celanese's policies and practices in areas of public concern, including fair employment; Vernon E. Jordan, Jr., the new executive director of the National Urban League, was one of the committee's members. In 1974, Celanese appointed a vice president for equal employment opportunity.

Along with these initiatives came steady progress in minority employment. From 5.6 percent of the total work force in 1966, the figures rose to 9.3 percent in 1970 and 14.6 percent in 1975. The gains came not only in lower-level jobs; the minority share of managerial and supervisory posi-

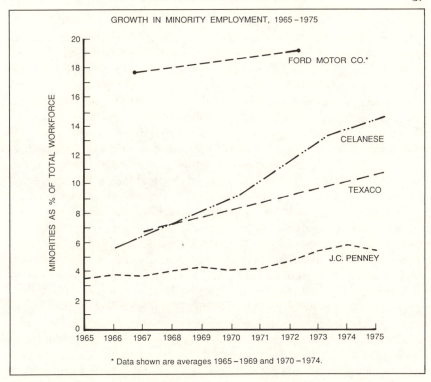

GROWTH IN MINORITY EMPLOYMENT, 1965–1975

MINORITIES AS % OF TOTAL WORKFORCE

FORD MOTOR CO.*

CELANESE

TEXACO

J.C. PENNEY

* Data shown are averages 1965–1969 and 1970–1974.

tions grew from 0.4 to 4.4 percent, and in professional positions there was an increase from 2.6 to 7.1.[25]

As the example of General Motors suggests, Young also used his corporate connections in the interests of black businessmen. John H. Johnson, president of Johnson Publishing Company, said that Young provided "entrées into the white establishment." On one occasion, Young introduced Johnson to Thomas J. Watson, Jr., the chairman of IBM. Johnson remembered their conversation. "Whitney said, 'Tom, this is John Johnson, he's the publisher of *Ebony* magazine. Have you ever heard of *Ebony* magazine?' " Watson said that he had, and that he thought well of the magazine. " 'I wish your advertising people felt the same way as you do,' " Johnson interjected. "Whitney said, 'Tom, you mean you don't advertise in *Ebony*?' Mr. Watson said, 'Well, I haven't, but maybe I will.' And he took out a little notebook . . . and he jotted down *Ebony* magazine in it, and two weeks later I got my first ad from IBM. I've been getting them ever since."[26]

Most intangible but in many ways most significant were the effects on corporate leaders of knowing Whitney Young. Even limited exposure to Young seems to have made some difference in their attitudes toward and willingness to try to do something about the racial situation in the United States. Again and again Young's speeches elicited strong testimony that that was so. From the executive vice president of the Stouffer Foods Corporation, Young heard, "I have been groping for some time for the idea that you have presented in the words 'compensatory action,' but have been unable to put the idea into words. I am deeply grateful for your having done this and I will do what I can to carry the thought forward to other groups." From an executive at General Electric came: "My wife and I have already had an opportunity to apply our new-found understanding of the problems, and the results strengthened our determination to do more." An insurance agent at Massachusetts Mutual Life in Buffalo wrote: "I certainly appreciate the additional insight you were able to give to me in the very pressing social problems with which we are faced today. You have helped me rededicate myself to do more about this." The organizer of a meeting of members of the National Association of Life Underwriters explained: "You so impressed me that I'm getting in touch with our local Urban League [to] find out what I can do to help."[27]

Such testimony notwithstanding, the longer-term impact of one-day stands is difficult to measure. More telling is Young's effect on the corporate leaders with whom he had more sustained contact. James R. Kennedy of Celanese was a case in point. Of his service on the Corporate Support Committee and later on the board of the National Urban League, Kennedy said emphatically, "I got more out of it than I gave." The experience broadened him, made him more tolerant, and gave him a more sophisticated understanding of racial problems and the means necessary to deal with them. He used to assume, he said, that the problems would be taken care of through social evolution. His involvement in the National Urban League made him realize that activists had a place in the overall scheme of things; he discovered that "evolution is a little too slow, you have to rev it up."[28]

In a time of racial turmoil, close acquaintance with Whitney Young provided a means of lining up on the side of progress and justice. Young frequently repeated a story that Mil Batten had told him. Batten was having breakfast with his children one morning, and they asked him about his plans for the week. He told them that he was going out on the road with Young to talk with corporate leaders about expanding employment opportunities for blacks and giving money to the Urban League. His son said, "You're going to do what?" Batten explained his plans again. His son came back with, "You mean you're not going to maximize the profits of J. C. Penney today! You're not going out this week to undercut Woolworth's; you're not going out to see if you can get something a little cheaper and increase the margin of profits of some product?" His father answered, "No."

Without saying a word, Batten's daughter ran over and hugged and kissed him, tears in her eyes. Batten said to Young, "I never had as much respect and affection and admiration from my kids [as] I had in that one moment."[29]

Young was the first black with whom a number of corporate leaders had ever dealt on anything approximating an equal basis. Exposure to him was a novelty for them, and they were struck by his ability to behave as a peer. "He came in as an equal," remarked Henry Loeb, the investment banker who served on the board of the National Urban League. "He had no inferiority concept at all." He had no hesitation about making connections with the chairmen and chief executive officers of the nation's largest corporations, and there was nothing self-effacing or obsequious about the way he related to the men he came to know. Enid Baird remembered one occasion when Henry Ford came to Young's office. Young had offered Ford a drink when he arrived, but Ford had declined. Baird could overhear their conversation from her desk. "I heard Whitney jumping on him," she said; he kept telling Ford, " 'You're wrong, you're wrong, you're wrong.' " Then Ford yelled to her, " 'Mrs. Baird, get me that drink, this man is driving me crazy!' "[30]

Young was the first black friend some corporate leaders had ever had— someone they felt comfortable having a drink with, someone who came from time to time to their houses. In part the evolution of that friendship was a phenomenon of the times. Because civil rights had become a major issue, there was a cachet in having a relationship with a prominent black leader. Young was the perfect candidate. A relationship with Young gave his corporate friends the ability to talk intelligently about the civil rights movement. Young was able to translate, to make comprehensible, the disturbing and sometimes baffling things people were seeing on television and reading in the newspapers. Friendship with him meant being plugged in, knowledgeable, in touch with the major currents of the time.[31]

But one ought not to underestimate the sheer force of personality that cemented those relationships. While the times may have made corporate leaders newly receptive to friendship with a black man, it was Whitney Young himself who evoked such a strong personal response. Doubtless charm had a great deal to do with it; so did Young's self-assurance, his ability to approach influential whites as an equal, and the fact that he so obviously fit in. Corporate leaders felt comfortable with him. He was personally attractive; he talked their language and to a great extent shared their values.

Whatever the source of the impulse, there is ample evidence of the strength of corporate leaders' regard for Young as a human being. Donald Kendall called him "a great guy." Henry Loeb said he was "good company, a nice fellow, a good man to be with." Mil Batten said that Young was "a person you could look up to, regardless of where you came from." David Rockefeller described him as a "highly educated, articulate, charming human being that one enjoyed being with." In the words of W. P. Gullander, president of the National Association of Manufacturers, "He was a man easy to respect, admire, and want for a personal friend." Henry Ford said that Young's gregariousness and sense of humor made it fun to be with him. James Linen called him "one of the most able, charming people I ever met in my life."[32]

More than that, though, prominent white executives responded to the rationality of his message, and they were affected by the ideas and experiences to which friendship with Young exposed them. Rockefeller remarked on Young's balance, sensitivity to issues, and ability to look at the race problem from the broadest possible perspective. Roche commented on the realism of his approach and his constructive, positive attitude. Ford said that he especially admired the originality of Young's thinking and his gift for making the problems of blacks comprehensible to people like Ford.[33]

Friendship with Whitney Young had to make a difference in these men's sensitivities, in their fundamental outlook on the world. At the very least, exposure to Young and his message tended to neutralize strong white voices that might otherwise have been real obstacles to racial progress. More often, he enlarged people's horizons, broadened them, sensitized them, made them more tolerant and more understanding, quickened their social consciences, influenced the way they thought about business decisions, and affected the way they talked to their peers. At best, Young played a critical role in motivating white leaders to act to address the racial crisis in the United States. Andrew Heiskell put it succinctly: "I started the Urban Coalition. Would I have done it if I hadn't known Whitney? Probably not." Ford, who headed the National Alliance of Businessmen, made the same point: "Knowing Whitney Young got me more interested in [urban and racial problems] and doing more [about them] than I would have done otherwise."[34]

To be sure, not all of the corporate leaders Young met behaved this way. He found his share of foot-dragging, of thinly veiled, patronizing, racist attitudes. And the positive responses to him as an individual did not necessarily translate into more enlightened racial views. Roger Wilkins remembered an occasion during the Johnson administration when one of a group of corporate leaders said to his colleagues, as they were leaving the White House, "God, I wish all of THEM were like Whitney. Then, maybe we could get somewhere." Close contact with Young could be a double-edged sword: on the one hand, a bridge toward broadened racial understanding, but on the other, a means of distancing oneself from other blacks who did not fit Young's mold.[35]

Young had no illusions that he had transformed the way American businessmen thought and acted on the race question. He knew that behind a "facade of fine-sounding words" about opening up jobs for blacks and improving conditions in the ghettos, too many companies were "doing next to nothing to fulfill their responsibilities." Then, too, the opportunity created by a booming economy and the spread of urban riots proved to be short-lived. By the early 1970s, with the economy in recession and the popular mood increasingly hostile to what was left of the black movement, corporations no longer showed the same zeal about attacking social problems. As Young wrote in March 1971, in what would turn out to be the last article he published, "The 'great involvement' in the social arena is beginning to look like the 'great cop-out.' " By the end of his life, Young would be looking toward the federal government, not the private sector, as the principal source of support for programs to benefit black Americans.[36]

X

The Kennedy and Johnson
Administrations

WHITNEY YOUNG was in and out of the White House for meetings on civil
rights and other issues, bill-signing ceremonies, and social occasions. He
held conferences with cabinet officials, testified from time to time before
congressional committees, and lobbied personally on Capitol Hill. Strong
as it was, Young's relationship to the federal government differed in important ways from his ties to the corporate establishment. The corporations were his special province. Alone among the civil rights leaders, he
had the contacts, the privileged access, the close ties that enabled him to
function persuasively as an interpreter for black America. In Washington
he was by no means the sole—indeed, even the chief—black operator.
There were blacks in government, black advisers in the White House, and
established black lobbyists. The civil rights leaders often counseled with
the president as a body, and individuals among them had their own channels of communication with the president and his advisers. Within that
framework, Young carved out a significant personal role.

Going to Washington was not unknown to Young's predecessors at the
National Urban League, but the variety and regularity of contacts with the
administration marked a significant departure from past practice. Eugene
Kinckle Jones, the executive secretary of the league during the New Deal,
never had an opportunity to meet with Franklin D. Roosevelt, who tried
hard to keep a safe distance from anything related to race. Still, Jones took
a leave from his post at the league to serve as adviser on Negro affairs in
the Department of Commerce in the mid-1930s. The National Urban
League, drawing on its traditional strengths in research and analysis, sent
Roosevelt detailed reports on the economic status of the black population
in 1933 and again in 1937, and it learned, thanks to the New Deal, to
lobby the federal government in the interest of the social and economic
welfare of black Americans. The practice of preparing carefully documented memoranda on racial matters continued into the Truman and Ei-

senhower administrations, and when Truman named a Committee on Equality of Treatment and Opportunity in the Armed Forces to recommend ways of implementing his executive order abolishing discrimination in the military, Jones's successor at the league, Lester B. Granger, was among its members.

The strength of the civil rights movement made race a national political issue in the 1960s in ways that it had not been before. At the same time, blacks and whites who were fighting for racial justice began to look to the federal government as their best hope for progress. The *Brown* decision had demonstrated the possibility of the beneficent assertion of federal power; the passage in 1957 and 1960 of the first civil rights legislation since Reconstruction, weak as it may have been, gave hope of further progress. State and local governments offered no such reassurance. Liberals mistrusted them as agents of reaction, and with good reason. The massive resistance that had greeted the *Brown* decision in the 1950s had come with the acquiescence, if not leadership, of public officials throughout the South. The efforts of blacks to exercise the franchise had been frustrated repeatedly by the ineffectiveness, if not active obstruction, of local authorities. And the civil rights demonstrations of the 1950s and 1960s had repeatedly shown those authorities to be unwilling or unable to ensure the rights and physical safety of the demonstrators. While the hopes of the civil rights movement focused increasingly on federal power, the federal government, in the administrations of John F. Kennedy and Lyndon B. Johnson, embarked on a period of activism in social justice and economic reform. All of these circumstances brought the executive director of the National Urban League to Washington to advance the interests of his constituency.

The prominence of the civil rights issue in the campaign of 1960 led Urban League officials to anticipate increased receptivity to racial concerns in the new Democratic administration. At Christmas time, 1960, the league sent Kennedy a detailed statement calling for federal action to attack the social and economic inequities suffered by black Americans. The document pointed up specific areas of discrimination against blacks in employment, housing, public welfare, and education, and proposed a range of policies and practices that the new administration might undertake to remedy them.[1]

League officials hoped to meet with Kennedy in the early months of his presidency to discuss the document, but a meeting was difficult to arrange. In the meantime, Young made other connections with administration officials, and he also made plans to open a Washington office of the National Urban League, with a full-time director to monitor legislation, maintain close communication with the federal departments, and help implement economic and social welfare programs so as to provide the maximum benefit for black Americans.[2]

Still, it seemed essential—both symbolically and substantively—to make direct contact with the president. Finally, in January 1962, thanks to the intervention of Louis E. Martin, vice chairman of the Democratic National Committee and a former trustee of the National Urban League, a meeting was scheduled. Young and the president of the league, Henry Steeger, went to the White House on January 23. They had a five o'clock appointment, the last on Kennedy's calendar, which gave them the chance for an hour and a quarter of relaxed, unhurried conversation.

Young and Steeger asked the president for a federal commitment to assure black Americans better education, equality of employment, better housing, and improvements in health and welfare, and they pledged the full resources and facilities of the Urban League to assist in the effort. Kennedy responded immediately: "I'll go for that." Young asked him which administration official he would designate to coordinate the effort. Kennedy said that it would be the vice president. Young and Steeger suggested that it would be useful to bring members of the Urban League's professional staff to Washington for a briefing on government programs and discussion of ways of involving league personnel in the planning and implementation of programs and services. Kennedy liked the idea. He promised to cover some of the expenses from government funds and instructed one of his aides to arrange appointments with the appropriate cabinet officers and agency heads.

The result was a three-day conference in May 1962, which brought eighty-nine National and local Urban League staff members and volunteers to Washington to meet with Secretary of Labor Arthur Goldberg, Secretary of Health, Education, and Welfare Abraham Ribicoff, Housing and Home Finance Administrator Robert C. Weaver, and their top aides. The president himself did not attend, but he sent a message pledging the administration to the promotion of "equality of opportunity for all Americans." The conference gave league officials the chance to learn about federal programs of direct relevance to the agency's concerns; at the same time, federal officials gained information about the problems and needs of blacks in cities across the country. Perhaps most important, the meetings gave the league the opportunity to establish personal as well as institutional relationships with those people at the federal agencies who had the greatest potential for influence over the economic and social welfare of black Americans.[3]

Otherwise, the relationship between Young and the Kennedy White House was never especially close. There were minor presidential appointments for Young—to the president's committees on Equality of Opportunity in the Armed Forces and on Youth Employment—and repeated, though unsuccessful, invitations to the president to speak at major Urban League gatherings. It was not that there was any particular tension. Close identification with the civil rights movement did not come easily to the president. Kennedy's reading of political realities led him to shy away from taking the vigorous action on civil rights that he had promised in his campaign. His early tests in the Eighty-seventh Congress made him all too aware of the power of Southern Democrats and conservative Republicans hostile to civil rights. Kennedy had won election in 1960 by the narrowest of margins, and he was untested politically; to put all his chips at the outset on the explosive issue of civil rights—a political contest he was quite sure he did not have the political strength or public support to win in the early years of his presidency—risked jeopardizing his entire legislative program. Given to a cool, analytic style, Kennedy was uneasy with protest as a mode of expression, and he was slow to warm to civil rights as a moral cause.

Like other civil rights leaders, Young prodded and pushed the Kennedy administration to take action in support of civil rights. He urged the president and the attorney general to intervene in behalf of demonstrators who fell victim to the hostility of Southern white law enforcement officials and the violence of white mobs. He called on the president to issue his long-promised executive order prohibiting discrimination in housing; later, he joined other critics in pointing to Kennedy's failure to enforce it. The trouble generally was that the president was too slow to act, Young thought; his civil rights program was clearly too timid. Angry at the Kennedys for dragging their feet on an issue of such overriding importance, Young lost his patience. The president and the attorney general, he declared sharply in early June 1963, "have only reacted, they have not acted" in dealing with civil rights. "Their attitude has been: How can we keep people from revolting and demonstrating and embarrassing us?" When would Kennedy throw off the shackles of political caution and give first priority to the demands of human rights, Young wondered; when would he demonstrate "the kind of guts" he had written about in *Profiles in Courage*? Later that month, when Kennedy went on national television to call for omnibus civil rights legislation, Young praised the president's message as historic and courageous, but in the same breath, he rebuked Kennedy for suggesting that a moratorium on demonstrations in Washington would hasten favorable congressional action on the measure. Shortly afterward, Young helped to plan the March on Washington in the face of Kennedy's fears of violence and disruption. In July, Young joined other black leaders in a television panel discussion critical of Kennedy's civil rights program for not going far enough; in October, when the House Judiciary Committee reported the civil rights bill to the full House, Young said that it represented "only the bare minimum of what these crucial times demand."[4]

On Friday, November 22, 1963, Young was in Cleveland to address a luncheon meeting of the National Association of Intergroup Relations Officials. He had just concluded his speech when the word came that President Kennedy had been assassinated in Dallas. Young returned to New York, and that weekend, like so many Americans, he and Margaret watched the continuous television coverage of the assassination and its aftermath. On Sunday night, he received a telephone call from the new president, Lyndon B. Johnson. It was one of many calls Johnson was making to establish contact with important leaders in many fields across the nation. He was eager to reassure Young of his intention to carry forward the fight for civil rights legislation that President Kennedy had begun. He told Young that he hoped they would have an opportunity to visit in Washington very soon. And he asked if Young would be attending Kennedy's funeral the next day. Young said he had expected to receive an invitation, but that there must have been some mix-up, since no invitation had come. Johnson said he would have his aide Bill Moyers find out what had happened; he was sure that it was "just a slip-up" and that Young ought to be making plans to come to Washington.

The Youngs went back to watching television. Twenty minutes later, the phone rang again. It was probably Moyers or a White House secretary, they thought. In fact, Johnson was on the line again. "I checked into that matter and there has been a slip-up," he said. "You come down tomorrow." He told Young that a White House car would meet him at the plane, and that the chauffeur would have his invitation.[5]

The Johnson administration brought a distinct change in the relationship between the White House and the civil rights movement. Johnson, a Southerner with a long history of racial conservatism, had begun to change his position on civil rights as his political ambitions grew. As Senate majority leader during the Eisenhower administration, he had engineered the passage of the civil rights acts of 1957 and 1960. The 1957 act empowered the federal government to bring suits in federal court in behalf of blacks denied the right to vote. It elevated the civil rights section of the Department of Justice to the status of a division under the leadership of an assistant attorney general. In addition, it created the United States Commission on Civil Rights and authorized it to investigate allegations of discrimination and denial of the right to vote, as well as to study and collect information about denials of equal protection under the law. The 1960 act strengthened the hand of the Justice Department in bringing voting suits and provided for the appointment of federal referees to register voters in the absence or in case of the nonfeasance of state registrars. The two laws were important, though tentative, first steps toward enlisting the power of the federal government in behalf of black rights.

As vice president, Johnson had been well acquainted with the leaders of the racial advancement organizations through his chairmanship of the president's Committee on Equal Employment Opportunity. As difficult as it was to get to see the president, it was easy to see the vice president, and the communications were frequent and cordial. Johnson took his chairmanship of the president's committee seriously, and his efforts surprised and delighted civil rights leaders. "He took a very personal concern in the fair employment business," Roy Wilkins said; "he called all manner of people—unions and employers and all over the country on the matter of increasing their employment of Negroes. Now, for a Vice President of the United States to do this, and especially a man who knew his way around and where the bodies were buried, so to speak, in Washington, this was very effective." Young, who had first met Johnson in the 1950s when he testified before the Senate on the 1957 civil rights bill and other proposed legislation, also had good feelings about the vice president. "I was impressed with what he said and the kind of people he was getting around him and the determination that he exhibited" to make the president's committee "much more effective" and "to really do something," he said. The two men stayed in close touch—"I suppose we visited on the phone at least once a week and in person at least once a month."[6]

Relying on well-honed political instincts, the vice president made gestures carefully designed to cultivate black leaders. Shortly after Young's appointment as executive director of the Urban League, Wilkins had a reception for him at a hotel in New York. Johnson was in town, and Theodore W. Kheel, the former president of the league, invited him to the party. As Young interpreted it, Johnson had "personally [come] over to welcome me in my new job." In November 1961, Young asked Johnson to speak at what he considered to be the National Urban League's most important event, the Equal Opportunity Day Dinner at the Waldorf-Astoria Hotel in New York. Johnson agreed and made a speech that made Young's "sound like the moderate!"[7]

Those kinds of contacts with civil rights leaders allowed Johnson to hit the ground running when he became president in November 1963. In the days following the assassination, he moved immediately to reach out to the leaders and publicly pledge his commitment to the cause of civil rights. He phoned each of them personally, in itself an unusual gesture. On November 27, addressing a joint session of Congress, Johnson called for swift enactment of civil rights legislation as a memorial to the slain president. On November 29, he began a series of meetings with individual black leaders.

The main theme of those conversations was Johnson's reaffirmation of his commitment to the Kennedy civil rights program. The civil rights bill that Kennedy had introduced in June 1963 was still tied up in Congress. Johnson knew the obstacles that stood in the way of passage, and he gave the leaders his appraisal of what it would take to get the bill out of the House Rules Committee and to break the filibuster in the Senate. He expressed his determination to move the bill forward as rapidly as possible and asked for the help and understanding of the civil rights leaders in the process.[8]

Young took advantage of his hour in the oval office to bring up the subject of unemployment among blacks. He told Johnson that it had reached catastrophic proportions, and he urged him to establish a massive public works program to combat it. Johnson did not commit himself on the proposal, but he asked Young to explain it further in a memo. Johnson convinced Young that he was "committed to carrying out the Kennedy program," and that he also had deep convictions of his own about civil rights. "Ten years ago," Young told the press, "if we had heard a new President speaking in a deep southern drawl, there might have been so much fear among Negro leaders that some of us might have gotten on the next boat for Ghana. But we know where Lyndon Johnson stands and we realize that he is a sincere and dedicated supporter of civil rights. A magnolia accent doesn't mean bigotry."[9]

Meetings with the president became a common experience for the civil rights leaders. Johnson invited them in all the time, Louis Martin recalled; he "felt he had to do more because of his background," and he "never would miss an opportunity to cement the relationship."[10] The leaders went to the White House as a group on numerous occasions. There was a session in January 1964 to discuss Johnson's campaign for civil rights legislation and the proposed war against poverty; an off-the-record meeting in advance of the leaders' testimony before the Platform Committee at the Democratic National Convention in August 1964; another following the election in November; a series of discussions beginning in the summer of 1965 to plan the June 1966 White House Conference, "To Fulfill These Rights"; an off-the-record meeting in advance of Johnson's civil rights message to Congress in March 1966; a similar discussion in advance of Johnson's civil rights message to Congress in February 1967; and an emergency gathering following the King assassination in April 1968.

Among the civil rights leaders, the president's closest ties were to Wilkins. The NAACP was still the preeminent civil rights organization, and Wilkins's vast experience in the political and legislative arena naturally appealed to Johnson. After Wilkins, Young was certainly Johnson's favorite. The president respected Young's leadership, and he liked his style.[11] Young wrote Johnson frequently, praising speeches, commenting on legislation, and recommending people for government jobs. Through White House staff members and other administration officials most directly concerned with the race issue, Young offered strategic advice on how best to deal with the movement and its leaders. In turn, they looked to Young to advance their purposes. Robert C. Weaver, the highest-ranking black official in the Johnson administration, described his working relationship with Young and Wilkins as a two-way street: they would get in touch with Weaver when they wanted something done, and Weaver would call them when he wanted their support either to push for something or "to raise a little hell" to block an action.[12]

As he did with so many other people, Johnson used Young as a sounding board, often telephoning him personally to ask advice and test ideas. When a major speech or a major policy initiative was coming up, Johnson made sure that Young knew about it and had a chance to offer suggestions in advance. What should Johnson say about the civil rights bill in his state of the union address in 1964? Who would be good candidates for appointment to the Civil Rights Commission? Who could Young and his board try to influence to back policies for which Johnson was seeking support?[13]

At critical junctures, Johnson turned to Young for help on Capitol Hill. Young and Wilkins were among the people Johnson mobilized in the successful effort to persuade Senate Minority Leader Everett M. Dirksen to help break the filibuster that was holding up the 1964 civil rights bill. "When are you going to get down here and start civil-righting?" Johnson cajoled over the phone. He told Young and Wilkins that they needed to convince Dirksen that supporting the bill would be in the interest of the Republican party. They should make plain that if Dirksen helped them, they would return the favor.

Rosa Keller, a trustee of the National Urban League, was in Young's office when Johnson called. She recalled that Young initially resisted Johnson's suggestion—Dirksen was so conservative that it was hard to imagine having a useful conversation with him about civil rights. Young volunteered to send a member of his staff, but Johnson insisted that the only person who could influence the senator would be Young himself.[14]

Young's appointment with Dirksen was arranged through the Washington lobbyist for Mobil Oil. Malcolm Andresen, Mobil's tax counsel and a trustee of the National Urban League, gave the instructions. Young also had the endorsement of the chairman of Mobil, Albert L. Nickerson, who knew Young through his work on the league's corporate support committee and thought well of him. The appointment was set for the late afternoon of Tuesday, March 10, in Dirksen's office at the Capitol. The director of public relations at Mobil would accompany Young and introduce him to the senator.

Young was well prepared for the meeting. He had familiarized himself with recent magazine and newspaper stories about Dirksen; he knew about Dirksen's personal life and interests, and he knew the history of Dirksen's positions on civil rights. Andresen had supplied him with legal arguments in favor of the public accommodations section of the proposed bill. There is no record of what went on in the meeting, but Andresen remembered it as extending well beyond the scheduled time. As he put it, "Whitney must have made one hell of a pitch." According to one report, Young told the senator that he "would go down in history as a 'blond Moses' " if he supported the bill. When he returned to New Rochelle, Young told Margaret, "I don't know what he's gonna do, Momma, but he looked at me and he said, 'Mr. Young, I thank you for coming.' " Later,

Young told the National Urban League board "that while no one thing changes a person this interview went far toward changing the Senator's attitude on many things."[15]

Access to the White House was heady stuff. Young "liked being able to pick up the phone and talk to Lyndon Johnson," Enid Baird said. His longtime Urban League colleague Ann Tanneyhill put it this way:

He was not without some ego—a truly human quality—and I like to imagine that some morning, as he was shaving preparatory to a trip to Washington, he would look in the mirror and say to himself: "I can't believe it! This little black boy from Kentucky has been called to the White House to sit down face to face with the President of the United States, to give him some advice . . . and I certainly will!"[16]

The aura of the power structure was seductive, but it was kept in check to some degree by the leveling influence at home. Margaret Young remembered a time when Whitney came home and announced, with great excitement, that he had been called to see the president at the White House. "So what's the big deal about the White House?" Lauren asked. "Lots of people talk to the President, Daddy."[17]

Johnson appointed Young to numerous advisory panels and presidential commissions, "many of which," Young later commented, "I didn't want."[18] There was frequent talk of Young joining the administration. Not only was he a prominent black leader, but he had attracted considerable attention by articulating a case for compensatory action to make up for past discrimination against black Americans, a position that bore considerable resemblance to the social philosophy of Johnson's Great Society.

Young believed that blacks needed more than equality of opportunity. Almost immediately after he assumed the executive directorship of the National Urban League, in speeches and in discussions with the staff, he began to make a case for compensatory action to help blacks move toward full and equal participation in American life. He had first begun to formulate the concept during his year at Harvard. In the course of his reading, reflection, and conversations with faculty members in the social sciences, it had begun to occur to him that what blacks needed was "compensatory—I even said preferential—treatment," he later told an interviewer. It had struck him, too, that "there might be some wisdom in using the Marshall Plan concept" to give some concreteness to what he had in mind.[19]

Young tried out his ideas in various forums. At the National Urban League's annual conference in September 1961, for example, he said, "I contend, over many protests, that as the Negro for over 300 years has been given the special consideration of *exclusion*, he must now be given by society special treatment, through services and opportunities, that will insure his inclusion as a citizen able to compete equally with all others."

In an interview with newsmen before the annual conference a year later, he spoke of the need for "10 years of special consideration." "If you're sincere about equal opportunity," he said, "10 years of special considera- tion is small enough exchange for 300 years of being 'specially ignored.' "[20]

At the annual convention of the Negro American Labor Council in No- vember 1962, he argued that "the disappearance of old barriers and the establishment of new laws" would not in themselves "erase the 300 years of deprivation" suffered by black Americans. He used a homely analogy to make his point: "The back wheels of a car cannot catch up with the front wheels unless something special happens. . . . If those who make the de- cisions in this country are really sincere about closing the gaps," he con- tinued, "then we must go further than fine impartiality." Blacks needed "better schools, better teachers, better facilities," and "special priority in employment"—in short, "special consideration" to "compensate for the scars left by 300 years of deprivation."[21]

To the City Club of Cleveland in January 1963, Young used another analogy: "It would be unfair to give a runner a pair of track shoes when the race is half over and expect or demand that he cross the finish line at the same time as a competitor who had track shoes for the entire race." Blacks could not be expected to perform as others could if they had not had the same opportunity for preparation. Compensatory action or preferential treatment would give blacks the chance to "catch up with others in all areas of living."[22]

Translating the call for special consideration into a fleshed-out, work- able plan became one of Young's major preoccupations during the winter and spring of 1963. Partly the issue was one of substance: What should government and industry be called on to do for black Americans? Partly it was a matter of philosophy: How could the league reconcile the call for special consideration with its historic emphasis on equality of treatment for blacks and whites? The challenge also had to do with language: Should the program be framed in terms of special or preferential treatment, or compensatory activity or consideration, or was it preferable to stick to widely accepted terms such as equal rights and equal opportunity? How could the statement be couched to minimize the possibility of misinter- pretation? Members of the board and staff had different ideas on those questions; in an effort to find a formulation that would satisfy as many of them as possible, the proposal went through five drafts between February and June.[23]

The president of the National Urban League, Henry Steeger, noted the unease that many of the whites on the board felt, at least initially, with what seemed to them to be an inflammatory proposal. They feared that it would tarnish the image of the league as an interracial agency, and they urged Steeger to do everything he could to influence Young to drop the matter. Steeger himself had doubts about Young's idea. The two men had several conversations on the subject. Young clung tenaciously to his proposal and ultimately convinced Steeger that he was right. His doubts assuaged, Steeger joined Young in promoting the concept.[24]

Finally, in June 1963, the National Urban League issued a major policy statement calling for a decade of special effort in employment, education, health and welfare services, and housing to compensate blacks for past discrimination. "Such special effort," the statement said,

which may appear to be in conflict with the principle of equal treatment for all, is required to overcome the damaging effects of generations of deprivation and denial and to make it possible for the majority of American Negroes to reach the point at which they can compete on a basis of equality in the nation's increasingly complex and fast-moving industrial economy.

The primary justification for such special effort lies in the fact that the nation itself is in jeopardy as long as it has within its body politic a large group of citizens who are socially and economically handicapped, often dependent, poorly educated and unable to assume the normal responsibilities of citizenship. And with the impact of automation, it appears possible that these conditions will become worse before they improve and that we may well create a permanent underclass of dependents unable to make a useful contribution to our way of life.

The second reason for such an effort arises from the fact that the intense needs and problems which are evident in so many Negro communities around the country are a direct result of past and present discrimination and exclusion based on race. Thus, as a matter of historic equity, compensatory effort is justified and may well be the only means of overcoming the heavy aftermath of past neglect. . . . A large segment of the American Negro population continues to lag seriously behind other Americans in almost every type of measurement which can be used to determine social and economic well being. And in certain categories the gap is widening rather than closing.

To remedy the problem, the league called for "a massive 'crash' attack" on the part of public and private agencies, an investment of energy and resources in education, employment, housing, social services, and leadership development that would ultimately "realize savings of millions of dollars in the cost of welfare services and public hospitalization . . . reverse the widespread social deterioration of urban families and communities," and help "develop the tools and understanding which will prevent the development of such deterioration in the future." The crash program had a shorthand label: the Domestic Marshall Plan.[25]

In articulating a case for compensatory action, Young went beyond the limits of the national consensus on civil rights. Whereas 80 percent of whites polled in 1963 agreed that the law should guarantee equal opportunities for blacks in employment, 97 percent said that they did not favor preference to make up for past discrimination. The notion of reverse discrimination made many whites uneasy; so did talk of measuring progress in terms of numbers, with its implication of quotas. "People who all of these years have never said anything about preference the other way, now suddenly have become very sensitive about preference," Young said. "People, who all of these years have never said anything about zero percent quotas of Negroes and one hundred percent quotas of white people, now suddenly get awfully upset when . . . we have to talk about numbers."[26]

Young spent considerable effort trying to calm those fears. "Preferential treatment," "indemnification," "special consideration," and "compensatory activity" were all " 'scare' phrases," he explained—in fact, they actually obscured the meaning of the Urban League's call for "special effort" (not, he emphasized, "special privileges") and went against the grain of people's native sense of fair play. The league's proposals were "necessary and just corrective measures"—they needed to be taken in order to give equal opportunity real meaning. They were necessary in order to prepare blacks to assume their full responsibilities in an integrated society. They were just, "because such an effort alone can repair the devastation wrought by generations of injustice, neglect, discrimination and indifference, based on race." The National Urban League's annual report later that year argued that the Domestic Marshall Plan was wholly American in purpose and concept; in no way was it a radical departure from historical practice. With black median family income half that of whites, and with the percentage of black workers in the lowest occupational categories, the rate of high school dropouts among blacks, and the rate of black unemployment all twice those of whites, "merely decreeing equality by law or fiat" was not enough to correct the grave imbalance between the races. It would take "special, intensive effort" to close the gap.[27]

Young's strong intervention in the public policy debate over compensatory action made him a logical candidate for deputy director of the poverty program, a position offered to him in February 1964. The *New York Times* reported that members of the National Urban League board urged Young not to take it. They were said to have cautioned Young that he might be used as window dressing in Washington and to have argued that Young's leadership was essential to the civil rights movement—especially since radical elements in CORE and SNCC were testing the limits of the integrationist consensus. The league, distressed at the *Times'* reporter's unfortunate reference to Young's "ability to contain the 'radicalism' " in the movement, tried to soften the impact of the story. The report was premature; no firm offer had been made. Young decided to say no to the offer, and in discussions with his board, he shaped an explanation for his refusal: he would say that he could serve best from the outside.[28]

Serving from the outside did not stop Young from having some influence on administration policy. While the federal government never directly embraced the proposal for a Domestic Marshall Plan, the social programs of the Great Society—for example, Manpower Development and Training, the War on Poverty, Head Start, and Model Cities—picked up some of its major themes. Young was not the architect of the administration efforts, but the National Urban League claimed as the War on Poverty got underway that it included "weapons conceived and created by the Urban League," and Young himself later boasted that parts of the Great Society were stolen from the Domestic Marshall Plan. Those claims involved an element of hyperbole; still, by repeatedly communicating his vision to policymakers—in private memoranda, in meetings with the president and other members of the administration, as an expert witness at congressional hearings, and as an adviser to the poverty program, among other ways—Young helped to shape the results.[29]

Similarly, Young's ideas about compensatory action came at an important stage in the evolution of public policy on affirmative action. The term "affirmative action" had first entered the public vocabulary in 1961, when the executive order creating the president's Committee on Equal Employment Opportunity required government contractors to take affirmative action in hiring. At that point its meaning was vague—positive efforts, certainly, but in the main the word was equated with nondiscrimination. The question of preferential treatment or quotas for hiring minority workers first began to be widely discussed in the summer of 1963. Young's was not the only voice in that discussion, but his was one of the first and most articulate.

By 1965, President Johnson had begun to speak publicly of the need not only for equality of opportunity for blacks, but for equality of results. In his commencement address at Howard University that June, Johnson drew directly on the language and logic of Young's argument for compensatory action. "Freedom is not enough," he said.

You do not wipe away the scars of centuries by saying: Now you are free to go where you want, and do as you desire, and choose the leaders you please.

You do not take a person who, for years, has been hobbled by chains and liberate him, bring him up to the starting line of a race and then say, "You are free to compete with all the others," and still justly believe that you have been completely fair.

Thus it is not enough just to open the gates of opportunity. All our citizens must have the ability to walk through those gates.

Young, along with Wilkins and King, reviewed and approved the Howard University speech. An Urban League spokesman claimed that the two men who wrote the speech, Richard N. Goodwin and Daniel Patrick Moynihan, used Young's book, *To Be Equal*, in the course of their drafting, a contention borne out by the strong similarity in language and metaphor.

By the late 1960s, affirmative action had come to be widely understood in terms of the special effort, or compensatory activity, that Young had described.[30]

As Young tried to influence the direction of public policy, he found new ways to make his views more widely known. The *Amsterdam News* (New York) began publishing a biweekly newspaper column, "To Be Equal," under his byline in April 1964. The column soon appeared on a weekly basis; by September, it had been picked up by thirty-seven newspapers, white as well as black. Young's longtime speechwriter, Dan Davis, wrote the columns, initially after close consultation with Young, who would provide ideas and review drafts; later, Young's direct involvement became more and more marginal, to the point that he sometimes would not even have read the columns before they were published. By the time of Young's death, the column appeared in more than one hundred newspapers across the country. In 1967, "To Be Equal" also began to be broadcast in the form of brief radio commentaries; by 1971, it was heard on over forty radio stations.[31]

In the summer of 1964, the publication of Young's book, *To Be Equal*, provided another vehicle for communicating his views. The case for a Domestic Marshall Plan was one of its central themes. "Page for page this is probably the best of the books so far published by Negroes on their civil rights struggle," wrote a white reviewer in the *New York World-Telegram*. The *New York Times* reviewer, himself black, said that the book "should be required reading for every corporation executive and government official."[32]

There continued to be talk of Young joining the Johnson administration. Malcolm Andresen arranged for Young to meet with James Rowe, the Washington lawyer who was one of Johnson's senior political advisers, to see whether he could be considered for a cabinet post. Rowe said maybe; he wanted to be sure that there would be a lot of support for the appointment from "the establishment." Johnson aide Hobart Taylor told Deputy Attorney General Ramsey Clark that Young "want[ed] to be a Cabinet officer, preferably HEW, but might be interest[ed] in a good Ambassadorial assignment."[33]

In late December 1964, at the request of the White House, the Federal Bureau of Investigation did a background check of Young for an unidentified presidential appointment. The results were transmitted to the White House in mid-January. There was considerable speculation in the national press that Johnson intended to name Young to replace Anthony Celebrezze as secretary of Health, Education, and Welfare.[34]

In a long column about the prospective appointment in the *New York Herald Tribune*, Jimmy Breslin said that an unidentified source in Harlem had told him that the leaders of the major civil rights organizations had agreed that Young would be their first choice if President Johnson was going to name a black man to the cabinet, and that everyone expected the Young appointment to be announced fairly soon. Interested in pursuing the story, Breslin found Young coming out of his office on East Forty-eighth Street and invited him to have a drink in a bar across the street. Young "let out a loud hollar when he found out what the conversation was to be about." He told Breslin that he had had a call at four o'clock that morning from a relative in Detroit who said to him, " 'Whitney, I couldn't sleep and I just had to pick up the phone and call you about this.' I told him he ought to get sleeping pills. I know enough about President Johnson, and about history, to know that the surest way to hurt things, and I mean my present position as a Negro leader, is to have a lot of speculation and people running around trying to help."[35]

As if to lend credibility to Breslin's informant, Martin Luther King telephoned Johnson to urge Young's appointment. White House aide Lee C. White suggested that the president tell King that any hint of pressure from black leaders for the appointment would only harm Young's cause. If the appointment was then made, it would appear that the president was succumbing to pressure; if not, blacks would believe that Johnson had let them down. White emphasized that no one in a position of authority in the administration had indicated to Young or to anyone else that he was under consideration for the post.[36]

Amid the flurry of publicity and rumors, Young took up the subject of the prospective appointment with the National Urban League's executive committee. No official offer had been made, he said; should one be forthcoming he would have to do "much 'soul-searching,' " since he believed that he could "render his best service to the country and the cause of civil rights" by remaining at the league.[37]

While Young may have wanted his board to believe that, he was obviously tempted by the possibility of going to Washington, and he was not always successful in hiding his interest. Roger Wilkins remembered taking Whitney and Margaret to his house after the inauguration ceremonies in January. As they drove past HEW, Whitney said, "Look, Margaret, this is HEW, on both sides of the street," the childlike exuberance clearly signaling what was on his mind.[38]

Whether to leave the Urban League for Washington turned out to be a decision Young did not have to make. In the summer of 1965, Johnson announced the appointment of John W. Gardner to succeed Celebrezze. The creation later that year of the new Department of Housing and Urban Development once again brought speculation that Young would be named to a cabinet post, but the job went to the administrator of the Housing and Home Finance Administration, Robert C. Weaver.[39]

Young later told an interviewer (with perhaps some exaggeration) that he had been "offered several jobs by Mr. Johnson. He's talked to me—his people have—about cabinet positions, about heading OEO, on a variety of occasions." Young said that each time he had managed to resist the president's arm twisting by reminding him "that I was better able to serve both his own objectives and the country's objectives in my present spot." He had told the president, he said, that he had a unique position as executive director of the National Urban League, one that allowed him to exercise maximum influence. It was better to keep some distance—and with it, independence—than to join the administration. Those closest to Young thought he was right. He had "a freedom of movement as head of the League that he wouldn't have had in Washington," Enid Baird reflected. Margaret Young put it this way: "Whitney could not have stood the bureaucracy of Washington, except for being President."[40]

The relationship between Johnson and Young stemmed from several sources. For one thing it reflected Johnson's style of doing business. A master of one-on-one communication, he flattered and cajoled, making people believe that theirs was the most important voice or view, artfully using pressure to get what he wanted. Then too it was a matter of chemistry: Johnson and Young liked and felt comfortable with each other, and Young made no secret of his admiration for the president. The friendship was also the result of a shrewd appraisal of the civil rights movement by Johnson and his aides. They knew who was for him and who was against him, and they quickly identified Young as one of the leaders who could be counted on to serve their purposes.

The war in Vietnam became the most extreme example of Johnson's proclivity for finding public ways of drawing prominent supporters around him in an attempt to isolate, or at least overshadow, his critics. Here Young, who backed the president's policies in Vietnam, found himself caught in a difficult situation.

The war split the civil rights leadership in dramatic, highly publicized ways. Convinced that racial injustice, poverty, and the war were all closely related, Martin Luther King began in August 1965 to voice his anguished conviction that the war must be stopped. In speeches, press conferences, and television interviews, he repeatedly urged the United States to halt the bombing of North Vietnam and to try to negotiate an end to the war.

Johnson reacted angrily to such statements. Members of the administration warned King to back off. "They told me I wasn't an expert in foreign affairs," King recalled, "and they were all experts. I knew only civil rights and should stick to that."[41]

Within the civil rights movement, the controversy over King's opposition to the war had less to do with views on the war itself than with a tactical question. What would be the effect on the movement of mixing opposition to the war with support for civil rights? Young believed firmly that linking the two together did a disservice to civil rights. In March 1966, following a regular meeting of CUCRL, he met privately with King and James Forman of SNCC to press his case. Young argued that civil rights and Vietnam ought to be treated as separate issues. " 'Johnson needs a consensus,' " he said. " 'If we are not with him on Vietnam, then he is not going to be with us on civil rights.' " King and Forman remained unmoved. "We understood that, given the corporations from which Whitney got support, his position on the war in Vietnam had to be different from ours," Forman said later. "We pointed out that we were probably not going to change his mind and that he certainly was not going to change ours. I told Brother Whitney that it was indeed sad if civil rights organizations had to go around trying to please this person in the White House and then that one, hoping to win some concessions."[42]

A Harris poll in April 1966 found that 41 percent of those surveyed said that opposition to the war on the part of a civil rights group made them "more against rights for Negroes." Concerned that King's new tack might harm the fortunes of the movement, more moderate civil rights leaders dissociated themselves from his position. When delegates from CORE tried to introduce a resolution calling for United States withdrawal from Vietnam at the White House Conference on Civil Rights in June 1966, Young, together with Wilkins, took the lead in heading off the move. Vietnam was not an appropriate issue to raise at the conference, Young said. In his opinion, it was possible for the United States to meet its international commitments and invest at the same time in domestic antipoverty programs. The conference ought to focus on the problems of greatest concern to black Americans, "rats tonight and jobs tomorrow," and not on the war in Asia. In August, on "Meet the Press," Young said, "The Urban League takes no position on Vietnam. We know this, that we had a race problem in this country before Vietnam; we will have a race problem after it is gone."[43]

Instead of diminishing, tensions within the movement over Vietnam rose as time went on. In February 1967, in a major speech in Los Angeles, King intensified his criticism of the war. In March, Julius Hobson, the Washington, D.C., activist, said that he was "ashamed of the black men who cry, 'let me in at the head table' " by supporting administration policy, and singled out Young and Massachusetts senator Edward Brooke "as examples of 'derelict civil rights leaders.' " That same month, King and Young clashed in a heated quarrel in the wake of a fund-raising event in Great Neck, Long Island. Asked by someone in the audience how he felt about Vietnam, King made plain his concern about the morality of the war and its effect on the United States. Asked the same question, Young replied differently. The war that concerned the National Urban League was here at home, in the ghettos. As for Vietnam, he could not speak for the league, but his personal view was that communism had to be stopped. As the evening drew to a close, Young and King exchanged angry words. Young admonished King that his opposition to the war would alienate Lyndon Johnson and make it impossible to get anything more from him for the benefit of blacks. King responded angrily: "Whitney, what you're saying may get you a foundation grant, but it won't get you into the kingdom of truth." Young retorted that *he* cared about the ghettos—King, it seemed, did not. "You're eating well," he cracked. King shot back that he opposed the war precisely *because* of what it was doing to the ghettos. King's lawyer, Harry Wachtel, broke up the argument and took King to his home. King kept berating himself for failing to control his temper. Wachtel said later that he had never seen King so disgusted at himself.

Late that night, King called Young at home to apologize. The two men talked for more than an hour. King insisted that he had a moral obligation to oppose the war. Young answered that it was wrong of King to try to use the influence he had built up as a civil rights leader for some other purpose. He argued, too (incorrectly, as it later became clear), that King was making a tactical mistake by telling people that domestic social programs would necessarily continue to suffer because of war spending. Young repeated his conviction that the nation could afford both guns and butter—a position that war-induced inflation would prove to be ill-founded.[44]

Undeterred by such criticisms, on April 4, 1967, King delivered a major address explaining his position on Vietnam that drew widespread criticism. Young struck his by-now-familiar theme. "I believe strongly that the urgent domestic problem of civil rights and the issue of the war in Vietnam should remain separate," he declared in a public statement. "The masses of Negro citizens . . . have as their first priority the immediate problem of survival in this country. . . . The limited resources and personnel available to civil rights agencies for work in their behalf should not be diverted into other channels."[45]

In an effort to heal the deep divisions in the movement over King's statements on Vietnam, Kenneth Clark called the principal black leaders to an off-the-record meeting in late May at his house in Hastings-on-Hudson, New York. The talk lasted all day. But instead of calming tensions, the discussion threatened to exacerbate them. King confronted Wilkins about some disparaging public statements that he had made about King. As Wilkins repeated his denials, King became increasingly upset. Then Young stepped in to mediate. He probed for common ground, reminding the two men that underneath their differences over Vietnam, they still shared important common goals. He did it so skillfully that Clark later accused him of "bringing his social work background and training into those discussions." Clark said that "it was Whitney's victory that these two men came together."[46]

The discussion ended with an agreement that the group would reconvene in the middle of June. This time the leaders kept their tempers in check, but there was no mistaking their continuing differences over Vietnam. Bayard Rustin underscored the importance of not splitting with the Johnson administration; Young told King that he wished he could give more attention to civil rights and less to the war.[47]

In the midst of the much-publicized battle within the movement, Young made two trips to Vietnam. He was the first civil rights leader to go there. The first trip, to investigate the situation of black servicemen, was his own idea. Administration officials cleared the way by allowing access to military installations and personnel and providing protection during the trip, and Young left for Saigon on Monday, July 18, 1966. At a news conference prior to his departure, he explained his purposes in going. He wanted to brief black military personnel on racial developments at home, ascertain their aspirations, skills, and career plans, and let them know about the National Urban League's intention to develop a program to help Vietnam veterans find jobs, pursue further education, retrain for civilian employment, and gain access to housing and social services. "Someone should let them know," he said, "that we back home care about them, love them and await the opportunity to serve them upon their return home."[48]

Young visited military units in Danang, Pleiku, An Khe, Nha Trang, and elsewhere. He met black soldiers along the streets and in the restaurants and bars of Saigon, visited wounded men in a field hospital, and met black civilians working for the Agency for International Development and the United States Information Service. He got an enthusiastic reception as a black leader who had come to Vietnam in order to meet black Americans stationed there and find out what his organization could do for them. A soldier Young encountered on a street in Saigon typified their response: " 'Don't tell me! Don't tell me! I know who you are! Urban League! Urban League! Yeah! Whitney Young! Whitney Young! I sure am glad to see you.' "[49]

In a confidential cable to the White House, the United States ambassador to Vietnam, Henry Cabot Lodge, gave his account of the trip. Young had had "ample opportunity to talk to Negro soldiers of all types and levels without prearrangement." He "maintained [a] questioning attitude throughout the trip, especially in contacts with higher officers," including the commander of the American forces, General William C. Westmoreland. He made the point that while blacks welcomed the "present colorblindness" of the military services, generations of discrimination made it necessary to be "a little color conscious the other way" by promoting blacks into higher ranks and professional specialties in proportion to their numbers. That Saturday night, in Saigon, Young held a news conference to outline what he had seen. He said that he found black servicemen "more concerned about black progress than black power." He criticized the military for not promoting black officers rapidly enough and for not fostering integration during off-duty hours. In general, though, he thought that the situation of blacks showed "drastic improvement" over World War II and the Korean War. Young's presentation appeared to make a favorable impression on the press corps, Lodge thought, and he urged that Young see the president and Acting Secretary of Defense Cyrus Vance on Monday morning when he got back to the United States.[50]

Young spent an hour and a half at the White House Monday morning with the president, Secretary Vance, special assistants to the president Walt W. Rostow and Joseph A. Califano, and deputy special counsel to the president Clifford L. Alexander, Jr. Young reported that the morale of black servicemen in Vietnam was extremely high, and he praised the unprecedented degree of integration that had been achieved among the American troops. He declared himself especially pleased by the evidence he had seen of interracial teamwork. He said, too, that the overrepresentation of blacks in the American fighting forces seemed to be the result not of discrimination in the draft but of a dramatically higher enlistment and reenlistment rate among blacks.

Young also reported on the things he had seen that disturbed him: the lack of black officers, the difficulty of securing promotions for blacks in the lowest grades, the de facto segregation during off-duty hours, and the lack of knowledge and concern of officers about the lives of their men when they were off duty. He declared his intention to seek endorsement for a new Urban League program to help returning veterans readjust to civilian life when the league's annual conference convened in Philadelphia the following week. In turn, Johnson promised to investigate the complaints Young reported and pledged his support for the Urban League's efforts to aid the returning servicemen.[51]

Young wrote about his trip in his newspaper column in a four-part series in August 1966, and again in an article in *Harper's* in June 1967.[52] At the end of August 1967, to his surprise and consternation, he found himself back in Vietnam as one of a team of observers sent by Johnson to monitor the South Vietnamese elections.

It was the fourth week in August, and Young was at the Urban League's annual conference in Portland, Oregon. He had just finished telling the delegates that he was no longer sure that it was possible to have both guns and butter and that if there had to be a choice, "the first priority ought to be peace and justice here at home." Then a call came from the president:

the South Vietnamese government had invited official foreign observers to monitor their elections, and Johnson wanted Young to go to Vietnam as a member of the American delegation. Young demurred: he was in the middle of the annual conference; he would need the permission of his board; it was a bad time for him to leave the country. In typical Johnson fashion, the president left him no choice. "Whitney, you wanted a Negro on the Supreme Court and I put on one," he said, referring to the recent appointment of Thurgood Marshall. "Now I want a Negro on this group going to Vietnam." Johnson quickly closed the conversation: "Well, Whitney," he said, "I'm going to announce you as one of the team, and if you feel you can't serve your country, you explain it to the press."[53]

The twenty-two observers included senators, governors, mayors, religious leaders, and labor, business, and news executives. They traveled to Saigon on Air Force One. Young sat next to W. P. Gullander, president of the National Association of Manufacturers. Dave Sullivan, a vice president of the AFL-CIO, sat behind them. To Sullivan the juxtaposition of civil rights leader and industrialist seemed ironic; as he said later, "I couldn't understand why that guy would ever sit next to the president of the NAM."[54]

The group got to Saigon on Wednesday, August 30. The observers inspected polling places, interviewed officials about the technicalities of election procedures, attended campaign rallies and a pre-election press conference given by the eleven presidential candidates, spoke privately with some of the candidates, and met with American military officers and diplomats. Picking up a ballot box in a polling place in a hamlet outside Phucuong, a provincial capital twenty-five miles north of Saigon, Young exclaimed, "Hey, it's got a real bottom in it." Asked if he was surprised, Young answered, "Well, I went through this in Mississippi."[55]

The observers came away persuaded that, despite their imperfections, the elections were "more free than fraudulent." Young scribbled his reactions on the back of an envelope. He had been "seriously concerned about the war—lives lost, resources diverted—dividing of country," and he had gone to Vietnam "prepared to be critical, suspicious, [and] cynical of [the] election procedure." He came away mindful of the unusual conditions under which the election was being held, aware of the advantages enjoyed by the incumbents but still impressed with the effort. He was struck especially by the absence of censorship, the provision of equal time for candidates on radio and television, the underwriting of campaign costs for all candidates, and the enthusiasm and interest in voting. As for irregularities in the election process, he told the press, "We have problems in Mississippi too. After all, what do you expect? How can you tell, anyway?"[56]

The observers met with the president on Wednesday morning, September 6, immediately after their arrival at Andrews Air Force Base.

They spent an hour in the Cabinet Room with Johnson, Secretary of State Dean Rusk, and Secretary of Defense Robert McNamara. Individual members of the delegation volunteered their impressions of what they had seen in Vietnam. "I left here with some cynicism and skepticism based on newspaper accounts which I read," Young said. "However, I returned completely satisfied that these were free elections [conducted] as well as could be expected under the conditions." Later, at a luncheon of the observers and a group of newspaper editors and publishers in the executive mansion, Young asked the president whether increased expenditures for Vietnam would make it necessary to cut back on spending for domestic programs. Johnson, refusing as always to acknowledge the difficulty of paying for both guns and butter, assured him, "We have not cut back anything."[57]

As Young had anticipated in his reluctance to go to Vietnam, there were costs associated with the trip. He got caught in the wash of general criticism that many of the members had much better things to do at home. He had already been attacked for letting himself be used "as a tool of LBJ" when he delivered "glad tidings" about integration in the armed forces and patriotism among black servicemen the summer before. Now a fellow member of the National Association of Social Workers wrote, "I am ashamed of your support of the USA Vietnam war by participating in that 'white wash' commission and thus contributing to the spurious and illegal election in S. Vietnam. . . . You certainly permitted yourself to be exploited."[58]

Civil rights activists, too, decried Young's participation in the mission. It further complicated his relationship with Martin Luther King. King's people had not undertaken any private efforts to get Young and Wilkins to change their position on Vietnam; they did not want the civil rights movement to break completely with the president, and it was helpful to them if Young and Wilkins maintained good relations with Johnson. But Johnson's efforts to use Young to balance King's position on Vietnam put additional strains on Young's relationship with King. The King forces had made a systematic effort to educate themselves about Vietnam by doing research, traveling there, and getting information from a wide variety of sources beyond the government. No wonder it rankled when Young, whom they regarded as inexperienced and not terribly well informed about Vietnam, came back from the election trip supporting Johnson's policies.[59]

The experience of the election observers made clear the complexity of the relationship between the civil rights movement and the war in Vietnam. Sharply critical of American policy in Vietnam, King lost the respect of the White House and the ability to exert influence there on behalf of the movement. Mindful of the benefits that had come to blacks under the

Great Society, Young was reluctant to jeopardize future gains for civil rights by distancing himself from the president on the war. Johnson understood that, and he used it to his advantage. Young ended up with little maneuvering room or opportunity for critical distance.

While disagreement over Vietnam drove a sharp wedge between Johnson and King, the president and Young remained entirely cordial. In the late autumn of 1968, Johnson made an unexpected appearance at the Urban League's Equal Opportunity Day Dinner in New York. He sketched the civil rights accomplishments of his administration and spoke eloquently about the job still to be done to achieve genuine equality of opportunity for black Americans. Young later described the occasion: "It was really a beautiful gesture on his part. . . . There was a room of 2000 people and there was hardly a dry eye in the place. . . . It gave us a real opportunity to say 'Thanks' to what we all feel has been the greatest leadership job in civil rights done by any President." Young announced that the league was establishing a scholarship fund in Johnson's name to enable blacks to study public affairs at the University of Texas. Johnson, he wrote in his newspaper column in January 1969, would "go down as a great President whose domestic accomplishments far outweighed the international policies that divided the nation. . . . I think that many black people already rank Lyndon Johnson as the President who has done the most for the black men." Later that month, just before he left office, Johnson awarded Young the Medal of Freedom. Some months later, Young sent Johnson a copy of his newly published book, *Beyond Racism*. "To Lyndon B. Johnson," he inscribed it, "who more than any President almost made this book unnecessary."[60]

XI

The Strains of Celebrity

YOUNG'S CELEBRITY carried costs, personal as well as political. He was no different in this respect from any other prominent national figure, as the constant pull of public responsibility kept him away from home and competed with his family for time and attention. But the strains of his celebrity had another, more distinctive dimension. The more successful he became in ingratiating himself with the economic and political power structure of the country, the more he opened himself to criticism from black Americans.

Family had always been extraordinarily important to Whitney. The security and self-confidence that he had gained from the family of his childhood had been the most significant shaping influence of his life. The close ties with his parents continued into adulthood. Laura died in 1962, soon after her son took up his responsibilities at the National Urban League, but Whitney, Sr., remained a loving, supportive presence. The father could scarcely contain his pleasure at what he saw. Whitney, Jr., had made the long, long step from Lincoln Ridge to New York City, and there he was, "one of the nation's leading servants of the people," with "one of the most responsible jobs of any individual in our group." Over the years, as Whitney, Sr., aged and Whitney, Jr., came into his own as a national figure, their relationship naturally shifted. The son was careful to keep his father informed about what he was doing. He sent him copies of speeches and itineraries, phoned him, and stopped to see him in Kentucky whenever he could. Whitney, Sr., continued to offer encouragement and advice. The son frequently spoke about the lessons he had learned from his father, but they tended to be youthful ones rather than on-going guidance to the mature man.[1]

A second source of support was Whitney's older sister, Arnita. Their relationship continued to be extremely close. They talked regularly on the phone, perhaps several times a week, usually early in the morning when Whitney first got to his office. On his trips to Chicago, he typically made time to see Arnita and her husband, Paul. The talk was personal as well as professional. As Arnita's daughter put it, "They were very close, very close. . . . He was her confidante and vice versa."[2]

Young's closest ties were with his wife and daughters. The pressures of his public roles, together with his deepest private needs, strained and shaped the life they shared.

When Whitney took up the executive directorship of the National Urban League, as his daughter Lauren remembered it, "it was like a rocket had taken off. . . . One minute he was there . . . and we were all together, and the next minute . . . he was . . . gone. It was that abrupt." The many demands of Young's public life meant that he was rarely at home. He traveled incessantly, sometimes visiting two or three cities in a single day. Even during an ordinary week in New York there was an endless round of telephone calls, meetings, press conferences, receptions, and dinners. If he got home at all on a weeknight, it was usually well after dinner, with time for little else but to glance at the mail and memoranda that stuffed his briefcase. Family life was largely postponed until the weekends.[3]

Even then, changing gears was not easy for him. "He didn't know how to stop; he didn't know how to relax," Marcia reflected about her father. As Whitney himself told an interviewer, "Weekends we try to relax together, and I pretend to do everything else but be the dignified, exact executive director who holds forth on weighty problems most of the time. But after a weekly conference with Vice President Humphrey, lunch with key executives of Socony-Mobil, and perhaps an afternoon meeting with bright and vibrant Urban League delegates from all parts of the country, weekend unwinding can be my hardest job."[4]

Their home was "off bounds to anybody," Margaret said; it was "the only place where Whitney could refuel and get it back together." She tried to keep the weekends low-key and unplanned in order to give him a chance to relax and enjoy some simple pleasures. She prepared his favorite foods—chili or pot roast or navy bean soup for supper; on Sunday mornings, before church, he usually made waffles. He loved watching football or baseball games on television—sometimes two or three at the same time. For a special treat, he might take Lauren to the city to see the Knicks play at Madison Square Garden. When he could, he swam, sometimes with Lauren, often with his good friend Bill Trent. He had little interest in serious literature or in cultural events; as Marcia put it, "His idea of a really terrific book was Harold Robbins. He also thought the Rockettes were great ballet."[5]

It was other people, above all, who provided stimulation and regeneration. Whitney enjoyed relaxing with friends at backyard swimming pools. He liked having people in for dinner. In fact, when the family moved in

1969 to Oxford Road, in an older New Rochelle neighborhood of substantial two-story houses, the space to do more entertaining was one of the attractions. This time there was none of the uncertainty that had attended the move to Mohegan Place, but Young was still keenly aware of his impact as a black person in a previously all-white area. He used to joke about it: "Well, there goes the neighborhood." He quickly made friends, and droppping in on them on weekends became a ritual. As Margaret remembered, "Whitney would get up and go out, and when he would come back he would have visited with just about everybody on this block."[6]

Anxious to keep what little time Whitney had at home as free of tension as possible, Margaret cajoled, implored, even bribed Lauren to behave herself when her father was around. Spirited, outgoing, quick to show her feelings, Lauren stood out in a family in which strong emotions were ordinarily kept under careful control. Not quite eight when her father became a national figure, she came to have complicated feelings about his public role. She liked many of the trappings that went with it—living in a nice neighborhood, traveling first class, meeting famous people, dining at elegant restaurants. But she hated being set apart from other people her own age, and she fought being singled out, being treated as special and different because of who her father was. She resented his frequent absences and envied her older sister, who had grown up before the family was thrust into the public eye. "Daddy and I were like friends," Marcia said. "Lauren and Daddy, I think, had more of an adversarial relationship. She was always angry that I'd had . . . Daddy during the best years." Alone so often with her mother, Lauren developed a close bond with Margaret. As Marcia described it, "Lauren and Mother were almost buddies in their anger together—Mother being resentful that Daddy was never around, and Lauren being resentful that Daddy was never around and the two of them were there together."[7]

When he was at home, especially as Lauren entered adolescence, her tensions festered. "Emotionally, he was so spent," she reflected, "and I was so wired." Bright, aggressive, moody, she was "into feelings." But her father kept their exchanges at a more superficial level. What was new at school? What had she been doing while he was away? If Lauren tried to turn the conversation to an issue that was important to her, "invariably he'd have a flight to catch or the phone would ring." "To get into my feelings," she said, "took more time and energy than he had."

Child of a black man who moved so comfortably in the highest echelons of the white world, Lauren suffered acutely when other blacks criticized her father. When some of her peers gave her a hard time about being "Whitey" Young's daughter, it hurt her deeply. She loved her father and admired what he stood for, but she was also embarrassed that he was the target of criticism, and she sometimes wished that he would take a more popular position. Influenced by the affirmations of black pride of the late 1960s, she grew a huge, unruly Afro and pasted "Free Angela Davis" stickers on the refrigerator door. Her father bent over backward to be tolerant; he would not forbid her to keep the Afro, for instance, but he cautioned her not to confuse symbols and substance—her hair was nothing more than a fad, and it would not make a whit of difference to people who were in need of jobs or food or shelter. Her closest friends found it difficult to understand how he could fail to identify with expressions of black identity that they valued. "I caused him a lot of problems," Lauren reflected years later. "On the one hand, I think, he really admired my spirit, he appreciated the gusto with which I charged off after things. But on the other hand, he was totally perplexed by it. I was probably one of the few elements in his life that was not within his control."[8]

For Marcia, the situation was different. Older, away at Bryn Mawr College from 1964 to 1968, and then, after graduation, married and living in Iowa, she was removed from the day-to-day pressures of her father's public role. Self-contained and less open than her sister, Marcia was less likely than Lauren to let her feelings show. Even at a distance, though, she conveyed her admiration for Whitney. "To Daddy, one of the few great men on earth," she wrote on a birthday card. On a Father's Day card she told him that "the press only gets half the story. I know there are more wonderful things to you than they'll ever see." On another Father's Day card she wrote, "I live by your example & I don't think I could do much better than that." On receiving a copy of one of her father's speeches, she wrote him, "It is truly beautiful. So are you."[9]

Marcia's relationship with Whitney was close, comfortable, and strongly intellectual. From an early age, she had felt included in his world. At first she was allowed to listen to "grown up conversations about big issues," and later was encouraged to participate in them. He talked with her about his work, sometimes shared his speeches with her, and gave her the feeling that he took her views seriously. She responded in kind in letters from college with comments on civil rights issues and on her father's role in the movement.

Insofar as there were any tensions between them, they grew largely from Marcia's strong feelings against the Vietnam war. She remembered one occasion when, at home from college for the holidays, she went with her father to an Urban League dinner where he sat next to McGeorge Bundy, who had been the national security adviser in the Kennedy and Johnson administrations. Rather than expressing his own personal opinions about the war, Young told Bundy at some length about Marcia's opposition to it. Later, he introduced them and promptly walked away, leaving them to argue.[10]

Deciphering Whitney's relationship with Margaret is more complicated. Early on, they had divided the responsibility for their family in a
conventional way: he was the breadwinner, she was the one to maintain
their home and attend to the needs of the children. Much as she missed
him when he traveled, she usually chose to stay at home. The traveling
was typically so frenetic and fast-paced that Margaret felt that there was
not much point in trying to go. More important, with Whitney's frequent
absences, she thought that the girls needed a steady source of love and
care. It was hard to trust someone else to make the right judgments. Margaret decided to adjust her own life for her family and to make the most of
the limited time she and Whitney were able to share.

Despite their frequent physical separations, Margaret felt herself to be
an important part of Whitney's world. A writer in her own right, she edited and commented on the things he wrote, corrected his grammar and
spelling, and gave him ideas and clippings from the things she read. He
turned to her regularly as a sounding board and adviser.[11]

The two shared a closeness bred during decades of common experiences. There was a strong bond between them, as Whitney made plain.
"Dearest Margaret," he wrote from Los Angeles in 1962. "Just to let you
know I love you and am thinking about you. . . . This has been a good trip
for the Urban League but rough on me here. It will be kinda nice to get
our family back together again. It is a wonderful family and you deserve
90% of the credit. You are truly a wonderful wife and mother, which has
been the big difference in my own career. Every day I love and appreciate
you more." From Bucharest, in the midst of the Time tour of Eastern
Europe in 1966, he wrote, "I hope someday we can visit these countries
together. This is a most valuable trip in so many ways. I would not have
missed it for the world. . . . Only thing wrong is that I miss you and the
kids. I do love you very much and you are truly a beautiful, wonderful wife
and mother." From Rome in 1967 came: "I love you very much. You have
been most brave, patient, and understanding of my crazy schedule and
work habits. I am looking forward to spending more time with you this
summer. Be sweet." And from Tunis in 1969 there was: "I miss you as
usual. Seems more so when I am so far away or I can't call you every nite.
But I do think about you and do love and admire you in growing degrees
every day."[12]

At a dinner dance celebrating their twenty-fifth wedding anniversary in
1969, Whitney gave Margaret a brooch modeled on the Urban League's
"equal" sign—a circle pin ringed with twenty-five pearls. Presenting the
gift in front of four hundred guests, he recited verses from Elizabeth Bar-
rett Browning's "How Do I Love Thee?" Two years later, for what would
be their last anniversary, he wrote,

Each year I appreciate you more and more as wife, lover, friend, and mother of our two wonderful daughters.

I know the nature of my work and travel has not made it easy for you. They meant you had many unshared decisions and responsibilities plus lonely hours. You have shown much understanding and patience.

For all of these things I am deeply grateful but most of all I am grateful to the fate that brought us together many years ago. I have never had a regret.[13]

Together with the closeness went real tension. Some of that tension was inherent in the imbalance in their roles. No matter that Margaret's was of her own choosing. Here was a highly intelligent, well-educated woman who had given up a professional career of her own to assume a subordinate role as helpmate and supporter. She did it well, but over time, it rankled. As Marcia said about her mother, "She was very conscious of being a background person. The only trouble with that is that often . . . one tends to resent the person who's in the foreground if you feel you're doing all the propping up."[14]

That was true especially because Margaret got so little of Whitney's time. She hated his frequent absences, hated being left alone. She resented the competing claims of his public position, and she made her frustrations abundantly clear.

Obviously troubled by Margaret's complaints, Whitney expressed his unease in a variety of ways. In public settings, he joked about the tensions inherent in the life of a highly visible national figure. One of the stock stories he used to soften up his audiences was about Margaret's unhappiness over his traveling. He said that he had told her that what counted was the quality of their time together, not the quantity. One night, he said, he came home after a long, exhausting trip; as he crawled into bed, Margaret tapped him on the shoulder and said, "All right, Mr. Quality."

Joking was one way of handling discomfort, but it was best suited to large, public settings. When Whitney and Margaret were among friends, the humor more often gave way to subtle sniping. Margaret made no secret of her resentment, nor Whitney of his exasperation at his inability to calm her. To his closest confidants, Whitney despaired of Margaret's persistent nagging. He had no interest in a public break; more than anything, he wanted her to be more accepting of the way he lived his life.[15]

At home, in the presence of their children, Margaret and Whitney usually handled their disagreements behind closed doors. Lauren noted, with some surprise, that she really could not recall her parents raising their voices or showing anger to one another. "They had what they called 'discussions,'" Marcia said. "They didn't have fights, but they would discuss things furiously."[16]

Some of those discussions surely concerned the other women in Whitney's life. He had had an eye for pretty women ever since the earliest years of his marriage. As he became a public figure, his relationships grew more complex. His position gave him ready access to a wider range of women, especially white women of economic influence and social standing. He was the consummate pursuer, successfully courting attractive women of both races. He did it, in part, for the pleasure of the conquest, in part as an escape from the terrific pressures of his job, in part to fill the loneliness of so many nights on the road. And as Margaret became more difficult to deal with, other women became a welcome refuge from the tensions he experienced at home.

There was nothing subtle about the way Young dealt with the women he fancied. He could be astonishingly bold in his approach. He was not restrained about expressing physical affection, even in public places and with women he knew only casually. Nor was he shy about making clear his desire for intimate companionship.

Young's brashness and persistence surprised and sometimes offended some of the women he sought. But others succumbed to his directness and his charm and electricity. At the same time, women pursued him. Like other important public figures, his celebrity and influence gave him a powerful sexual appeal, and there was an extraordinary magnetism about him in any case. Women did not hesitate to make him aware of their interest in knowing him much better. The temptations were abundant, and Young took ample advantage of them.

Just what the relationships meant to Young is difficult to say. Some of them seem to have been long-lasting and emotionally intense; others were briefer, no more than flirtations. Doubtless they satisfied deep-seated emotional and sexual needs. Doubtless, too, they reflected the intense pressures of the kind of public life Young led. On the road, under constant criticism, facing the ever-present threat of attack or assassination, he yearned for distraction from his problems, for comfort and reassurance. He looked for validation and affirmation; he needed constant attention and reinforcement, needed to be cared for and nurtured, needed constantly to be told that he was loved.[17]

"He loved and he loved to be loved," his sister Arnita reflected. "That's one of the key factors in his [emotional] life." Lauren described her father as "like a puppy who needed people around to pat him on the head and tell him he was great." Marcia thought of him as a prototypical Leo: "He loved to be lionized." She said that "in a lot of ways, he was a very modest person, and he needed to be reassured that he was as terrific as he was." She recalled an occasion when her father visited her in Iowa: "I had a party for him, and he was sitting there surrounded by all these sort of middle-aged, middle western women who were just—you know, whatever he said was fabulous—and he was just *loving* it, he just loved that kind of stuff, loved an audience and loved adoration."[18]

Hand in hand with the need for attention, for adoration, went a need to flaunt his conquests. Young advertised his triumphs and his infatuations, boasted about them, joked about them. Surrounded by good-looking white women at an Urban League conference, for instance, he exclaimed to Lindsley Kimball, "This is black power!" He was both the gleeful little boy and the proud, macho man—striking in his boldness, in his seeming disregard for consequences, in his willingness to live dangerously. Time after time, Young went out of his way to make certain that his friends were aware of the prominent white women he attracted. As one of them put it, "He'd always let you know."

Young's reputation with women "made him a baaad brother," one Urban League executive reflected. "It gave him a certain legitimacy." The belief that he could have any white woman of power and position and influence whom he wanted became part of his aura as a leader, almost inextricably intertwined with his image and influence. "It was part of an illusion which he encouraged."[19]

One can only speculate about the effects of Young's preoccupation with other women. Most of his friends and associates say that the woman issue had little if any negative effect on his discharge of his public responsibilities. If anything, some of the relationships may have worked to the advantage of the Urban League, as wealthy, influential white women gave more freely of their time, money, and connections than they might have had it not been for their personal ties to Young.

For Margaret, Whitney's involvement with other women was, at best, a persistent irritant, plainly an integral part of the way he lived his life, and yet not disruptive enough to shake her strong belief in the fundamental solidity of their marriage. Her sensitivities on the subject were well known. As the years went by, she presented herself increasingly as the neglected wife, disturbed not only by her husband's relationships with other women, but by the competing demands of his public role.[20]

The tensions he experienced at home were one part of the price Young paid for his particular brand of celebrity. The other part came in the form of public criticism of the authenticity of his blackness. It was a common theme. Whitney Young, so the popular perception had it, had sold out to the white establishment.

To a significant extent, Young brought the criticism on himself by virtue of the way he lived. Even his white friends liked to twit him about his establishment ways. Lyndon Johnson once tracked him down at lunch at the '21' Club in New York. Young picked up the phone and heard the familiar Texas voice: "You're a hell of a leader of the poor blacks, having lunch at '21'." One summer afternoon, when Young was relaxing in banker Morris D. Crawford's swimming pool, floating lazily, scotch and soda in hand, Crawford snapped a photograph. Later, he gave Young a copy.

"Now, Whitney, you behave yourself," he joked, "because I'm gonna show that picture all around Harlem."[21]

There is no doubt that Young got a kick out of conferring with corporate chieftains and counseling presidents. Skeptics took a cynical view. As one civil rights leader commented to the social psychologist Thomas F. Pettigrew, "Whitney sells out for a bottle of champagne." Even some of Young's friends worried that he enjoyed it all too much; if he got along *that* well with the white establishment, what was he really doing behind those closed doors? To an extent, they had a point. Young was human, and he had a healthy ego. "He got a charge out of the circles he was traveling in," Marcia said. It was hard not to get carried away. Young could hardly wait to boast about visiting Henry Ford in his private office; "he *just loved it*" when he was drinking with corporate leaders in a New York hotel; he showed a childlike delight at his appointment to the board of the Federal Reserve Bank of New York; he got a thrill out of seeing his face on the cover of *Time* magazine. "Sometimes he was excited by the aura of the power structure," Margaret reflected. "Whitney wasn't beneath being intrigued with being able to manipulate [it]."[22]

Like most powerful people, Young sometimes had difficulty distinguishing between what was necessary to sustain his own influence and prestige and what was necessary to advance his cause. At times, celebrity and prestige became their own reward. That was what many of his critics sensed.

The more Young succeeded in building close contacts with powerful whites, the more he drew criticism from skeptical blacks. He addressed the issue of his life-style directly. He often told the story of the train ride between his home in New Rochelle and his office in Manhattan. "I think to myself," he said, "should I get off this morning and stand on 125th Street cussing out Whitey to show I'm tough? Or should I go downtown and talk to an executive of General Motors about 2,000 jobs for unemployed Negroes?" Of course he kept company with white corporate chiefs; as he put it, "*Somebody's* got to talk to the people who have something to give." To blacks who derided his decision to live in a predominantly white, middle-class suburb, he responded, "I never promised to live in the ghetto with you. I said I would work to ensure every one of you the right to live in decent housing wherever you choose. The solution isn't for me to come and join you and the rats; it's for you to come on out here and join me and these white folks."[23]

Young defended himself by insisting that the high living had its purposes. A woman he met at an elegant party might be asked to take a table at a future Urban League function. Dinner at a fancy restaurant with another couple might provide a good chance for argumentation and persuasion. When a young black militant told Young that traveling first class on airplanes was not "being with the people," Young said that the Urban League's income never grew when he rode in tourist but that he could show some healthy gifts as a result of conversations with fellow passengers in first class. He argued that knowing what happened in the sauna bath at the Harvard Club actually helped him do his job. He claimed that he kept his objectives plainly in sight: "I don't get so flattered by floating around on some yacht," he said, "that I lose sight of my goal." His point was that the more compatible he became with the white establishment, the more successfully he could use it to advance his goals.[24]

Those explanations contain a germ of truth, but they were clearly self-serving. The high living was more an expression of Young's own ego needs than it was a vehicle for realizing his social goals. Those needs were strong, and they influenced the nature of his relationships with the leaders of the white establishment just as they did his relationships with women. While Young's private, personal needs were sometimes compatible with his larger objectives, that was not always the case. The more he satisfied the demands of his ego, the more they threatened to become ends in themselves. Some of the people who knew him best worried that the larger objectives were, at times, overshadowed. Even Young himself must have understood, on some level, the dissonance between his life-style and his public role. Had that not been the case, it would have been unnecesary to do quite so much explaining.[25]

The most significant challenge to Young's standing as a black leader came in the latter part of the 1960s. The issue was ideology, not life-style. The question, as the public discourse broadened to include cries of black power, was how Young would position himself in an increasingly politicized racial environment.

XII

Black Power

WHITNEY YOUNG'S close ties to the economic and political leadership of the country stamped him as increasingly suspect in the eyes of many blacks as the racial climate heated up in the late 1960s. "Moderate" was the polite way to characterize him. Ed Brown, the brother of H. Rap Brown, and his colleagues in SNCC, for example, regarded Young as "the most establishment kind of civil rights leader," one who represented an older style. He was a reformer rather than a revolutionary, attempting to move blacks into the mainstream instead of effecting significant political change. Less restrained critics used derisive forms of description: "Uncle Tom," "oreo cookie," "Uncle" Whitney, "Whitey" Young. Daniel Watts, editor of the Harlem newspaper *Liberator*, dismissed Young, along with Wilkins and King, as "house niggers." Cecil Moore, once the head of the Philadelphia branch of the NAACP, described Young and others like him as "the white man's black errand boys." The writer Julius Lester called Young one of the "black con men" of "White Power." While the indictments came chiefly from blacks, some white radicals took a similar view— Saul Alinsky, for one, compared Young to cooperative natives in the Congo whom colonial rulers used to keep the other natives quiet.[1]

In the racial climate of the 1960s, it would have been difficult to imagine describing Young as anything but a moderate. He was committed to integration, and he believed in the democratic process. He sought to work within the system to change it, not to opt out of it or overturn it. Still, he disliked the label. Just because someone did not "shout and scream or throw bricks and Molotov cocktails" did not mean that he was a moderate, Young insisted. In his own writings, in interviews, and in response to repeated questioning, he explained his position. There were no moderates in the civil rights movement; "we are all militant when it comes to demanding our full rights." The Urban League was just as angry at racial injustice as anyone else. The proper distinction was not between "moderate" and "militant," but between "burners and builders, between insane and sane leadership."[2]

That distinction was never really accepted in the 1960s. On the spectrum of civil rights ideologies and tactics, Young's position *was* moderate. His early public posture on black separatism and racial violence made that plain. While he and his organization became more militant as the racial crisis grew more intense, they always lagged behind the radicals in the movement. "Moderate" may not have captured the full complexity of Young's position, but the label was hard to shake. It was easier to categorize blacks in broad terms as moderates and militants than to explicate the more complex roles within the movement. (Young tried calling himself a responsible militant; not surprisingly, the label never stuck.) Moreover, Young's own role was hard to understand. To young blacks in particular, his easy access to the power structure meant that he had sold out to the white establishment. In a time of intense passion, this man who operated quietly seemed out of sync. Appreciating the contribution of such a role to the struggle for civil rights took a more sophisticated understanding of processes of social change than could have been expected of most people.

The demonstrations of the early 1960s had afforded opportunities for Young to identify himself with the main thrust of the civil rights movement. Always careful to make clear the special functions of the National Urban League and to specify the limits of its role, he nevertheless associated the organization with the nonviolent direct action protests that dominated the movement.

As more radical elements within the civil rights movement came to reject nonviolence and integration, Young was no longer able to identify himself with the most visible expressions of protest. In the early and mid-1960s, the news was the Urban League's presence at the March on Washington, Montgomery, and Jackson. Now the headlines announced Young's criticisms of violence and separatism. In October 1966, he joined A. Philip Randolph, Bayard Rustin, Roy Wilkins, and Dorothy Height in a public statement reiterating the fundamental principles of the civil rights movement: "*We are committed to the attainment of racial justice by the democratic process. . . . We repudiate any strategies of violence, reprisal, or vigilantism, and we condemn both rioting and the demagoguery that feeds it.*"[3] The following summer, in the wake of riots in Newark and Detroit, Young, Randolph, Wilkins, and Martin Luther King issued a joint statement affirming their opposition to racial violence and deploring riots as "ineffective, disruptive and highly damaging to the Negro population, to the civil rights cause, and to the entire nation."[4]

In the context of the times, calling for an end to violence meant staking out an unmistakably moderate position. It was Rap Brown, calling riots "dress rehearsals for revolution" and urging blacks to grab their guns and set fire to Washington, who defined the outer limits of black protest. As those limits stretched in the late 1960s, the moderation of a stance like Young's was inevitably underscored.[5]

Young's views on violence were more complex than plain opposition. He rejected as simplistic the popular perception that the riots were the work of a handful of extremists or outside agitators. "You don't need Mao or Castro or some Russian to tell you your baby just got bitten by a rat," he said in the summer of 1966. He understood that the violence expressed the depths of hopelessness and despair in the black community. At the same time, he rejected the possibility that violence could be an effective agent of social change. As he put it on "Face the Nation" in the summer of 1967, "We do not believe that the Negro is going to solve the problem by tearing up his own communities and killing his own people."[6]

Perhaps most important, Young pointed out again and again that the riots were distracting attention from the pressing needs of blacks in the ghetto. When the House of Representatives took up antiriot legislation in July 1967, he chided them for not focusing instead on the economic and social conditions that spawned the violence. "I'm getting pretty annoyed the way some people are using this summer's riots as an excuse to avoid doing anything about the basic social problems which caused them," he wrote in a newspaper column shortly thereafter. People ought to be working to "create more jobs and better housing and decent education." That, not reprisals, was the way to ward off future riots.[7]

The analysis was sophisticated; by deploring violence but simultaneously insisting on an attack on the conditions that bred violence, Young was staking out a position not easily categorized as moderate or militant. But the complexity of his position was often forgotten or too rarely understood. Instead, the simplified version, in slogans or catchphrases (as in his exhortation to blacks to reject "the Pied Pipers of destruction"—the extremists—as their leaders in the drive for racial equality), drew the headlines and defined popular perceptions of his point of view.[8]

Even more than the explosion of race riots, the call for black power redefined the boundaries of the civil rights movement in the late 1960s and created a new standard by which to measure militancy and moderation. Outspoken champions of black rights might draw the line at violence and still retain credibility, but unwillingness to embrace black separatism and black pride became, in the eyes of many younger blacks, a litmus test for commitment to the black cause.

With Stokely Carmichael of SNCC and Floyd McKissick of CORE leading the cry for black power in the summer of 1966, other civil rights leaders were forced to take a stand. Black power made headlines, and it gave the media as well as younger blacks a new standard by which to measure the militancy of the older leaders. Roy Wilkins made his position clear at the NAACP's annual convention: " 'Black power' means antiwhite power," he said; "we of the NAACP will have none of this." Young deplored the media's preoccupation with the new slogan of black power at the expense of serious discussion of the problems of poverty and discrimination. "The

National Urban League does not intend to invent slogans, however appealing they may be to the press," he declared in a statement issued in July. "What we will continue to do . . . is expand and develop positive programs of action which bring jobs to the unemployed, housing to the dispossessed, education to the deprived, and necessary voter education to the disenfranchised. In the final analysis, these are the things . . . which bring power to both black and white citizens, and dignity and pride to all."[9]

But for all of Young's insistence on the unwillingness of the Urban League to become involved in a "fruitless dispute over the value of a slogan which has not even yet been clearly defined by its originators," he could not escape taking a more specific stand. Appearing on a radio interview show in New York on July 31, he called black power "a chant and a slogan in the absence of concrete, tangible programs." It was "vague enough . . . to be all things to all people," dramatic enough to win the attention of the media and so "rescue what were dying groups." Appearing on a special edition of "Meet the Press" with other civil rights leaders three weeks later, he said, "The Urban League takes a position that power is something that one acquires through having sufficient economic means, educational resources, and political know-how. We do not feel that one gets pride or dignity or power simply by being white or being black."[10]

Throughout the next two years, Young repeated two basic arguments about black power. One—a plausible point—related to the nature of power. As he put it at a press conference at Wilberforce University, where he received an honorary degree in January 1967, "Power is not the result of . . . skin color. . . . Power is the green of a one dollar bill; it is the brown of a textbook; it is the white of the ballot." Young's second theme, one which was at odds with the facts, was that proponents of black power represented only a tiny fraction of the nation's black population.[11]

Young frequently joked that he believed so strongly in equality that he was convinced that blacks had "as much right to have [their] extremists as the whites," and he made plain his willingness to work with black power advocates and black nationalists alike toward the achievement of common goals. But he was always careful to spell out the convictions that kept him apart from the militants. Explaining his opposition to separatism, he declared, "I don't go along with setting up a separate nation for Negroes. I don't believe in withdrawing from the main stream of society. I don't believe we should buy boats and go back to Africa." Explaining his opposition to violence, he told angry young blacks, "Personally I am not nonviolent, but I'm not a fool, either, I can count. I know you can't fight a tank with a beer can nor destroy a regiment with a switch."[12]

Such views bespoke a hard-headed appraisal of practical realities. But many blacks, frustrated by the dead weight of reality and energized by the cries of black power, had little use for sober assessments. "Roy Wilkins and Whitney Young have ceased to speak for Negroes," a black woman in Denver wrote in the summer of 1967, doubtless voicing the impatience and expectation of many others. "They speak to white people. They tell the white people about peaceful demonstrations, gradual integration, and a lot of other things that have lost their sting. We've had 100 years of peace with no freedom. Now we'll try a few long hot summers. Whatever happens, with what we have now, we can't lose."[13]

The assassination of Martin Luther King and the explosion of the ghettos in April 1968 shook Young and provided the catalyst for some changes in his thinking and for a reorientation in the Urban League's emphases.

More than any other public event, the King assassination troubled Young profoundly. The murder was "unspeakably shock[ing]," he told the press the night King was shot. "Those of us who have remained loyal to his concept of nonviolence have been dealt a mortal blow." It was difficult for him to conceal his frustration and anguish. Questioned by reporters at an Urban Coalition press conference four days later, he said that he was not "remotely concerned with how white people feel or how sorry they are" but only with what they did. If whites failed to take action to address the desperate needs of blacks in the nation's ghettos, there would be more deep despair and anger. Even "people like me may be revolutionists," Young said. "And I'm not going to be a stupid revolutionist." To another question, he responded, "If you think that I am not as angry as Rap Brown, then you misread me. I'm just no fool. I'm not going to give them an excuse to kill all Negroes with all the new weapons and practice they have." The sharp anger did not dissipate easily. To a YMCA meeting later that month in Colorado, Young declared that the assassin who shot King "pulled the trigger rather comfortable with the knowledge that he had the approval of millions of white Americans." The gunman, he said, "was spawned in a society that has been, at best, indifferent to the terrible discriminations and injustices against the Negro" and, at worst, "a participant in this type of brutality."[14]

In a more extended interview, Young revealed the severe strain the King assassination imposed on his reformist convictions:

I have tried with great difficulty—having no tangible, concrete victories that are significant—to remain a sane, responsible leader. I continue to feel that way.

But if the large majority of Negroes, including people like me, are forced to give up hope and to feel that this country—the white people particularly—is congenitally, morally bankrupt, then I have no choice. I can't continue to stand by and see my people out of work, living in ghettos, their kids bitten by rats.

If the assassination of Martin Luther King . . . doesn't shock America into doing the things that it should have done years ago, then I have no choice. Either I get out of it and go to Africa, or I just conclude that America has no capability of responding in a moral tone to anything but violence.[15]

Young's anguish over the explosion of racial violence led him to embrace the proposal of the executive director of the Washington, D.C., Urban League, Sterling Tucker, for a significant change in the Urban League's program.

The demand for change was not new in 1968. As early as 1966, as black power made the headlines, some Urban Leaguers had begun to express discontent with the direction of the agency's activities. At the annual conference in Philadelphia that August, outside protesters picketed the opening session, making plain their impatience with the league's safe, establishment-oriented nature. Young was part of the problem; as one placard jibed, he was "Whitney Young—Boss Kimball's son." At one point, with Kimball presiding, the protesters marched into the assembly hall. Young whispered to Kimball to let them have their say. When they finished, Young thanked them for speaking their minds. He liked to think, he said, that the Urban League was always open to the expression of different points of view.[16]

Outspoken delegates to the conference criticized the agency for its cautiousness. As David Rusk, the young associate director of the Washington, D.C., Urban League, put it, the league was suffering from "too much reasonableness." Rusk (the son of Secretary of State Dean Rusk) insisted that the league needed to give up its "traditional role as an interracial communications link, a mediator, an interpreter." Instead, he urged that it embrace lobbying, community organizing, and direct action.

Rusk offered pointed examples of the kinds of activities he had in mind. He acknowledged that the league might "take an awful beating in the process"; greater activism carried a range of risks, from loss of tax-exempt status, to ouster from the local United Fund, to building enemies. But he insisted that the crisis of the cities demanded that the league transform itself into "a relentless, dedicated, driving force at the heart of social change."[17]

Rusk's words struck a resonant chord. Frank Stanley, an associate director of the National Urban League, called on the organization to mobilize the masses of blacks in the ghetto. Wyatt Tee Walker, the former executive director of the Southern Christian Leadership Conference who had joined the staff of New York governor Nelson A. Rockefeller as a special assistant on urban affairs, said that the league "must retool, adapt itself to today's needs," adding, "They have no alternative."[18]

Young agreed that the league needed to focus more directly on the problems of the ghettos, but he disagreed with the call for a massive reorientation of the organization's approach. It was all well and good for militant civil rights groups to try to organize the ghettos, but direct action was not the Urban League's way. Young fell back on rhetoric he had used before. The league "can't be the Army, Navy and Air Force of the civil rights movement," he said; the agency's approach provided a valuable supplement to that of more militant organizations. In the next year, as if to shift the terms of the debate, he revived his call for a Domestic Marshall Plan as a way of dealing with the crisis in the cities.[19]

The King assassination narrowed the gap between Young and the dissidents within the league. He called an emergency meeting of national board and staff members as well as local executives and board presidents on the last weekend in April. "Abnormal times," he said, "call for abnormal action." The nation stood perilously close to catastrophe, and the National Urban League could be of some help in averting disaster. The point of the meeting was not "to change the Urban League from moderate to militant," or to endorse black power, or "to discredit or minimize any of our past history or contributions," but to consider some reorientation of the agency's focus in order to make it more effective. The discussion centered on a proposal that Sterling Tucker had drafted for a "New Thrust" to bring the Urban League more directly into the ghetto. The proposal went to the national board at its meeting in May. By midsummer, a committee of local and national board and staff members had completed a revised draft of Tucker's working paper for distribution to the affiliates, and Tucker, on leave from the Washington Urban League to run the new program, had assembled a staff to design and implement it. At the end of July, at the league's annual conference, the Delegate Assembly added its endorsement.[20]

The New Thrust started from the premise that most blacks, for the foreseeable future, would continue to live in segregated communities. The league was not so much abandoning its historic commitment to integration as acknowledging that real integration was a distant dream. The New Thrust committed the agency "to sink roots deep in the ghetto"—to develop a range of special projects aimed at building economic and political power where most blacks were concentrated. The emphasis would be on community organizing, on bolstering indigenous political and economic leadership, on promoting economic self-sufficiency, and on gaining community control of ghetto institutions. The Urban League would provide technical assistance and professional expertise to facilitate confrontations between ghetto dwellers and the power structure. Instead of acting as spokesman for blacks, the league would help them to speak effectively for themselves. Instead of merely providing social services, it would function as a direct agent of social change.[21]

Reporting on the league's new direction, the *Wall Street Journal* announced, "The National Urban League, long scored by radicals as the 'Uncle Tom' of the civil rights movement, is crossing the railroad tracks into the ghetto." While the *Journal* was talking metaphorically, that was precisely what most Urban Leagues did, either moving their offices or, more frequently, opening additional outposts in the heart of the ghetto. Within a year, the National Urban League had initiated new projects in voter registration, entrepreneurial development, and leadership development, and most of the affiliates had launched an array of special New Thrust projects.[22]

As Young explained on a number of occasions, the New Thrust meant building ghetto power. "What we are talking about . . . is a sharing of power . . . between the haves and have nots. . . . We are talking about one group of people giving up some of their economic, social and political power to another group—to insure peace—to insure the domestic tranquility, to insure the good life in America for all Americans—even the black ones." That sharing of power would be an investment in the stability of American society, in the country's survival as a nation.[23]

By the summer of 1968, Young was clearly moving toward a different point of view. His basic thinking had not changed dramatically, but there was a sufficient change in emphasis, a sufficient reorientation of perspective, to lead to something new. He still insisted that a Domestic Marshall Plan best embodied the massive effort necessary to "undo the vicious network of racism and poverty" and close the widening gap between the races. But now he began to couch his vision in terms of an open, not an integrated, society—a pluralistic society that permitted the healthy persistence of ethnic and cultural differences, a world in which blacks would have their fair share of power and wealth, but would be free to choose between integrated and segregated living. As he explained in an interview in 1968, blacks ought to have "the same rights to live in any neighborhood, select any job, go to any school" as any other Americans. In the event that they chose, as other ethnic groups had, to live among their own people, they ought not to pay the price of "the worst garbage collection, the worst police protection, and the worst housing." What blacks wanted was freedom of choice. "Integration for integration's sake is not an objective of any black man I know today."[24]

Young elaborated the idea in his book, *Beyond Racism*, published in June 1969. Instead of spending their energies on "futile attempts to emulate white people," blacks had come increasingly to focus on developing the black community. That did not signify a retreat into separatism. The goal of most black Americans was "full equality in an open society in which blacks and whites are equals, with the same choices open to all."[25]

Similarly, while Young never gave up his commitment to nonviolent strategies and interracial cooperation, he articulated a new position on black power that seemed to place him much closer to those blacks who were the most impatient with the capacity of the system to deliver social change. He understood that impatience. As he told the National Urban League's executive committee in June 1967, he had found in the black community "a hopelessness and a despair, a complete lack of confidence in the ability of white America to address itself seriously to the problems of the day." Increasingly, he shared the belief that the nation respected only those who could mobilize their own resources. If he reacted that way, he pointed out, "it should not be hard to understand why the masses of Negroes feel as they do."[26]

For all of his sympathy with the anguish and frustration that underlay the cry for black power, Young had never liked the term. More than anything, he deplored its connotations of violence and separatism. Besides, black power gave whites who were growing increasingly uncertain about their commitment to civil rights a perfect excuse for backing off. Letting whites off the hook was exactly the wrong approach. "After all white people got us into this mess," Young said. "I think they ought to be a part of getting us out of it."[27]

Young had hoped that black power "would just sort of fade away," but when that did not happen, he decided to find some way to "defang" the term and "to give it a positive overtone."[28]

The annual convention of CORE in Columbus, Ohio, in July 1968 gave Young the platform to begin the effort. Roy Wilkins had already addressed the delegates; while he had said that the NAACP was " '100 per cent' behind building black pride, black economic power and black political strength," it was his disavowal of the most extreme forms of black separatism that had drawn the headlines the next day. Now it was Young's turn. The atmosphere at the convention was tense, and he knew that he was on the spot. Some of the more militant delegates were reported to have threatened a walkout in response to Young's appearance. That protest did not materialize; still, the audience came with a heavy skepticism shaped by the white press's consistent portrayal of Young as a moderate. What he said astonished and delighted them. "Brothers and sisters," he greeted them ("I didn't say 'ladies and gentlemen,' " he later pointed out). "I come to this convention believing that the goals and objectives we have in common are far greater than those on which we may differ. . . . The Urban League," he said, "believes strongly in that interpretation of black power which emphasizes self-determination—pride—self respect—participation and control of one's destiny and community affairs." He brought the delegates to their feet, applauding loudly and shouting, "The brother has come home."[29]

The speech caused something of a sensation. The national press, headlining the emergence of a "New Whitney Young," called it a "sharp reversal" of Young's previous position. Requests for copies poured into the Urban League's offices in New York. Many blacks hailed what one psychiatrist described as Young's "impressive and courageous" statement; in the words of a young black social worker, "You have made the decision to walk among your people without fear and to be a true leader rather than being a tool of the establishment." The *Baltimore Afro-American* praised Young for demonstrating that he understood "the aggressive, self-deter-mining mood of today's black people." Floyd McKissick, national director of CORE, declared that the speech demonstrated that there were "not the differences that people thought" in the black movement.[30]

While the CORE speech enhanced Young's image in certain quarters, it also caused nervousness and dismay among longtime supporters of the National Urban League. Some of them took the speech to mean that the league had changed its course, and they wrote to express their regrets at the reversal. Others could not quite believe that Young had really meant to take as extreme a position as press accounts seemed to suggest. The publisher of the *Scottsdale Daily Progress*, formerly a member of the board of the Phoenix Urban League, asked Young to clarify his position. "What does your support of 'Black Power' mean? Does this mean that the Urban League approach is being changed? . . . Does it leave any place in the civil rights movement for the white person of good will, and if so where?" Troubled by what he had read about the speech in the *New York Times*, the chairman of Montgomery Ward asked for a copy of the com-plete text "as I find it difficult to believe this newspaper's account." The vice chairman of the New Jersey advisory committee to the United States Commission on Civil Rights wrote to say that she had read the *Times'* account of the speech "with great disappointment and concern. . . . I hope—and believe—it must be a mis-quotation."[31]

Young's response illustrated the complexity inherent in his multiple roles. Having made a move that won him plaudits among blacks, he needed to make certain that he had not done any significant damage to his credibility among influential whites. In a radio editorial for Metromedia Broadcasting in New York, he tried to strike a safe middle ground. The speech did not represent "a reversal of the Urban League's position on 'Black Power,' " he declared. That position remained unchanged. "I made quite clear my opposition to any interpretation of the phrase which in-cludes violence, or a retreat into separatism." What he was advocating, however, was "that interpretation of 'Black Power' which holds it to mean the development of pride and self-respect, and which encourages partici-pation in community affairs and control of one's own destiny." To worried correspondents, he sent a copy of the speech along with an assurance that he had not really changed his stance. He had simply tried, he said, to give a much-used phrase "a realistic and constructive interpretation." That seemed to satisfy the people who wondered at what they had read in the newspapers. "There was absolutely nothing in what you said that I find myself in any disagreement with," the chairman of Pitney-Bowes wrote after reading the text. "I think it is an excellent speech and the original press treatment of it must have been garbled to cause me any concern."[32]

By trying to strike a middle ground comprehensible to integrationists as well as to proponents of black power, Young added a new dimension to his familiar roles of bridge and interpreter. To militant blacks, he showed that a black man who frequented corporate boardrooms could share in the vision of dashiki-clad youths in the streets. To establishment whites, he suggested that beneath their inflammatory rhetoric, advocates of black power were expressing legitimate aspirations.

"I had to make a rather basic decision," Young explained in an interview in 1969. "One is of no value to a society or to institutions as a leader unless he has the respect of his people, his constituency, the people he would lead." He could have condemned black power, he said, or he "could try to reinterpret it, redefine it, sanitize it a bit if you will, and give it a positive connotation." He chose the latter course.[33]

What difference did it make that Whitney Young took it upon himself to provide a positive reinterpretation of black power? Who was listening? The columnist Charles Bartlett wrote that in endorsing black power, Young was "rescuing a valuable concept from irresponsible hands. . . . 'Black power' under its new sponsorship will be torn away from its tarnishing association with the pseudo-leaders, the anti-white militants who talk of 'honkies,' 'getting the gun,' and a separate black state. It will be construed to mean 'black pride' instead of 'black coercion.' " Young had performed a service, the *Milwaukee Journal* concurred, by asking "white America, unsettled by a confusing chorus of 'black power' sloganeering, to look and listen with greater sensitivity."[34]

Young's reinterpretation of black power made it easier for prominent whites to embrace the doctrine. But it was also possible for whites to find in his words justification for distancing themselves from what seemed to them its worst connotations. In "rescuing 'Black Power,' " the *New Rochelle Standard-Star* emphasized, Young had not aligned himself "with the extremists who espouse 'black power' in the sense of fostering hatred, violence and separatism." The *New Orleans States-Item* pointed out that "although Black Power has come to connote violence in the minds of many, Mr. Young emphatically rejected the concept of violence." Even more important than that, he also rejected "the concept of separatism, the notion that the black man has a destiny apart from that of other Americans."[35]

In sum, whites took from Young's words on black power the message they were prepared to hear. In some cases, his reinterpretation helped them to grasp the frustrations and aspirations embodied in the slogan and to redouble their commitment to the black movement. In others, Young's words provided reassurance that the most extreme expressions of black power were as abhorrent as they had believed.

Blacks, too, were divided in their response to Young's sanction of black power. The political scientist Charles V. Hamilton, coauthor with Stokely

Carmichael of the book *Black Power*, said that Young "was never scared off or frightened by the term black power, in the way that I think a lot of people were." Young "thought there was a lot of bravado about it," but still understood "some of the important symbolic, emotional . . . aspects of [the] term."[36]

But most blacks, not privy, as Hamilton was, to long discussions with Young on the subject, took a more skeptical view. Young still remained a moderate—too moderate. No matter that he embraced black power, no matter that he reoriented the league with the New Thrust. Even as the New Thrust was being ratified at the league's annual conference in New Orleans in 1968, some fifty young protesters disrupted the meetings. It was the first time that the league had held an annual conference in the South. The Jung Hotel, the headquarters for the meeting, had a history of racial discrimination; even though its work force was no longer segregated, the hotel still had too few black employees. A number of local Urban League executives agreed that the league had made a mistake in meeting there. To the young protesters, the choice of the Jung simply confirmed the league's middle-class orientation; how could it pretend to understand the needs of people in the streets? As the youths grabbed the microphone, Young responded coolly. As one of the Urban League executives in the audience recalled, "He didn't raise his voice. He didn't seem angry. He just gave them the mike and let them talk." A spokesman for the group read a list of demands: the league should move the conference out of the Jung, make the membership of its policy-making bodies 80 percent black and 20 percent radical white, and get young people more involved in the movement. "These are people who may not have degrees from college," Young explained to the delegates. "But they have degrees in being hurt." Later, Young invited the protesters to his suite, ordered sandwiches and drinks, and heard them out. "He disarmed them," said a local executive who sympathized with the demonstrators and sat in on the conversation. "Disarmed them." The protesters came back the next day and talked some more. "He took what was, at best, an embarrassing situation for the movement . . . and made it a positive situation."[37]

The next summer, in Washington, demonstrators again disrupted the league's annual conference. This time they were black college students, heads of the black student unions on sixty campuses, who were working for the Urban League during the summer as organizers in ghetto communities around the country. At the first conference session, thirty-five of the students interrupted the welcoming remarks of the league's president, James A. Linen, called him irrelevant to the needs of blacks, and criticized the league for inadequate involvement of "grass roots" people in the proceedings. Two days later, all sixty students invaded the Delegate Assembly, grabbed the microphone away from Young, called for the ouster of white industrialists from the National Urban League board, demanded greater representation of young people in the affairs of the organization, and insisted that the league make good on its rhetorical commitment to build ghetto power. "How can we allow James Linen to be president of the Urban League?" one student shouted. "He doesn't give a damn about black people." Another cried out: "We should jam Whitney Young up against the wall and force him to implement [our] programs." Still another said that "the Urban League is controlled by Whitey. It has been since it started, and it still is. Urban League workers are only an extension of Whitey's arm with Whitey's mind."[38]

Once again, Young handled the confrontation calmly. To the students, he made plain that while he understood the depth of their anger, the league could not share in their total indictment of white society. He told them that some of their proposals were infeasible, but that some made good sense. He pledged that the league would try to be responsive to their concerns and, especially, to involve young people more fully in its activities. To Ronald H. Brown, the organizer of the summer program, who was extremely embarrassed by the behavior of his charges, Young offered reassurance—it was important for the league to hear what the young people had to say. To the trustees who were singled out for personal attack, Young apologized, expressing the hope that "they would not 'cop out' but would react with even greater determination to serve the cause." As offensive as the students' language may have been, he said, it was important to "try to separate the 'rhetoric of revolution' from the substance of the issues." The upshot of the confrontation was a significant change in Urban League policy; 25 percent of the members of the national board, as well as the boards of the affiliates, would now be under the age of thirty.[39]

The challenges to Young's standing as a black leader came in other contexts as well. In September 1970, Young addressed the International Congress of African Peoples in Atlanta. He had not attended the black power conferences that had been held annually since 1967, but the congress, with its emphasis on forging a black united front, had a broader focus; moreover, it promised to move beyond rhetoric to action. And so he decided to accept the invitation of Imamu Amiri Baraka (formerly LeRoi Jones, a prominent black poet and playwright) to participate in the gathering. "I make no apologies at all for attending a conference where only blacks are," Young explained when questioned about it. "We are a family and it is appropriate and essential that family members get together before they plan to go elsewhere."[40]

Young and Baraka had come to know each other the previous year, when Young had agreed to help Baraka's Committee for Unified Newark secure foundation support for a drive to register black voters in advance of the 1970 municipal election in Newark. Baraka was frank about his reasons for approaching Young: "He had access to the folks with the money." For his part, Young had apparently agreed to endorse the effort on the grounds that participation in the political process was a more effective means of accomplishing social change than the more confrontational methods being advocated in some quarters.[41]

Baraka believed that Young belonged at the Congress of African Peoples, although the two men by no means agreed. Baraka saw Young as closely tied to the white establishment, representing the interests of big business and the black elite. But he found him to be more open, less inflexible and dogmatic, than some of the other established black leaders. Despite their differences, it was possible to *talk* with Young. Besides, the point of the congress was to forge a united front; convinced of the value of inclusiveness, Baraka thought that Young, speaking for significant numbers of blacks, ought to be there. As he told the delegates, "I would rather make a political alliance with Whitney Young than with Abbie Hoffman [the white yippie leader, with whom Black Panther Eldridge Cleaver and other militants were making common cause] because Whitney Young controls masses of black people's minds."[42]

To the black activists and intellectuals participating in the congress, however, Young stood out as an anomaly. A commitment to black nationalism was the driving force behind the congress. If there were any doubts about where Young stood, one had only to look to the pages of the previous month's *Ebony*, where he had declared emphatically that the resurgence of black separatism bore "little real relevance to the solution of the black man's problems. . . . The fact," Young had asserted, "is that there are no virtues to be found in segregation, whether imposed by white racists or sought out by ourselves. . . . Separatism as a strategy for equality has never worked and it never will. . . . I believe in the need for an integrated society," Young summed up, "not because associating with whites is, of itself, a good thing, but because it is only through participation in the mainstream that full equality can be won."[43]

Views of that sort grated with black nationalists. Chuck Stone, a former assistant to Congressman Adam Clayton Powell and one of the original organizers of the black power conferences of the late 1960s, spoke for many of the delegates who opposed Young's participation in the Congress of African Peoples. "Young shouldn't even have been allowed to speak," he declared the day before his scheduled appearance. "He wouldn't have invited LeRoi Jones to speak at an Urban League conference. Neither Young nor Wilkins are heroes to these blacks here. Let them run the NAACP and the Urban League because those two organizations are losing out anyway."[44]

Stone said that he was acquiescing in Young's appearance for the sake of unity. But as Young rose to speak on the night of September 5 in the packed Morehouse College gymnasium, others in the crowd of more than four thousand made plain their displeasure by heckling and booing. The chairman of the congress, Heyward Henry, a young lecturer in black studies at Harvard and MIT, urged them to let Young speak.[45]

At the outset, Young struck a conciliatory note:

I would hope by our very presence . . . that we are saying loud and clear for the whole world to hear that we are through publicly bickering among ourselves for the entertainment of other folks—that instead, we are moving toward a new unity based on those things we have in common and our desire not just to survive, but to survive with equity and dignity for ourselves and for our children.

Turning to his main theme, "Realities of Power," Young made clear his opposition to separatism as a strategy for racial advancement. Dismissing firepower as ineffective, he emphasized the importance of economic power, political power, and brain power as the essential weapons in the black struggle. At the end, the crowd gave him an ovation.[46]

The Congress of African Peoples incident encapsulates many of the central themes that characterized Young's relationships with the most militant blacks. Strongly committed as he was to interracial action, he was willing to reach out to and work with those who thought otherwise. Secure about himself and his own role, he could tolerate public criticism with a certain amount of dispassion. That was true partly because of his own self-assurance, partly because of his ability to distinguish symbols and substance, partly because he understood and kept a sense of humor about the rhetoric of some of the younger militants. He liked to tell the story of the black student at Columbia University who had declared in a television interview that his leaders were Rap Brown, Stokely Carmichael, and Eldridge Cleaver. The student feared that his draft board in Columbia, South Carolina, was about to call him, and he wanted help in avoiding military service. Two days after his television appearance, he came to see Young. Young told him that he had heard what he had said about his leaders. "Why didn't you go see them? Why do you come to me? I'm not powerful." The young man responded, "Oh, Mr. Young, come on. You know I'm just rapping."[47]

Young was not afraid to call young militants on the disjunction between their rhetoric and their behavior. He told a story about his meeting with a group of black students at Yale University, during which he listened as they condemned him for his moderation. Finally, he told them, "You are only a stone's throw from hundreds if not thousands of black boys in New Haven who don't have fathers. How many of you have brought one of them up here to the campus, just once, for a good meal or just some companionship?" None of them had. "The hell with y'all," he told them.[48]

Young sometimes succeeded in bridging the gap between himself and more militant blacks. Close exposure facilitated cutting through public rhetoric, understanding each other's purposes, and seeing beyond stereotypical images. But most militants saw Young at a distance, not up close, and they continued to snipe at him, despite the evolution of his views on black power, despite his reorientation of the Urban League, despite his efforts at communication.

Distancing themselves in a noisy public fashion from more established civil rights leaders gave more radical blacks a means of carving out their own niche in a movement where recognition came as much from headline grabbing as from real influence. Young clearly had the influence; others built themselves up by tearing him down. Criticizing Young was a way of saying to whites that they could not solve the problems of black America by dealing with him. They needed, instead, to deal directly with the militants.

A more important reason for the militants' persistent attacks on Young was their fundamentally different view of the world. Reformist, dedicated to the American capitalist system, Young sought to make it more equitable, more open, and more just. To young radicals who wanted to topple that system, his efforts to patch it up seemed wrongheaded, if not counterproductive.

Not only was Young trying to patch up the system, but he was doing so in ways that usually kept him off the front lines. His role in the movement virtually guaranteed that he would be the object of scorn. He was the negotiator, the man who rode the wake of the confrontations to wrest concessions from the white establishment. To do his job, he had to move slowly and speak quietly. That made him anathema to many of the young people in the movement; for them, working behind the scenes in the way Young did looked all too much like selling out.

XIII

The Nixon Administration

As THE 1960S DREW to a close, Young did more than confront persistent tensions within the black movement; with the change of administrations in Washington, he also found new battles to fight.

For most black Americans, the election of 1968 seemed bereft of victory. No other candidate managed to evoke the intense emotional commitment that so many blacks had felt for Robert F. Kennedy. Still, when the choice came down to Richard M. Nixon, Hubert H. Humphrey, Eugene J. McCarthy, and George C. Wallace, those blacks who went to the polls voted overwhelmingly for Vice President Humphrey. A longtime champion of civil rights, Humphrey had led the fight for a strong civil rights plank at the Democratic National Convention in 1948; more recently, he had played a major role in the passage of the Civil Rights Act of 1964. By contrast, Wallace was openly racist, and most blacks saw McCarthy as the candidate of the white intellectual elite. Nixon had no previous record of support for civil rights. Moreover, the themes of his campaign—opposition to school busing and open housing, the promise to appoint only conservative justices to the federal courts, the emphasis on restoring law and order—seemed deliberately calculated to appeal to whites who were tired of black protest.

Congratulating Nixon on his election, Young made plain that he would have to work to win black confidence. Nixon needed to move quickly to allay the widespread fears about his insensitivity to the problems of blacks. The Urban League stood ready to help him to become president "not of some Americans, but of *all* the people."[1]

In an effort to overcome the skepticism, if not hostility, toward him in the black community, Nixon began directly after the election to open lines of communication with black leaders. On November 15, he met privately with Young for a little more than an hour in the president-elect's suite at the Pierre Hotel in New York City. At a news conference scheduled by the Nixon transition team following the meeting, Young declared himself encouraged by their discussion. Nixon had clearly conveyed his "concern about the divisions in the country," Young told reporters. He said that he was willing to give Nixon the benefit of the doubt, adding somewhat guardedly that "a man is innocent until proved guilty," and that he saw no insurmountable obstacles to Nixon's "quest to gain the trust of the black community." The columnist Mary McGrory noted that "Young's endorsement of the new leader" was "cautious in the extreme."[2]

It soon became widely rumored that Young was in line for a cabinet appointment. Before the Johnson presidency, there had been no reason to expect the president to name a black to his cabinet. But with the appointment of Robert C. Weaver as secretary of Housing and Urban Development in 1966, expectations changed. Now political observers naturally weighed the likelihood that the cabinet would include a black appointee. With minimal support from black voters in the election, Nixon did not owe blacks a slot; yet the need to enhance his credibility among blacks made such an appointment a matter for serious consideration. The *Wall Street Journal* considered that the new administration would need a black in at least one high post, and that Young seemed a plausible choice. He had met with the president-elect; he had "contact with white businessmen as well as Negro slum-dwellers." The *Journal* thought him a likely candidate for secretary of Health, Education, and Welfare.[3]

In mid-December, the *New York Times* reported that the Nixon forces had tried unsuccessfully to interest Young in a top job. According to the *Los Angeles Times* News Service, the blacks under consideration for the cabinet included Young, Massachusetts senator Edward W. Brooke, and New York lawyer Samuel R. Pierce, Jr., but the appointment of a black man of stature seemed fraught with difficulty. On the one hand, other black leaders were said to be exerting great pressure on the men in question not to join the administration. At the same time, it was not clear how hard the Nixon people had worked to make such an appointment happen, given the likelihood of objection from some of the whites Nixon was anxious to court.[4]

Asked about the reports on "Meet the Press" the Sunday before Christmas, Young denied that he had actually been offered a cabinet post. Would he have accepted if an offer had been made? That would have depended on the position, how he was approached, what kinds of commitments the administration was prepared to make. Still, he said, "I am inclined to believe that what I am doing at the present time is more important to the country and to my people." Nixon's version of what had happened was that he had discussed with Young the possibility of joining the cabinet, and that Young had told him "that he could do more for those things he believed in outside of government than inside of government."[5]

Young took a pragmatic attitude toward doing business with the new administration: Nixon was president; "he's the only one we've got." Given the acute nature of the problems facing black Americans, trying to work with him was the only practical choice.[6]

In the interests of influencing the administration's policies and priorities, the National Urban League marked the inauguration by sending Nixon a detailed memorandum urging a massive crusade to tackle the urban-racial crisis. It laid out a number of specific recommendations, including full implementation of national manpower policy, an increase in the minimum wage to $2 an hour, vast expansion of manpower training programs, and replacement of the public welfare system with a system of income maintenance. "The prime need is for real and pervasive national commitment, one that draws on all our resources, public and private, and on all our richest talents," the league exhorted. "We need a demonstration from the top that the nation is totally committed to the fight against racism and the products of racism, against second-class citizenship and urban decay."[7]

But the early months of the administration gave no evidence of such a commitment. At first, Young took the position that Nixon deserved some time to prove his intentions. Most blacks were already pessimistic about the new administration, he told his board in February 1969, but he thought it premature to render a judgment. To be sure, the administration had failed to appoint blacks to high-level jobs, but the real test would come in the kinds of legislation proposed and the funds appropriated for implementation. By May, he was increasingly skeptical; while he had had conversations with a number of administration officials about following up on the league's memorandum to the president, he told the board that he was "less than wildly enthusiastic" about the first hundred days of the Nixon presidency.[8]

By summer, Young had moved away from his initial balanced, wait-and-see approach. There was already ample evidence of the administration's intentions, and he did not like what he saw. At every opportunity Nixon seemed to play to the fears and emotions of whites, especially Southerners, working-class ethnics, and northern suburbanites, who had had enough of black protest and racial violence. The administration pushed for a congressional moratorium on court-ordered school busing, lobbied against an extension of the Voting Rights Act of 1965, and declined to enforce desegregation guidelines by cutting off federal funds for schools that were out of compliance. The president dramatically weakened the Offices for Civil Rights in the Department of Justice and in the Department of Health, Education, and Welfare, fired government officials seeking to implement integration guidelines, and vetoed bills and impounded funds designed to assist blacks. It was hard to avoid the conclusion that the

Nixon administration meant to roll back the gains that had previously been realized in civil rights.[9]

Like other black leaders, Young began to criticize the administration for failing to face up to "the urban-racial problems that should be at the top of the list of priorities," and for encouraging a national mood of polarization, indifference, and repression. At the same time, he distanced himself from Nixon on the Vietnam war. Perhaps the fact that Lyndon Johnson had left the White House freed Young to think about the war in ways that had not been possible for him before; perhaps, influenced by the course of events and by his own daughters' strongly held views against the war, he had simply come to change his mind.[10]

After the Tet offensive in January 1968, American public opinion shifted increasingly against the war. By early 1969, for the first time, more than half of those surveyed in national polls said that America's involvement in Vietnam had been a mistake from the outset. Whereas 56 percent of those questioned in January 1968 called themselves hawks, 55 percent in November 1969 said that they were doves. Antiwar activists planned a nationwide moratorium for October 15, 1969, with a massive rally in Washington on the grounds of the Washington Monument. They invited Young to speak.[11]

The invitation came in the midst of Young's reconsideration of his position on the war. He had come to believe that Martin Luther King was more right than he was, and that it was difficult to separate the war from domestic problems. The war was polarizing the country and diverting attention from critical needs at home. After long discussions with board and staff members, he decided to make his change of heart public. He wired the organizers of the Vietnam moratorium that he was already committed for October 15, but that he was preparing a statement in support of the moratorium.[12]

Before issuing the statement, Young sent a draft to the members of the National Urban League board. The board included many powerful whites who had been staunch supporters of the war effort, and Young was understandably cautious about antagonizing them. But opinion on the war had shifted sufficiently to diminish the risk. He told the board that he had been under a great deal of pressure to take a position on the war. He would not officially commit the organization, but he was ready to make a personal statement. The situation had changed significantly since his decision three years earlier to remain neutral, and he expected more favorable response and support than he did opposition. He hoped that the board would agree that it was no longer possible to remain silent and still maintain credibility.[13]

Young issued the statement on October 13. "For some time now," he said,

I have viewed this country's agony in Vietnam with a sense of deepening distress.

Day after day, month after month, our involvement in this war on distant Asian soil has sharpened the divisions and frustrations among the people of this country as no other issue has in recent history.

I am totally convinced that Vietnam is tragically diverting America's attention from its primary problem—the urban and racial crisis—at the very time that crisis is at flash point.

Young said that involvement in Vietnam had intensified America's domestic crisis and created a disastrous drain on national resources. It was time to turn away from Vietnam and pour those resources back "into our own land, our own cities, our own people."[14]

The *New York Times* noted that Young was the first black leader "to align himself squarely with the antiwar forces" since King had done so in 1967. "Welcome home, baby," exclaimed the director of CORE, Roy Innis, a long time critic of the war, when he learned about Young's shift.[15]

The Nixon administration failed to listen to the message of the moratorium. Nor did it take any steps to respond to critics who accused it of ignoring or even inflaming a growing sense of domestic crisis. For all his strong reservations about the president's policies, Young was still reluctant to break with Nixon, since there was little to be gained in closing off the possibility of constructive communication with the administration. What Young wanted was action on the pressing social and economic needs of black Americans, and he was ready to keep talking to people in the White House and the federal agencies in the hope of making some headway. Private discussions with some of the more sympathetic officials gave some encouragement, but the administration's public pronouncements were inconsistent and confusing. On the one hand, Nixon had promised to do more for blacks than any president had ever done. But this was the president whose administration had distanced itself from the Voting Rights Act and from enforcement of federal guidelines for school desegregation; the president who encouraged the "Silent Majority" of middle Americans, who channeled their frustrations over crime, the war, and the economy into hatred of blacks and young whites; the president who nominated to the Supreme Court G. Harrold Carswell, a Southern appeals court judge who was known to have supported segregation. Anxious to communicate with the administration but unable to find an effective means, Young urged National Urban League trustees who had contacts with those in authority to urge them to think carefully about the effect on blacks and the country at large of what seemed to be administration policy. The present course, he told the board, could "lead only to moral suicide."[16]

In private discussions over the winter and spring of 1970, Young continued to express his frustration at doing business with Nixon. "I feel very discouraged," he said off the record, in an interview in March. "I think there has been a clear decision made to go backwards. They're going to follow the political route and [do] whatever is expedient. [T]hey're going to reflect the fears, the panic, the prejudice. . . . They aren't going to provide leadership." It was not that the administration was uniformly hostile; the administration consisted of many parts, and there were some good men in the White House and the cabinet who shared the Urban League's concerns about the domestic crisis. But Nixon himself seemed impervious to the race problem. The access to the president that Young had previously enjoyed was no longer available. Nixon was isolated from firsthand sources of information. Since he had been in office he had never talked to Young, or, for that matter, to Roy Wilkins. Either the White House believed, naively, that if there was no contact with black leaders, the leaders—and the race problem—would disappear, or it did not care what black leaders thought.[17]

At the end of June 1970, public criticism of Nixon by prominent blacks reached a crescendo when Bishop Stephen G. Spottswood, chairman of the board of the NAACP, charged in the keynote address at the organization's annual conference that the White House was conducting "a calculated policy to work against the needs and aspirations" of black Americans. A Gallup poll published in early July revealed widespread black dissatisfaction with the president.[18]

Dismayed, moderates on the White House staff sought ways of redeeming the administration. It had been (and would continue to be) common for Leonard Garment, special consultant to the president, and others privately to encourage people like Young to see the administration in a more favorable light. Now, in the wake of Spottswood's attack, Garment initiated discussions with Young about joining the administration on a temporary basis as an adviser on racial issues. The possibility of such an appointment became the subject of considerable speculation in the press. In early July, NBC reported that there had been informal White House staff discussions about making an appointment, and that Young had already been approached; shortly thereafter, United Press International reported that the president had actually asked Young to take the post. According to the wire service account, officials at the Western White House in San Clemente, California, described the invitation to Young as "part of a new administration drive to improve the channels of communication between the President and minority groups." Young would be an " 'ambassador' on [the] home front," one of a group of people to be appointed "to heal the divisions with dissident minorities."[19]

Amid the public speculation and private negotiations between Young and the administration, intermediaries made a suggestion to Young. If, in his forthcoming speech to the National Urban League's annual confer-

ence, Young would moderate his criticism, if he would say that he believed that the president might be willing to make some accommodation
with black America, the administration would be prepared to provide substantial programs to benefit blacks.

Where the suggestion originated within the administration, and on
what authority it was communicated, remains unclear. Nor is it known
how Young responded privately to the idea. But the July 19 speech can
easily be interpreted as containing a signal. "As critical as I have been of
Administration actions," Young declared, "I do admit that there are some
signs that elements of this Administration are moving forward to bring
about change. . . . [I]t would be a mistake for us to fail to recognize that
within every Administration there are contending forces."[20]

Within the context of an otherwise critical speech, it was no great departure from what Young had said before. In fact, he had made precisely
the same point at Urban League gatherings in late spring and early summer. But in the wake of Spottswood's attack, Young's speech was widely
construed as a defense of the administration. Whether or not he had
framed his remarks as a calculated response to the administration feeler,
Young drew criticism from other blacks for being soft on Nixon.[21]

What negotiations may have followed are unknown, but it seems clear
that the signal failed, at least in the short run, to bring out the positive
response for which Young may have hoped. At the same time, the possibility of an advisory post in the administration failed to materialize. At a
news conference at the outset of the league's annual meeting, Young acknowledged that there had been some discussion about his joining the
administration, but he made clear that there had been no formal invitation. He said, further, that he would consider any offer carefully, but that
he would not take such a job without the approval of the black community.
The *Amsterdam News* reported that Young had been "sounding [out]
black leaders to determine whether they would allow him to represent
their views to the White House inner circle." Whether or not that was
true, the publicity itself generated advice on what Young should do. Jesse
Jackson, national director of SCLC's Operation Breadbasket, applauded
the idea; he thought that it was important for blacks to have "access to
inside counsels [*sic*] of the White House," and Young seemed well-suited
for the role. "The United States could only bring honor to itself by having
you serve in such capacity," Jackson told Young. "Your longstanding contributions to [the] cause of racial justice has more than qualified you both
for such ranking governmental service and for the trust of the nation's
black people." Charles Kenyatta, an outspoken militant who had been one
of Malcolm X's bodyguards, took the opposite view. "Whitney wants to be
a spokesman," he sneered. "Every Administration [has] had a black man
as an overseer of the plantation." And the national vice president of the

Negro American Labor Council, Troy Brailey, cautioned, "In my opinion, a leader of one of the major civil rights organizations should not join the Nixon administration in any capacity."[22]

No one can be sure what happened next. As Jackson told the story, it was Young who declined the appointment. "I wanted to accept that post," Jackson said Young told him; "I could have done the job. But the brothers would not have understood." Margaret Young insisted that Whitney "had no notion of going with the administration." According to another account—that of Sterling Tucker, at that time assigned to the National Urban League to run the New Thrust, who had talked with Garment about the possibility of a post for Young—the job was never actually offered.[23]

It is known that by late August, the issue was closed. At a press conference, Young said that he had not been asked officially to take a post in the administration, and that he would not be willing to be considered for such an appointment. The president "doesn't need advice from Whitney Young," he said, "and Whitney Young has no desire to be a single black Moses." He delivered a stinging attack on the administration for its indecisiveness and flabbiness on civil rights. Nixon's record was "sort of like Jell-o," he said. "You can't really get ahold of it. . . . It's what I call white magic, you know, now you see it, now you don't." As for the mood among blacks, "I've never seen the black community quite as universally disillusioned and lacking in confidence about an Administration as I have this one."[24]

While Young continued to be sharply critical throughout the fall, he made another private attempt to come to terms with the administration. This time his efforts were more effective. He was increasingly alarmed that the deepening urban crisis in the country was receding from the general consciousness and that public and private responses to it seemed to be weakening. He wanted to meet with the president and members of the cabinet to talk about what could be done. Young's purpose was twofold. He wanted to convey information about the economic and social plight of black Americans and the mood in the black community. But he also wanted to recommend programmatic initiatives on the part of the administration, and here his interest was in shoring up the Urban League as well as in promoting governmental attention to the needs of blacks. The league was having money problems, and Young thought that having the government subcontract federal programs would be a way of stabilizing the organization's financial condition.[25]

In part the money situation reflected insufficient allocations to local Urban Leagues from local united and community fund agencies. With the expansion of Urban League programming as a result of the New Thrust, affiliates needed more money to finance their activities. But local funding agencies, squeezed by inflation and tight money, were likely to be cutting back their appropriations. United Way officials were also put off by the assertive, confrontational stance of Urban Leagues in some communities. In November, at the behest of local executives, representatives of the National Urban League and of the ninety-seven affiliates met in emergency session in St. Louis to address the funding crisis. At a press conference at the conclusion of the two-day meeting, Young called for an immediate 50-percent increase in United Way allocations to local Urban Leagues. How could the United Way be serious about the desperate problems of the cities when it gave the Urban League only 1 1/2% of its allocations? "I am saying to the United Way today, and to all citizens who give to the United Way, that we cannot and will not continue to participate in this fraud being perpetuated [sic] on the American public."[26]

The Urban League movement also had to face the fact that private contributions to the national organization were coming in more slowly than usual, due to the general state of the economy and to uncertainty about the consequences of new tax reform legislation. In December, Young ordered a freeze on new hiring and a review of each staff position with an eye to possible reductions. The next month, he announced that the league would be unable to pay raises to those professional staff members who would have merited them.[27]

Probably the biggest financial blow came with the news in the fall of 1970 that the Ford Foundation's next grant to the National Urban League would be substantially smaller than it had been the year before. Foundation money had become extremely important to the league; whereas it raised $1,973,000 from private industry in 1970, its income from foundations totaled $5,054,000.[28]

Under the leadership of McGeorge Bundy, the Ford Foundation in the late 1960s became the most significant source of Urban League funding. In August 1966, at Young's invitation, Bundy made his first major public address as president of Ford at the Urban League's annual conference. There he announced the foundation's new commitment: "We believe that full equality for all American Negroes is now the most urgent domestic concern of this country," he said. "We believe that the Ford Foundation must play its full part in this field."[29]

The activities of the Urban League and the strength and effectiveness of Whitney Young made the organization a logical vehicle for Ford's support. Without the Urban League, Bundy later explained, Ford would have been unable at that time to undertake urban projects "through someone respected and respectable." In 1966 and 1967, within the first year of Bundy's presidency, Ford gave the Urban League $1,500,000 for a fair-housing project, as well as $430,000 for general support and $600,000 toward the purchase of a new national headquarters at 55 East Fifty-

second Street, a building that it would share with the United Negro College Fund. In 1968 and 1969, Ford made grants to the league totaling
$4,700,000, the bulk of the money designated to support the New
Thrust.[30]

The various Ford grants were less an endorsement of a particular set of
programs than an investment in the continuing strength of the National
Urban League. In the words of Mitchell Sviridoff, the foundation's vice
president for national affairs, that investment was "a vote of confidence in
Whitney Young," a means of supporting "a powerfully effective national
leader." It was also a way of strengthening the center in the civil rights
movement; "if that center ever came apart," Sviridoff observed, "I think
there would be unholy chaos in the civil rights community."[31]

By the fall of 1970, however, Ford officials were ready to put stricter
limits on their beneficence. The foundation was facing leaner times. Simultaneously, program officers in the Urban Affairs Division who had
worked most closely with the National Urban League were skeptical
about the rationale for the agency's newest funding requests and, more
generally, about the way the league was being run. "I thought that the
New Thrust conceptually was a wonderful idea, because I believed that
the Urban League was the best network we had for really getting at the
problems of the inner-city poor," Roger Wilkins said. Accordingly, he had
facilitated the foundation's big grant for the New Thrust (in fact, it was the
largest grant he made during his time at Ford). But he was disappointed
at the results. "I did not see a reorientation of effort or a sharpening of
focus that warranted a repeat of that giant grant." Sviridoff agreed with
Wilkins that the New Thrust programs were not particularly effective.[32]

In October, Wilkins reported to Bundy that he had talked with Young
and told him that while the foundation was not yet ready to settle on a
figure for its next grant to the Urban League, it was likely to be in the
neighborhood of a million dollars. That could not have come as a total
surprise, since Wilkins had made plain in earlier conversations that the
new Ford grant would be substantially smaller than the $3.6 million of the
previous year. Still, Young expressed shock and dismay. Wilkins justified
the cut in terms of the limited resources currently available to the foundation and said that he could not consider anything beyond the range of $1
to $1.5 million. Young told him that anything below $1.5 million would be
disastrous. "It is my guess that the cut will really not hurt the League very
much," Wilkins confided to Bundy, "and that Whitney's anguish stems
more from the fact that much of his self-image is based on his ability to
raise funds. In my judgment, what the League needs now is not a rich
treasury but sharp, hard administration and clear program guidance.
Whitney knows I feel this strongly, but if he's done anything about it, it is
not discernible to the naked eye."[33]

Young was looking for $5.7 million in foundation grants for 1970–1971, and he had hoped that Ford would provide $3.8 million. In view of his conversations with Wilkins and later with Bundy, he trimmed the total foundation budget to $5.2 million and asked Ford for $3.2 million. The Ford grant finally came in at $1,725,000.[34]

The insufficiency of United Way appropriations, the slowing of private contributions, and the dramatic decrease in the level of support from the Ford Foundation all disposed Young to think about the federal government as a source of funding for Urban League programs. The idea was not as far-fetched as it might have seemed in light of the Nixon administration's record on race. After all, Young reasoned, if the administration was willing to spend millions to bail out major industries that were in financial difficulty (as it intended to do with Lockheed), it also had an obligation to support nonprofit agencies that were vital to the nation's welfare.[35]

Through the efforts of Leonard Garment and the assistant to the president for domestic affairs, John D. Ehrlichman, a meeting with the president and members of the cabinet was arranged for Tuesday, December 22. With little time to spare, Young, Sterling Tucker, Betti Whaley, the league's program director, and Cernoria Johnson, director of the Washington Bureau, worked furiously to prepare the presentation. Young arrived in Washington on Monday and rehearsed his presentation over dinner with Tucker and Whaley. On Tuesday morning, they went to the White House.[36]

Nixon opened the meeting by noting that Young had been a frequent and harsh critic of administration policies. He said that the Urban League was "a vitally important organization whose views should be heard." Young spoke first of the disillusionment many blacks felt with administration policies. Some people, he said, believed that change could come only with the election of new faces in 1972. Others, more pessimistic, had given up hope, convinced that the system would collapse because of the inequities it perpetuated. The Urban League believed, however, that it was imperative to act immediately to address the "crisis of disaster proportions" confronting the black community.[37]

The bulk of Young's presentation focused on the crushing impact on blacks of unemployment and poverty and the desperate need for intensified efforts to alleviate the urban crisis. He sketched its dimensions in graphic detail. The rate of black unemployment in major cities—25 percent—was from two to four times greater than the rate among whites. Among black teenagers, the rate of unemployment was 35 percent. Blacks were three times more likely to be in poverty than whites; median black family income was less than two-thirds that of whites. Not only were blacks suffering disproportionately from the economic conditions of the moment, but they stood at a significant disadvantage in other major indices of social well-being, such as education, health, and housing. Fifty-eight percent of black children completed the eighth grade, as compared with 78 percent of whites. Forty percent of black students graduated from high school, as compared to 62 percent of whites. Blacks had higher rates of infant mortality and lower life expectancies than whites. Black families suffered the hardships of inadequate housing and ineffective community services.[38]

With greater cooperation between the public and private sectors, there would be some chance of making headway in combating those problems. The government seemed not to recognize the gains that could be realized through an intelligently conceived joint strategy. There were already good models. Young used the analogy of Lockheed: when the government wanted airplanes built, it contracted with experienced manufacturers in the private sector. But when the government wanted to deliver social services, it ignored private agencies and created its own delivery systems. That made no sense. Why not subcontract social programs to established agencies that had the experience to run them? That would allow for more effective delivery of services, improve the credibility of the administration in the black community, and, not incidentally, strengthen the agencies.[39]

The president responded favorably to Young's suggestion, and he directed the cabinet to develop cooperative arrangements along the lines Young had proposed. Nixon designated Garment and the office of budget and management director George P. Shultz to serve as contact men for the effort in the White House, and he asked each cabinet secretary to designate a liaison person in his department to work with the league. He told Young to call back in a month to report on the progress that had been made in implementing the plan.[40]

Young left the White House greatly encouraged. To Garment he wrote, "We all came out winners." To the president, he sent thanks for the positive leadership he had demonstrated and proclaimed himself "more confident and optimistic" than he had been in some time that "tangible and concrete results will be forthcoming."[41]

Young's new optimism about Nixon struck a discordant note among black critics of the White House, but at least some commentators were willing to suspend judgment to see what the administration delivered. As the newspaper columnist Carl T. Rowan put it, "Even allowing for the possibility that Young was suffering from intoxication brought on by the high altitude of the White House, let us hope he is right."[42]

The Urban League began immediately to develop proposals for cooperative ventures with the federal government in the areas of employment, education, housing, and social welfare. Working feverishly for thirty days, often around the clock, staff members reviewed the catalog of federal as-

sistance programs to figure out how and where the league could participate in training, evaluation, and provision of direct services. After elaborate negotiations, the league won commitments for $28 million in federal
funds for at least fifty different programs to be implemented by itself and
other agencies. In February, the National Urban League board ratified
the league's new "Federal Thrust," setting the pattern for the massive
infusion of federal money into the organization in the next decade. The
new relationship between the league and the national government was
"possibly the most important systems change" that the Urban League had
ever been engaged in, Young told his executive committee. Still, it carried a risk: the infusion of federal funds might mean that the private sector
would no longer feel obligated to support the organization. Young's caution about the potential drawbacks to greater dependence on federal funding proved prophetic, but he would not live to see the fruition of the new
arrangements he set in motion.[43]

XIV

Doubts, Pressures,
Prospects for the Future

AFTER NEARLY a decade at the National Urban League, Young was ready to move on to something else. His restlessness had not reached the stage of a public announcement, but those who were closest to him knew that he wanted a change. He had accomplished his major objectives for the Urban League, and the job had lost its challenge. He was getting bored, and he was tired. Ten years at the league struck him as about right. He would turn fifty in the summer of 1971; he did not want to follow Lester Granger's pattern and stay until he retired. "He really wanted to take a year off," Margaret said, "and just travel and think, read, and . . . retool, kind of just get it back together."[1]

There were so many different pressures in his life. Within the league, the crisis over funding—a source of grave concern in recent months—had been most urgent. The new arrangements with the Nixon administration gave some hope of significantly alleviating the problem, but the real impact on the league of Federal Thrust would not be clear for some time to come.

At the same time, there had been persistent concerns about the internal management of the organization. Administration was not Young's greatest strength; nor was it where he devoted the largest part of his attention. Over the years, as he moved the Urban League into the civil rights movement, made it a factor in debates over public policy, and strengthened its connections to the corporate establishment, he necessarily spent most of his time on matters other than running his organization. Simply staying on top of the varied, far-flung activities of a growing national organization kept him traveling much of the time. As he became more influential, demands on his time from outside groups increased. It was hard to say no, particularly if it was a group he believed in or a cause he wanted to advance. So much of minority group leadership was built around an individual personality that it was difficult for anyone to stand in for him. He would come home and say to Margaret, "Momma, everybody's pulling at me."[2]

Young seemed always to be on the road making speeches and attending meetings. It was not only the federal government and the corporate sector that captured his energies. When he had a chance to connect with another part of the white establishment, he seized the opening. The possibility of changing attitudes and affecting practices, coupled with the seductiveness of greater visibility, overcame practical calculations about available time.

Young took on the establishment in all of its forms: voluntary associations, the professions, the schools, the churches. To the Episcopal Diocese of Manhattan in 1963, he said that it was not enough for the clergy to stop discriminating. "You have to reach out to the Negro and say I want you. You have to meet us 75 or 80 percent of the way." Speaking to the Union of American Hebrew Congregations the same year, he took the rabbis to task for "mouthing platitudes and salving the people's conscience" instead of leading their congregations in working for civil rights. An audience with the pope in 1967 was a chance to urge the pontiff to issue an encyclical on racism and to make every Catholic institution in the United States "a model for racial justice."[3]

To the National Association of Housing and Redevelopment Officials in 1965, Young threw out a challenge to "really come out and fight for integration." Even heads of major corporations—"not exactly bleeding heart idealists"—had taken up the cause. Why not NAHRO? Or were its members among the "wholly inadequate insecure frightened little people" who were afraid to "run the risk of diversity"?[4]

To the National Council of the YMCAs in 1966, he said that he saw plenty of blacks working in Y kitchens, basements, and locker rooms, but almost none in responsible staff and board positions. "If the Boston Celtics can integrate, and even the Rockettes at Radio City Music Hall," he chided, "surely an association of Christian gentlemen can integrate." To the National Association of Broadcasters in 1969, he issued the same challenge: "If we can integrate sports and houses of prostitution, why can't we integrate broadcasting?"[5]

Opportunities like these were appealing because they gave Young a chance to preach to white leaders whom he believed needed to be converted to his cause. They were appealing, too, because he was a master of the art; he had a gift for capturing the attention of his audiences, and he could not have been immune to the reinforcement that came when they told him how effective he had been. The president of NAHRO, for instance, responded to his speech by commenting, "Seldom has the needle been inserted so deeply and effectively as you did today." A television reporter for the *New York Times* wrote that in Young's speech to the National Asso-

ciation of Broadcasters, he had "laid it on the line" with "vigor and candor" and "twist[ed] the stiletto with a subtlety and humor that make businessmen take heed." Young was no different from anyone else in liking
approval.[6]

But the opportunities were appealing to Young chiefly because they
held the promise of actually stimulating his audiences to grapple with racial issues more directly than they might have done otherwise. The pay-
offs were never immediate, or even always obvious, but when they came,
they made the expenditure of time and effort worthwhile.

Young's involvement with two groups of professionals—engineers and
architects—illustrates the point. At the annual meeting of the National
Society of Professional Engineers in January 1968, Young challenged his
audience to bring young blacks into the profession and to apply the prob-
lem-solving techniques of engineering to the urgent problems of the
ghetto. In response, the society passed a resolution calling on engineers
to become actively involved in tackling urban problems and to encourage
minorities to enter their field. Along with the resolution came testimo-
nials to Young's effectiveness. "Please register one Professional Engineer
who *is* willing to stand up and be counted," one man wrote. "Your wonderful talk . . . indicates a direction and intelligent leadership that I would
be proud to follow." Another engineer wrote to say that he and some of his
colleagues wanted to do what they could to encourage more blacks to
enter the profession. "We are first trying to educate ourselves on the subject. We seek your help."[7]

The annual convention of the American Institute of Architects in June
1968 provided a similar opportunity to raise the collective consciousness
of a group of white professionals. Young thought that architects had distinguished themselves by their "thunderous silence" and "complete irrele-
vance" when it came to civil rights, and he minced no words in telling
them so. Once again, his speech provoked a set of resolutions, this time
establishing a national scholarship program for minorities to study architecture and calling on architects to become more actively involved in addressing urban and environmental problems. The AIA set up a task force to
explore ways of improving opportunities for blacks in architecture, and it
cooperated with the National Urban League in some projects toward that
end.[8]

Speeches were one way of reaching the white establishment. Another
was to join boards and committees in the nonprofit and public sectors.
Young belonged to a long list, among them the presidential commissions
to which Lyndon Johnson appointed him, the boards of the Urban Coalition and Urban America, and, later, the boards of the Massachusetts Institute of Technology, the New York Federal Reserve Bank, and the Rockefeller Foundation. (He declined to join corporate boards on the ground

that such appointments might inhibit his freedom to criticize the practices and policies of major corporations.) In his own profession, he was elected president of the National Conference on Social Welfare and, subsequently, of the National Association of Social Workers.

In the worst of these cases, Young, stretched too thin, lent his name but failed to pull his weight. Kenneth Clark remembered their joint tenure on the board of the Urban Development Corporation in New York. Young never showed up for meetings. Perhaps, Clark mused, he might have behaved differently if the businessmen on the board had been bigger names.[9]

In the best instances, Young invested time and energy, and his efforts made a difference. As a member and later president of both the National Conference on Social Welfare and the National Association of Social Workers, Young pushed insistently for greater sensitivity to the problems of minorities and poor people and for greater involvement in social and political action. "Social work," he said in his presidential address to the National Conference on Social Welfare in 1967, "was born in an atmosphere of righteous indignation, of divine discontent." But in their zeal to become professional and respectable, social workers had lost the urgency of the challenge and the passion of the crusader. Instead, they had "made a fetish of methodology, a virtue of neutrality and objectivity." Too many social workers looked down their noses at the poor; too many were uncomfortable with issues of race and religion. They had come to be seen not as crusaders but as "experts in adjustment and accommodation," professionals who busied themselves with applying means tests and ferreting out unauthorized men in welfare households. Young exhorted his colleagues to recapture their lost heritage: "We must plant the spark of change and the seeds of indignation in the mind of every citizen suffering in want. We must be the catalysts of change, not the maintainers of the status quo."[10]

Young's professional colleagues credit him with pushing the NCSW toward greater activism. The same was true of the National Association of Social Workers, where, in the words of James R. Dumpson, the movement toward political action "got a terrific thrust from Whitney's presidency." Dumpson, a black executive at the New York Community Trust, said that Young "made a major contribution in validating social action [and] protest" as legitimate techniques for social workers. Mitchell I. Ginsberg, dean of the School of Social Work at Columbia University and Young's successor as president of the NASW, saw a discernible difference in the association's "interest and involvement and concern with the poor and the disfranchised and minorities" because of Young's influence.[11]

Young's involvements beyond the National Urban League were good for his organization in many ways. His visibility rubbed off on the league by heightening its prestige and augmenting the range of its connections.

But his outside activities also carried costs for the league, since they made it difficult for him to devote as much attention as he might have to managing the organization. Part of the problem was simply a matter of time, but part was shifting gears. Margaret reflected on how hard it was for Whitney to come down from the high of his outside life to focus on the mundane business of running the Urban League: "I think there were times when after he had been in the public eye so much Whitney dreaded the day-to-day drudgery of administering that organization. He thought it was too much to expect for him to be out there, puddle hopping from one city to another, giving speeches, receiving the applause, and then come back in and say to somebody, 'Now what about this department? I want a run-down on the budget tomorrow. Who is doing this fund-raising?' "[12]

As Young's longtime speechwriter, Dan Davis, evaluated his boss, "He was best outside. . . . As an administrator, he was—he was a social worker." James R. Kennedy, one of the businessmen on the National Urban League board, said that "he wasn't a businessman. He didn't think like a businessman." Young was not good at making the Urban League operate efficiently; as Kennedy put it, the league "was not as well organized as a businessman would like it."[13]

For one thing, Young was too tolerant of inadequate performance. He hated to tell people that they were not doing a good job and found it almost impossible to fire anyone. That meant that the league was carrying staff members who failed to pull their weight. "To a fault," Young kept people on when he should not have, Betti Whaley said. "I told him, 'Whitney, you run the grandest welfare program of all. This has become a sheltered workshop.' "[14]

Along with a disposition to be soft on weak performance, Young lacked the temperament and personal style to be a hands-on administrator. He was impatient with detail. Desk work bored him. Sitting in an office, shuffling papers, giving orders and supervising their execution—none of that appealed to him.[15]

The sense that Young was overcommitted and that there was need for some improvement in the way the league was being run led the league's board to hire a management consulting firm, Cresap, McCormick and Paget, to study the agency's organization and management practices. The consultants began their work in the fall of 1968 and submitted a detailed report in the spring of 1969. They found, not surprisingly, that Young could not function effectively as both "Mr. Outside and Mr. Inside."[16]

The consultants said that Young was spending too much time away from the office, and that he had failed to organize the league so that it could function effectively in his absence. In 1968, he was out of the office nearly 60 percent of the time, and activities not directly related to the administration of the league or to fund-raising accounted for 45.5 percent of his time. Two factors intrinsic to the way Young had organized the Urban League further handicapped the way it operated. One was the inadequacy of systems for reporting on programs and finance, which meant that the executive director got too much undigested information. The other was the quality of Young's supporting staff. Young had simply never mastered the art of surrounding himself with good people. The consultants noted that the overall caliber of the top staff below the level of executive director was not impressive, and they pointed to the need for additional staff assistance in the areas of planning, staff coordination, and fund-raising.

The report recommended, among other things, the appointment of a deputy executive director who would take on direct responsibility for planning and staff coordination; the revision of program and financial reporting systems; the clarification of responsibility for programs; the reconstitution of the national staff to improve the quality of personnel and to clarify their roles and responsibilities; the strengthening of personnel administration and staff training functions; and a strengthening of the relationships between the national and regional offices and the regional offices and the affiliates.[17]

Ersa Poston, a trustee of the National Urban League and a close personal friend of Young's, said that the report was "a little difficult" for him to handle. He resisted especially delegating significant authority to a deputy. Developing a strong second-in-command had never been his style. But the board made it clear that he had to make some changes. "I think this bothered him a great deal," Poston said. "It wasn't that we were saying that we didn't have confidence in his ability to handle the operation, but that the operation could not function the way we had expanded." Sensitive to criticism, Young interpreted the report as "an affront to his leadership. . . . That's about the only time I saw him feel uncomfortable with the board," Poston added.[18]

Once the board made clear that he had no choice, Young moved promptly to implement the recommendations. In September 1969, he announced the appointment of Harold R. Sims, former deputy to Sargent Shriver at the Office of Economic Opportunity, as deputy executive director. (Vernon E. Jordan, Jr., had applied for the job, but had not been selected; "I think we all consider you a more likely candidate for the Executive Director spot rather than the deputy," Young wrote him, "but that isn't vacant yet!") Young consolidated and upgraded the league's personnel and training functions under the leadership of a new director of personnel. At the same time, he appointed a new director of research to oversee the expanded functions of that department. By the spring of 1970, steps had been taken to reorganize and consolidate the league's program operations in an upgraded program department, and to strengthen the relationship between the national and the regional offices. That fall,

Young ordered the creation of a unit within his office to engage in long-range planning for the Urban League movement. Other problems identified in the Cresap, McCormick and Paget report—for example, difficulties in the relationship between the National Urban League and the affiliates; the lack of a functional mechanism to remove personnel who were not pulling their weight; the absence of systematic methods of gathering, recording, utilizing, and disseminating information—continued to be discussed among the leaders of the league for the remainder of Young's tenure in office.[19]

Along with the crisis in funding and the complications of internal management came a challenge of a different kind. The white press, through its most influential organ, the *New York Times*, seemed to be engaged in a deliberate effort to undercut Young's standing as a civil rights leader. Young had tried for years to get the communications industry to focus on responsible civil rights organizations and leaders; its habit of paying constant attention to the most outspoken separatists had seemed to him "a deliberate attempt to destroy the constructive, meaningful organizations." But the white media had continued to indulge their penchant for creating instant black leaders, and Young had not been shy about expressing his annoyance. "Something happens in civil rights and the newspapers call up outstanding personalities like James Baldwin or Louis Lomax or Willie Mays and ask what they think," he said in an interview in *Editor & Publisher* in 1964. "I don't question the integrity of their statements. But do newspapers call Frank Sinatra to comment on foreign policy? Or John O'Hara to comment on wheat to Russia? The racial situation is complex and it takes organization [and] know-how to comment on it."[20]

The black separatism and racial violence of the late 1960s threw up all manner of self-styled black spokesmen, and the white media gave the angriest, most militant among them their attention. As Young told a staff writer for the *Los Angeles Times* in 1966, "It's reached the point where it's a big joke in Harlem how to get on the front page. . . . Newspapers make these 'leaders' into Frankensteins and then say to us, 'Control them.' " In an interview in *U.S. News & World Report* in 1968, he lambasted the news media for its detailed coverage of Stokely Carmichael. "His following right now amounts to about 50 Negroes and about 5,000 white reporters," he said. "They have created him. There is no organization; there is no following. They have projected him, and this has kept him alive. . . . When I make a speech about co-operation between whites and Negroes, I'm given about four or five inches of space," Young continued. "When Stokely talks about 'killing whitey,' his whole speech is reprinted and gets television coverage."[21]

Now, in September 1970, the *New York Times Magazine* ran a long feature story on Young, but the publicity was not the kind he would have chosen. The title gave away the article's slant: "Whitney Young: Black Leader or 'Oreo Cookie'?" The author, Tom Buckley, painted Young as an uneasy man, worrying about his reputation in the black community while he sauntered along the corridors of power. Buckley said that Young was the leader of few blacks and that he was "frequently derogated as 'Uncle Whitney' or '*Whitey* Young' or 'the Oreo cookie.' " Young's speech that summer at the National Urban League's annual conference, suggesting some optimism about the Nixon administration, was only one of many examples Buckley gave of his questionable standing as a black leader. "No black figure I spoke to seemed to take the speech very seriously," Buckley wrote. "Their comments ranged from 'publicity stunt' to 'con game' to the assertion that Young was making a blatant attempt to get a top job in Washington."[22]

The Buckley article drew angry protests from blacks as well as whites. It was "not only a personal insult to Whitney Young but also an affront to all black leaders," A. Philip Randolph said. "Buckley's attitude is typical of all too many whites who are trying to be 'with it.' In order to be where the action is, or where they think it is, they have to put down the responsible black leadership." The columnist Carl T. Rowan objected strongly to "white liberals arrogating unto themselves the right to decide which black man is a soul brother and which is an Uncle Tom." "Tom Buckley and the *Times* can pick their own heroes," he said; "we black people will pick the black ones." Why did the *Times* "go out of its way to seek to destroy Whitney Young in the eyes of both blacks and whites?" the *New York Courier*, a black weekly, wondered. "The obvious question to every thinking black is 'Has Whitney Young lost his usefulness to the power structure?' " M. Moran Weston, rector of St. Philip's Episcopal Church in Harlem, put it this way: "The errand boys of the racist power structure have an uncanny way of going for the jugular vein of every Black man who is serious about basic change and in position to do something about it."[23]

The intensity of the black reaction to the Buckley piece was especially interesting in light of the fact that Buckley's characterization of Young was not very different from anything that had been said many times elsewhere. Actually, Buckley's depiction of Young's comfort with the white establishment probably represented the feelings of a great many blacks. But what blacks believed privately or talked about among themselves was one thing; what rankled here was the fact that a white reporter had written the piece, and that influential blacks, often speaking without attribution, had helped him.

The Buckley article clearly upset Young. He had become accustomed to being characterized as a moderate—not that he liked it, but he knew he had to live with it. But the Buckley piece was different. Buckley had managed to do a sophisticated job of undercutting him, and he had done it with the cooperation of some people Young thought were his friends. The article "really bothered him," Vernon Jordan said. Young thought it was "an unfair characterization of his leadership."[24]

The many pressures of Young's life, public as well as private, had a lot do to with his readiness to change jobs. While he had pretty much decided to give up the executive directorship, he had not yet determined what he wanted to do next. One job he would have liked fell beyond his reach. J. George Harrar would be retiring as president of the Rockefeller Foundation, and Young, a trustee of the foundation since 1968, hoped to succeed him. When he learned that he was not among the final candidates, it was a major disappointment. He had counted on Lindsley Kimball to help him get the job—this time in vain. Young never really had a chance at it, not because of lack of ability but because of his particular area of expertise. He knew nothing about science or medicine and had no experience working overseas. Given the directions in which the foundation wanted to move, that meant that he did not have the right qualifications for the job. Young heard the reasons why he had not been chosen; still, Kimball said, "he just couldn't see why not." Young confided to Sterling Tucker, "I don't think they're ready for a black man to handle that much money."[25]

He found it difficult to shake his feeling of frustration. Margaret urged him to get away from New York for a while. She had done what she could to comfort him, but the nature of their relationship made it hard for her to do much more to raise his spirits. With her encouragement, however, Young traveled west with Bill Trent. The two friends spent the better part of a week at Winthrop Rockefeller's house in Palm Springs, California. Young kept talking about the Rockefeller presidency: What he had done wrong? Why had someone else been chosen? Trent asked him, "Where did you get the notion you were going to get it anyhow?" Trent wondered aloud why Young wanted the job. After all, as head of the Urban League, he had as many accomplishments, as much recognition and prestige, as a man could hope for. He remembered asking Young, "What more do you want?"[26]

With a major foundation out of the question, Young's intimates disagree over the direction he would have taken. A corporate post? Unlikely. Politics? Some say he had his eye on a Senate seat; others believe that he would eagerly have accepted a cabinet position—HEW, most likely, or perhaps HUD. He used to joke about his political prospects, but underneath friends discerned a serious intent. Finding the right job would not have been easy. Young was accustomed to being in charge, and he would have wanted a job big enough to fit his sense of his own importance. As he sometimes joked, "I'm the only head of the National Urban League; New York has *two* senators."[27]

There had not yet been much chance for black leaders to move beyond the racial arena to assume significant leadership positions on the broader national scene. Young was "uniquely situated to do that," Vernon Jordan said; he would have been able "to transform, to parlay all of his Urban League experiences of ten years into something bigger and better that would have impacted the nation and the world." But his trip to Africa in 1971 meant that the chance would never come.[28]

XV

Lagos

❧

In March 1971, Young went to Lagos, Nigeria, to participate in the African-American Dialogue. He should not have made the trip. He was overtired, and the trip would be exhausting. His doctor had urged him to slow down. He suffered from a chronic kidney condition, called glomerulonephritis, and he had a bad back; if he took better care of himself, there was no reason why he could not live out a normal life, but the pace he ordinarily kept was overdoing it. Moreover, Margaret had just come home after two weeks in Aurora, where her father had died on March 1. The ordeal—days of watching as he grew steadily weaker, ending, finally, with his burial on March 4—had left her emotionally and physically spent. She wanted Whitney at home with her, but he insisted on going to the dialogue. It seemed to her that he rarely had time for her needs. That was a well-established pattern in their lives, at least of late, but Margaret had never come to accept it; now, unusually vulnerable because of her father's death, she was especially resentful.

Lauren, worried about her mother, fearful of taking responsibility for her when she was in such a fragile emotional state, begged her father not to go. He said that the trip was important—"this was one he had to do." Lauren was so angry that she refused to say goodbye when he came into her room before he left for Kennedy Airport early on the morning of Saturday, March 6.[1]

Sponsored by the African-American Institute in New York, the dialogue brought together delegates from the United States and from Africa to talk about African-American relations in the 1970s. The American delegates included a U.S. senator, members of Congress, a former U.S. attorney general, civil rights leaders, and leaders from the media, business, and the professions. The African participants included a current and a former head of state, cabinet ministers, ambassadors, and a university president, among others. The meetings took place at the Nigerian Institute of International Affairs.[2]

Others among the American delegation had clear recollections of Young's participation in the conference. John Conyers, the black congressman from Detroit, described him as a major force in discussions about the connections between racism and poverty in an international context. Louis Stokes, the black congressman from Cleveland, thought especially of Young's intervention in the heated debate over whether, in the light of limited sensitivity to the problems of blacks in the United States, that country could adopt a proper foreign policy toward Africa. What struck Stokes was "the articulate way in which he was able to dispassionately approach the perspectives and views of the disparate groups and at the same time be able to make his own point."[3]

The black journalist, Ernest Dunbar, remembered Young as the artful mediator, the skillful communicator between blacks and whites. He recalled Young's intervention on behalf of Jesse Jackson. Jackson had not been among the people originally invited to the conference, but he had traveled to Ghana at his own initiative and had asked to be included. The conference secretariat had agreed, despite the fact that the Nigerian military government did not think well of him. At one session, Jackson unleashed a blistering indictment of white America in the blunt language of the ghetto. Young spoke up, not to refute what Jackson said but rather to explain it in more refined terms. Whereas Jackson raised the hackles of his white listeners, Young, conveying essentially the same message, could leave the conference room and go swimming or drinking with the very people he had indicted.[4]

The Africans respected Young because of the particular role he played in the civil rights movement. They knew that he could communicate directly with the leaders of the business community as well as the elected political leadership of the country, and they saw him as a likely person to carry their message about the importance of American aid to the future of Africa. Moreover, the Africans took to Young as a human being. Bayard Rustin remembered especially one morning when the formal session was a little late getting underway. Joking, he said to Young, "What will we do, dance or sing?" Young laughed, and they began to sing the old spiritual, "Sometimes I Feel Like A Motherless Child." The Africans loved it, so they sang three verses, to enthusiastic applause. It was all part of the spirit of the dialogue; "it was a kind of celebration of friendship," Rustin said, "and Whitney always seemed to be at the center of it."[5]

Young found the experience thoroughly exhilarating. To members of the conference staff, he spoke enthusiastically of what "Mother Africa" meant to him. "So much of what we have read or heard has been so distorted," he wrote to Margaret on March 9. "The strengths, beauty and positives have been ignored. . . . The Africans are young, intense, highly intelligent and beautifully articulate. . . . I am learning a lot." The next

day, he struck a similar note in a conversation with an American graduate
student who was in Lagos working on a doctoral dissertation. Relaxing in
an armchair, a cigarette in one hand, a glass of soda in another, he remarked on how much the conference had taught the black American delegates about African problems. "Now we can take the message back home
to the people."[6]

On Thursday, March 11, the fourth day of the conference, there was a
working session in the morning, but the afternoon—unlike the previous
days—was free of business. Young decided to skip the formal luncheon
and join a small group of conference participants and staff for a swim and
a picnic lunch. "We can talk about the world," he said, in mock justification, "but mostly we can talk about how happy we'll be not to be at that
reception." Swimming was one of Young's favorite forms of relaxation, and
the hot, humid Lagos climate made playing hooky all the more appealing.
Just the day before, Young had gone swimming with Edmund S. Muskie,
the U.S. senator from Maine. The chance for an outing on Thursday afternoon seemed irresistible. Afterward, he planned to meet Rustin, a knowledgeable collector of African art, and the two of them would go shopping
for some gifts for Margaret and his daughters. An official reception that
night, hosted by the military governor of Lagos State, would give Young
plenty of opportunity for socializing, so his absence at lunch would hardly
be noticed.[7]

Nigerians warned the Americans about the dangerous undertow at the
beach closest to their hotel, the elegant Federal Palace, overlooking
Lagos Lagoon. So instead, they set out in a U.S. Embassy outboard motor
launch for Lighthouse Beach, about twenty to twenty-five minutes across
the harbor. In addition to Young, the party included former U.S. attorney
general Ramsey Clark and his wife, Georgia; William W. Broom, Washington bureau chief for Ridder Publications, and his wife, Birdsall;
Thomas H. Wyman, vice president of the Polaroid Corporation; and two
interpreters for the conference, Monique de Gravelaine and Madeleine
Hurel, whom Young had invited to join the group. They arrived at the
island, disembarked at Tarqua Bay, and set out for Lighthouse Beach,
about ten minutes away.

The group put its picnic lunch, shirts, and towels under a palm-frond
beach shelter and went immediately into the ocean. Wyman recalled their
pleasure not only in being cool, but in their successful truancy. He said,
"Whitney called out at one point, 'I wonder what's going on at the reception.' " For all the beauty of the setting, the surf was more challenging
than they had anticipated. Ramsey Clark described the water as "fairly
rough and choppy." William Broom called it turbulent—"very little roll
and all chop"—and said that "the riptide pulled constantly at your legs like
a large elastic band so that you had to put out effort even when standing

in thigh-deep water." Clark added, "None of us were in water that was very deep or over our heads except when large waves rolled in. There was a fairly strong cross-current that seemed to divide about where we were swimming."

After ten or fifteen minutes, some of the swimmers started back to the beach, hungry for the sandwiches and beer they had brought with them from the hotel. The Brooms were the first out of the water; Wyman followed, then de Gravelaine. The last four in the water were Ramsey and Georgia Clark, and Young and Hurel, who had swum out the farthest, perhaps fifty yards from the beach. "This is great," Young called to Hurel. From the beach, the Brooms could see Young breast-stroking toward the shore.

As the Clarks made their way out of the ocean, Ramsey looked back: Whitney was nowhere in sight. Hurel turned and came toward them. "He is playing," she said, "playing dead." Clark looked once again and saw Young floating on his back in two feet of water, about thirty or forty feet from the shore. Twice Clark saw Young lift his arm, and then he turned over, facing down.

On the beach, the Brooms and Wyman had made their way to the shelter and dried themselves off. The three were talking when Broom pointed toward the water and said, "I don't see Whitney." Wyman ran quickly to the water's edge; he spotted Young just at the point when he lifted his arm out of the water. Reassured, he signaled to the Brooms that Young was all right. Within a few seconds, Wyman realized that he was mistaken, as he saw the Clarks run into the water and begin to pull Young into shore against the tide.

When they reached the beach, Clark and Wyman began a desperate effort to revive Young through mouth-to-mouth resuscitation. Broom went immediately to get some help. With two Nigerian lifeguards as guides, he headed for a nearby police post. But it was siesta hour, and he could find neither a policeman nor a telephone. Villagers said there was no doctor on the island. Broom ran about three hundred yards to the point where the boat was anchored and set out for the Federal Palace Hotel. Once there, he located the hotel's house physician, Dr. A. O. Senbanjo, who quickly prepared a medical kit. Broom had sent the embassy boat back to Lighthouse Beach to provide immediate transportation in case Young had been revived, so he and Senbanjo and his nurse returned to the island by charter.

The charter boat was an outboard, slower and smaller than the embassy launch. The tide was running against them, and the trip took much longer than it had before. To compound the problem, the boatman said that his craft was too fragile to go around the jetty to Tarqua Bay; over Broom's protest, he insisted on putting into a landing farther inland, on the lagoon side of the island. The result was to double or even triple the distance that had to be covered on foot.

The three hiked more than a half mile across blistering-hot sand. By the time they arrived, it was about 3:40 P.M., perhaps seventy to seventy-five minutes from the time Broom had first set out for help.

Dr. Senbanjo felt Young's pulse and listened for a heartbeat, and then announced that Young was "gone." Wyman insisted that the doctor try to revive him. Senbanjo and his nurse worked on Young, but nothing helped.

The party found an old, tattered stretcher, and with the help of some young men who had gathered earlier to watch the effort at resuscitation, they carried Young's body to the embassy launch at Tarqua Bay. The boat set out for the wharf closest to Lagos State General Hospital. En route, Senbanjo prepared a medical report; he said that he thought the cause of death was a heart attack, a tentative diagnosis that would be widely reported in the first accounts in the American press.[8]

While Clark and Wyman accompanied the body from the wharf to the morgue at the hospital, Broom went to the embassy to report the accident and get help in informing Margaret and in making the necessary local arrangements. Clark and Wyman met him there later and arranged for a mortuary to handle preparation of the body. Clark asked the embassy doctor, W. Foster Montgomery, an American surgeon serving as regional health officer for the U.S. Department of State, to attend the autopsy the next morning. Montgomery said that he would see to it that the autopsy was performed by a respected forensic pathologist, Dr. A. O. Laja, head internist at the hospital.[9]

The men then returned to the Federal Palace Hotel, where they began the process of notifying the delegates to the conference of the tragedy. Ernest Dunbar was sitting on the terrace. He remembered vividly how "an ashen Ramsey Clark, still in bathing trunks and with a towel around his neck, rushed up the steps and announced: 'Whitney is dead.' " John Lewis said, "We were stunned, literally shocked"; the news left him feeling terribly alone and very far from home. *Newsweek* editor-in-chief Osborn Elliott went to break the news to Rustin; "Bayard just sat there in his hotel room, overcome with grief."[10]

That evening, the black Americans attending the conference gathered in Clark's room at the Federal Palace. Jesse Jackson was the first to arrive. "I can't believe it," he said. "My insides are crawling with grief." He and Clark embraced. The others came, and Clark and Wyman recounted in detail what had happened that afternoon. The men discussed arrangements for a memorial service in Lagos, as well as plans for the trip back to the United States. As the meeting began to break up, Jackson asked the group to stand in a circle. They crossed arms and clasped each other's hands as Jackson offered a prayer. "It was a prayer of healing and comfort to us," one of the men told Broom later, "and when it was over, none of us thought to drop the other's hand. We just stood there in silence holding on to each other."

Later, the men met with the press in a conference room downstairs. Clark spoke briefly about the tragic events of the afternoon, and Conyers, speaking on behalf of the delegates, described Young's contributions to justice.[11]

The embassy cabled the State Department to report the tragedy and asked for help in notifying Margaret Young. Barbara Watson, a good friend who was the administrator of the department's Bureau of Security and Consular Affairs, reached her by phone at midday. The call woke Margaret; still exhausted from the ordeal of her father's death, she had been napping on the sofa. She refused to believe what Watson told her. Angrily, she hung up on her. Shortly afterward, the White House called and asked Margaret to stand by for the president. Again she was absolutely unwilling to acknowledge what had happened.

Ersa Poston, Margaret's college roommate and a trustee of the National Urban League, was having her hair done at a beauty parlor in Albany when she heard the news on the radio. Watson reached her there and asked how to get some close friends to the Youngs' house as quickly as possible. Poston told her to try Harvey Russell and Bill Trent, and that she would get there as fast as she could.

Russell was in his office at Pepsico in Purchase, New York. As vice-chairman of the African-American Institute, he should have been in Lagos attending the dialogue, but at the last minute something had come up at work, and he had been unable to go. A friend phoned to say that one of the wire services was carrying a report that Young had died. Russell called the National Urban League but was unable to get any information. Then he called Margaret and left immediately for New Rochelle.

By now people had begun to come to the house on Oxford Road, and Margaret was no longer able to avoid facing the reality that Whitney was dead. She called New Rochelle High School to ask that someone bring Lauren home. Lauren's guidance counselor found her, by chance, in the hall. She had decided to skip class, and she was on her way outside to meet her boyfriend. The counselor insisted that she come to the office with him and demanded that she turn over her car keys to guard against the possibility that she might hear the news on the car radio. "For cutting class you're taking my car keys?" she exclaimed. Oblivious to what was going on, Lauren kept telling her counselor that he was overreacting—surely cutting class was not that big a deal. Finally he got her to settle down and told her that her mother had called and needed to see her, and that he was going to take her home. It was "like a comedy of errors," Lauren reflected, years later. He was trying to explain, she was laughing and carrying on, "not giving him a chance."[12]

Francis Kornegay, the longtime executive of the Detroit Urban League, was meeting with his board when a secretary came to interrupt the meeting. "Something terrible must have happened," Kornegay thought to himself. The Indianapolis executive, Sam Jones, had just come home from work when a news bulletin flashed over the air. "I just stood there and cried like a baby." In New York, James D. Williams, just three months into his job as director of public relations at the National Urban League, was summoned from a meeting by a shaken secretary, who reported that Harold Sims had just gotten a call from the State Department. Williams's staff began the arduous task of putting together packets of information to send to the press and the local affiliates. After hours, staff members from other departments came to help prepare mailings and answer phones. They worked almost around the clock; one staff member remembered a chauffeured limousine, lent by McGeorge Bundy, taking her home to Bedford Stuyvesant in the early hours of the morning. Amid all the activity, what she recalled most vividly was the silence, "absolute silence"—"it was like somebody had dropped the atomic bomb on the Urban League."[13]

In Washington, the White House ordered an air force jet to Nigeria. When he learned about Young's death, Brigadier General Daniel ("Chappie") James, Jr., the highest-ranking black man in the air force who was serving as deputy assistant secretary of defense for public affairs, broke down in tears in his office at the Pentagon. James went to Secretary of Defense Melvin Laird and volunteered to fly Young's body home. When the plane left Andrews Air Force Base for the eleven-hour, six thousand-mile flight to Lagos, in the cockpit, along with James, were three southern white pilots and a black navigator.[14]

In Lagos, Young's death touched both officials and ordinary citizens. John Lewis remembered people walking up to him on the street and saying, "We're sorry about Brother Young. We're sorry about the American." On Saturday afternoon, a memorial service for Young drew three hundred mourners to the Anglican Christ Church Cathedral. The first speakers were Africans: Okoi Arikpo, the Nigerian commissioner for external affairs, and Emile-Derlin Zinsou, the former president of Dahomey. William Clyde Truehart, the U.S. ambassador to Nigeria, read a statement from President Nixon. Ramsey Clark described Young as a "giant, laughing man" who combined "steel and velvet" as he "strove mightily all the days of his life to heal the divisions of inequality and injustice." John Lewis paid homage to "a brave, courageous warrior for freedom, justice, and the realization of human dignity" who had the ability to move white men "on Wall Street in New York City" and black men "on no street in Jackson, Mississippi."

Next John Conyers spoke on behalf of American political leaders. Then Bayard Rustin told the mourners of the thousands of times he had called Young to ask for help for individual blacks who needed shelter, or decent clothing, or scholarships to go to school. "Never once did he say no." Cutting his remarks short, Rustin closed his eyes, threw back his head, and broke into the haunting strains of the old slave spiritual, "Death Ain't Nothing But a Robber." One of the mourners later captured the scene for Margaret: "Tears streaming down his cheeks," Rustin "sang his heart out for his friend."

Now Tom Wyman rose on behalf of the American business community. Of all the black leaders, he said, Young had "assumed the special responsibility for opening the eyes of the business world to the crying needs of his people." As Wyman put it, "He built a thousand bridges over the canyons of racism in his special pursuit of equality for all men."

Next Charles J. Hamilton, the young Urban League trustee, spoke for the league, making plain all the while the depth of his feelings for the man he had come to love and respect as a son would a father.

Finally, Jesse Jackson, gowned in white vestments, delivered the principal eulogy. Just days before, at the dialogue, Young had described Jackson as his spiritual leader; now the young minister returned the compliment, speaking of his "frank and open admiration" for a man he called "a father figure in the civil rights movement." Finally, led by Jackson, Africans and Americans joined hands to sing the anthem of the civil rights movement, "We Shall Overcome."[15]

Following the service, a number of the Americans went by boat with Young's older sister, Arnita Boswell, to Lighthouse Beach. There Jackson revealed that the autopsy performed the day before had shown that Young had suffered a subarachnoid hemorrhage. He said that Young had taken in a quantity of water and that his heart was enlarged, a sign of high blood pressure, often a contributing factor in a brain hemorrhage. The National Urban League later issued a statement explaining that subarachnoid hemorrhage meant a break in the blood vessels in a blood-and-fluid filled space around the brain, which resulted in loss of consciousness. It said that the hemorrhage could have been caused by the rough surf, by tumbling in the heavy water, or by hitting solid debris.[16]

Early Sunday morning, the jet bearing Young's flag-draped coffin took off from Lagos. On board were Boswell and the Urban Leaguers who had made the trip from the United States, as well as a number of the Americans who had been attending the dialogue. The plane stopped in Dakar, Senegal, to pick up Young's daughter, Marcia, who was living in Morocco with her husband, Robert Boles, a Fulbright scholar, and their ten-month-old son, Mark. Then it proceeded to New York, where it landed at Kennedy Airport late Sunday afternoon. Mayor John V. Lindsay was waiting at the airport, along with some two hundred other dignitaries, colleagues, and friends of Young's. Later, addressing a predominantly black student audience at San Francisco State College, Stokely Carmichael would draw laughter and applause when he sneered, "Some (blacks) love the slavemaster so much that even when they die in Africa they have their body shipped here."[17]

Young's body was taken immediately to the Unity Funeral Home in Harlem, and from there to the mortuary of the Office of the Chief Medical Examiner of New York City. The circumstances of his death seemed sufficiently ambiguous to warrant a second autopsy. The death certificate registered in Lagos said that death had occurred from subarachnoid hemorrhage, without any mention of the fact that Young had been swimming at Lighthouse Beach. There would be an advantage to a finding of death by drowning, since Young's life insurance policy provided for double indemnity in case of accidental death. Alexander D. Forger, a partner in Milbank, Tweed, Hadley & McCloy and the Young family lawyer, asked the chief medical examiner, Milton Helpern, to conduct another autopsy. Assisted by Deputy Chief Medical Examiner Michael M. Baden, Helpern did so at the city morgue at Bellevue Hospital on the evening of March 14.[18]

Helpern's findings, made public a month later, disputed Laja's ruling of death by hemorrhage. Helpern saw no evidence that Young had suffered a blow to the head. He found no subarachnoid hemorrhage, or any hemorrhage anywhere in the brain. There was a very slight amount of blood in the furrows of the brain surface on the right side, but it seemed to him more reasonable to attribute the appearance of the brain's surface to the effect of the vigorous attempts at resuscitation than to subarachnoid hemorrhage. Helpern found only slight evidence of atherosclerosis and discerned no damage to any other organ. The appearance of the lungs was consistent with inhalation of water. In light of the story of Young's death, which he had heard from Ramsey Clark, Helpern concluded that he must have drowned. Death from drowning could occur very rapidly; it did not require the inhalation of large amounts of water. "In view of the circumstances and the absence of any other competing cause of death and any other significant disease or traumatic injury . . . that would unequivocally explain the disability and fatal submersion of the deceased," Helpern summed up, "one is compelled to the conclusion that the death resulted from submersion while the deceased was swimming in a fairly strong ocean surf for reasons which are not demonstrable. Such cases of drowning in persons who can swim are not unusual and the circumstances and the post mortem findings do not always provide the explanation of why the victim loses control of the situation even though he can swim."[19]

The contradictions between the Laja and Helpern accounts, together with the circumstances surrounding the Helpern autopsy, leave a measure of ambiguity about how Whitney Young actually died. Given the relatively recent assassinations of Malcolm X and Martin Luther King, it would have been surprising had there not been some speculation about the possibility of foul play. Young himself had been one of the targets of a highly publicized assassination plot on the part of a small group of black terrorists, known as the Revolutionary Action Movement (RAM), in 1967.[20] The next year, in the wake of the King assassination, the National Urban League began to look into security precautions in order to protect the executive director. The agency took out a double-indemnity insurance policy on Young's life, and, whenever he traveled, it generally arranged through local police departments to have two plainclothesmen meet him at the plane, accompany him to his hotel, attend any gathering in which he participated, and see to it that he returned safely to the airport. In New York, beginning in the summer of 1969, the league employed a staff assistant for security to act as Young's chauffeur and bodyguard.[21]

In Lagos, however, there had been no special security. There were rumors and questions about the possibility of foul play. Had Young become too effective, too powerful? Was it in the interest of the establishment to have him taken care of? Might black radicals in the United States have wanted him killed? Black Africans? The American government? For all the talk at the time, with the exception of an article in *Jet* in April, none of the speculation ever found its way into print. To all intents and purposes, the publication of the Helpern findings seemed to settle the matter in the public mind. Since those findings were consistent with the interests of the Young family, no further effort was made to clarify apparent uncertainties and contradictions.[22]

On Monday, March 15, the Helpern autopsy having been completed, Young's body was returned to the funeral home and made ready to lie in state at Riverside Church. Teams of executive directors of Urban League affiliates took turns standing as sentries around the casket. The doors of the stately church were opened to the public at noon on Monday; by the time they were closed early Tuesday morning to prepare for the funeral, some eighteen thousand mourners had come to pay their respects. They were black and white, people of all ages and economic stations; the largest number, however, appeared to be "mainstream Blacks." A reporter for *Jet* described them as middle-income adults whose average age was forty, men and women "who still believe that they can make it in the system." A reporter for the *Atlanta Journal* interviewed two of the younger men waiting in the long line. A twenty-nine-year-old Bronx resident commented, "Young found jobs for blacks. He wanted people to know what it is to go out and earn your own money rather than go on welfare." A nineteen-year-old Columbia University student said, "Young was a man working for change through the system. He was a quiet man." Fittingly, the

crowd, too, was quiet, subdued, and orderly. "One noticed immediately,"
the *Jet* reporter commented, "that there was a lack of the intense, all-
enveloping emotionalism which characterized the funerals of Malcolm X
and Martin Luther King." That was not surprising; "in life Whitney Young
just didn't arouse such feelings, pro or con."[23]

The funeral service brought together the many complicated strands of
Young's personal and professional life. The honorary pallbearers represented the full range of his associations. From the spectrum of black leadership came Roy Wilkins, executive director of the NAACP, Vernon E. Jordan, Jr., executive director of the United Negro College Fund, George
Wiley, executive director of the National Welfare Rights Association, and
Imamu Amiri Baraka, of the Committee for Unified Newark; from the top
echelons of business came James A. Linen, chairman of the executive
committee of Time Inc. and Joseph F. Cullman III, chairman of the board
of Philip Morris, Inc. The major foundations were represented by J.
George Harrar, president of the Rockefeller Foundation, and McGeorge
Bundy, president of the Ford Foundation; from the Urban League, in
addition to Linen, past board presidents Theodore W. Kheel and Lindsley
F. Kimball were among the pallbearers, along with the acting executive
director, Harold R. Sims. Ramsey Clark was also an honorary pallbearer,
as were three old friends—Carl T. Rowan, Harvey C. Russell, and William J. Trent, Jr.—and a black high school student from New Rochelle,
Eric H. Vinson, who had been a great admirer of Young's. An estimated
forty-five hundred mourners filled the church—Urban League staff and
volunteers, civil rights leaders, community activists, heads of federal
agencies, elected officials, and representatives of industry, large foundations, and voluntary agencies. "I studied the faces of the many people in
the vast congregation," said Howard Thurman, dean emeritus of Marsh
Chapel at Boston University, who delivered one of the eulogies. "I could
think of no other occasion which, by choice, would bring together the very
rich and the poor, the black separatist and the white segregationist, those
who had abandoned all hope for the internal reordering of society on the
basis of equality of opportunity and privilege, and those who were dedicated to an orderly reshuffling of priorities which would give maximum
participation to all in the fruits of a good society."[24]

The service began with the String Quartet from Dvorak's *New World
Symphony*. The Rev. Ernest T. Campbell, minister of Riverside Church,
delivered the invocation and read the scripture selection and prayer.
There were two solos by the great soprano Leontyne Price—"Climb
Every Mountain" from *The Sound of Music*, and the familiar spiritual,
"Well Done"—and the congregation sang the hymn "Oh God Our Help in
Ages Past." Three men with close associations to Young delivered eulo-
gies: Benjamin E. Mays, president emeritus of Morehouse College; Thur-

man; and Peter H. Samsom, pastor of the Community Unitarian Church of White Plains, where the Youngs worshiped. Years before, Young had said to Thurman that if anything happened to him, he wanted Thurman to take part in his funeral service. Thurman, almost old enough to be Young's father, had brushed Young's comment aside. "Oh, that will never happen," he told him.[25]

The common theme of the eulogies was Young's role as conciliator and bridge-builder. Campbell established it in his opening prayer: "How blessed are the peacemakers—God shall call them His sons." Mays said, "Whitney Young believed that blacks and whites cannot elude each other and that we must live together and work together." Thurman spoke about Young's twofold commitment: on the one hand, he dedicated himself to the "overwhelming task of feeling his way into the grain in the wood of the dominant white man and to rationalize the insight into a technique of understanding and negotiation"; on the other, he identified "with the plight of the poor," seeking to bring them "into direct contact with resources of the very rich, thereby creating a community of common sharing, mutual dependence and effective economic participation." Young was "a bridge between," Thurman said; "he was not a beggar."

Samsom, the last of the speakers, recalled that Young had "often said, 'There are always ways not to do what you don't want to do. . . . A nation that can send men to walk on the moon can eliminate its ghettos, if it wants to'—and he tried to make us want to enough." Young, he said, "went quietly and steadily about his unromantic task of opening doors between people in the great house of mankind. . . . Separation was the evil he strove in all his ways to overcome," Samsom said: "Peacefully, persistently, he prodded us and the corporations and the government toward the better way of building bridges between people, who together with each other and with the rich resources of this gifted land, must tackle the enormous problems that none of us can hope to meet alone, let alone solve."[26]

The mourners filed out onto Riverside Drive as the organist played one of Young's favorite songs, "The Impossible Dream" from *Man of La Mancha*. He had long carried the words on a piece of paper that he kept in his wallet, and he often quoted them in his speeches. Now the familiar music echoed hauntingly through the church. Outside, a crowd of fifteen hundred had gathered—some, doubtless, out of curiosity, many drawn there to pay their respects to Young.[27]

The funeral procession formed outside the church. Young would be buried in Lexington, Kentucky, beside his mother. On the way to La Guardia Airport, the motorcade made its way along Broadway; then it traveled the full length of 125th Street, in the center of Harlem. Thousands of people lined the streets and sidewalks or leaned out of apartment windows; as the cortege passed by, some of them gave the clenched-fist salute. Some Harlem schools had closed to honor Young's memory, and children as well as adults clustered on the street in the bright sunshine. Groups of school children sang "The Battle Hymn of the Republic." Here and there there were hand-lettered signs: "Whitney Young, A Great Civil Rights Leader," one of them said. A tone of reverence hushed the normally lively neighborhood; the loudspeakers that usually brought rock tunes from the music shops into the main streets of Harlem now played hymns and spirituals.[28]

The demonstration of affection and respect was particularly striking in light of the persistent allegation that Young was out of touch with the common people. The role that he played in the civil rights movement deprived him of popular adulation during his lifetime. What he did best, he accomplished quietly. In an age of dramatic gestures and strident voices, his deeds and his message were usually overshadowed. While he was alive, popular convention made it unfashionable for blacks to applaud his role. Still, the throngs of people who lined 125th Street gave a clear sense of Young's impact on those for whom he strove to speak.

A party of one hundred league staff, board members, and friends went to Kentucky with the Young family for the interment service. When they arrived at the airport in Louisville, Young's body was taken to the A. D. Porter & Sons Funeral Home, where a public viewing was set for late Tuesday afternoon. Members of Psi Boule and Alpha Phi Alpha fraternities and the executive directors of the Louisville and Lexington Urban Leagues alternated as honor guards. People had begun lining up on West Chestnut Street as early as 3:30 P.M. It was a cold, damp afternoon, but the crowd of mourners waited patiently until the doors to the funeral home opened at 5:30. By the time the viewing ended three hours later, some five thousand people had filed past the open, steel gray casket.

The next morning, a motorcade of three hundred cars, escorted by city and county police, left the funeral home for the seventy-five-mile trip to Lexington. Across the street, students from the sixth, seventh, and eighth grades at Pope Paul and John Catholic School assembled to watch the procession. Some of them held up signs: "Though gone he is, he shall reign on, right on. We need more Whitney Youngs"; "A man who gives me hope. Thanks, Whitney." Along Chestnut Street between Thirteenth and Eleventh streets, students from two nearby elementary schools and Central High School stood quietly watching the motorcade.

The procession left the city and headed east on U.S. 60. It passed Lincoln Ridge, slowing briefly in front of the Lincoln Institute campus, where a good-sized crowd had assembled. Then it moved on to Frankfort, where it circled through the campus of Kentucky State University, past large groups of students, as the university band played the alma mater. From there the cortege drove on to Lexington. As it approached Greenwood Cemetery, the streets were lined with onlookers; a few businesses and homes displayed memorial wreaths in their windows, some of them accompanied by Young's picture.

Greenwood Cemetery had been founded in the first decade of the twentieth century. Segregated, like virtually all such facilities in the South, it had separate sections for whites and blacks. Even in the 1970s, when civil rights legislation had made such separation a thing of the past, a sturdy wire fence divided the two halves of the cemetery. In the years since desegregation, a few blacks had been buried on what used to be the all-white side, but no whites had been buried in the all-black section. As CBS newsman Dan Rather reported during his coverage of Young's burial service, "the private group that owns the cemetery says that they simply had no applications . . . for white funerals on this side of the fence. A waitress at a local coffee shop said this morning that Greenwood Cemetery and the segregated overtones that remain here are, as she described it, 'one of our old scars.' "

The cemetery was located in a low-income black neighborhood on the north side of the city. It was poorly tended, overgrown with weeds and littered with debris. The decision to bury Young there in the family plot spurred a massive cleanup effort. Not only would the condition of the cemetery be distressing to the Young family, but the service would have a great many dignitaries in attendance, and the eulogy would be delivered by the president of the United States. Then too, the burial would be widely covered on television as well as in the newspapers. A city crew of fifty workers spent three days hauling away debris, and a group of volunteers, white as well as black, pitched in to prune the trees and clean away the underbrush. Similar pains had been taken by city officials to spruce up the route that the funeral procession would follow on its way to the cemetery, prompting one group of onlookers to display a large banner made out of a bedsheet. "It took a great man to die before we got our street clean," the banner read. "Mr. Nixon, what will it take to get a sewer line?"

Flecks of snow had been falling throughout Wednesday morning, but the slowly rising temperature had kept the ground clear. Shortly after noon, with the temperature up to forty-two degrees, the sun broke through the clouds, warming the raw, chilly day. More than an hour before the service was set to begin, a crowd of three thousand, most of them black, had gathered at the cemetery. Most of the onlookers were there to pay tribute to Young, but some had come out of curiosity. "I just came to see what was going on," an older man acknowledged to a reporter. "I heard there was gonna be big doings." Doubtless others shared the motivation of the high school student who said he "came to see the Prez."

Shortly before the service began, a loudspeaker played recordings of some of Young's speeches, bringing a hush to the crowd. The cortege moved toward the grave site, beneath a large oak tree. Pallbearers carried the casket, covered with a wreath dotted by red roses and white carnations, to its place beside the freshly dug grave. Ushers from the local Urban League, wearing black armbands emblazoned with the league's equal sign, showed the mourners to their seats. The Young family sat on one side of the grave, friends and dignitaries on the other. Then the presidential party arrived at the cemetery. Nixon placed a wreath at one end of the casket and took his seat beside Margaret Young. The crowd of onlookers, now numbering close to five thousand, pressed in around the grave site.[29]

The White House had originally suggested that the president attend the funeral in New York, but the strength of anti-Nixon feeling at that time had led Harvey Russell, who was coordinating the funeral arrangements along with Ersa Poston and Bill Trent, to suggest that he come to Kentucky instead. Even so, having the president deliver the eulogy in Kentucky was a complicated matter. However genuine Nixon's desire to pay tribute to Young, there was no denying his political motive: honoring Young might improve the president's credibility with blacks. That put Margaret in a difficult position. If she accepted the tribute, she could not escape the related implication of identification with Nixon's policies. Whatever her personal preferences, she refused to put herself in the position of saying no to the president. After the burial service, a widely circulated photograph showing Margaret leaning close to Nixon carried the caption: "Mrs. Young embracing the President after the service." What she had actually been doing was whispering to Nixon that she expected him to live up to the commitments he had made to Young in the December meeting with the cabinet. Still, the public impression would be shaped by the press's interpretation of what the photograph portrayed.[30]

Nixon's eulogy formed the centerpiece of the brief grave-side ceremony. "Whitney Young's genius," he said, lay in knowing "how to accomplish what other people were merely for." Nixon said that Young was neither patient nor moderate, but that he understood the uses of patience and moderation in achieving his goals. "Whitney Young's message," Nixon concluded,

was this: "What can I do? What can I do to make this a better country? What can I do through helping others, through recognizing their equality, their dignity, their individuality, to realize the American dream?"

His dream, if I may paraphrase, was one nation, under God, indivisible, with liberty and justice and opportunity for all. To fulfill his dream is the responsibility of each of us. It is a commitment that each of us makes in his heart on this day.[31]

Following the reading from scripture and the offering of prayers, a black bugler from the Thirteenth Army Band at Fort Knox blew taps, and Whitney Young was laid to rest in his native Kentucky.[32]

When Margaret returned to New Rochelle, she found a letter from Whitney, written from the Federal Palace Hotel. It was postmarked March 11, the day he had gone swimming at Lighthouse Beach. "Dearest Margaret," it read. "The only negative thing so far about this trip is your not being with me and the heat. The latter I can adjust to, the former I cannot. I really look forward more and more to our visits together to these kinds of new, different and historic places and people." He knew that the trip to Lagos had been ill-timed, and he tried to make amends. "I hope you are making gains in recovery from the terrible strain and ordeal of your father's passing. I worried so much about you. Have done some thinking and am going to try much harder to be more considerate. This I know I can and must do. No one deserves it more than you. My travel I can't help but so much, but maybe you can go more with me. I love you dearly."[33]

Epilogue

WHITNEY YOUNG spent his life making the needs and interests of black Americans comprehensible and compelling to the whites who had the power to do something about them. Consummate politician, salesman, and interpreter, he goaded and challenged the white establishment to redress the effects of segregation, discrimination, and poverty. In the process, he bridged the gulf between the ghetto and the power structure in ways that no other black man of his generation was able to duplicate.

That was Young's special role in the civil rights movement, and it required that he execute a delicate balancing act. The blacks who knew him best thought that he did it well. In Bayard Rustin's words, Young had a "unique talent for dealing with the white power structure without losing touch with the grass-roots movements in the black community." Carl Stokes reflected that "he managed to be militant, but not to the point of identification with the militants that would jeopardize his relations with white corporate America. . . . That takes a skill that there haven't been many around to do."[1]

The balancing act can be construed in different ways. One way is to suggest that Young was equally at home in a bar in the ghetto and in a corporate boardroom, a common theme among many of his friends. As an unnamed black journalist put it, "He was urbane enough to talk with the fat cats downtown and hip enough to talk with the tough cats uptown and he never seemed out of place doing either."[2]

That interpretation, however, overstates the case for Young's identification with the ghetto. Plainly, he spent most of his time with "the fat cats downtown." He clearly had the ability to deal with "the tough cats uptown," but he did much less of it. The corporate boardroom, not the ghetto bar, was his typical milieu. The more prominent Young became, the more walking the streets of the ghetto lost its place in his regular routine. It was not that he lacked sympathy for ordinary blacks, or that his sensitivity to their plight diminished. But daily immersion in the ways of the ghetto was just not part of his life.

More to the point in understanding the balancing act that Young managed is to emphasize his role as a builder of bridges between two quite different worlds. That was the way contemporaries understood him, across the spectrum of race and ideology. *Newsday* labeled him "the Negro ambassador." Roy Wilkins described him as "a salesman for Negro rights" who "spread his wares and made his persuasive arguments" before "the mighty men of his country." Imamu Amiri Baraka said that Young "unified all forces"; Floyd McKissick called him "one of those rare individuals who could communicate on almost all levels." Most expressive of all was the simple formulation of the *Los Angeles Times*: "So Whitney Young Jr. tried to build bridges. That was what he was all about."[3]

Ironically, the role that Young played so effectively made it inevitable that he would be undervalued during his lifetime. He never scored high in national measures of black opinion. When pollsters asked about blacks' views of civil rights organizations and leaders, Young and the National Urban League typically came up with middling ratings. In a 1965 Harris poll, for example, Martin Luther King had a 94 percent approval rating, the NAACP got 90 percent, CORE received 70 percent, and the National Urban League was approved by only 60 percent of those polled. In 1970, when Harris asked blacks whom they respected, 93 percent said they had "a great deal" or "some" respect for the NAACP. The same questions brought a positive response from 91 percent for SCLC, 79 percent for Roy Wilkins, 78 percent for the National Urban League, and 68 percent for Young.[4]

What Young did best, he accomplished quietly. In an age of dramatic gestures and strident voices, his deeds and his message were usually overshadowed. At a time when the masses of blacks measured blackness by time spent on picket lines and by intensity of antiwhite rhetoric, he was bound to fall short. By associating with people who were not part of the struggle, he aroused skepticism or disdain. The very nature of the role he had carved out for himself meant that he would be mistrusted among his own people.

Could it have been otherwise? Some of Young's staunchest admirers believe that if he had only worked harder at communicating with ordinary blacks, they would have recognized how much he had done to make things better for them, how deeply he cared, what he really stood for. But Young could not have explained convincingly the importance of what he did in boardrooms to blacks who had only minimal understanding of the nature of power in corporate America. He could not have publicized his private conversations with business and political leaders and still have expected those leaders to heed his message the next time he came to call. The perceptual gap between him and the people in the streets was built into the very nature of his role. The more effective he was as bridge and interpreter, the more likely he was to be misunderstood. As Andrew Young put it, "The more that white folk trust and respect a black leader, the greater the suspicion in the black community. It was inconceivable to alienated blacks that Whitney Young could deal with the big business establishment or government without 'selling out.' From their bitter perspective, 'if you were telling it like it is, you wouldn't be tolerated long.' "[5]

Young accepted the reality that popularity would not be his lot. "The test of what makes a Negro leader," he insisted, "is not who shouts the loudest or gets the angriest but who *gets the most results*." He knew that he could "play up to the despair and the anger among black people, and probably go up in the polls," but that struck him as "a cheap shot." He told an interviewer toward the end of his life, "I resist the temptation for momentary popularity for the long haul. I leave to history and to my own conscience to know whether I've been effective."[6]

Young was the civil rights leader who walked the thinnest of edges between two disparate constituencies, the man in the middle who belonged fully to neither camp. "Bridge builders are, by the nature of their work, neither on one side or the other," the black journalist William Raspberry wrote when Young died. "And Whitney Young could never be either a member of the 'power structure' or a true-blue 'soul brother.' It was a sacrifice he knowingly and willingly undertook because he believed it had to be done." Young chose the role deliberately. "Someone," he often explained, "has to work within the system to try and change it," and that someone was Whitney Young.[7]

But working within the system carried genuine personal costs. Kenneth Clark, a longtime friend, said that the role Young played in the movement "was one of the most difficult roles a man could have chosen. He was sniped at from all sides, but he realized the importance of maintaining bridges of understanding, no matter how difficult." Carl Holman of the National Urban Coalition, who had been one of Young's colleagues in Atlanta, said that "he spent much of his adult life crossing fire zones between armed camps, and he could not have enjoyed being caught as he often was in the crossfire. But he continued to do it, and in large and small ways it paid off."[8]

As the preceding chapters have suggested, that payoff expressed itself in a number of ways. Through jobs and training programs, Young enlarged the economic opportunities available to black Americans. He gave powerful whites in the private sector a means of comprehending the problems of the ghetto and, in the most successful instances, making some contribution toward their amelioration. He threw his weight behind public policies to combat discrimination and poverty. He encouraged communication and understanding across racial lines at a time when turmoil and misunderstanding were driving whites and blacks apart.

Still, for every powerful white whose eyes Young opened, there were others whose social consciences lay dormant. For every corporation or professional association whose employment practices and social policies Young affected, there were others that took refuge in tokenism and inaction. Despite his best efforts at influencing public policy, there were too few effective federal efforts to wipe out racism and poverty. No one black leader, no matter how skillful an interpreter, no matter how strong a bridge, could dramatically change the face of American race relations.

But Young made a significant dent. He excelled as a mediator at a time when mediators were in short supply. He understood power, and he knew what it took to accomplish social change. When others set change in motion by marching in the streets, in Chuck Stone's words, "he helped to guide it and orchestrate it, . . . to give it direction, shape, and a certain stability." In a time of intense passion and upheaval, he was a steady source of reason and calm. As a young neighbor put it at the time of his death, "He was one of the very, very few strong and just and clearsighted men who put his arms around our country and held it together, to heal it, so that it would not explode."[9]

And despite the feelings in some quarters that Young did not measure up on a scale of militancy, he showed whites and blacks a range of possibilities for equal opportunity and racial justice that they might not otherwise have come to see. That was true of the leaders with whom he spent so much of his time, but it was also true of others, young as well as old, who were inspired by his vision and his example. A woman from Little Rock, who described herself as a "typical 'white liberal do-gooder,' " said that Young was "the one person who could help me . . . begin to understand some of our deepest problems and what part I might play in their solution." A young man who was a friend and contemporary of Young's daughter, Marcia, put it this way:

He represented to us . . . much more than a dedicated fighter for justice, much more than mere commitment to a vital cause. . . . Whitney Young was an exemplar of an ideal that existed nowhere else in my world. He was articulate, unafraid, and strong in his faith in a cause and the people who would pursue that cause. . . . I admired and respected him, for that strength and faith, and felt from him and learned from him that I too could pursue that just cause that he strove for. In this way I feel that he was almost a father to me, that he fathered something in me, something which my own parents could not have kindled, something which is both a goal and a method for achieving that goal, something he left to many, many people.

Or, in the words of a black high school student in Lansing, Michigan, "Whitney Young started out a brother and died a brother. He was one cat that could run with rich white people and still look out for us."[10]

Whitney Young liked to think of himself as "a voice for the voiceless, a hope for the hopeless." Certainly he succeeded in bringing the voiceless and the hopeless to the attention of the power structure, in representing their needs in the most intelligible, effective ways that he could imagine. A builder of bridges between blacks and whites, he did what he could to change attitudes and practices, promote communication and understanding, and contribute to the goal of a fairer, more egalitarian society.[11]

Abbreviations

❦

AUC	Division of Special Collections/Archives, Robert W. Woodruff Library, Atlanta University Center
Barnes/MBY interview	Transcript, Betty Barnes interview with Margaret Buckner Young, courtesy of Margaret B. Young
Ford	Ford Foundation Archives
GEB	General Education Board Papers, Rockefeller Archive Center
KSU	Special Collections, Blazer Library, Kentucky State University
MBY	Margaret B. Young
MLK	Martin Luther King, Jr., Papers, Library and Archives, Martin Luther King, Jr., Center for Nonviolent Social Change, Atlanta
MSRC	Moorland-Spingarn Research Center, Howard University
NUL	National Urban League
NUL, followed by part, series, and box number	National Urban League Papers, Manuscript Division, Library of Congress
Parris	Guichard Auguste Bolivar Parris Papers, Manuscript Division, Library of Congress
SCRBC	Schomburg Center for Research in Black Culture
WMY	Whitney M. Young, Jr.
WMY, followed by box number	Whitney M. Young, Jr., Papers, Rare Book and Manuscript Library, Columbia University
WMY interview, RJBOHC	Tape, Whitney M. Young, Jr., interview, May 6, 1970, Ralph J. Bunche Oral History Collection, Moorland-Spingarn Research Center, Howard University
WMY Sr.	Whitney M. Young, Sr.
WMY Sr., followed by box number	Whitney M. Young, Sr., Papers, Blazer Library, Kentucky State University

Notes

PREFACE

1. *Louisville Courier-Journal*, Mar. 12, 1971, NUL new series.
2. Jackson quoted in *Duluth News Tribune* (Minn.), Mar. 14, 1971, NUL new series.
3. Quoted in *Atlanta Constitution*, Mar. 18, 1971, WMY biographical file, AUC.

PROLOGUE

1. Bernhard M. Auer, "A Letter from the Publisher," *Time*, Nov. 11, 1966, WMY 7.
2. *New York Times*, Jan. 8, 1967, p. 54.
3. "Report from East Europe," "To Be Equal" column no. 46, Nov. 16, 1966, and Special Notes, Personalities on *Time-News* Tour, Oct. 20–Nov. 1, 1966, WMY 7; handwritten notes in Briefing Book, Time News Tour, WMY 2b; Heiskell interview.
4. *New York Times*, Jan. 8, 1967, p. 54; Irwin Ross, "The Black Power of Whitney Young," *Reader's Digest* 94 (Jan. 1969): 117.
5. Leonard Lyons, "The Lyons Den," *New Orleans Times-Picayune*, Nov. 11, 1966, WMY 223; Baird interview no. 1; Henry Ford to WMY, n.d. [Dec. 21, 1966], NUL new series.

CHAPTER I

1. Quoted in Richard Bruner, *Whitney M. Young, Jr.: The Story of a Pragmatic Humanist* (New York, 1972), pp. 11–13.
2. See *Kentucky's Black Heritage* (Frankfort, 1971), pp. 61–67, 83, Kentucky Division, Louisville Free Public Library; George C. Wright, *Life Behind a Veil: Blacks in Louisville, Kentucky, 1865–1930* (Baton Rouge, La., 1985).
3. Tape no. 10, WMY Sr. Box 10; Peggy Mann, *Whitney Young, Jr.: Crusader for Equality* (n.p., 1972), pp. 16, 18.
4. On WMY Sr.'s early life history: George C. Wright, "The Founding of Lincoln Institute," *Filson Club History Quarterly* 49 (1975): 57–70; tape no. 10, WMY Sr. Box 10; WMY Sr. resume, n.d., WMY Sr. Box 9; Love interview no. 1; unidentified newspaper clipping (obituary of Laura Ray Young [October 1962]), courtesy of Eleanor Young Love; untitled, undated clipping in scrapbook no. 13, WMY Sr.

Box 1; WMY to Ralph Edwards, Jan. 10, 1957, WMY 1; *Kentucky's Black Heritage*, p. 78.

5. Mann, *Whitney Young, Jr.: Crusader for Equality*, pp. 18–22.

6. On WMY Sr. and Lincoln's financial problems: Lincoln Institute faculty meeting minutes, Mar. 22, 1934, and Wm. Bembower, Annual Report to the Board of Trustees of Lincoln Institute, June 5, 1935, both in WMY Sr. unnumbered box; tape no. 10, WMY Sr. Box 10; untitled typed sheet for Founder's Day, n.d., "History of Lincoln Institute of Kentucky," n.d. [1952?], and Annual Report of Administration of Lincoln Institute for 1937–1938, all in Scrapbook no. 12, WMY Sr. Box 1; WMY speech, Frederick Douglass Sesquicentennial Lectures, University of Rochester, Mar. 2, 1967, WMY 150; WMY Sr. quoted in Love interview no. 1; Carroll interview; *Kentucky's Black Heritage*, pp. 64–65.

7. WMY quoted by WMY Sr., tape no. 3, WMY Sr. Box 10 ("My father taught me"); WMY to Ralph Edwards, Jan. 10, 1957, WMY 1.

8. Boswell interview no. 1 and no. 2; Love interview no. 1; Bruner, *Whitney M. Young, Jr.*, p. 17.

9. The quotes are from WMY, article prepared for book tentatively titled "This I Believe" for Howard University, Feb. 28, 1967, WMY 206; WMY speech, Frederick Douglass Sesquicentennial Lectures; and WMY interviewed by Sterling Brown, n. d., tape no. 15, WMY Sr. Box 10, respectively.

10. WMY, "This I Believe"; Bruner, *Whitney M. Young, Jr.*, pp. 13–15; WMY, "A Vanishing Era," *Harper's* 230 (April 1965): 172.

11. Kidd interview; Love interview no. 2; Poston interview; certificate of appointment signed by Postmaster General Walter F. Brown, Apr. 5, 1929, framed picture no. 36, WMY Sr. Papers.

12. Love interview no. 1; Boswell interview no. 2; B. B. Hamilton interview.

13. Quoted in Bruner, *Whitney M. Young, Jr.*, p. 11.

14. Ibid., pp. 7–8; WMY, "This I Believe" (source of the quote).

15. WMY quoted in Irwin Ross, "The Black Power of Whitney Young," *Reader's Digest* 94 (Jan. 1969): 120; Boswell interview no. 1; "Which Way, America?" [Jan. 16, 1971], p. 11, transcript in WMY biographical file, AUC.

16. WMY Sr. quoted in tape no. 8, WMY Sr. Box 10; Love interview no. 1; WMY, "This I Believe."

17. Love interview no. 2; WMY interviewed by Sterling Brown; WMY Sr., tapes no. 3 (source of the quotes) and no. 10, both in WMY Sr. Box 10; WMY Sr. resume, n.d., WMY Sr. Box 9; Wright, *Life Behind a Veil*, pp. 270–72.

18. WMY, "This I Believe" ("My mother's love of humanity"); WMY interviewed by Sterling Brown ("appreciation for study"; "feeling for people"); Love interview no. 1; Boswell interview no. 2.

19. Russell interview; Shobe interview; Harvey G. Russell tribute in "Whitney Young—One Year Later," transcript of service, White Plains Community Church, Mar. 12, 1972, James A. Linen Papers, courtesy of James A. Linen, Greenwich, Conn.; Wright, *Life Behind a Veil*, pp. 274–80.

20. Love interview no. 1; Russell interview; Baird interview no. 1 (Thomas story).

21. WMY Sr., tape no. 3, WMY Sr. Box 10; WMY interviewed by Sterling Brown; Love interview no. 1; B. B. Hamilton interview.

22. WMY interviewed by Sterling Brown; Boswell interview no. 1 and no. 2; Love interview no. 1 and no. 2; Russell interview; WMY to Ralph Edwards, Jan. 10, 1957, WMY 1; transcript, WMY interview, "Speaking Freely," WNBC Television, Nov. 8, 1969, p. 4, WMY 194; WMY Sr., quoted in WMY speech, "Reason and Responsibility in the Elimination of Bigotry and Poverty," National Conference on Social Welfare, May 31, 1968, WMY 165.

23. Love interview no. 1; Boswell interview no. 2; Kidd interview; Russell interview; Poston interview; Shobe interview.

24. On student life at Lincoln Institute: Semi-Annual Report of the Directors of Lincoln Institute, Nov. 1, 1935, Regulations for Morris B. Belknap Hall, typescript, Nov. 24, 1933, Regulations for Extein [sic] Norton Hall, Nov. 24, 1933, Annual Report of the Dean of Women, 1934–1935, attached to Wm. Bembower, Annual Report to the Board of Trustees of Lincoln Institute, June 5, 1935, and Faculty meeting minutes, Lincoln Institute, 1933–1936, all in WMY Sr. unnumbered box; Annual Report of Administration of Lincoln Institute for 1937–1938, Scrapbook no. 12, WMY Sr. Box 1, *The Tower*, 1939, KSU; Wright, "The Founding of Lincoln Institute," pp. 66, 69; Love interview no. 1; Kidd interview; Carroll interview (source of the quote); Poston interview.

25. WMY interviewed by Sterling Brown; WMY quoted in *Atlanta World*, Feb. 14, 1968, WMY biographical file, AUC ("My father . . . and LaMont"); WMY quoted in John Molleson, "Whitney Young Talks About: A Man to Remember," *Parade*, Feb. 11, 1968, WMY biographical file, AUC ("great lessons"); WMY speech, Golden Key Awards Presentation, Annual Conference, American Association of School Administrators, Feb. 17, 1968, WMY 160 ("I was somebody").

26. WMY to Ralph Edwards, Jan. 10, 1957, WMY 1; WMY interviewed by Sterling Brown.

CHAPTER II

1. Love interview no. 1; Kentucky State College, *Ten Year Report, 1929–1939* (May 1939), pp. 10, 12, KSU.

2. Shobe interview; Kentucky State College, *Ten Year Report*, p. 63.

3. Kentucky State Industrial College, *Annual Catalogue, 1937–1938* [*The Bulletin*, vol. 9, no. 3], pp. 45–46, 66–67; WMY Record Card, College Department, Kentucky State Industrial College, transcript obtained from Registrar, Kentucky State University.

4. WMY Record Card; Barnes/MBY interview, Nov. 13, 1975, p. 9, Jan. 8, 1976, pp. 31–32, courtesy of MBY.

5. Kentucky State Industrial College, *Annual Catalogue, 1937–1938*, pp. 28–30; *Kentucky Thorobred* 10 (Nov. 1939): 3; Kentucky State Industrial College, *Hand Book, '37–'38*, pp. 26–27, 37–46, KSU.

6. Kentucky State Industrial College, *Hand Book, '37–'38*, pp. 5–20; Shobe interview; Poston interview, Russell interview; *Kentucky Thorobred* 10 (Nov. 1939): 5 (source of the quote).

7. Kentucky State Industrial College, *Hand Book, '37–'38*, p. 47; Poston interview; Shobe interview; *Kentucky Thorobred* 10 (Oct. 1939): 1.

8. Shobe interview; Russell interview.

9. Shobe interview ("equip yourself"); Walters interview; WMY quoted in Richard Bruner, *Whitney M. Young, Jr.: The Story of a Pragmatic Humanist* (New York, 1972), p. 20.

10. Shobe interview; Love interview no. 1; Russell interview; WMY quoted in Bruner, *Whitney M. Young, Jr.*, p. 19.

11. Russell interview.

12. Bruner, *Whitney M. Young, Jr.*, p. 19; Russell interview; WMY, address at Commencement Convocation, Kentucky State College, June 3, 1962, WMY 123.

13. On WMY's campus life: Kentucky State Industrial College, *Annual Catalogue, 1937–1938*, p. 38; *Louisville Courier-Journal*, Aug. 5, 1964, clipping in WMY file, Western Branch, Louisville Free Public Library; Shobe interview; Russell interview; Walters interview; Love interview no. 1 and no. 2; Bruner, *Whitney M. Young, Jr.*, p. 18; *Kentucky Thorobred* 10 (Dec. 1939): 1; 12 (Dec. 1940): 1, 5; and 9 (May–June 1941): 8.

14. Mrs. John J. Jones, quoted in *Greeneville Sun* (Tenn.), Mar. 22, 1971, NUL new series; Poston interview.

15. For MBY's account of her early life and her experiences at Kentucky State, see Barnes/MBY interview, Nov. 13, 1975, pp. 1–7, Jan. 8, 1976, pp. 19–22, and MBY interview no. 3 and no. 6. Her accomplishments at Kentucky State are documented in *Kentucky Thorobred* 10 (Oct. 1939): 1; and 10 (April–May 1942): 3; and Kentucky State College, *Fifty-Fourth Annual Commencement*, Program, May 19, 1942, KSU. On Aurora, Illinois, see U.S. Department of Commerce, Bureau of the Census, *Sixteenth Census of the United States: 1940, Population*, vol. 1, *Number of Inhabitants* (Washington, D.C., 1943), p. 292; U.S. Department of Commerce, Bureau of the Census, *Negroes in the United States, 1920–1932* (Washington, D.C., 1935), p. 57.

16. On WMY and MBY: WMY note quoted in Peggy Mann, *Whitney Young, Jr.: Crusader for Equality* (n.p., 1972), p. 36; Ersa H. Poston tribute in "Whitney Young—One Year Later," transcript of service, White Plains Community Church, Mar. 12, 1972, James A. Linen Papers, courtesy of James A. Linen, Greenwich, Conn.; Poston interview; Love interview no. 1; MBY quoted in *Louisville Defender*, July 27, 1972, p. C1 ("it was too late"); MBY interview no. 7; *Kentucky Thorobred* 12 (Dec. 1940): 6; and 9 (Jan. 1941): 6; WMY Record Card.

17. Kentucky State College, *Baccalaureate Services*, Program, June 8, 1941, and Kentucky State College, *Fifty-Third Annual Commencement*, Program, June 10, 1941, KSU; *Kentucky Thorobred* 9 (May–June 1941): 2.

CHAPTER III

1. WMY speech, Frederick Douglass Sesquicentennial Lectures, University of Rochester, Mar. 2, 1967, WMY 150.

2. WMY Sr., tape no. 3, WMY Sr. Box 10; editorial, *Madisonville Messenger* (Ky.), Mar. 22, 1971, NUL new series; Peggy Mann, *Whitney Young, Jr.: Crusader for Equality* (n.p., 1972), pp. 38–39; MBY interview no. 3.

3. Transcript, WMY interview, "Speaking Freely," WNBC Television, Nov. 8, 1969, p. 4, WMY 194; Report of Special Inquiry on Whitney Moore Young, Jr., Dec. 30, 1964, Federal Bureau of Investigation, Field Office File SL 161–1604,

Federal Bureau of Investigation Papers obtained through the Freedom of Informa-tion/Privacy Act; WMY quoted in Tom Buckley, "Whitney Young: Black Leader or 'Oreo Cookie'?" *New York Times Magazine*, Sept. 20, 1970, p. 80 ("My motiva-tion"); WMY speech, Frederick Douglass Sesquicentennial Lectures.

4. Ulysses Lee, *The Employment of Negro Troops* (Washington, D.C., 1966), p. 270.

5. WMY speech, Frederick Douglass Sesquicentennial Lectures ("At first . . . "; "Of course . . . "); Mann, *Whitney Young, Jr.: Crusader for Equality*, p. 40 (officer-soldier dialogue); WMY quoted in Irwin Ross, "The Black Power of Whit-ney Young," *Reader's Digest* 94 (Jan. 1969): 120 (ultimate gesture).

6. Barnes/MBY interview, Nov. 13, 1975, p. 11; MBY interview no. 3 and no. 6 ("Whitney said"); Mann, *Whitney Young, Jr.: Crusader for Equality*, pp. 41–43 ("I'm like every other mother"); Report of Special Inquiry on Whitney Moore Young, Jr., Dec. 30, 1964, Federal Bureau of Investigation, Field Office File SL 161–1604.

7. Young told the story of his experiences in the 1695th in Buckley, "Whitney Young: Black Leader or 'Oreo Cookie'?" p. 80, and WMY speech, Frederick Douglass Sesquicentennial Lectures. The journey to England and his time there are described in a letter to his parents, May 21, 1945, WMY 268. His service record is documented in Army of the United States, Enlisted Record and Report of Separation, and Army of the United States, Separation Qualification Record, both in WMY 268, as well as in Report of Special Inquiry on Whitney Moore Young, Jr., Dec. 30, 1964, Federal Bureau of Investigation, Field Office File SL 161–1604. The activities of the 1695th are documented in historical data supplied by the U.S. Army Reserve Personnel Center under the Freedom of Information/Privacy Act, and in 1695th Engineer Combat Battalion, After Action Report, May 22, 1945, Record Group 407, Records of the Adjutant General's Office, World War II Operations Reports, ENBN–1695–0.3, Military Reference Branch (NNRMS), National Archives. For Margaret's visit, see MBY interview no. 3.

8. WMY, article prepared for book tentatively titled *This I Believe* for Howard University, Feb. 28, 1967, WMY 206 ("first flicker of hope"); WMY speech, Frederick Douglass Sesquicentennial Lectures ("I was convinced").

9. WMY, "A Negro Soldier's Memory," *McCall's* 95 (Dec. 1967): 168.

10. WMY, World War II log, Dec. 16–29, 1945, courtesy of MBY.

11. Dale Carnegie, *How to Win Friends & Influence People*, rev. ed. (1936; New York, 1981).

12. WMY, World War II log, Jan. 1–3, 1946.

CHAPTER IV

1. Barnes/MBY interview, Jan. 8, 1976, p. 33; MBY interview no. 6; Hen-don interview; Army of the United States, Separation Qualification Record, WMY 268.

2. MBY interview no. 6; Gaskins interview; transcript, WMY interview, WNBC Television's "Speaking Freely," Nov. 8, 1969, p. 5, WMY 194; WMY speech, "Social Work Education for What End?" 50th Anniversary Dinner, School of Social Work, University of Minnesota, Jan. 24, 1968, WMY 260; Kidneigh inter-

view; C. J. Dunkle letter, Jan. 3, 1946, WMY 268; Peggy Mann, *Whitney Young, Jr.: Crusader for Equality* (n. p., 1972), pp. 48–49.

3. WMY transcript, University of Minnesota Graduate School, WMY 265; Kidneigh interview; Whitmore interview.

4. James T. Wardlaw, Intermediate Report on Field Assignment, Mar. 18, 1947, WMY 259.

5. WMY, "History of the St. Paul Urban League," Plan B Report, University of Minnesota School of Social Work, Aug. 1947, Social Welfare History Archives, Walter Library, University of Minnesota. The quotes are from p. 1.

6. U. S. Department of Commerce, Bureau of the Census, *Sixteenth Census of the United States: 1940, Population*, vol. 2, *Characteristics of the Population*, pt. 3, *Kentucky* (Washington, D. C., 1943), pp. 173, 175, pt. 4, *Minnesota*, pp. 13, 14, 173, 180; WMY, "History of the St. Paul Urban League," p. 15; Earl Spangler, *The Negro in Minnesota* (Minneapolis, 1961), p. 158.

7. Governor's Interracial Commission, *The Negro Worker's Progress in Minnesota* (St. Paul, 1949), pp. 5–6, 20–29, 38; WMY, "History of the St. Paul Urban League," pp. 46–49; Spangler, *The Negro in Minnesota*, pp. 131–33, 138–40; St. Paul Urban League, *22nd Annual Report* (1945), p. 9, *24th Annual Report* (1947), p. 6, St. Paul Collection, St. Paul Public Library; Wardlaw interview; Rogers interview; Hendon interview; Gaskins interview.

8. St. Paul Urban League, *24th Annual Report* (1947), p. 10, St. Paul Collection, St. Paul Public Library; Rogers interview (source of the quote); Gaskins interview; G.S.E. Williams interview.

9. St. Paul Urban League, *A Quarter Century of Progress in the Field of Race Relations, 1923–1948*, Minnesota Historical Society; WMY, Speech Notes, Guidance Workshop, June 25, 1959, WMY 191a; minutes of exploratory meeting, St. Paul Urban League Vocational Committee, May 19, 1948, NUL Series 13, Box 27.

10. Mann, *Whitney Young, Jr.: Crusader for Equality*, pp. 52–53; St. Paul Urban League, *A Quarter Century of Progress in the Field of Race Relations, 1923–1948*, pp. 5, 7–8; Report of the St. Paul Urban League, Dec. 1947, and St. Paul Urban League board minutes, Apr. 29, 1948, NUL Series 1, Box 125; St. Paul Urban League, *26th Annual Report* (1949), p. 7, *27th Annual Report* (1950), p. 6, St. Paul Collection, St. Paul Public Library; Rogers interview; Spangler, *The Negro in Minnesota*, p. 136 (source of the quote). There were approximately eight hundred firms in St. Paul.

11. Rogers interview; Governor's Interracial Commission, *The Negro Worker in Minnesota* (St. Paul, 1945); letter of transmittal, Francis J. Gilligan to Governor Luther W. Youngdahl, Apr. 11, 1949, in Governor's Interracial Commission, *The Negro Worker's Progress in Minnesota*.

12. Konopka interview; S. Vincent Owens to Ann Tanneyhill, May 26, 1949, WMY 259.

13. S. Vincent Owens to Ann Tanneyhill, May 26, 1949, WMY 259; Rogers interview; Hendon interview.

14. MBY interview no. 3; Barnes/MBY interview, Jan. 8, 1976, pp. 39–40; *Omaha World-Herald*, Feb. 1, 1950, WMY biographical file, W. Dale Clark Library, Omaha.

15. MBY interview no. 3; Barnes/MBY interview, Jan. 8, 1976, pp. 36–37; Gaskins interview; G.S.E. Williams interview; Hendon interview. Williams claims that Young organized the Young Marrieds Club. On Young's salary, see S. Vincent Owens to Ann Tanneyhill, May 26, 1949, WMY 259. The $3,500 salary would have put him in the top 6 percent of black wage-earners in the United States. See E. Franklin Frazier, *Black Bourgeoisie* (Glencoe, Ill., 1957), p. 51.

16. Gaskins interview.

17. Hendon interview; Gaskins interview.

18. Barnes/MBY interview, Jan. 8, 1976, p. 45; Granger quoted in Ann Tanneyhill to S. Vincent Owens, May 23, 1949; Owens to Tanneyhill, May 26, 1949, WMY 259.

19. M. Leo Bohanon to Lester B. Granger, Oct. 27, 1949, Bohanon to [R.] Maurice Moss, Nov. 16, 1949, Alfred C. Kennedy to Granger, Dec. 3, 1949, Moss to James Paxson, Dec. 9, 1949, Marion M. Taylor to Moss, Dec. 30, 1949, all in NUL Series 1, Box 116; Paxson to WMY, Dec. 30, 1949, WMY 1a; Paxson interview ("Whitney was a charmer"); Skinner interview. The salary put Young in the top 1.3 percent of black wage-earners. See Frazier, *Black Bourgeoisie*, p. 51.

20. WMY to R. Maurice Moss, Dec. 23, 1949, NUL Series 1, Box 116; WMY to Moss, Jan. 10, 1950, NUL Series 1, Box 126; editorial, *St. Paul Sun*, n.d. [1950], WMY 229a.

21. Barnes/MBY interview, Jan. 8, 1976, pp. 37–38, 40–41; MBY interview no. 3; McCaw interview; Skinner interview; Additional Personnel Data on Whitney M. Young, Jr., typescript prepared for R. Maurice Moss, as per WMY to Moss, Dec. 31, 1952, WMY 259; *Omaha Star*, Dec. 21, 1951, p. 1.

22. U.S. Department of Commerce, Bureau of the Census, *Census of Population: 1950*, vol. 2, *Characteristics of the Population*, pt. 27, *Nebraska* (Washington, D.C., 1952), pp. 47, 166–69; Omaha Urban League, *22nd Annual Progress Report, 1949*, pp. 3, 7, and *Annual Report, 1952*, both in NUL Series 13, Box 21; Omaha Urban League Reports, May 1950, and George H. Robinson to Lester B. Granger, Aug. 9, 1954, both in NUL Series 1, Box 116; *Omaha Star*, Mar. 6, 1953, p. 1; Additional Personnel Data on Whitney M. Young, Jr.; Racial Policies in Public Housing, WMY memorandum to National Urban League, NUL Affiliates, Nov. 23, 1951, NUL Series 6, Box 93; Bohanon interview; G. Robinson interview; Dodge interview; R. R. Brown interview; McCaw interview; Abrahams interview; Skinner interview.

23. McCaw interview ("go-getter"); WMY quoted in: *Omaha World-Herald*, Feb. 18, 1951, *Omaha World-Herald* Library; ibid., Feb. 1, 1950, WMY biographical file, W. Dale Clark Library, Omaha; *Omaha Evening World-Herald*, n.d. [ca. Feb. 14, 1950], NUL Series 1, Box 116.

24. On WMY's efforts with respect to black employment: Omaha Urban League, *23rd Annual Report, 1950*, pp. 3, 4, *24th Annual Report, 1951*, and *Annual Report, 1953*, all in NUL Series 13, Box 21; Omaha Urban League, Report of the Activities of Local Urban Leagues for Year of 1952, and Omaha Urban League Reports, n.d. [stamped Sept. 8, 1952], both in NUL Series 5, Box 46; Additional Personnel Data on Whitney M. Young, Jr.; *Omaha Star*, Mar. 10, 1950, p. 1, Sept. 15, 1950, p. 1, June 16, 1950, pp. 1, 5, Mar. 16, 1951, p. 1, June 8, 1951,

p. 1, July 27, 1951, p. 1, May 15, 1953, p. 1; Abrahams interview; Ramsey interview; WMY quoted in *Omaha World-Herald*, Oct. 4, 1953, *Omaha World-Herald* Library ("they were crusaders"), and in *North Omaha Sun*, Apr. 21, 1966, WMY 204 ("how pleased we were").

25. Omaha Urban League Reports, n.d. [stamped Sept. 8, 1952], and Sept. 1953, NUL Series 13, Box 21; Additional Personnel Data on Whitney M. Young, Jr.; G. Robinson interview.

26. WMY memorandum, Racial Policies in Public Housing; Additional Personnel Data on Whitney M. Young, Jr.; *Omaha Star*, Nov. 23, 1951, p. 1; *Omaha World-Herald*, Nov. 11, 1953, *Omaha World-Herald* Library; N. Phillips Dodge to Nancy J. Weiss, Mar. 11, 1987.

27. Jeffrey Harrison Smith, "The Omaha De Porres Club" (unpublished master's thesis, Creighton University, 1967), pp. 40–43, W. Dale Clark Library, Omaha.

28. Holland interview; Smith, "The Omaha De Porres Club," pp. 56–60; *Omaha Star*, June 15, 1951, p. 1.

29. Corbin interview; McCaw interview; G. Robinson interview.

30. McCaw interview; Omaha Urban League, *23rd Annual Report, 1950*, pp. 8–9, and *Annual Report, 1953*.

31. Abrahams interview; Ramsey interview.

32. Ramsey interview; Tyler interview; N. Phillips Dodge to Nancy J. Weiss, Mar. 11, 1987; Skinner quoted in Abrahams interview.

33. Transcript, Robert L. Myers oral history interview, Mar. 21, 1979, pp. 14–17, W. Dale Clark Library, Omaha; Tyler interview; Skinner interview; WMY quoted in *Omaha World-Herald*, Apr. 28, 1966, *Omaha World-Herald* Library.

34. N. P. Dodge, Jr., remarks for Whitney Young Dinner, May 19, 1961, WMY 1a; Dodge to Nancy J. Weiss, Mar. 11, 1987.

35. Quoted in *Omaha World-Herald*, June 18, 1972, *Omaha World-Herald* Library.

CHAPTER V

1. McCaw interview.

2. *The Reflections of Florence Victoria Adams* (1981), pp. 3–11; Clarence A. Bacote, *The Story of Atlanta University: A Century of Service, 1865–1965* (Atlanta, 1969), pp. 328–29, 353–54; "The South's Foremost School of Social Work," *Ebony*, Oct. 1959, pp. 84–88, WMY 273.

3. Bacote, *The Story of Atlanta University*, p. 318; WMY quoted in Richard Bruner, *Whitney M. Young, Jr.: The Story of a Pragmatic Humanist* (New York, 1972), p. 44 ("shouldn't be permitted to flounder"); WMY to Rufus Clement, Sept. 17, 1953, WMY 1a; Barnes/MBY interview, Jan. 8, 1976, pp. 46–48 ("that far south"); MBY interview no. 3 ("hated the thought").

4. WMY quoted in Bruner, *Whitney M. Young, Jr.*, p. 44 ("second Emancipation"), and in *Atlanta World*, Nov. 17, 1953, clipping in scrapbook, Atlanta University School of Social Work ("I was born in the South").

5. Lester B. Granger to WMY, Oct. 8, 1953, R. Maurice Moss to WMY, Jan. 13, 1953, WMY to Moss, Feb. 3, 1953, WMY 1a.

6. Additional Personnel Data on Whitney M. Young, Jr., typescript prepared for R. Maurice Moss, as per WMY to Moss, Dec. 31, 1952, WMY 259; Edythe K. Hall to Lester B. Granger, Nov. 11, 1953, NUL Series 1, Box 116; Paxson interview.

7. WMY to Lester B. Granger, Oct. 9, 1953, WMY 1a.

8. WMY interview, RJBOHC ("I was challenged"); Rufus E. Clement to WMY, Nov. 10, 1953, WMY to Clement, Sept. 17, 1953, WMY 1a; *The Reflections of Florence Victoria Adams*, p. 17. A total income of $7,000 put Young in the top 0.3 percent of blacks in the United States. See E. Franklin Frazier, *Black Bourgeoisie* (Glencoe, Ill., 1957), p. 51. By 1959–1960, Young's last full year as dean, his nine-month salary had increased to $8,300.

9. Quoted in *Omaha Star*, Nov. 13, 1953, p. 1.

10. Barnes/MBY interview, Jan. 8, 1976, p. 48; MBY interview no. 3.

11. G. Hill interview.

12. Ibid.; Coleman interview; Ross interview; WMY to Nelson C. Jackson, May 3, 1958, NUL Series 2, Box 15; *The Reflections of Florence Victoria Adams*, pp. 17, 31–33; Bacote, *The Story of Atlanta University*, p. 355; Frankie [Florence] V. Adams to WMY, July 31, 1960, WMY 1a (source of the quote).

13. WMY, Orientation Message, 11th Annual Out-of-Town Supervisors' Conference Report, Nov. 21–23, 1957, Atlanta University School of Social Work, AUC; Bacote, *The Story of Atlanta University*, p. 357; Ross interview; Katherine A. Kendall to WMY, Dec. 23, 1955, WMY 1a.

14. Mack interview ("the most instrumental person"); John W. Mack to MBY, Apr. 2, 1971, WMY 251; Wade interview.

15. On the desegregation of the library system: memorandum, WMY to Executive Committee, Greater Atlanta Council on Human Relations, n.d. (source of the quotes), and unidentified newspaper clipping, n.d., WMY 32; Howard Zinn, *The Southern Mystique* (New York, 1970), pp. 42–51; Zinn interview.

16. Williamson interview; Paul Douglas Bolster, "Civil Rights Movements in Twentieth Century Georgia" (doctoral dissertation, University of Georgia, 1972; xerographic copy published by University Microfilms), pp. 173–74.

17. Williamson interview; Holman interview. The participants are unable to date the organizing meeting of ACCA; it would be sometime before November 1957, by which time NBC had decided to drop the Nat King Cole show.

18. On ACCA: WMY interview, RJBOHC; J. Hill interview; Holman interview; Warner interview; Williamson interview.

19. Foreword, *A Second Look: The Negro Citizen in Atlanta* (Atlanta, Jan. 1960).

20. Holman interview; Distribution (Geared to Brochure Sections), typescript, n.d., WMY 32; Atlanta Committee for Cooperative Action to Dear Friend, Feb. 14, 1960, Clarence D. Coleman Papers, courtesy of Clarence D. Coleman, Atlanta; *Atlanta Daily World*, Feb. 14, 1960; *Atlanta Constitution*, n.d., WMY 229a.

21. James P. Brawley to WMY, Mar. 9, 1960, WMY 1a; editorial, *Atlanta Daily World*, Feb. 16, 1960, *New York Times*, Feb. 14, 1960, *Atlanta Constitution*, n. d., all in WMY 229a; Bond interview.

22. *Atlanta Daily World*, Mar. 9, 1960, WMY 229a; Bond interview; WMY interview, RJBOHC; Holman interview.

23. Howell Raines, *My Soul Is Rested: Movement Days in the Deep South Remembered* (1977; pb. ed., New York, 1983), p. 85; Bond interview; Williamson interview; Mack interview; Parham interview.

24. WMY interview, RJBOHC; Mack interview; Bond interview; J. Hill interview.

25. Bond interview; Parham interview; Mack interview.

26. Parham interview; Mack interview; Scott quoted in Holman interview.

27. WMY, "Student Protest Movement," undated speech, WMY 7.

28. M. Carl Holman, "Whitney Young: 'A vital link, a unique human coupling has been lost,' " *Contact* 2 (July 1971), 25, WMY vertical file, SCRBC; G. Hill interview.

29. Barnes/MBY interview, Jan. 8, 1976, pp. 50–51; MBY interview no. 3 ("I hated it"; "I was angry").

30. In each telling, the details of the conversation varied slightly. So did the name of the housekeeper, which Young deliberately fictionalized in order to protect her privacy. This version is a composite of WMY, *Beyond Racism* (New York, 1969), pp. 226–27, and a WMY speech, "Reason and Responsibility in the Elimination of Bigotry and Poverty," National Conference on Social Welfare, May 31, 1968, WMY 165.

31. Barnes/MBY interview, Jan. 8, 1976, pp. 49–53; MBY interview no. 3 (Rich's); Cantarella interview; Casteel interview.

32. WMY to James L. Cox, Mar. 22, 1958; WMY to Alfred Kennedy, June 5, 1959, WMY 1.

33. Joseph Golden to Clara A. Kaiser, Jan. 2, 1959, WMY 1a; unidentified clipping [1959], WMY 229a.

CHAPTER VI

1. WMY to Donald S. Howard, Feb. 25, Apr. 22, 1958, and Howard to WMY, Mar. 3, 1958, WMY 1a; WMY to Howard, Mar. 21, 1958, WMY 1.

2. WMY to Rufus E. Clement, Apr. 22, 1958, WMY 1a; WMY to Lester B. Granger, June 9, 1958, WMY 1.

3. WMY, "The Role of the Urban League in the Current American Scene," speech delivered at NUL annual conference, Sept. 8, 1959, WMY 121a.

4. Kimball interview no. 1; Allen interview no. 1; G. Robinson interview; Wolfe interview; Berry interview; Hall interview; Mervis interview; Steele interview; Jacobs interview; Lindsley F. Kimball to J. George Harrar, Aug. 28, 1961, GEB Series 628, Box 276, Folder 2878.

5. Lindsley F. Kimball to WMY, Sept. 8, 1959, WMY 263; Nancy J. Weiss, *The National Urban League, 1910–1940* (New York, 1974), pp. 81–82, 156–57, 242; Kimball interview no. 1. Kimball joined the board in January 1959.

6. "Dr. Whitney Young—Dean of School of Social Work of Atlanta University," interoffice memorandum, L[indsley] F. K[imball] to F[lora] M. R[hind], Dec. 16, 1959, GEB Series 950, Box 529, Folder 5663 ("immediately struck"); Kimball quoted in Tom Buckley, "Whitney Young: Black Leader or 'Oreo Cookie'?" *New York Times Magazine*, Sept. 20, 1970, p. 82 ("active arena").

7. Kimball quoted in Trent interview no. 3; Lindsley F. Kimball to WMY, Oct. 27, 1959, WMY to Kimball, Nov. 23, 1959, GEB Series 950, Box 529, Folder 5663.

8. WMY to Lindsley F. Kimball, Oct. 23, Nov. 23, 1959, Kimball to WMY, Nov. 25, 1959, all in GEB Series 950, Box 529, Folder 5663.

9. WMY to Lindsley F. Kimball, Nov. 23, 1959, GEB Series 950, Box 529, Folder 5663.

10. Flora M. Rhind to WMY, Dec. 9, 28, 1959, WMY to Rhind, enclosing General Education Board, Personal History Record and Application for Fellowship, both Dec. 11, 1959, and Lindsley F. Kimball to WMY, Dec. 29, 1959, all in GEB Series 950, Box 529, Folder 5663.

11. [Hylan Lewis,] "The Case for Harvard" (typescript, n.d., on Health and Welfare Council stationery), WMY 265; WMY to Lindsley F. Kimball, Dec. 7, 1959, Feb. 5, 1960, GEB Series 950, Box 529, Folder 5663.

12. Lindsley F. Kimball to WMY, Apr. 25, 1960, WMY to Dean Rusk, May 6, July 20, Aug. 27, 1960, Rusk to WMY, July 26, 1960, Rusk, memorandum on interview with WMY, Sept. 7, 1960 (source of the quotes), all in GEB Series 950, Box 529, Folder 5663.

13. G. Hill interview.

14. Barnes/MBY interview, Jan. 15, 1976, pp. 74–75, 77–81.

15. WMY to Dean Rusk, Sept. 29, 1960, GEB Series 950, Box 529, Folder 5663; WMY to Gordon W. Allport, May 13, 1960, Allport to WMY, June 1, 1960, WMY 263; Thurman interview; Barnes/MBY interview, Jan. 15, 1976, p. 83. WMY Notebooks, WMY 1a, show the courses for the fall semester and summer school. It is not entirely clear which courses Young concentrated on in the spring term; the choices, along with some indication of his preferences, are outlined in two handwritten lists of courses in WMY 265.

16. WMY interview, RJBOHC.

17. Mack interview; Parham interview; Zinn interview; Holman interview; Martin interview; J. H. Johnson interview.

18. WMY to Lester B. Granger, Nov. 25, 1959, WMY 1; WMY to Lindsley F. Kimball, Dec. 17, 1959, WMY 263.

19. Lester B. Granger to Henry Steeger, Sr., Mar. 7, 1960, WMY 2.

20. Transcript, Guichard Parris/Lester Brooks interview with Sophia Y. Jacobs, Apr. 18, 1969, Parris Box 48; Kimball interview no. 1 and no. 2.

21. NUL board minutes, Sept. 9, 1959, NUL Series 11, Box 5; Jan. 21, 1960, WMY 12; Guichard Parris and Lester Brooks, *Blacks in the City: A History of the National Urban League* (Boston, 1971), p. 395.

22. Lester B. Granger to Henry Steeger, Sr., Mar. 7, 1960, WMY 2; Granger to WMY, Mar. 7, 1960, WMY 12. There is no reason to believe that Granger wrote only to Young, but there is no written evidence to substantiate the assumption that he must have sent letters to other prospective candidates.

23. WMY to Henry Steeger, Sr., Mar. 28, 1960, Steeger to WMY, Apr. 12, 1960, WMY 12.

24. Memorandum, Lester B. Granger to the Executive Committee, May 3, 1960, and memorandum, Henry Steeger to the Executive Committee, National Urban League, Inc., May 24, 1960, WMY 12.

25. Memorandum, Lester B. Granger to Regina M. Andrews, Theodore W. Kheel, Mollie Moon, Burns W. Roper, Henry Steeger, June 10, 1960, and Granger to WMY, June 3, 1960, WMY 12; Allen interview no. 2; Berry interview.

26. NUL board minutes, Sept. 6, Dec. 2, 1960, NUL Series 11, Box 5; NUL executive committee minutes, Oct. 27, 1960, memorandum, Lester B. Granger to the Members of the Executive Committee, National Urban League, Nov. 9, 1960, both in WMY 12.

27. On the selection of WMY: Roper interview; J. H. Johnson interview; Andresen interview; H. L. and M. Moon interview; Kimball interview no. 1 and no. 2.

28. Butler interview.

29. Henry Steeger to WMY, Dec. 9, 1960, WMY to Steeger, Dec. 15, 1960, NUL board minutes, Jan. 26, 1961, memorandum, Lester B. Granger to Executive Directors of Affiliated Organizations, Jan. 27, 1961, all in WMY 12.

30. These comments come from two sets of undated, handwritten notes, one in WMY 7, the other in WMY 12.

31. Henry Steeger to WMY, Jan. 27, 1961, WMY 1a; NUL press release, "National Urban League Picks New Executive Director," Jan. 30, 1961, WMY 12.

32. Thomasina Norford to WMY, n.d. [1961], WMY 1; Roy Wilkins to WMY, Feb. 16, 1961, National Association for the Advancement of Colored People Papers, Group 3, Series B, Box 456, Manuscript Division, Library of Congress.

CHAPTER VII

1. Tanneyhill interview; "The Big Five in Civil Rights," *Time* 81 (June 28, 1963): 16 (source of the quotes).

2. The responses are all in WMY 1.

3. Wallace interview.

4. Homer A. Jack to WMY, Feb. 13, 1961, WMY 1; MBY interview no. 6; Barnes/MBY interview, pp. 85–88; U. S. Department of Commerce, Bureau of the Census, *Census of Population: 1960*, vol. 1, *Characteristics of the Population*, pt. 34, *New York* (Washington, D. C., 1961), p. 34.

5. John Kaplan, "Segregation Litigation and the Schools—Part I: The New Rochelle Experience," *Northwestern University Law Review* 58 (Mar.–Apr. 1963): 1–72.

6. MBY interview no. 6; WMY interviewed by Sterling Brown, tape no. 15, WMY Sr. Box 10.

7. Barnes/MBY interview, Jan. 15, 1976, pp. 88–89; WMY speech, "The Antipoverty Program—Its Strengths and Weaknesses," Thirtieth National Conference, National Association of Housing and Redevelopment Officials, Oct. 27, 1965, WMY 131 (source of the quote).

8. WMY interviewed by Sterling Brown.

9. Barnes/MBY interview, Jan. 15, 1976, p. 91; Peggy Mann, *Whitney Young, Jr.: Crusader for Equality* (n.p., 1972), pp. 60–61 (source of the quotes).

10. WMY to Frankie V. Adams, Aug. 11, 1961, WMY 2.

11. WMY speech, NUL Annual Conference, Sept. 7, 1961, NUL Pt. 2, Series 5, Box 29; WMY to WMY Sr., Oct. 5, 1961, WMY 2.

12. Kheel interview; NUL board minutes, Nov. 17, 1961, WMY 12; Lindsley F. Kimball to J. George Harrar, Aug. 28, 1961, Henry Steeger, Sr., to Harrar, Aug. 29, 1961, Janet M. Paine to Steeger, Sept. 6, 1961, all in GEB Series 628, Box 276, Folder 2878; Income Comparison by Source, National Urban League, courtesy of the League's Fund Department; WMY quoted in Guichard Parris and Lester Brooks, *Blacks in the City: A History of the National Urban League* (Boston, 1971), p. 402.

13. NUL board minutes, Nov. 17, 1961, WMY 12; memorandum, David R. Hunter to Dyke Brown, Nov. 3, 1961, Ford L 61-1416.

14. Excerpt, Lindsley F. Kimball to [Henry T.] Heald, Aug. 21, 1961, Ford L 61–1417 ("forlorn causes"); Kimball to J. George Harrar, Aug. 28, 1961, GEB Series 628, Box 276, Folder 2878; Kimball to Heald, Oct. 11, 1961, Ford L 61-1417 ("a little more privacy").

15. Foundation gifts increased from $62,000 in 1961 to $239,000 in 1962. See Income Comparison by Source, National Urban League.

16. Andresen interview; Background Information on Projected Financial Program, National Urban League, Oct. 30, 1961, WMY 12; Income Comparison by Source, National Urban League; Proposed Formula for Calculating "Fair-Share" Giving to National Urban League by Commerce and Industry Sources, revision of Nov. 3, 1961, WMY 12.

17. WMY quoted in Kimball interview no. 1; NUL board minutes, May 25, Nov. 17, 1961, executive committee minutes, Oct. 19, 1961, all in WMY 12.

18. NUL executive committee minutes, Apr. 11, 1963, WMY 12; Steeger interview; Puryear interview; Andresen interview; Jacobs interview.

19. Steeger interview; Kimball interview no. 1; Puryear interview; Selected List of Corporation Contributions (Showing 1961–1962 Comparison), Dec. 1962, attached to WMY to Maxwell Hahn, Dec. 3, 1962, NUL new series; NUL board minutes, Feb. 16, 1962, May 16, Nov. 19, 1963, Feb. 20, 1964, WMY 12; Income Comparison by Source, National Urban League.

20. WMY notes for staff meeting, Oct. 11, 1961, WMY 2; memorandum, WMY to Executive Directors of Local Urban Leagues, Nov. 10, 1961, NUL Pt. 2, Series 5, Box 13; NUL board minutes, Nov. 17, 1961, Nov. 19, 1962, WMY 12; Allen interview no. 1; Parris interview; memorandum, WMY to NUL Professional Staff, June 18, 1965, NUL Pt. 2, Series 1, Box 28.

21. Statement of WMY, Meeting of Special Committee, Commerce and Industry Council, National Urban League, Oct. 30, 1961, WMY 265 (source of the quote); Mervis interview; Wolfe interview; Walters interview; W. J. Brown interview; Trent interview no. 3; Steele interview; Barkstall interview; Odom interview; Dixon interview; Talbert interview.

22. Notes on WMY conversation with Council [of Executive Directors], Sept. 2, 1961, Parris Box 40.

23. WMY to Frankie Adams, Dec. 12, 1961, WMY 2.

24. "Urban League Programs," memorandum, Nelson C. Jackson to Executives and Staff, Local Urban Leagues, Mar. 23, 1962, Ford L 61–1417; NUL board minutes, Sept. 6, 1962, WMY 12; R. R. Brown interview.

25. See in NUL Pt. 2, Series 5: NUL cabinet notes, Nov. 4, 1963, Box 2; NUL board minutes, Nov. 19, 1963, Box 18; memorandum, Henry Steeger and WMY

to Presidents and Executive Directors, Apr. 7, 1964, Box 14; NUL press release, Apr. 9, 1964, Box 31.

26. NUL, *Year-End Report*, 1961, and *Annual Report*, 1964–1965, 1966, National Urban League Library, New York City; Gene Grove, "The Urban League Turns a Corner," *Los Angeles Herald-Examiner, Tuesday Magazine*, Aug. 1966, pp. 6–7, WMY 233b; memorandum, Ruth Allen King to A. J. Allen, Sept. 22, 1961, NUL Pt. 2, Series 1, Box 30; *Amsterdam News* (N.Y.), Mar. 20, 1971, p. 5.

27. For a brief account of these programs, see NUL, *Annual Report*, 1964–1965, 1966, 1967, 1968, 1969, NUL Library.

28. WMY to Lester B. Granger, Apr. 18, 1962, NUL Pt. 2, Series 1, Box 86; NUL, *Annual Report*, 1966, NUL Library; WMY, "Developing Negro Leaders," *Outlook*, Sept. 1966, pp. 14–15, WMY 204.

29. Allen interview no. 1; Whaley interview no. 2.

30. NUL press release, "Obituary," Mar. 11, 1971, WMY vertical file, SCRBC; Hall interview ("stepped . . . up"); WMY to Frederick W. Richmond, Feb. 10, 1961, WMY 1.

CHAPTER VIII

1. Quoted in *Memphis Commercial Appeal*, Sept. 11, 1958, WMY 229a.

2. "Policy Statement on Non-Violent Direct Action Techniques," Jan. 11, 1962, NUL Pt. 2, Series 1, Box 25.

3. WMY speech, annual convention, Southern Christian Leadership Conference, Sept. 27, 1962, WMY 124; memorandum, WMY to Executive Directors of Urban League Affiliates, June 7, 1963, NUL Pt. 2, Series 1, Box 26.

4. "Demonstrations and Picketing," WMY memorandum to Executive Directors of Urban League Affiliates, July 3, 1963, NUL Pt. 2, Series 1, Box 26.

5. A. Philip Randolph to WMY, Mar. 26, 1963, NUL Pt. 2, Series 1, Box 25; Jervis Anderson, *A. Philip Randolph: A Biographical Portrait* (New York, 1973), chs. 16, 21; David J. Garrow, *Bearing the Cross: Martin Luther King, Jr., and the Southern Christian Leadership Conference* (New York, 1986), pp. 265–67.

6. WMY to A. Philip Randolph, Apr. 2, 1963, NUL Pt. 2, Series 1, Box 25; WMY interview with Dr. Albert E. Gollin of the Bureau of Social Science Research, Inc., July 26, 1967, WMY 9 (source of the quote). By April 4, Young had made clear to Randolph that the league would be willing to participate in the march. See Meeting with Brother A. Philip Randolph, Apr. 4, 1963, NUL Pt. 2, Series 1, Box 26.

7. WMY interview, RJBOHC ("pretty shaken up"); Andresen interview ("nervous as hell"); NUL executive committee minutes, Apr. 11, 1963, WMY 12.

8. NUL executive committee minutes, Apr. 11, 1963, WMY 12; WMY to A. Philip Randolph, Apr. 30, 1963, NUL Pt. 2, Series 1, Box 25; *New York Times*, July 24, 1963, p. 15; WMY interview with Dr. Albert E. Gollin; WMY interview, RJBOHC.

9. Allen interview no. 1; WMY and Johnson quoted in NUL program staff minutes, July 18, 1963, Parris Box 40.

10. Andresen interview ("really going to be left out"); Allen interview no. 1; Parris interview.

11. Transcript, National Educational Television's "For Freedom Now," July 22, 1963, pp. 3–4, NUL Pt. 2, Series 5, Box 49; WMY speech, NUL annual conference, July 31, 1963, WMY 125. As late as August 12, Young was writing local executives to reassure them that it was all right to participate ("August 28th Demonstration in Washington," WMY memorandum to Executive Directors of Urban League Affiliates, Aug. 12, 1963, NUL Pt. 2, Series 1, Box 26).

12. J. Lewis interview; Abernathy interview; Rustin interview no. 1; Height interview.

13. Rustin interview no. 1 and no. 2.

14. Carl M. Brauer, *John F. Kennedy and the Second Reconstruction* (New York, 1977), pp. 271–73.

15. Transcript, Whitney Young, Jr., oral history interview, June 18, 1969, p. 7, Lyndon B. Johnson Library; Rustin interview no. 2.

16. Rustin interview no. 1 and no. 2.

17. J. Lewis interview; James Forman, *The Making of Black Revolutionaries* (New York, 1972), pp. 332–37.

18. The leaders' itinerary appears in Frank Montero memorandum to WMY, n.d. [Aug. 1963], NUL Pt. 2, Series 1, Box 25.

19. Platform Guests—Lincoln Memorial, National Association for the Advancement of Colored People Papers, Group 2, Series B, Box 373, Manuscript Division, Library of Congress; WMY speech at the March on Washington, Aug. 28, 1963, WMY 126.

20. Ruth U. Swayze to WMY, Aug. 29, 1963, Hobart Taylor, Jr., to WMY, Sept. 4, 1963, NUL Pt. 2, Series 1, Box 26.

21. WMY interview with Dr. Albert E. Gollin.

22. NUL board minutes, Feb. 20, 1964, WMY 12; WMY speech, NUL Annual Conference, July 31, 1963, WMY 125.

23. WMY quoted in "The Big Five in Civil Rights," *Time* 81 (June 28, 1963): 16 ("go to jail"); WMY notes for a speech on the occasion of the March on Montgomery, Mar. 25, 1965, WMY 131.

24. Zinn interview; NUL board minutes, May 18, 1965, p. 8, president's office, National Urban League, New York City.

25. On the Meredith march: Garrow, *Bearing the Cross*, pp. 476–87 (Carmichael quotes); WMY statement, "Four Points," June 14, 1966, WMY 140 ("black nationalist overtones"; "lack of respect"); Cleveland Sellers, *The River of No Return: The Autobiography of a Black Militant and the Life and Death of SNCC* (New York, 1973), pp. 162–63.

26. On WMY in Jackson: NUL executive committee minutes, June 21, 1966, WMY 16; WMY, Statement to the Press, June 26, 1966, Jackson, Miss., WMY 1a; WMY remarks prepared for delivery at Jackson, Miss., June 26, 1966, WMY 140 ("we are marching . . . "; "I have no intention of retreating"); *New York Times*, June 28, 1966, p. 22; A. Young interview.

27. NUL press release, June 14, 1966, WMY 209. The confidential report appears in neither the Young Papers nor the National Urban League Papers, so one

can only infer its contents from letters thanking Young for sending it. See, for example, G. D. Bradley to WMY, July 12, 1966, Francis S. Quillan to WMY, July 11, 1966, Howard H. Jones to WMY, July 18, 1966, Craig Thompson to WMY, July 11, 1966, WMY 143.

28. Allen interview no. 1; Andrew J. Young, "Whitney Young: Working from the Middle," *Life* 70 (Mar. 26, 1971), p. 4.

29. Eddy interview; *New York Times*, Jan. 19, 1967, p. 18, Jan. 26, 1967, p. 22.

30. Eddy interview; Height interview; NUL board minutes, Jan. 22, 1959, NUL Series 11, Box 5; record of Taconic Foundation giving to the National Urban League, Taconic Foundation records; record of Stephen R. Currier's personal gifts to the league, both in Taconic Foundation records; Currier to WMY, Jan. 4, 1961, WMY 12.

31. An Assessment Project, n.d., WMY to Stephen R. Currier, Apr. 11, 1963, Currier to Edward Bryce, Apr. 24, 1963, WMY to William J. Trent, Jr., May 7, 1963, all in Roy Wilkins Papers, Box 32, Manuscript Division, Library of Congress; Farmer interview; Height interview. The papers and other documents relevant to the project are in Assessment Project File, Taconic Foundation records.

32. Eddy interview.

33. Stephen R. Currier to Martin Luther King, Jr., June 12, 1963, MLK 1:1, 8:3; Eddy interview (source of the quotes). SNCC was not invited to join the group until later; it objected to being ignored and got King to intercede in its behalf. See Forman, *The Making of Black Revolutionaries*, pp. 364–65.

34. Eddy interview; *Newsday*, July 17, 1963, WMY 220; Height interview; Currier to Henry Steeger, July 25, 1963, WMY 38.

35. Height interview.

36. Wiley A. Branton to A. Philip Randolph, Aug. 13, 1964, WMY 38, Mar. 4, 1965, MLK 1:1, 7:30; Council for United Civil Rights Leadership, Report no. 1, July 16, 1963, WMY 38 (source of the quote).

37. NUL executive committee minutes, June 20, 1963, president's office, National Urban League, New York City.

38. Quoted in *Danville Register* (Va.), July 9, 1963, WMY 220.

39. Editorial, *New York Herald Tribune*, July 17, 1963, WMY 38. See also *New York Times*, July 10, 1963, p. 24; and *Detroit Free Press*, July 17, 1963, and *Spartanburg Herald* (S.C.), July 9, 1963, both in WMY 220.

40. Draft of letter from Stephen R. Currier and WMY, Sept. 11, 1963, and *New York Times*, July 18, 1963, WMY 38. The formula for distribution of funds, which gave each organization roughly 10 percent of its budget for the previous year, left SNCC with by far the smallest allocation, a decision that rankled SNCC leaders. See Forman, *The Making of Black Revolutionaries*, p. 366.

41. CUCRL press release, Oct. 22, 1963, MLK 1:1, 7:29; Equality Button Card, NUL Pt. 2, Series 5, Box 12; Martin Luther King to Wiley Branton, Jan. 13, 1965, NUL Pt. 2, Series 1, Box 13.

42. J. Lewis interview; Farmer interview; Height interview; Branton interview; A. Young interview. For a much more critical view, see Forman, *The Making of Black Revolutionaries*, pp. 366–70.

43. Stephen R. Currier to Dorothy I. Height, Aug. 14, 1964, MLK 1:1, 7:30; Eddy interview.

44. CUCRL minutes, Apr. 28, 1965, WMY 38; Arthur Q. Funn to Roy Wilkins, Jan. 30, 1967 (the same letter went to the other members of the council), NAACP Group 3, Series B, Box 455.

45. On WMY as moderate: J. Lewis interview; Rustin interview no. 1; Height interview; Farmer interview; Branton interview; Baird interview no. 1; Logan interview; Conyers interview; Parris interview.

46. Jackson quoted in *Duluth News Tribune* (Minn.), Mar. 14, 1971, NUL new series; Harold R. Sims, "Whitney Young's Open Society," *Annals* 396 (July 1971): 71; Jacob interview; Baird interview no. 1.

47. J. Lewis interview; Rustin interview no. 1.

48. McKissick interview; August Meier and Elliott Rudwick, *CORE: A Study in the Civil Rights Movement, 1942–1968* (New York, 1973), pp. 406–12.

49. Quoted in *Christian Science Monitor*, Sept. 3, 1968, WMY 207.

50. Farmer interview; R. H. Brown interview; WMY speech, Annual Meeting, Wichita Urban League, Mar. 13, 1962, WMY 124 ("It isn't Urban League *or*"); WMY speech, "Civil Rights Action and the Urban League," Wayne State University, Feb. 13, 1963, NUL Pt. 2, Series 5, Box 42 ("Most advocates of civil rights"); WMY, "Race Relations Leadership—1963," speech to Capital Press Club, Feb. 21, 1963, WMY 126 ("a single Messianic leader").

51. Quoted in "The Big Five in Civil Rights," p. 16.

52. Dumpson interview; Height interview.

53. WMY speech, National Association of Social Workers, Apr. 24, 1969, WMY 91.

54. *The Autobiography of Malcolm X* (1965; reprint, New York, 1966), pp. 243, 244, 385; Peter Goldman, *The Death and Life of Malcolm X*, 2d ed. (Urbana, Ill., 1979), pp. 6, 16, 232 ("mealy-mouth . . . action"; "I don't see why they hate me").

55. Goldman, *The Death and Life of Malcolm X*, pp. 228–29; Shabazz interview; Sutton interview; K. Clark interview no. 2; J. H. Johnson interview.

56. James Farmer, *Lay Bare the Heart: An Autobiography of the Civil Rights Movement* (New York, 1985), p. 216 ("iron fist"); Farmer interview.

57. Martin interview; McKissick interview.

CHAPTER IX

1. P. L. Prattis column, *Pittsburgh Courier*, June 9, [1962], courtesy of Eleanor Young Love.

2. WMY speech to Milwaukee businessmen at Schlitz Brown Bottle, Jan. 9, 1968, William R. Simms tape, courtesy of William R. Simms.

3. See, for example, transcript of WMY speech, Equal Opportunity Panel, American Bankers Association, Sept. 26, 1967, WMY 155; WMY speech, "Business, Race Relations, and the Community," New York Chamber of Commerce, Mar. 7, 1968, WMY 170.

4. WMY speech, Institute of Life Insurance, Dec. 12, 1967, WMY 147.

5. WMY speech, "Business, Race Relations, and the Community" ("high visibility"; "late on Monday"; "Exhibit A") and WMY speech, "Can the City Survive?" Robert Morris Associates, Oct. 28, 1968, WMY 167 ("they, too, can move up-

stairs"); WMY speech, "Community Communications," National Industrial Conference Board, Jan. 10, 1968, WMY 165 ("the Lena Hornes"); transcript, WMY speech, Equal Opportunity Panel, American Bankers Association.

6. WMY speech, "Business, Race Relations, and the Community."

7. *New York Times*, Dec. 3, 1964, p. 55; WMY speech, "Community Communications"; WMY speech, American Iron and Steel Institute, May 22, 1968, WMY 160.

8. Mr. Hill's reply, attached to WMY speech, National Association of Mutual Savings Banks, May 26, 1969, WMY 179.

9. WMY speech, Institute of Life Insurance.

10. Transcript, WMY speech, Economic Club of Detroit, Sept. 30, 1968, WMY 172.

11. WMY speech, Institute of Life Insurance.

12. Transcript, WMY speech, Public Affairs Forum, First National City Bank, Jan. 31, 1968, WMY 169.

13. Kenneth L. Meinen to MBY, Mar. 22, 1971, WMY 250 (hotel story); WMY quoted in Mary McGrory column, *Washington Evening Star*, Nov. 23, 1965, WMY 221 (airline story).

14. WMY addressing NUL board, May 1970, Kansas City, William R. Simms tape, courtesy of William R. Simms (Wallace story); MBY interview no. 1.

15. Transcript, WMY speech, Businessmen's Employment Luncheon, sponsored by the Greater Newark Chamber of Commerce and Greater Newark Development Council, Feb. 7, 1968, WMY 165 ("own best interest"); WMY speech to Milwaukee businessmen, Schlitz Brown Bottle ("I know of no group"; "productive consumers"); WMY speech, "Can the City Survive?" ("You are the one that suffers").

16. Kendall interview; Linen interview no. 1; Crawford interview; Ewing interview ("a very skillful way").

17. C. V. Hamilton interview; K. Clark interview no. 2.

18. WMY to Robert S. Oelman, Nov. 18, 1966, WMY 7.

19. Baird interview no. 1; Steeger interview ("I can't take it").

20. Batten interview.

21. Reed O. Hunt to Charles de Bretteville, May 20, 1969, James A. Linen Papers, courtesy of James A. Linen, Greenwich, Conn.; National Urban League, 1965 Corporate Contributors $500 & over, WMY 8; 1966 Corporate Honor Roll, WMY 165; Gary M. Bloom memorandum to Roger Stone, Feb. 20, 1970, and Keryn King to WMY, June 26, 1970, both in Linen Papers.

22. Income Comparison by Source, National Urban League, courtesy of Fund Department, National Urban League.

23. Jonas interview.

24. Richard T. Erickson to Nancy J. Weiss, June 27, 1988; R. R. Hailes to Nancy J. Weiss, June 29, 1988; M. Louis Camardo to Nancy J. Weiss, July 1, 1988; Roche interview.

25. "Celanese Luncheon," William R. Simms memorandum to WMY, Sept. 21, 1966, WMY 7; Kennedy interview; Cora Drewry, "Celanese Corporation Affirmative Action Employment Activities, 1960–1975," Sept. 22, 1988.

26. J. H. Johnson interview.

27. Donald S. Carmichael to WMY, Jan. 24, 1963, WMY 126 (Stouffer Foods); Earl E. Spencer to WMY, June 24, 1968, WMY 163; Fred H. White to WMY, Mar. 13, 1970 (Massachusetts Mutual Life), and Walter J. Shields to WMY, Mar. 19, 1970 (National Association of Life Underwriters), both in WMY 188.

28. Kennedy interview.

29. WMY, "Man and His Social Conscience," *AIA Journal*, Sept. 1968, p. 49, NUL new series.

30. Loeb interview; Baird interview no. 1.

31. Forger interview; Davenport interview; Logan interview.

32. Kendall interview; D. Rockefeller interview; Loeb interview; Batten interview; Gullander interview; Ford interview; Linen interview no. 1.

33. D. Rockefeller interview; Roche interview; Ford interview.

34. Heiskell interview; Ford interview.

35. Roger Wilkins to Nancy J. Weiss, Aug. 31, 1987.

36. WMY, *Beyond Racism* (New York, 1969), p. 111 ("fine-sounding words"); WMY column, *New York Times*, Mar. 13, 1971, p. 29.

CHAPTER X

1. "The Time Is Now," A Statement of the National Urban League to John F. Kennedy, President-elect, Dec. 29, 1960, NUL Pt. 2, Series 5, Box 11.

2. On the administration connections, see correspondence in Whitney M. Young, Jr., folder, John F. Kennedy Presidential Papers, White House Central Name File, Box 3098, John F. Kennedy Library. On the League's Washington office, see NUL board minutes, Feb. 16, 1962, WMY 12; *Washington Evening Star*, Feb. 12, 1962, WMY 220.

3. Henry Steeger, *You Can Remake America* (Garden City, N.Y., 1969), pp. 47–49 ("I'll go for that"); Summary of Points Discussed by the Officers of the National Urban League . . . with the President of the United States, Jan. 23, 1962, attached to Henry Steeger and WMY to the President, Jan. 23, 1962, NUL Pt. 2, Series 1, Box 55; NUL press release, "Roundup on Three-Day Urban League Conference in Nation's Capital," May 25, 1962, NUL Pt. 2, Series 5, Box 28 (JFK message).

4. NUL press releases, Aug. 2, 10, Sept. 20, 1962, NUL Pt. 2, Series 5, Box 29; May 8, 14, June 20, 1963, ibid., Box 30; *New York Times*, Apr. 27, 1963, p. 1, June 10, 1963, p. 1 ("only reacted"; "kind of guts"), July 23, 1963, p. 15, Oct. 30, 1963, p. 22 ("bare minimum").

5. The account of the Johnson phone call comes from Michael Amrine, a man who interviewed Young for a book he proposed to write about Johnson's first days in the White House. It is contained in a rough draft of a small section of the book, attached to Amrine to WMY, May 8, 1964, WMY 203.

6. Transcripts, Roy Wilkins oral history interview, Apr. 1, 1969, p. 5, and Whitney Young, Jr., oral history interview, June 18, 1969, pp. 1, 3, 4, Lyndon B. Johnson Library.

7. Kheel interview; A. Wilkins interview; transcript, WMY oral history interview, pp. 3–4, LBJ Library.

8. Transcript, Wilkins oral history interview, p. 12, LBJ Library; material relating to Nov. 29, 1963 meeting with Wilkins, in President's Appointment File [Diary Backup], Box 1, Lyndon B. Johnson Papers, Lyndon B. Johnson Library.

9. *New York Times*, Dec. 3, 1963, pp. 1, 20 ("the Kennedy program"), Dec. 8, 1963, Sec. 4, 3 ("magnolia accent").

10. Martin interview.

11. This assessment is based on interviews with Martin, Mitchell, Weaver, Farmer, Kheel, J. Lewis, Parris, and A. Young, as well as Lady Bird Johnson to Nancy J. Weiss, Dec. 14, 1984.

12. Telegrams and letters from Young to Johnson in WMY Name File, WHCF, LBJ Library; Weaver interview.

13. Weaver interview; Kheel interview; Martin interview; Steeger interview; memorandum, Anne to Bill, Jan. 10, 1964, re WMY response to telephone request from LBJ, Ex SP2–4, Box 133, LBJ Library.

14. Transcript of conversations with Young and Wilkins, quoted in Doris Kearns, *Lyndon Johnson and the American Dream* (New York, 1976), p. 192; Keller interview.

15. Andresen interview; Edmund P. Hennelly to Malcolm Andresen, Feb. 25, 1964, Andresen to WMY, Mar. 6, 1964, folder marked 1964 Personal: Senator Everett Dirksen, all in WMY 2; Keller interview; "Whitney Young: He Was a Doer," *Newsweek* 77 (Mar. 22, 1971): 29 ("blond Moses"); MBY interview no. 1; NUL board minutes, May 21, 1964, WMY 12.

16. Baird interview no. 1; Ann Tanneyhill, "Whitney M. Young, Jr., The 'Voice of the Voiceless,' " *Columbia Library Columns* 26 (May 1977): 6–7.

17. MBY interview no. 1.

18. Transcript, WMY oral history interview, p. 15, LBJ Library. Johnson appointed Young to the President's Commission on Law Enforcement and the Administration of Justice, the National Advisory Council to the Office of Economic Opportunity, the National Commission on Technology, Automation and Economic Progress, the White House Conference on Education, the President's Special Panel on Cities, the Kaiser Committee on Urban Rehabilitation, the United States delegation to the General Conference of the United Nations Educational, Scientific and Cultural Organization, and the United States delegation to the United Nations General Assembly.

19. WMY interview, RJBOHC.

20. WMY speech, NUL annual conference, Sept. 7, 1961, NUL Pt. 2, Series 5, Box 29; *Grand Rapids Press*, Sept. 1, 1962, WMY 229a.

21. WMY speech, "Unless Something Special Happens," Third Annual Negro American Labor Council Convention, Nov. 9, 1962, WMY 123.

22. WMY speech, "The Challenges of Race Relations," City Club of Cleveland, Jan. 19, 1963, WMY 126.

23. See NUL board minutes, Feb. 7, 1963, president's office, National Urban League, New York City; the correspondence and drafts in NUL Pt. 2, Series 5, Box 7; NUL executive committee minutes, Apr. 11, 1963, WMY 12; NUL board minutes, May 16, 1963, NUL Pt. 2, Series 5, Box 18; Guichard Parris/Lester Brooks interview with Henry Steeger, Parris Box 48.

24. Steeger, *You Can Remake America*, pp. 43–44.

25. A Statement by the Board of Trustees of the National Urban League urging a crash program of special effort to close up the gap between the conditions of Negro and white citizens, June 9, 1963, NUL Pt. 2, Series 5, Box 7.

26. Harris poll, reported in "How Whites Feel About Negroes," *Newsweek* 62 (Oct. 21, 1963): 45; WMY speech, "New Challenges in Today's Race Relations," White Plains Community Church, Unitarian, Sept. 23, 1963, WMY 127.

27. "Should There Be 'Compensation' for Negroes?" *New York Times Magazine*, Oct. 6, 1963, p. 129; NUL, *1963 Annual Report*, p. 4, NUL Library, New York City.

28. *New York Times*, Feb. 23, 1964, p. 34; memorandum, Guichard Parris to NUL Staff, Feb. 24, 1964, NUL Pt. 2, Series 5, Box 14 (source of the quote); Parris, Outline to serve as basis for discussion with Mr. Frank Adams, New York Times, Feb. 24, 1964, WMY 7; NUL board minutes, Feb. 20, 1964, WMY 12.

29. NUL, *Annual Report*, 1964–1965, NUL Library; WMY interview, RJBOHC. On Young's role as an adviser to Sargent Shriver in the early stages of the development of the poverty program, see, for example, *New York Times*, Feb. 15, 1964, p. 8; memorandum, Guichard Parris to Local League Executives and Staff, Mar. 3, 1964, NUL Pt. 2, Series 5, Box 14; Walter W. Heller to WMY, Mar. 14, 1964, WMY 128; NUL board minutes, May 21, 1964, WMY 12. Transcripts of his testimony on Capitol Hill in support of the program appear in WMY 198, 199, and 200.

30. Peter H. Weiss, "The Origins of Affirmative Action: The Federal Equal Employment Opportunity Program, 1961–1969" (senior thesis, Princeton University, 1979), pp. iv, 9–12, 45; Lyndon B. Johnson, Commencement Address at Howard University, June 4, 1965, in James MacGregor Burns, ed., *To Heal and to Build: The Programs of President Lyndon B. Johnson* (New York, 1968), pp. 218–19; Lee Rainwater and William L. Yancey, *The Moynihan Report and the Politics of Controversy* (Cambridge, Mass., 1967), pp. 4, 188. Compare the Howard University address with *To Be Equal* (New York, 1964), pp. 22–23, 25.

31. Davis interview no. 1.

32. *To Be Equal* was published by McGraw-Hill and written by Lester Brooks. For the reviews, see *New York World-Telegram*, Aug. 11, 1964, and *New York Times Book Review*, Oct. 11, 1964, WMY 233c.

33. Andresen interview; memorandum, Ramsey Clark to the President, Jan. 7, 1965, WMY Name File, WHCF, LBJ Library.

34. Teletype, Director FBI to SACS, Dec. 21, 1964, Federal Bureau of Investigation File 161–3190–1, and J. Edgar Hoover to Lee C. White, Jan. 14, 1965, Federal Bureau of Investigation File 161–3190–54, Federal Bureau of Investigation Papers, obtained through the Freedom of Information/Privacy Act. The file on the investigation is an inch thick. For press accounts, see, for example, *Denver Post*, Nov. 8, 1964, *New York World-Telegram and The Sun*, Nov. 20, 1964, both in WMY 220, and *Amsterdam News* (N.Y.), Jan. 9, 1965, WMY 221.

35. Jimmy Breslin column, *New York Herald Tribune*, Jan. 8, 1965, clipping in Federal Bureau of Investigation File 161–3190–A, FBI/FOIPA.

36. Memorandum, Jack Valenti to the President, Jan. 12, 1965, and Lee C. White, "Notes for Discussion with Martin Luther King," memorandum for the President, Jan. 13, 1965, both in Ex PE2, WHCF, Box 8, LBJ Library.

37. NUL executive committee minutes, Jan. 18, 1965, WMY Box 15.

38. Roger Wilkins to Nancy J. Weiss, Aug. 31, 1987.

39. "Washington Whispers," *U.S. News & World Report*, Nov. 1, 1965, and *New York Herald Tribune*, Nov. 9, 1965, both in WMY 221.

40. Transcript, WMY oral history interview, p. 9, LBJ Library; Baird interview no. 1; MBY interview no. 1.

41. Quoted in Stephen B. Oates, *Let the Trumpet Sound: The Life of Martin Luther King, Jr.* (New York, 1982), p. 376.

42. James Forman, *The Making of Black Revolutionaries* (New York, 1972), pp. 369–70.

43. Harris poll reported in *New York Post*, Apr. 11, 1966, and WMY quoted in *Boston Traveler*, June 2, 1966 ("rats tonight"), both in WMY 221; transcript, "Meet the Press," Aug. 21, 1966, p. 62, WMY 192.

44. Hobson quoted in *Washington Post*, Mar. 30, 1967, WMY 223; WMY and King quoted in David Halberstam, "The Second Coming of Martin Luther King," *Harper's* 235 (Aug. 1967): 49; *Providence Journal*, Apr. 23, 1967, WMY 224; Oates, *Let the Trumpet Sound*, p. 432.

45. Oates, *Let the Trumpet Sound*, pp. 437–38; WMY quoted in NUL press release, Apr. 5, 1967, WMY 205.

46. K. Clark interview no. 1.

47. *New York Times*, June 15, 1967, p. 31; David J. Garrow, *Bearing the Cross: Martin Luther King, Jr., and the Southern Christian Leadership Conference* (New York, 1986), p. 566.

48. *New York Times*, July 22, 1966, p. 4; memorandum, George Christian to the President, July 9, 1966, WMY Name File, WHCF, LBJ Library; NUL press release, July 18, 1966, WMY 209 (source of the quote).

49. "To Be Equal" column no. 32, Aug. 10, 1966, WMY 211.

50. Text of cable from Lodge, for Bundy from Sieverts, July 23, 1966, President's Appointment File [Diary Backup], July 26, 1966, Box 40, LBJ Library; *New York Times*, July 24, 1966, p. 49.

51. *New York Times*, July 27, 1966, p. 24; NUL press release, July 27, 1966, WMY 211.

52. "To Be Equal" columns no. 32–35, Aug. 10, 17, 24, 31, 1966, WMY 211; WMY, "When the Negroes in Vietnam Come Home," *Harper's* 234 (June 1967): 63–69.

53. WMY quoted in *Providence Journal*, Aug. 27, 1967, WMY 224; Johnson quoted in David Halberstam, "Notes from the Bottom of the Mountain," *Harper's*, June 1968, p. 41, NUL new series ("I want a Negro"), and in MBY interview no. 1 ("you explain it to the press").

54. Gullander interview.

55. Itinerary for Group 3, American Observer Group, Aug. 31, 1967, WMY 8; *New York Times*, Sept. 1, 1967, WMY 224.

56. WMY handwritten notes on envelope of invitation to reception from U.S. Ambassador to South Vietnam, Sept. 1, 1967, WMY 8; *Washington Post*, Sept. 4, 1967, WMY 224.

57. "Meeting with Vietnam Election Observers in the Cabinet Room," memorandum, Jim Jones to the President, Sept. 6, 1967, and "Summary of the Presi-

dent's Meeting with News Publishers and Columnists and the Vietnam Election Observers," memorandum, Larry Levinson to the President, Sept. 6, 1967, both in President's Appointment File [Diary Backup], Sept. 6, 1967, Box 75, LBJ Library.

58. Mary McGrory column, *Chicago Sun-Times*, Sept. 3, 1967, WMY 224; K. E. Wallach to WMY, July 25, 1966, WMY 3 ("tool of LBJ"); Charles H. Alspach to WMY, Sept. 5, 1967, WMY 8 ("I am ashamed").

59. Zinn interview; A. Young interview.

60. White House press release, "Remarks of the President at the Urban League Dinner," Nov. 19, 1968, WMY 29a; transcript, WMY oral history interview, p. 4, LBJ Library ("beautiful gesture"); *New York Times*, Nov. 20, 1968, p. 30; WMY, "LBJ Steps Down," "To Be Equal" column no. 2, Jan. 8, 1969, WMY 216; *New York Times*, Jan. 21, 1969, p. 29; inscription quoted in Nicholas C. Chriss, "The LBJ Library," *Chicago Sun-Times*, May 9, 1971, NUL new series.

CHAPTER XI

1. WMY Sr. and Laura Ray Young to WMY, Aug. 17, 1962, WMY 263 ("leading servants"); WMY Sr. to WMY, Jan. 30, 1961, WMY 1 ("one of the most responsible jobs"); Love interview no. 1; Boswell interview no. 2.

2. Boswell interview no. 2; B. B. Hamilton interview; Cantarella interview.

3. Casteel interview; Baird interview no. 1; MBY interview no. 1 and no. 3.

4. Cantarella interview; WMY quoted in "The Man Who Didn't Want to be the First Negro in the Cabinet," *Pageant*, Apr. 1966, p. 115, WMY 221.

5. MBY interview no. 1 and no. 3; Casteel interview; Trent interview no. 1 and no. 3; Cantarella interview.

6. Casteel interview; MBY interview no. 3 and no. 6; Shelley interview ("there goes the neighborhood").

7. MBY interview no. 3; Casteel interview; Cantarella interview.

8. Casteel interview; Vinson interview.

9. Cantarella interview; undated birthday card, undated Father's Day card, Father's Day card postmarked June 17, 1966, and Marcia and Bobby Boles to WMY, postmarked May 12, 1970, all in WMY 263.

10. Cantarella interview; Marcia Young to WMY and MBY, Aug. [21], 1966, and to WMY, postmarked Oct. 15, 1966, WMY 263.

11. MBY interview no. 1 and no. 3; Casteel interview; Cantarella interview; Davis interview no. 1; Baird interview no. 1; Russell interview; Trent interview no. 3; Roper interview; Compton interview.

12. WMY to MBY, postmarked July 1962; Oct. 24, 1966; n.d. [1967]; and postmarked Oct. 22, 1969, respectively, all in WMY 263.

13. MBY interview no. 4; *New York Times*, Jan. 3, 1969, p. 23; WMY to MBY, Jan. 2, 1971, WMY 265.

14. Cantarella interview.

15. Maude Kimball to MBY, Sept. 5, 1967, WMY 263; MBY interview no. 3; MBY quoted in Dunbar S. McLaurin, "The Whitney I Knew," *Sphinx* 57 (May–June 1971): 43, courtesy of Eleanor Young Love; Allen interview no. 2 ("Mr. Quality"); Wolfe interview; W. J. Brown interview; K. Clark interview no. 3.

16. Casteel interview; Cantarella interview.

17. H. Lewis interview no. 1 and no. 2; Mervis interview; Barney interview; Linen interview no. 3; Tree interview; Jacobs interview; Wallace interview; Freeland interview; G. Hill interview; Jones interview; Farmer interview; Coleman interview; Wardlaw interview; Poston interview. Many other people spoke about Young's relationships with women, but did so only after the tape recorder had been turned off.

18. Boswell interview no. 2; Casteel interview; Cantarella interview.

19. Maude Kimball, in Kimball interview no. 2; H. Lewis interview no. 1 ("he'd always let you know"); Mervis interview; Barney interview ("baaad brother").

20. See, for example, K. Clark interview no. 2; Farmer interview; H. Lewis interview no. 1; R. H. Brown interview; Linen interview no. 3; Jacobs interview.

21. Baird interview no. 1 ('21' Club); Crawford interview.

22. Pettigrew interview no. 2 ("bottle of champagne"); Russell interview; Allen interview no. 1; Whaley interview no. 2; C. J. Hamilton interview; Cantarella interview; K. Clark interview no. 4; Pettigrew interview no. 3 ("he *just loved it*"); Davis interview no. 1; Kimball interview no. 1 and no. 2; WMY to Otto Fuerbringer, Aug. 10, 1967, WMY 3; MBY interview no. 1.

23. WMY quoted in "Whitney Young: He Was a Doer," *Newsweek* 77 (Mar. 22, 1971): 29 (125th Street; "people who have something to give"), and in Carl T. Rowan and Dreda K. Ford, "In Memory of Whitney Young," *Reader's Digest* 100 (Apr. 1972): 125 ("I never promised to live in the ghetto").

24. MBY interview no. 1; Baird interview no. 1; WMY quoted in Helen Mervis, remarks at New Orleans Urban League tribute to WMY, May 30, 1971, WMY 254 ("being with the people"); "Races: The Other 97%," *Time* 90 (Aug. 11, 1967): 15; WMY quoted in "Whitney Young: He Was a Doer," p. 29 ("floating around on some yacht").

25. K. Clark interview no. 4.

CHAPTER XII

1. E. Brown interview; Watts quoted in *Boston Traveler*, Sept. 30, 1966, WMY 223; Moore and Alinsky quoted in "Races," *Time* 90 (Aug. 11, 1967): 13; Julius Lester, *Look Out, Whitey! Black Power's Gon' Get Your Mama!* (New York, 1968), p. 115. For the use of the other racial epithets, see, for example, Adam Clayton Powell quoted in *New York Times*, Aug. 30, 1966, *Los Angeles Times*, Sept. 5, 1966, and *Washington Post*, Jan. 9, 1967, WMY 223; *Baltimore Sun*, June 22, 1967, p. A10, WMY 224; *Christian Science Monitor*, Sept. 3, 1968, WMY 207; William Raspberry column, *Louisville Courier-Journal*, Mar. 16, 1971, WMY file, Western Branch, Louisville Free Public Library; Tom Buckley, "Whitney Young: Black Leader or 'Oreo Cookie'?" *New York Times Magazine*, Sept. 20, 1970, pp. 32, 74; Claude Lewis column, *Philadelphia Bulletin*, Mar. 21, 1971, NUL new series; "Civil Rights: A Kind of Bridge," *Time* 97 (Mar. 22, 1971): 20; Calvin S. Morris column, *Chicago Daily Defender*, Mar. 26, 1971, NUL new series.

2. WMY, "We Are All Militants," "To Be Equal" column no. 29, July 10, 1968, WMY 215 ("shout and scream"; "we are all militant"); " 'We Need Tangible Vic-

tories,' " *U.S. News & World Report* 64 (Apr. 22, 1968): 45 ("burners and build-ers").

3. "Crisis and Commitment," statement released Oct. 14, 1966, WMY 209.

4. NUL press release, July 26, 1967, WMY 205.

5. *New York Times*, August 7, 1967, p. 1.

6. WMY quoted in *Long Island Press*, Aug. 11, 1966, WMY 223, and transcript, "Face the Nation," July 9, 1967, p. 19, WMY 192.

7. NUL press release, WMY Statement on the Anti-Riot Legislation Pending before the House of Representatives, July 14, 1967, WMY 209; WMY column, *Washington Daily News*, Aug. 7, 1967, WMY vertical file, MSRC.

8. Quoted in *New York Times*, Aug. 21, 1967, p. 24.

9. Wilkins quoted in "Negro Leaders Dividing—the Effect," *U.S. News & World Report* 61 (July 18, 1966): 31; WMY quoted in NUL press release, July 11, 1966, WMY 209.

10. WMY quoted in: *New York Times*, Aug. 5, 1966, p. 10; press release, WINS News Conference, July 31, 1966, WMY 192; transcript, "Meet the Press," Aug. 21, 1966, pp. 38–39, WMY 192, respectively.

11. *Springfield Sun* (Ohio), Jan. 20, 1967, WMY 223 (source of the quote); *Rochester Democrat and Chronicle* (N.Y.), Mar. 3, 1967, WMY 223; transcript, "Face the Nation," July 9, 1967, pp. 8–9, WMY 192.

12. WMY speech to Urban Coalition, quoted in *One Worker*, Sept. 3, 1967, WMY vertical file, SCRBC; WMY quoted in *New York Times*, Nov. 2, 1968, p. 24 ("not a fool").

13. Letter to the editor from Alice Alexander, *Denver Post*, July 16, 1967, WMY 224.

14. WMY quoted in: *New York Times*, Apr. 5, 1968, p. 1; *Washington Post*, Apr. 9, 1968, WMY 229; *Denver Post*, Apr. 21, 1968, NUL new series.

15. " 'We Need Tangible Victories,' " pp. 45–46.

16. Kimball interview no. 2; Lindsley F. Kimball to WMY Sr., Sept. 20, 1966, Scrapbook no. 6, WMY Sr. Box 1; Jackson interview.

17. Rusk quoted in *New York Post* [Aug. 1?, 1966], WMY 204 ("too much rea-sonableness"), and in Guichard Parris and Lester Brooks, *Blacks in the City: A History of the National Urban League* (Boston, 1971), pp. 443–44.

18. Quoted in *New York Post*, Aug. 3, 1966, WMY 204.

19. *New York Post* [Aug. 1?, 1966], Aug. 3, 1966 (source of the quote), WMY 204; UPI interview with Young in *Detroit News*, Aug. 16, 1967, WMY 224; WMY speech, NUL annual conference, Aug. 20, 1967, WMY 149.

20. WMY notes, Urban League Leadership Conference, Apr. 27, 1968, WMY 168; NUL board minutes, May 17, 1968, president's office, National Urban League, New York City; A New Thrust for the National Urban League, Aug. 1968, Ford PA 68–897; minutes, NUL Annual Delegate Assembly, July 31, 1968, WMY 19.

21. WMY speech to NUL annual conference, July 29, 1968, WMY 165; min-utes, Annual Delegate Assembly, July 31, 1968, WMY 19; WMY speech to NUL annual conference, July 28, 1969, WMY 180 (source of the quote).

22. *Wall Street Journal*, Aug. 12, 1968, p. 24, WMY 229. On some of the proj-ects, see Sterling Tucker, "New Thrust—One Year Later: A Report to the Dele-

gate Assembly" [1969], WMY 19; National Urban League, "1969–1970: A Discussion Prospectus," Sept. 17, 1969, NUL new series.

23. WMY speech, Equal Opportunity Day Dinner, Nov. 19, 1968, WMY 173.

24. WMY, "Needed: A Domestic Marshall Plan," *Saturday Review* 51 (Mar. 30, 1968): 18 ("vicious network"); *Christian Science Monitor*, Sept. 3, 1968, WMY 207.

25. WMY, *Beyond Racism* (New York, 1969), p. 62. The book was published by McGraw-Hill and written by Dan Davis.

26. NUL executive committee minutes, June 20, 1967, WMY 17.

27. Transcript, "Face to Face with Murphy Martin" [Aug. 13, 1969?], p. 4, WMY 194.

28. WMY interview, RJBOHC.

29. Wilkins in *Washington Post*, July 6, 1968, NUL new series; WMY interview, RJBOHC ("ladies and gentlemen"); WMY speech to 1968 CORE Convention, July 6, 1968, WMY 162; delegates quoted in *New York Times*, July 7, 1968, p. 1.

30. Editorial, *Trentonian*, July 15, 1968, WMY 229 ("New Whitney Young"); *New York Times*, July 7, 1968, pp. 1, 38 ("sharp reversal" and McKissick quote), Price M. Cobbs, M.D., to WMY, July 26, 1968 ("impressive and courageous"), and Thomas Adams (social worker) to WMY, July 9, 1968, all in WMY 162; editorial, *Baltimore Afro-American*, Aug. 20, 1968, WMY 229.

31. Jonathan Marshall to WMY, July 8, 1968, Robert E. Brooker to WMY, July 10, 1968, and Millicent H. Fenwick to WMY, July 7, 1968, all in WMY 162.

32. WMY editorial for Metromedia Broadcasting, July 9, 1968, WMY 194; WMY to Thomas Adams, July 15, 1968, WMY 162; W. H. Wheeler, Jr. to WMY, Aug. 13, 1968, WMY 162.

33. WMY quoted in transcript, WNBC Television's "Speaking Freely," Nov. 8, 1969, p. 6, WMY 194.

34. Charles Bartlett column, *Washington Evening Star*, July 11, 1968, and editorial, *Milwaukee Journal*, n.d. [July 1968], both in WMY 162.

35. Editorial, *New Rochelle Standard-Star*, July 15, 1968, WMY 229; editorial, *New Orleans States-Item*, July 30, 1968, WMY 273.

36. C. V. Hamilton interview.

37. Dixon interview ("didn't raise his voice"); Fair interview ("disarmed them"); Barkstall interview; Barney interview; W. J. Brown interview; F. Campbell interview; F. Williams interview; *New York Times*, Aug. 1, 1968, p. 48; WMY quoted in "Races," *Time* 92 (Aug. 9, 1968): 21.

38. *New York Times*, July 29, 1969, p. 22, July 31, 1969, p. 21 (Linen; "jam Whitney Young"); *Washington Post*, July 31, 1969, p. A–28, and *Washington Afro-American*, Aug. 2, 1969 ("controlled by Whitey"), as reported in Federal Bureau of Investigation report on National Urban League National Conference, Aug. 26, 1969, File 100–23217–64, Federal Bureau of Investigation Papers obtained through the Freedom of Information/Privacy Act.

39. *New York Times*, July 31, 1969, p. 21; WMY quoted in *Washington Post*, July 31, 1969, p. A–28, FBI/FOIPA; Mack interview; R. H. Brown interview; NUL board minutes, July 30, 1969, president's office, National Urban League, New York City (source of the quotes).

40. NUL executive committee minutes, Oct. 20, 1970, p. 8, president's office,

National Urban League, New York City; WMY quoted in *New York Times*, Mar. 12, 1971, p. 41.

41. Baraka interview; NUL executive committee minutes, Jan. 20, 1970, p. 2, president's office, National Urban League, New York City.

42. Baraka interview; Baraka quoted in *New York Times*, Sept. 5, 1970, p. 6, WMY 229a ("political alliance with Whitney Young").

43. WMY, "Separatism? 'We ARE Separated—and That's the Cause of All Our Woes,' " *Ebony* 25 (Aug. 1970): 90–91, 94.

44. Quoted in *New York Post*, Sept. 5, 1970, WMY 229a.

45. Stone interview; Jordan interview no. 2; Vinson interview.

46. WMY speech, "Realities of Power," Congress of African Peoples Conference, Sept. 5, 1970, WMY 188; Baraka interview; Stone interview.

47. WMY speech to NUL board, May 1970, Kansas City, William R. Simms tape, courtesy of William R. Simms.

48. Young told the story to Tom Buckley, who reported it in "Whitney Young: Black Leader or 'Oreo Cookie'?" p. 32.

CHAPTER XIII

1. Quoted in NUL press release, "Statement by WMY on the 1968 Election," Nov. 6, 1968, WMY 206.

2. *New York Times*, Nov. 16, 1968, p. 17 ("concern about the divisions"; "quest to gain the trust"); *Washington Post*, Nov. 16, 1968 ("a man is innocent"), and McGrory in *Washington Evening Star*, Nov. 18, 1968, both in NUL new series.

3. *Wall Street Journal*, Nov. 15, 1968, WMY 229.

4. *New York Times*, Dec. 13, 1968, p. 36; *Los Angeles Times* news service article in *Omaha World-Herald*, Dec. 12, 1968, *Omaha World-Herald* Library.

5. Transcript, "Meet the Press," Dec. 22, 1968, pp. 2–3, WMY 194; Richard M. Nixon, *Four Great Americans: Tributes Delivered by President Richard Nixon* (New York, 1972), pp. 42, 43.

6. WMY addressing NUL board, May 1970, Kansas City, William R. Simms tape, courtesy of William R. Simms (source of the quote); Ernest Tidyman, "Whitney Young: New Thrust for the Urban League," *Tuesday Magazine*, Jan. 1969, WMY vertical file, MSRC.

7. National Urban League, "A Call to Action: Recommendations on the Urban and Racial Crisis Submitted to President-Elect Richard M. Nixon," Jan. 10, 1969, Parris Box 42.

8. NUL board minutes, Feb. 11, 1969, p. 3, May 20, 1969, p. 9, president's office, National Urban League, New York City.

9. Jonathan Schell, *The Time of Illusion* (New York, 1976), pp. 39–41; Harvard Sitkoff, *The Struggle for Black Equality, 1954–1980* (New York, 1981), pp. 223–25.

10. Young first made the charges in his speech to the Urban League's annual conference (WMY speech, NUL annual conference, July 28, 1969, WMY 180). He repeated them in an address to the American Bar Association, reported in *New York Times*, Aug. 14, 1969, p. 17, and in a speech at the annual convention of the National League of Cities, reported in ibid., Dec. 7, 1969, p. 67.

11. Godfrey Hodgson, *America in Our Time* (Garden City, N.Y., 1976), pp. 384–85; telegram, Sam Brown, David Hawk, David Mixner to WMY, Sept. 30, 1969, and Susan Werbe to WMY, Oct. 1, 1969, WMY 21.

12. Transcript, Whitney Young, Jr., oral history interview, June 18, 1969, p. 12, Lyndon B. Johnson Library; Baird interview; telegram, WMY to Susan Werbe, Oct. 8, 1969, WMY 21.

13. Memorandum, WMY to NUL Trustees, Oct. 7, 1969, WMY 22.

14. NUL press release, "Statement by Whitney M. Young, Jr., on Vietnam," Oct. 13, 1969, WMY 22.

15. *New York Times*, Oct. 14, 1969, WMY 21.

16. NUL board minutes, Nov. 19, 1969, p. 15, Feb. 16, 1970, p. 8 (source of the quote), president's office, National Urban League, New York City; Schell, *The Time of Illusion*, pp. 23, 81–82.

17. Transcript, John Slawson interview with WMY, Mar. 16, 1970, p. 19, attached to Slawson to WMY, June 2, 1970, WMY 29a; WMY addressing NUL board, May 1970, Kansas City, Simms tape.

18. *New York Times*, June 30, 1970, p. 1, July 12, 1970, p. 42. One in four blacks approved of the administration, compared with six in ten whites.

19. Garment interview; *New York Times*, July 1, 1970, p. 1, July 4, 1970, p. 6 (NBC report); *Norfolk Journal & Guide*, July 11, 1970, WMY 209 (UPI report).

20. Shelley interview; WMY, "A Strategy for the Seventies: Unity, Coalition, Negotiation," keynote address, NUL annual conference, July 19, 1970, WMY 190. Young's close associates were unaware of the overture from the administration, and some of them find the story improbable (see, for example, Davis interview no. 2). But James A. Linen, who, as president of the National Urban League, would have been in a position to know about it, confirms the above interpretation (Linen interview no. 2).

21. *New York Post*, July 21, 1970, p. 12, July 23, 1970, p. 8, editorial, *Amsterdam News* (N.Y.), July 25, 1970, p. 1, and *New York Times*, July 25, 1970, p. 10, all in WMY 229a.

22. *Amsterdam News* (N.Y.), July 25, 1970, p. 1, WMY 229a; *Atlanta Daily World*, July 23, 1970, WMY biographical file, AUC; *New York Times*, July 20, 1970, p. 1, July 22, 1970, p. 27; Jackson quoted in Calvin S. Morris column, *Chicago Daily Defender*, Mar. 26, 1971, NUL new series ("access to inside counsels"), and telegram, Jesse L. Jackson to WMY, July 11, 1970, WMY 1a; Kenyatta quoted in *New York Post*, July 21, 1970, p. 12, WMY 229a; Troy Brailey to WMY, Aug. 1, 1970, WMY 4.

23. Jesse Louis Jackson, "The Brothers Would Not Have Understood," *Equal Opportunity* 3 (Sept. 1971): 22, WMY 1a; MBY interview no. 2; Tucker interview.

24. Quoted in *Washington Post*, Aug. 20, 1970, WMY vertical file, MSRC ("black Moses"), and in *New York Times*, Aug. 20, 1970, pp. 1, 20 ("sort of like Jell-o").

25. "Meeting with the President and the Cabinet," memorandum, WMY to NUL Board of Trustees, Presidents and Executive Directors of Local Affiliates, Jan. 4, 1971, and WMY to Leonard Garment, Dec. 14, 1970, both in NUL new series; NUL board minutes, Feb. 15, 1971, WMY 23; Tucker interview; Davis interview no. 1.

26. Bernard E. Garnett, "Local Urban Leagues Face Funding Crisis," *Race Relations Reporter*, n.d., attached to memorandum, Bill Perry to Enid [Baird], Sept. 24, 1970, WMY 209; "National Urban League Leaders Holds [*sic*] Emergency Conference," NUL press release, Nov. 11, 1970, WMY 212 (source of the quote).

27. Synopsis, Cabinet Session, Nov. 20, 1970, WMY 23; "Financial Position of the Agency," memorandum, WMY to NUL Staff, Dec. 15, 1970, WMY 24; "Salary Increments," memorandum, Executive Director to NUL Staff, Jan. 11, 1971, WMY 23.

28. Income Comparison by Source, National Urban League, courtesy of Fund Department, National Urban League, New York City.

29. Bundy interview; address by McGeorge Bundy, annual banquet, National Urban League, Aug. 2, 1966, Ford PA 66–139.

30. Bundy interview; Ford Foundation, *Annual Report, Oct. 1, 1965 to Sept. 30, 1966*, pp. 72, 91, 114, *Oct. 1, 1966 to Sept. 30, 1967*, pp. 16, 82–84, *Oct. 1, 1967 to Sept. 30, 1968*, pp. 6, 85, *Oct. 1, 1968 to Sept. 30, 1969*, p. 111, *Oct. 1, 1969 to Sept. 30, 1970*, p. 21. The $4,700,000 compares with a contribution of $1,604,000 to the NAACP.

31. Sviridoff interview.

32. "National Urban League's Proposal," memorandum, Ronald Gault to Roger Wilkins, Dec. 7, 1970, Ford PA 70–68, folder no. 1; R. Wilkins interview no. 3; Sviridoff interview.

33. "Urban League Renewal," memorandum, Roger W. Wilkins to McGeorge Bundy, Oct. 14, 1970, Ford PA 70–68, General Correspondence.

34. WMY to McGeorge Bundy, Oct. 19, Dec. 3, 1970, and Howard R. Dressner to WMY, Jan. 29, 1971, NUL new series.

35. *New York Times*, Mar. 12, 1971, p. 41, says that Young got the idea for the meeting when he became angry at reports of proposed industrial bailouts. See also Tucker interview.

36. Garment interview; Whaley interview no. 1; WMY to John Ehrlichman, Dec. 24, 1970, NUL new series; Tucker interview. For the jockeying within the administration over arrangements for the meeting, see the sheaf of documents in Ex HU2, White House Central Files, Nixon Presidential Materials Project, National Archives.

37. WMY, "New Role for Community Groups," "To Be Equal" column no. 50, Dec. 30, 1970, WMY 219.

38. NUL, *Annual Report, 1970*, National Urban League Library, New York City.

39. "Meeting with the President and the Cabinet," memorandum, WMY to NUL Board of Trustees, Presidents and Executive Directors of Local Affiliates, Jan. 4, 1971, NUL new series; Allen interview no. 1; WMY, "To Be Equal," *Amsterdam News* (N.Y.), Jan. 9, 1971, p. 14.

40. Office of the White House Press Secretary, transcript, Press Conference of Whitney Young, Dec. 22, 1970, WMY 212.

41. WMY to Leonard Garment, Dec. 24, 1970, NUL new series; WMY to Richard M. Nixon, Dec. 24, 1970, Ex HU2, WHCF, Nixon Presidential Materials Project.

42. *Amsterdam News* (N.Y.), Jan. 2, 1971, pp. 1, 14, 39; typescript, Rowan, Dec. 23, 1970, NUL new series.

43. Whaley interview no. 2; Recap of NUL Cabinet Discussion on White House Meeting, Dec. 28, 1970, NUL new series; NUL executive committee minutes, Jan. 19, 1971, pp. 4–5, WMY 24; NUL board minutes, Feb. 15–16, 1971, WMY 23; NUL board minutes, May 17, 1971, pp. 4–5, president's office, National Urban League, New York City; *New York Times*, Mar. 12, 1971, p. 41.

CHAPTER XIV

1. MBY interview no. 1; Compton interview; Baird interview no. 1; Tucker interview.

2. MBY interview no. 1.

3. WMY quoted in *New York Times*, Oct. 31, 1963, p. 23 (Episcopal Diocese), Nov. 22, 1963, p. 29 (Union of American Hebrew Congregations); WMY to Pope Paul VI, July 10, 1967, WMY 9.

4. WMY speech, "The Antipoverty Program—Its Strengths and Weaknesses," National Association of Housing and Redevelopment Officials, Oct. 27, 1965, WMY 131.

5. WMY speech, "Social Needs to Which Voluntary Organizations Like the YMCA Should Respond," National Council of the YMCAs, May 14, 1966, WMY 137; WMY quoted in *New York Times*, Mar. 25, 1969, p. 95.

6. NAHRO president quoted in *Providence Evening Bulletin*, Oct. 27, 1965, WMY 131; Jack Gould in *New York Times*, Mar. 30, 1969, p. 21.

7. Excerpts, WMY speech, "The Engineer's Role in Urban Problems," National Society of Professional Engineers, Jan. 11, 1968, National Society of Professional Engineers, News of the Engineering Profession, Jan. 26, 1968, Roger E. Goodwin to WMY, Jan. 29, 1968 ("stand up and be counted"), Lee Wright to WMY, Feb. 9, 1968 ("we seek your help"), all in WMY 165.

8. WMY, "Man and His Social Conscience" and "Business Session," *AIA Journal*, Sept. 1968, 47 (source of the quotes) and 114, NUL new series; "AIA Establishes Unique Task Force," *Builders Report/News & Features*, Sept. 2, 1968, WMY 206; "Status Report on Joint NUL-AIA Projects," memorandum, Nancy Lane to Gary Bloom, Apr. 23, 1970, WMY 11.

9. Clark interview no. 3.

10. WMY speech, National Conference on Social Welfare, May 24, 1967, WMY 149.

11. Dumpson interview; Ginsberg interview. See also WMY speech, National Association of Social Workers, Apr. 24, 1969, and *NASW News* 14 (May 1969): 13, both in WMY 91; WMY, "from the PRESIDENT," *NASW News* 15 (May 1970): 3, WMY 112.

12. MBY interview no. 4. See also Talbert interview; Romero interview; Kimball interview no. 2.

13. Davis interview no. 1; Kennedy interview. See also J. Williams interview; C. Thomas interview; Mervis interview; Glover interview; Kimball interview no. 2.

14. Whaley interview no. 2. See also Parris interview; Puryear interview; Baird interview no. 1.

15. Davis interview no. 1; Tucker interview; Ginsberg interview; Coleman interview; Whaley interview no. 2; Edmunds interview.

16. Poston interview; Martin interview; Jordan interview no. 1 (source of the quote).

17. Cresap, McCormick and Paget Inc., "National Urban League: Study of Organization and Management Practices," Mar. 1969, Ford PA 68–470.

18. Poston interview.

19. WMY to Vernon E. Jordan, Jr., Aug. 22, 1969, NUL new series; memorandum, WMY to Executive Directors of Urban League Affiliates, Aug. 28, 1969, and NUL press release, Sept. 15, 1969, both in WMY 212; memorandum, WMY to NUL Headquarters Staff and Regional Directors, Apr. 2, 1970, Ford PA 70–68, folder no. 1; "Master Planning for Long-Range Results," memorandum, WMY to NUL Cabinet Members, NUL Regional Directors, Local Executive Directors, Sept. 8, 1970, NUL new series.

20. NUL board minutes, May 16, 1963, p. 7, NUL Pt. 2, Series 5, Box 18 ("a deliberate attempt"), and Rick Friedman, "A Negro Leader Looks at the Press," *Editor & Publisher*, July 18, 1964, p. 38, WMY 205.

21. WMY quoted in *Los Angeles Times*, Oct. 23, 1966, WMY 204, and " 'We Need Tangible Victories,' " *U.S. News & World Report* 64 (Apr. 22, 1968): 46.

22. Tom Buckley, "Whitney Young: Black Leader or 'Oreo Cookie'?" *New York Times Magazine*, Sept. 20, 1970, pp. 32, 76.

23. A. Philip Randolph et al. to the Editor, *New York Times Magazine*, Sept. 25, 1970, and Carl T. Rowan, "White Liberals Who Pick Black Heroes," n.d. [between Sept. 20 and Oct. 7, 1970], both in WMY 1a; *New York Courier*, Sept. 26, 1970, WMY 229a; M. Moran Weston to WMY, Sept. 22, 1970, WMY 11.

24. Jordan interview no. 1 (source of the quote) and no. 2; MBY interview no. 1; H. L. Moon interview; Rustin interview no. 2; K. Clark interview no. 2; C. V. Hamilton interview; Sutton interview; N. B. Johnson interview.

25. Harrar interview; Freeland interview; Trent interview no. 1 and no. 3; Mervis interview; Kimball interview no. 2; Tucker interview. In September 1971, the Foundation announced that the job would go to Dr. John H. Knowles of Massachusetts General Hospital. The search for Harrar's successor, however, had begun well before Young's death.

26. Trent interview no. 3.

27. Quoted in Compton interview.

28. Jordan interview no. 1.

CHAPTER XV

1. Peggy Mann, *Whitney Young, Jr.: Crusader for Equality* (n.p., 1972), p. 86; MBY interview no. 5 and no. 6; Casteel interview (source of the quote).

2. "African-American Relations in the 70s," Report, Third Annual Conference, African-American Dialogues, Mar. 8–12, 1971, WMY 271.

3. Conyers quoted in transcript, CBS News Special Report, "Whitney Young Jr.: 1921–1971," pp. 11–12, MSRC; L. Stokes interview.

4. Ernest Dunbar, "The Lost Black Leader," *Look* 35 (Apr. 20, 1971): 76.

5. Bayard Rustin, "His Last Days," *Urban League News* 1 (Mar. 24, 1971): 1, 8.

6. Madeleine Hurel and Monique de Gravelaine to MBY, Mar. 13, 1971, WMY 264 ("Mother Africa"); WMY to MBY, Mar. 9, 1971, courtesy of MBY; interview reported in Associated Press dispatch, *Bluefield Telegraph* (W.Va.), Mar. 15, 1971, NUL new series.

7. Program, Third Annual Conference, African-American Dialogues, Mar. 8–12, 1971, WMY 264; Wyman interview (source of the quote); *New York Daily News*, Mar. 13, 1971, NUL new series; Rustin interview no. 2.

8. On the outing to Lighthouse Beach and WMY's death: *New York Daily News*, Mar. 13, 1971, NUL new series; transcripts, Ramsey Clark statement, Mar. 11, 1971 (Clark, Hurel, Senbanjo quotes), Thomas H. Wyman statement, Mar. 11, 1971 ("I don't see Whitney"), William W. Broom statement, Mar. 12, 1971, in Scrapbook no. 21, WMY Sr. Box 2; William Broom, "Eyewitness Recalls Last Minutes of Young," *Jet* 40 (Apr. 1, 1971): 20–21 ("This is great"); Simeon Booker, "America Mourns Whitney M. Young, Jr.," *Ebony* 26 (May 1971): 42–43, WMY 233e ("little roll and all chop"); Wyman interview ("I wonder what's going on"); R. Clark interview.

9. Transcripts, Ramsey Clark statement, William W. Broom statement.

10. Dunbar, "The Lost Black Leader," p. 76; J. Lewis interview; Elliott interview.

11. Jackson quoted in *Gary Post-Tribune* (Ind.), Mar. 18, 1971, and unidentified man quoted in *Duluth News-Tribune* (Minn.), Mar. 14, 1971, both in NUL new series; transcript, Ramsey Clark statement.

12. On the news of WMY's death: Simeon Booker, " 'It Can't Be True! It Can't Be!': Mrs. Young to State Dept. Aide," *Jet* 40 (Apr. 1, 1971): 7, WMY 233a; MBY interview no. 6; Poston interview; Russell interview; Casteel interview.

13. Kornegay interview; Jones interview; J. Williams interview; F. Williams interview ("absolute silence").

14. *New York Daily News*, Mar. 12, 1971, clipping in WMY vertical file, SCRBC; Booker, " 'It Can't Be True! It Can't Be!' " pp. 6–9.

15. J. Lewis interview; *Cleveland Call and Post*, Mar. 20, 1971, WMY 233d; Recording, Whitney Young Memorial Service, Lagos, Nigeria, Mar. 13, 1971, courtesy of MBY; George N. Lindsay to MBY, Mar. 14, 1971, WMY 251 ("sang his heart out"). See also Program, Memorial Service for Whitney Moore Young, Jr., Mar. 13, 1971, Christ Church Cathedral, Lagos, Nigeria, WMY biographical file, AUC.

16. *Louisville Courier-Journal & Times*, Mar. 14, 1971, NUL new series; NUL press release, Mar. 15, 1971, Percy H. Steele, Jr., Papers, courtesy of Percy H. Steele, Jr., Oakland, Calif.

17. Booker, " 'It Can't Be True! It Can't Be!' " pp. 8–9; *New York Times*, Mar. 15, 1971, p. 40; Carmichael quoted in *Oakland Tribune*, Mar. 18, 1971, NUL new series.

18. Forger interview. On the insurance arrangements, see Report no. 1, Estate of Whitney M. Young, Jr., Mar. 15, 1971, WMY 255.

19. Milton Helpern to Alexander D. Forger, Apr. 8, 1971, James A. Linen Papers, courtesy of James A. Linen, Greenwich, Conn. Writing years later, Baden recounted the story of the autopsy and pointed out flaws he saw in the procedures used in Lagos. He noted that Young had an enlarged heart and a history of high blood pressure, and hypothesized that the hot weather had caused cardiac arrhythmia, which had led to the drowning. See Michael M. Baden, M.D., with Judith Adler Hennessee, *Unnatural Death: Confessions of a Medical Examiner* (New York, 1989), pp. 155–57.

20. Roy Wilkins was another of the targets. The idea, apparently, was to blame the assassinations on whites in order to incite racial uprisings around the country. See, for example, "Assassination Incident," memorandum, Art Sears, Jr., to Guichard Parris, June 21, 1967, WMY 2; *New York Times*, June 22, 1967, WMY 224.

21. NUL executive committee minutes, Apr. 22, 1968, June 16, 1970, president's office, National Urban League, New York City; "Statement of Duties—Staff Assistant for Security," memorandum, Frank R. Steele to Security Committee, Oct. 28, 1969, WMY 31.

22. Shelley interview; J. Lewis interview; A. Young interview; Coleman interview; R. H. Brown interview; J. Williams interview; Jones interview; Glover interview; Vinson interview; Peter Bailey, "Young: 4th Black Leader to Die since 1963," *Jet* 40 (Apr. 1, 1971): 13–14, WMY 233a.

23. Bailey, "Young: 4th Black Leader to Die since 1963," p. 14; *Atlanta Journal*, Mar. 16, 1971, WMY biographical file, AUC; *Amsterdam News* (N.Y.), Mar. 20, 1971, p. 5.

24. "In Memoriam: Whitney Moore Young, Jr., 1921–1971," Riverside Church, New York City, Mar. 16, 1971, WMY 274; "Nixon Gives Eulogy at Graveside . . . ," *Urban League News* 1 (Mar. 24, 1971): 1; Bailey, "Young: 4th Black Leader to Die since 1963," p. 16; Howard Thurman, "What Can I Do?" eulogy to WMY at service of tribute, First Unitarian Church, San Francisco, Apr. 4, 1971, Steele Papers.

25. "In Memoriam: Whitney Moore Young, Jr., 1921–1971"; Thurman interview.

26. Campbell quoted in "Dr. Mays, Dr. Thurman Give Eulogies; Young Requested Both," *Jet* 40 (Apr. 1, 1971): 17, WMY 233a; "Whitney M. Young, Jr., 1921–1971: Texts of Eulogies Delivered by President Richard M. Nixon at Lexington, Ky., March 17 and Dr. Benjamin E. Mays, Dr. Howard Thurman and Dr. Peter H. Samsom at Riverside Church, March 16, 1971," WMY 261.

27. "In Memoriam: Whitney Moore Young, Jr., 1921–1971"; *New York Times*, Mar. 17, 1971, p. 1.

28. NUL press release, Mar. 14, 1971, WMY biographical file, AUC; *Amsterdam News* (N.Y.), Mar. 20, 1971, pp. 1 ("A Great Civil Rights Leader"), 5; *New York Times*, Mar. 17, 1971, p. 49; *Louisville Courier-Journal*, Mar. 17, 1971, Steele Papers.

29. On the viewing in Louisville and the burial in Greenwood Cemetery: *Louisville Times*, Mar. 17, 1971, Steele Papers (signs; banner; "big doings"; "came to see the Prez"), and transcript, CBS News Special Report, "Whitney Young Jr.: 1921–1971."

30. Russell interview; MBY interview no. 1; *New York Times*, Mar. 18, 1971, p. 42.

31. "Whitney M. Young, Jr., 1921–1971: Texts of Eulogies."

32. Transcript, CBS News Special Report, "Whitney Young Jr.: 1921–1971," p. 8. Young's interment in Lexington would be short-lived. Three months later, Margaret had his body moved back to Westchester, where it was reinterred at Ferncliff Cemetery in Hartsdale, an action that caused some tension between Margaret and Young's father and sisters.

33. WMY to MBY, Mar. 9, 1971, courtesy of MBY.

EPILOGUE

1. Rustin interview no. 1; C. Stokes interview.

2. "Civil Rights: A Kind of Bridge," *Time* 97 (Mar. 22, 1971): 20.

3. Patrick Owens column, *Newsday*, Mar. 12, 1971, and Roy Wilkins column, *Long Island Press*, Mar. 21, 1971, both in WMY 261; Baraka quoted in "Civil Rights: A Kind of Bridge," p. 20; Floyd McKissick column, *Amsterdam News* (N.Y.), Mar. 20, 1971, NUL new series; editorial, *Los Angeles Times*, Mar. 14, 1971, WMY 233f.

4. "The Negro in America—1965," *Newsweek* 65 (Feb. 15, 1965): 27; "Whom Do Blacks Respect?" *Time*, Apr. 6, 1970, p. 28.

5. Andrew J. Young, "Whitney Young: Working from the Middle," *Life* 70 (Mar. 26, 1971): 4.

6. WMY speech, "The American Dilemma—1965," Woman's Board, Chicago Urban League, Apr. 24, 1965, WMY 130 ("who *gets the most results*"); WMY interview, RJBOHC.

7. William Raspberry column, *Louisville Courier-Journal*, Mar. 16, 1971, WMY file, Western Branch, Louisville Free Public Library; WMY quoted in *New York Times*, July 21, 1970, p. 25.

8. Clark quoted in "Whitney M. Young Dies: Blacks and Whites Lose An Important Leader," *Negro History Bulletin* 34 (Apr. 1971): 94; M. Carl Holman, "Whitney Young: 'A vital link, a unique human coupling has been lost,' " *Contact* 2 (July 1971), 25, 28, WMY vertical file, SCRBC.

9. Stone interview; Carolyn Shelley to MBY, Mar. 12, 1971, WMY 250.

10. Martha Bass to MBY, Mar. 29, 1971; Howard Winant to MBY, Mar. 18, 1971, WMY 250; *Lansing State Journal* (Mich.), Mar. 12, 1971, NUL new series.

11. WMY interview, RJBOHC.

A Note on Sources

GIVEN the abundance of endnotes on the preceding pages, a full bibliography would be redundant here. This Note on Sources covers the manuscript collections, oral history interviews, videotapes, and recordings that comprise the most important primary sources for this book.

MANUSCRIPT COLLECTIONS

The principal sources for a study of Whitney M. Young, Jr., are Young's own papers, deposited in the Rare Book and Manuscript Library at Columbia University, and the National Urban League Papers, Manuscript Division, Library of Congress.

The Whitney M. Young, Sr., Papers, Blazer Library, Kentucky State University, contain important material on Young's family background and early life. A number of Young's colleagues and family members made available material in their private files: Clarence D. Coleman; Alexander D. Forger; Sam H. Jones; James A. Linen; Eleanor Young Love; Arthur B. McCaw; Eugene W. Skinner; Percy H. Steele, Jr.; Margaret B. Young. There is scattered biographical information in clipping files in the following repositories: Division of Special Collections/Archives, Robert W. Woodruff Library, Atlanta University Center; W. Dale Clark Library, Omaha; Western Branch, Louisville Free Public Library; Moorland-Spingarn Research Center, Howard University; Schomburg Center for Research in Black Culture. The Federal Bureau of Investigation's files on Young and on the National Urban League, obtained through the Freedom of Information/Privacy Act, include useful data.

Important supplements to the National Urban League Papers include the following: board of trustees minutes and executive committee minutes, in the president's office at the National Urban League in New York City; annual reports, in the National Urban League Library; the papers of the National Urban League's director of public relations, Guichard Auguste Bolivar Parris, Manuscript Division, Library of Congress. There are a few relevant items in the Chicago Urban League Papers, Special Collections Department, The University Library, The University of Illinois at Chicago.

On Young's role in the civil rights movement, there is additional material of importance in the following collections: the Martin Luther King, Jr., Papers, Library and Archives, Martin Luther King, Jr., Center for Nonviolent Social

Change, Atlanta; the National Association for the Advancement of Colored People Papers, Manuscript Division, Library of Congress; and, to a lesser extent, the Roy Wilkins Papers, Manuscript Division, Library of Congress.

For Young's ties to the federal government, see the John F. Kennedy Presidential Papers and the White House Staff Files of both Lee C. White and Harris L. Wofford, Jr., in the John F. Kennedy Library, Boston; the Lyndon B. Johnson Presidential Papers in the Lyndon B. Johnson Library, Austin, Tex.; the Nixon Presidential Materials Project in the National Archives, Alexandria, Va.

The records of the major foundations document their involvement with Young, the National Urban League, and the civil rights movement more generally. See the records of the Taconic Foundation, at the Taconic Foundation in New York City; the Ford Foundation Archives, at the Ford Foundation in New York City; and, at the Rockefeller Archive Center in Pocantico Hills, New York, the General Education Board Papers and the Rockefeller Foundation Archives.

On Young as a social worker, there are some scattered materials in a scrapbook at the Atlanta University School of Social Work and in the National Conference on Social Welfare Papers and the National Social Welfare Assembly Papers, Supplement 2, both in the Walter Library, University of Minnesota.

On Young's unit in World War II, there is scanty information in historical data supplied by the U.S. Army Reserve Personnel Center, St. Louis, under the Freedom of Information/Privacy Act, and in the Records of the Adjutant General's Office, Military Reference Branch (NNRMS), National Archives.

ORAL HISTORY INTERVIEWS

This book relies heavily on oral history of two kinds: interviews conducted expressly for this study, and tapes or transcripts of interviews deposited in research libraries or held privately.

The following interviews were conducted for this study:

Ralph David Abernathy, Aug. 4, 1983, Atlanta

Milton R. Abrahams, Jan. 7, 1987, Omaha

Alexander J. Allen, Oct. 29, 1979, Nov. 13, 1979 (by telephone), Jan. 31, 1980, New York City

Malcolm Andresen, Oct. 19, 1984, New York City

Enid C. Baird, Oct. 3, 1979, New York City; Jan. 30, 1980 (by telephone), Oct. 15, 1988 (by telephone), Brooklyn

Imamu Amiri Baraka, Sept. 25, 1984, Stony Brook, N.Y.

Vernon L. Barkstall, July 29, 1983, New Orleans

Clarence Barney, July 29, 1983, New Orleans

William M. Batten, Mar. 8, 1984, New York City

Edwin C. Berry, July 27, 1982, Chicago

M. Leo Bohanon, Jan. 29, 1984, St. Louis (by telephone)

Julian Bond, Aug. 16, 1983, Atlanta (by telephone)

Arnita Young Boswell, Feb. 27, 1980 (by telephone), July 27, 1982, July 28, 1987 (by telephone), Chicago

Junius A. Bowman, July 29, 1983, New Orleans

Wiley A. Branton, Jan. 2, 1980, Washington, D.C.
Hallie Beachem Brooks, Aug. 2, 1983, Atlanta
Ed Brown, Feb. 21, 1984, Atlanta (by telephone)
Raymond R. Brown, Jan. 21, 1984, Akron (by telephone)
Ronald H. Brown, Nov. 12, 1986, Washington, D.C.
William J. Brown, July 29, 1983, New Orleans
McGeorge Bundy, Dec. 5, 1979, New York City
George Butler, Aug. 7, 1986, Washington, D.C.
Frank Campbell, July 30, 1983, New Orleans
Marcia Young Cantarella, Aug. 11, 1983, New York City
Joseph and Kathelene Carroll, Aug. 31, 1983, Indianapolis (by telephone)
Lauren Young Casteel, July 31, 1982, Denver
Kenneth B. Clark, Oct. 29, 1979, Feb. 3, 1984, New York City; June 29, 1988,
    October 4, 1988 (by telephone), Hastings-on-Hudson, N.Y.
Ramsey Clark, July 12, 1983, New York City
Wilbur J. Cohen, Nov. 2, 1984, Louisville
Clarence D. Coleman, Aug. 2 and 3, 1984, Atlanta
James Compton, July 28, 1982, Chicago
John Conyers, Jr., Jan. 24, 1984, Washington, D.C.
Bettye Corbin, Feb. 12, 1987, Omaha (by telephone)
Morris D. Crawford, Jr., Sept. 26, 1979, New York City
Joseph F. Cullman III, Nov. 14, 1979, New York City
Roma Danysh, Oct. 26, 1988, Washington, D.C. (by telephone)
Ronald R. Davenport, May 11, 1984, Pittsburgh
Daniel S. Davis, Oct. 29, 1979, Feb. 26, 1980 (by telephone), New York City
Thomas Dixon, July 28, 1983, New Orleans
N. Phillips Dodge, Mar. 4, 1987, Ormond Beach, Fla. (by telephone)
James R. Dumpson, Oct. 12, 1979, New York City
Jane Lee J. Eddy, Nov. 30, 1983, New York City
Arthur J. Edmunds, July 31, 1983, New Orleans
Osborn Elliott, Sept. 1, 1983, New York City
Herman Ewing, July 29, 1983, New Orleans
T. Willard Fair, July 29, 1983, New Orleans
James Farmer, Aug. 17, 1983, Fredericksburg, Va.
Marvin Feldman, Feb. 8, 1980, New York City (by telephone)
Henry Ford II, Jan. 14, 1980, Detroit (by telephone)
Alexander D. Forger, July 12, 1983, New York City
Wendell G. Freeland, May 11, 1984, Pittsburgh
Leonard Garment, Jan. 30, 1983, Washington, D.C. (by telephone)
Laura G. Gaskins, Oct. 25, 1983, Minneapolis
Mitchell I. Ginsberg, Oct. 17, 1979, New York City
Gleason Glover, July 31, 1983, New Orleans
Jack Greenberg, Dec. 14, 1979, New York City
W. P. Gullander, Oct. 22, 1984, Green Valley, Ariz. (by telephone)
Mildred Hall, Feb. 3, 1984, New York City
Bonnie Boswell Hamilton, July 27, 1983, Burbank, Calif.

Charles J. Hamilton, Jr., July 11, 1983, New York City
Charles V. Hamilton, Oct. 20, 1983, New York City
Grace Townes Hamilton, Aug. 4, 1983, Atlanta
J. George Harrar, Feb. 5, 1980, Scarsdale, N.Y. (by telephone)
Dorothy Height, Dec. 4, 1979, New York City
Andrew Heiskell, Oct. 10, 1979, New York City
Bernese and Coleridge T. Hendon, Oct. 26, 1983, Minneapolis
Theodore M. Hesburgh, Aug. 31, 1983, Notre Dame, Ind. (by telephone)
Genevieve Hill, Aug. 1, 1983, Atlanta
Jesse Hill, Aug. 3, 1983, Atlanta
Denny Holland, Jan. 7, 1987, Omaha (by telephone)
Donald L. Hollowell, Aug. 2, 1983, Atlanta
M. Carl Holman, Jan. 4, 1980, Washington, D.C.
Hugh Jackson, July 29, 1983, New Orleans
John E. Jacob, Sept. 7, 1983, New York City
Sophia Yarnall Jacobs, Oct. 14, 1983, New York City
Cernoria Johnson, Jan. 24, 1984, Kensington, Md.
John H. Johnson, Oct. 29, 1984, Chicago
Napoleon B. Johnson II, Oct. 20, 1983, New York City
Gilbert Jonas, Sept. 26, 1988, New York City (by telephone)
Sam H. Jones, July 30 and 31, New Orleans
Vernon E. Jordan, Jr., Oct. 26, 1979, New York City; Oct. 21, 1983, Washington, D.C.
Rosa Keller, Aug. 25, 1983, New Orleans (by telephone)
Donald M. Kendall, Nov. 9, 1984, Purchase, N.Y. (by telephone)
James R. Kennedy, Oct. 18, 1984, Essex Fells, N.J.
Theodore W. Kheel, Oct. 26, 1979, New York City
Mae Street Kidd, Aug. 5, 1982, Louisville
John C. Kidneigh, Oct. 24, 1983, Minneapolis
Lindsley F. Kimball, Oct. 1, 1979, New York City; Aug. 22, 1983, Newtown, Pa. (with Maude Kimball)
Gisela Konopka, Oct. 24, 1983, Minneapolis
Francis A. Kornegay, Jan. 9, 1984, Detroit (by telephone)
Hylan F. Lewis, Feb. 17, 1984, Jan. 13, 1987, New York City
John Lewis, Aug. 3, 1983, Atlanta
John V. Lindsay, July 12, 1983, New York City
James A. Linen, Oct. 10, 1979, New York City; Feb. 22, 1980 (by telephone), Aug. 25, 1983, Greenwich, Conn.
Henry A. Loeb, Oct. 16, 1984, New York City (by telephone)
Marian B. Logan, Sept. 7, 1983, New York City
Eleanor Young Love, Aug. 4, 1982, Oct. 23, 1988 (by telephone), Louisville
John Mack, July 28, 1983, New Orleans
Stanley Marcus, Feb. 13, 1987, Dallas (by telephone)
Louis E. Martin, Jan. 3, 1983, Washington, D.C.
Benjamin E. Mays, Aug. 4, 1983, Atlanta
Arthur B. McCaw, Sept. 10, 1983, Washington, D.C.

Charles B. McCoy, Oct. 22, 1984, Wilmington, Del. (by telephone)
Floyd McKissick, Sept. 27, 1988, Oxford, N.C. (by telephone)
Helen Mervis, Aug. 29, 1983, New Orleans (by telephone)
Clarence M. Mitchell, Jr., Dec. 7, 1979, Baltimore
Henry Lee and Mollie Moon, Sept. 21, 1983, Long Island City, N.Y.
Constance Baker Motley, Sept. 15, 1983, New York City
Robert L. Myers, Jan. 7, 1987, Omaha (by telephone)
Vernon L. Odom, July 29, 1983, New Orleans
Johnny E. Parham, Jr., Oct. 14, 1983, New York City
Guichard Parris, Sept. 26, 1979, New York City
James M. Paxson, Jan. 26, 1987, Palm Desert, Calif. (by telephone)
Thomas F. Pettigrew, Nov. 16, 1984, Newark, N.J.; May 10, 1986, Palo Alto,
    Calif.; Sept. 13, 1986, Santa Cruz, Calif.
Ersa H. Poston, July 18, 1983, Maclean, Va.
Mahlon T. Puryear, Nov. 19, 1983, New Rochelle, N.Y.
William C. Ramsey, Jan. 6, 1987, Omaha
George H. Robinson, Jan. 26, 1984, Washington, D.C.
Samuel Robinson, Aug. 4, 1982, Louisville
James M. Roche, Oct. 19, 1984, Bloomfield Hills, Mich. (by telephone)
David Rockefeller, Sept. 15, 1983, New York City
Jeannette Rockefeller, Apr. 16, 1984, Seattle (by telephone)
Charles F. Rogers, Oct. 25, 1983, St. Paul, Minn.
Manuel Romero, Jan. 19, 1984, New York City
Burns W. Roper, July 11, 1983, New York City
Edyth L. Ross, Aug. 1, 1983, Atlanta
Donald Rumsfeld, Feb. 20, 1980, Skokie, Ill. (by telephone)
Harvey C. Russell, Aug. 29, 1983, Purchase, N.Y.
Bayard Rustin, Dec. 12, 1979, Feb. 1, 1984, New York City
Betty Shabazz, Feb. 17, 1984, Brooklyn
Edwin F. and Florence D. Shelley, Jan. 28, 1980, New Rochelle, N.Y.
James R. Shepley, Oct. 10, 1979, New York City
Benjamin F. Shobe, Aug. 6, 1982, Louisville
William R. Simms, Feb. 2, 1980, New York City
Harold R. Sims, Feb. 6, 1980, New Brunswick, N.J. (by telephone)
Eugene W. Skinner, Jan. 6 and 7, 1987, Omaha
Henry Steeger, Sr., Oct. 3, 1979, New York City
Percy H. Steele, Jr., July 30, 1983, New Orleans
Carl B. Stokes, Aug. 22, 1979, New York City
Louis Stokes, Jan. 25, 1984, Washington, D.C.
Chuck Stone, Feb. 3, 1980, Philadelphia (by telephone)
Percy Sutton, July 13, 1983, New York City
Mitchell Sviridoff, Oct. 19, 1979, New York City
Henry A. Talbert, Sr., July 29, 1983, New Orleans
Ann Tanneyhill, Oct. 19, 1979, New York City
Clarence E. Thomas, July 28, 1983, New Orleans
Sue Bailey Thurman, Jan. 5, 1984, San Francisco (by telephone)

Marietta Tree, July 12, 1984, New York City

W. J. Trent, Jr., Nov. 28, 1979 (by telephone), Feb. 22, 1980 (by telephone), Greensboro, N.C.; Apr. 14, 1982, New York City

Sterling Tucker, Oct. 30, 1979, Washington, D.C.

Charles E. Tyler, Jan. 7, 1987, Omaha (by telephone)

Verne W. Vance, Jan. 7, 1987, Omaha (by telephone)

Eric H. Vinson, June 17, 1988, New York City

Lyndon Wade, Aug. 16, 1983, Atlanta (by telephone)

Phyllis A. Wallace, July 27, 1986, Newark-Princeton, N.J.

Arthur Walters, July 29, 1983, New Orleans

James Tapley Wardlaw, Oct. 25, 1983, Minneapolis

Clinton Warner, Aug. 5, 1983, Atlanta (by telephone)

Rodney Wead, Jan. 7, 1987, Omaha (by telphone)

Robert C. Weaver, Oct. 12, 1979, New York City

Betti S. Whaley, Feb. 25, 1980 (by telephone), Jan. 24, 1984, Washington, D.C.

Dorothy A. Whitmore, Oct. 25, 1983, Minneapolis

Joyce Wiesner, Nov. 9, 1988, St. Louis (by telephone)

Aminda Wilkins, Sept. 7, 1983, Jamaica, N.Y.

Roger Wilkins, Oct. 6, 1979, New York City; Apr. 16, 1982, La Jolla, Calif.; Mar. 16, 1987, Washington, D.C. (by telephone)

Faith Williams, Feb. 3, 1984, New York City

George Sue Edmunds Williams, Oct. 26, 1983, St. Paul, Minn.

James D. Williams, Sept. 7, 1983, New York City

Sidney Williams, July 27, 1982, Chicago

Q. V. Williamson, Aug. 5, 1983, Atlanta

William Wolfe, July 28, 1983, New Orleans

Clarence Wood, Oct. 14, 1983, New York City

Thomas H. Wyman, July 11, 1983, New York City

Andrew Young, Aug. 4, 1983, Atlanta

Margaret Buckner Young, Oct. 13, 1979, Jan. 29, 1980 (by telephone), Oct. 31, 1982, Nov. 19, 1983, July 30, 1986, June 13, 1987, Sept. 12, 1988 (by telephone), New Rochelle, N.Y.

Howard Zinn, Oct. 16, 1984, Newton, Mass. (by telephone)

Tapes and transcripts of interviews that proved particularly helpful include:
In the Lyndon B. Johnson Library Oral History Collection:
James Farmer, Oct. 1969, July 20, 1971
Roy Wilkins, Apr. 1, 1969
Whitney Young, Jr., June 18, 1969
In the John F. Kennedy Library Oral History Program:
Simeon S. Booker, Apr. 24, 1967
Arthur A. Chapin, Jr., Feb. 24, 1967
Belford V. Lawson, Jan. 11, 1966
Burke Marshall, Jan. 19–20, 1970
Samuel V. Merrick, Oct. 17, 1966

Poverty and Urban Policy: Conference Transcript of 1973 Group Discussion of the Kennedy Administration Urban Poverty Programs and Policies, June 16-17, 1973

Hobart Taylor, Jr., Jan. 11, 1967

Harris Wofford, Nov. 29, 1965

In the Ralph J. Bunche Oral History Collection, Moorland-Spingarn Research Center, Howard University:

Edwin C. Berry, Feb. 22, 1968

Clarence D. Coleman, Jan. 24, 1968

Melvin King, Oct. 28, 1967

Guichard Parris, Nov. 3, 1967

Whitney M. Young, Jr., May 6, 1970

Others:

Betty Barnes interviews with Margaret Buckner Young, Nov. 13, 1975, Jan. 8, 15, 1976, courtesy of Margaret B. Young

Daniel S. Davis interviews with Whitney M. Young, Jr., in preparation for writing *Beyond Racism*, n.d, courtesy of Daniel S. Davis

Robert L. Myers interview, Mar. 21, 1979, Aug. 1, 1984, W. Dale Clark Library, Omaha

Whitney M. Young, Jr., speeches recorded by William R. Simms, tapes courtesy of William R. Simms

Whitney M. Young, Sr., and Whitney M. Young, Jr., speaking on undated tapes in Whitney M. Young, Sr., Papers, Blazer Library, Kentucky State University

VIDEOTAPES AND RECORDINGS

"Which Way, America?" transcript, KNBC Public Affairs Documentary, [Jan. 16, 1971], Division of Special Collections/Archives, Robert W. Woodruff Library, Atlanta University Center

"Whitney Young Jr.: 1921–1971," transcript, CBS News Special Report, Mar. 17, 1971, Ralph J. Bunche Oral History Collection, Moorland-Spingarn Research Center, Howard University

"Whitney M. Young, Jr.: The Force Behind the Man," videotape, Whitney M. Young, Jr., Memorial House, Lincoln Institute

"The Great Ones," Group W (Westinghouse Broadcasting Company), July 1971, recordings courtesy of Margaret B. Young

"In Memoriam: Whitney Moore Young, Jr., 1921–1971," Riverside Church funeral service, Mar. 16, 1971, recording courtesy of Margaret B. Young

Whitney Young Memorial Service, Lagos, Nigeria, Mar. 13, 1971, recording courtesy of Margaret B. Young

Whitney Young speech [to Pittsburgh Urban League], Sept. 17, 1968 (mismarked Dec. 23, 1968), courtesy of Margaret B. Young

Index